Communications
in Computer and Information Science   1997

Rationale

The CCIS series is devoted to the publication of proceedings of computer science conferences. Its aim is to efficiently disseminate original research results in informatics in printed and electronic form. While the focus is on publication of peer-reviewed full papers presenting mature work, inclusion of reviewed short papers reporting on work in progress is welcome, too. Besides globally relevant meetings with internationally representative program committees guaranteeing a strict peer-reviewing and paper selection process, conferences run by societies or of high regional or national relevance are also considered for publication.

Topics

The topical scope of CCIS spans the entire spectrum of informatics ranging from foundational topics in the theory of computing to information and communications science and technology and a broad variety of interdisciplinary application fields.

Information for Volume Editors and Authors

Publication in CCIS is free of charge. No royalties are paid, however, we offer registered conference participants temporary free access to the online version of the conference proceedings on SpringerLink (http://link.springer.com) by means of an http referrer from the conference website and/or a number of complimentary printed copies, as specified in the official acceptance email of the event.

CCIS proceedings can be published in time for distribution at conferences or as post-proceedings, and delivered in the form of printed books and/or electronically as USBs and/or e-content licenses for accessing proceedings at SpringerLink. Furthermore, CCIS proceedings are included in the CCIS electronic book series hosted in the SpringerLink digital library at http://link.springer.com/bookseries/7899. Conferences publishing in CCIS are allowed to use Online Conference Service (OCS) for managing the whole proceedings lifecycle (from submission and reviewing to preparing for publication) free of charge.

Publication process

The language of publication is exclusively English. Authors publishing in CCIS have to sign the Springer CCIS copyright transfer form, however, they are free to use their material published in CCIS for substantially changed, more elaborate subsequent publications elsewhere. For the preparation of the camera-ready papers/files, authors have to strictly adhere to the Springer CCIS Authors' Instructions and are strongly encouraged to use the CCIS LaTeX style files or templates.

Abstracting/Indexing

CCIS is abstracted/indexed in DBLP, Google Scholar, EI-Compendex, Mathematical Reviews, SCImago, Scopus. CCIS volumes are also submitted for the inclusion in ISI Proceedings.

How to start

To start the evaluation of your proposal for inclusion in the CCIS series, please send an e-mail to ccis@springer.com.

Hugo Plácido da Silva · Pietro Cipresso
Editors

Computer-Human Interaction Research and Applications

7th International Conference, CHIRA 2023
Rome, Italy, November 16–17, 2023
Proceedings, Part II

 Springer

Editors
Hugo Plácido da Silva
IT - Institute of Telecommunications
Lisbon, Portugal

Instituto Superior Técnico
Lisbon, Portugal

Pietro Cipresso
University of Turin
Turin, Italy

ISSN 1865-0929   ISSN 1865-0937 (electronic)
Communications in Computer and Information Science
ISBN 978-3-031-49367-6   ISBN 978-3-031-49368-3 (eBook)
https://doi.org/10.1007/978-3-031-49368-3

This Springer imprint is published by the registered company Springer Nature Switzerland AG
The registered company address is: Gewerbestrasse 11, 6330 Cham, Switzerland

Paper in this product is recyclable.

Preface

This volume contains the proceedings of the 7th International Conference on Computer-Human Interaction Research and Applications (CHIRA 2023), which was held in Rome, Italy as a hybrid event, from 16 to 17 November.

CHIRA is sponsored by the Institute for Systems and Technologies of Information, Control and Communication (INSTICC), and is held in cooperation with the European Society for Socially Embedded Technologies (EUSSET).

The purpose of CHIRA is to bring together professionals, academics and students who are interested in the advancement of research and practical applications of human-technology & human-computer interaction. Different aspects of Computer-Human Interaction were covered in four parallel tracks: 1) Human Factors for Interactive Systems, Research, and Applications; 2) Interactive Devices; 3) Interaction Design; and 4) Adaptive and Intelligent Systems. Human-Computer Interaction is getting renewed interest as human-AI interaction due to the increasing success of artificial intelligence and its applications.

In addition to paper presentations, CHIRA's program included three invited talks delivered by internationally distinguished speakers: Antonio Camurri (Università degli Studi di Genova, Italy), "Aesthetically Resonant Multimodal Interactive Systems", Andrea Gaggioli (Università Cattolica del Sacro Cuore, Italy), "Designing Transformative Experiences: Exploring the Potential of Virtual Technologies for Personal Change", and Wendy E. Mackay (Inria, Paris-Saclay, and Université Paris-Saclay, France), "Creating Human-Computer Partnerships".

CHIRA received 69 paper submissions from 30 countries, of which 20% were accepted as full papers. The high quality of the papers received imposed difficult choices during the review process. To evaluate each submission, a double-blind paper review was performed by the Program Committee, whose members were highly qualified independent researchers in the CHIRA topic areas.

In addition, the Special Session on "Enhancing the Esports Experience (E3)", chaired by Sven Charleer and Laura Herrewijn, was held together with CHIRA 2023.

All accepted complete papers are published by Springer in these conference proceedings, under an ISBN reference. The proceedings are abstracted/indexed in DBLP, Google Scholar, EI-Compendex, INSPEC, Japanese Science and Technology Agency (JST), Norwegian Register for Scientific Journals and Series, Mathematical Reviews, SCImago, Scopus and zbMATH. CCIS volumes are also submitted for inclusion in ISI Proceedings.

We express our thanks to all participants. First to all the authors, whose quality work is the essence of this conference; secondly to all members of the Program Committee and auxiliary reviewers, who helped us with their expertise and valuable time. We also deeply thank the invited speakers for excellent contributions in sharing their knowledge and vision.

Finally, we acknowledge the professional support of the CHIRA 2023 team for all organizational processes, especially given the needs of a hybrid event, in order to make it possible for the CHIRA 2023 authors to present their work and share ideas with colleagues in spite of the logistic difficulties.

We hope you all had an inspiring conference. We hope to meet you again next year for the 8th edition of CHIRA, details of which will soon be available at http://www.chira.scitevents.org/.

November 2023

Hugo Plácido da Silva
Pietro Cipresso

Organization

Conference Chair

Pietro Cipresso   University of Turin, Italy

Program Chair

Hugo Plácido da Silva   IT - Instituto de Telecomunicações, Portugal

Program Committee

Iyad Abu Doush	American University of Kuwait, Kuwait
Christopher Anand	McMaster University, Canada
Martin Baumann	Ulm University, Germany
Samit Bhattacharya	Indian Institute of Technology Guwahati, India
Paolo Bottoni	Sapienza University of Rome, Italy
Chris Bowers	University of Worcester, UK
John Brooke	Independent Researcher, UK
Kursat Cagiltay	Sabanci University, Turkey
Valentín Cardeñoso Payo	Valentín Cardeñoso Payo, Spain
Eric Castelli	LIG Grenoble, France
Sven Charleer	AP University of Applied Sciences and Arts Antwerp, Belgium
Christine Chauvin	Université de Bretagne Sud, France
Isaac Cho	Utah State University, USA
Yang-Wai Chow	University of Wollongong, Australia
Cesar Collazos	Universidad del Cauca, Colombia
Arzu Coltekin	University of Applied Sciences and Arts Northwestern Switzerland, Switzerland
Lizette de Wet	University of the Free State, South Africa
Andrew Duchowski	Clemson University, USA
John Eklund	UX Research, Australia
Vania Estrela	Universidade Federal Fluminense, Brazil
Jesus Favela	Cicese, Mexico
Peter Forbrig	University of Rostock, Germany

Marcus Winter   University of Brighton, UK
Floriano Zini   Free University of Bozen-Bolzano, Italy

Additional Reviewers

Fu-Yin Cherng   National Chung Cheng University, Taiwan,
                                 Republic of China
Anand Deshpande   Angadi Institute of Technology and Management,
                                 India

Invited Speakers

Andrea Gaggioli   Università Cattolica del Sacro Cuore, Italy
Wendy E. Mackay   Inria, Paris-Saclay, and Université Paris-Saclay,
                                 France
Antonio Camurri   Università degli Studi di Genova, Italy

Contents – Part II

Special Session on E3: Enhancing the Esports Experience

Contents – Part I

Main Event

I Am in Love with the Shape of You: The Effect of Mass Customization on the Human-Robot Relationship

E. Liberman-Pincu(✉) , A. Bulgaro , and T. Oron-Gilad

Ben-Gurion University of the Negev, 84105 Beer-Sheva, Israel
elapin@post.bgu.ac.il

Abstract. This study examined the effect of mass customization of a socially assistive robot (SAR) on older-adult users' attitudes and behaviors toward the robot. Mass customization, actively modifying aspects of a product by users before use, was proven to increase positive reactions towards products. Thirty-one older-adult participants were invited one at a time to explore new applications of personal robots for domestic use utilizing the Temi robot. We divided them into two groups that differed in their ability to manipulate the robot's visual design using various add-ons before starting the one-on-one interaction with the robot. Results of the thematic analysis and questionnaires suggest that allowing mass customization can increase users' enjoyment, help in forming human-robot relationships, and lead to proactive Interaction.

Keywords: Personal assistance robot · Mass customization · Product design · Human-robot interaction · Technology acceptance · User enjoyment · Human-robot relationship Older adults

1 Introduction

Mass customization is a process of producing and delivering products modified or adapted to satisfy individual customers' specific needs or preferences [1] by selecting predefined modules or using different add-ons. It combines the benefits of custom-made products with the low costs and efficiency of mass production [2]. Hence, it is considered valuable for both customers and manufacturers [3]. This approach leads to a positive reaction termed "I designed it myself," which leads to a significantly higher willingness to pay for the product [4, 5]. In the field of Socially Assistive Robots (SAR), customizing personal robots can contribute to a sense of ownership, establish relationships, and improve acceptance and engagement [6, 7]. People may use the robot's personalization to give it an identity (gender, name, etc.) or express their own identity [8]. Furthermore, it was found that when participants assembled the robot, they tended to have more positive evaluations of the robot and the interaction process [9, 10].

H. P. da Silva and P. Cipresso (Eds.): CHIRA 2023, CCIS 1997, pp. 3–12, 2023.
https://doi.org/10.1007/978-3-031-49368-3_1

As smart technologies become more commonplace and are increasingly used by older adults to improve or maintain their ability to perform important everyday activities, it is important to find ways to increase acceptance and overcome barriers that may impede people from wholly integrating these technologies into their lives [11]. Personalizing the robot's appearance can make it more appealing and engaging for the elderly and can ease its acceptance [12]. Studies have shown that people tend to develop connections with their SARs [13, 14]. These connections can be attributed to the SARs' ability to provide social support and companionship, as well as their ability to perform tasks that are difficult or impossible for the user. As robots become more common in our everyday environments, it will become increasingly important to form sustained and supportive human-robot relationships [15].

Furthermore, in a study that explored the design space of different contexts of SARs by asking users [16] and professional designers [17] to design the most suitable design for each use context, we found that while there was a level of agreement among professional designers regarding the designs of three of those contexts: a service robot for an assisted living facility, a medical assistant robot for a hospital environment, and a COVID-19 officer robot, the case of a personal robot for domestic use seemed to be unique. The designers' selections of visual qualities varied and were more influenced by personal preferences. Some even suggested that a personal robot should be customizable [18]. Users' design preferences were related to personal data such as age and gender [16, 18].

Previously, we evaluated this effect in the design process of a personal assistant robot using an online questionnaire [19], where participants were asked to design their own personal robot by selecting predefined elements of the robot's body and screen (body structure, outline, color, and GUI). Results suggested that allowing mass customization positively affects users' acceptance and leads to higher perceived enjoyment, intention for future use, and perceived robot usefulness. In this study, we aimed to explore the effect of mass customization on attitudes and behaviors in real interaction settings.

2   SARs' Morphology and Personality

The add-on designs were based on the outcomes of two studies: a deconstruction study of visual qualities (VQs) based on a market survey and a literature review [18], where we identified three typical morphologies for SARs: human-like, pet-like, and machine-like. To those, we added a fourth flower-like morphology and evaluated users' perceptions of each [20]. For this study we allowed participants to adjust the design of a machine-like robot and make it look human-like, pet-like, or flower-like according to their preferences and their desired relationship with the robot.

We designed two types of add-ons for the Temi robot (purchased via ONE robotix [21] its local distributor in Israel): 1) a screen frame (human-like, gold dog-like, black dog-like, or a flowery frame) and 2) eight options for an apron for the robot's chest. Further, we provided the selection of the robot's default screen display, offering ten different faces. Figure 1 presents the different design options we provided to the participants.

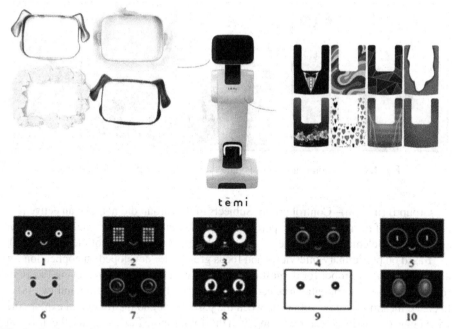

Fig. 1. Design options provided to the participants: four screen frames, eight aprons, and ten screen faces.

3 Aim and Scope

The study examines whether allowing older-adult users to customize the visual appearance of their robot by selecting predesigned add-ons will affect their perception and attitude toward it. To achieve this, we formed two groups of participants that differed in their ability to customize the robot's design before exploring and evaluating a new application.

4 Method and Study Design

The experiment was conducted in the "Palace Lehavim" assisted living in a public room. Thirty-one residents participated in the study voluntarily, all older adults aged 70–80 (18 women and 13 men), with each participant experiencing personal interaction with the robot. Participants were invited to explore and evaluate a new application for a personal robot developed for this study. To assess the effect of mass customization on users' acceptance of a personal robot, we conducted an experiment among subjects involving 31 subjects randomly divided into groups:

Group A (n = 15)– Customization group: Subjects in this group took an active part in the design of the robot, selected and assembled the appearance of the robot according to their personal preferences (using the design component presented in Fig. 1), and then performed a guided interaction with the self-designed robot. Figure 2 presents the customization process and three examples of modified robots.

Fig. 2. The customization process and three examples of modified robots.

Group B (n = 16)– Control group. Subjects of this group did not take an active part in the design of the robot and only performed a guided interaction with the robot without adding design elements (using the original machine-like appearance of the Temi robot).

Based on preliminary interviews and focus groups, we developed an application for a personal assistant robot for domestic use and an experimental setting using the Temi robot [22]. The experimental application contained a short conversation and two tasks to create meaningful interactions between the participant and the robot and explore the wide range of possibilities for working with the Temi robot. Table 1 details the different parts of the application. Figure 3 presents participants performing the two tasks.

Table 1. The different parts of the application we used for this study.

Conversation	Temi: "Hello, I'm Temi. What's your name? Subject's response Temi: "Nice to meet you (the subject's name). What a pleasure it is to be here at "Palace Lehavim". How old are you?" Subject's response Temi: "I wouldn't think you were over 25."
Task 1: remote controlling	Using tablet control, participants were asked to direct the robot out of the room to a prespecified location after being shown three pictures of objects: a flower, a house, and a ball. A picture of one of the objects was posted at this location on the floor. The participants were asked to locate and recognize which picture was on the floor. We used the robot's built-in video call function
Task 2: cognitive games	Participants were given several options for playing cognitive games on Temi's screen, including memory games, math exercises, Tetris, and Sudoku

The participants were asked to fill in two questionnaires before and after the interaction. The first contains demographic data and the Negative Attitudes towards Robots Scale (NARS) questionnaire [23]. After completing the task, participants completed an acceptance questionnaire based on the Technology Acceptance Model (TAM) using the

Fig. 3. Right: Controlling the robot's motion using a tablet. Left: Playing a cognitive game.

Almere model [24]. The Almere Model is a technology acceptance model designed to assess the acceptance of social robots. It is a Likert scale-based questionnaire that measures both functional acceptance (ease of use, usefulness) and social acceptance (acceptance of the robot as a conversational/interaction partner). Figure 4 illustrates the two groups' study structure.

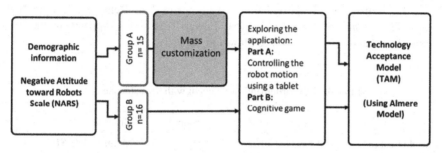

Fig. 4. Illustration of the two groups' study structures.

During the experiment, we collected behavioral observations of the participants. All observations and discussions were later transcribed and used for thematic analysis.

5 Results

5.1 Acceptance Questionnaire

We have found no notable differences in most acceptance factors among the two groups: Anxiety was very low among all participants (Mean = 1.74 SD = 0.54) on a [1–5] Likert scale. Intention to Use (ITU) and Perceived enjoyment (PENJ) were high regardless of the group (ITU mean = 4.1 SD = 0.64), PENJ mean = 4.16 SD = 0.42). Customizing also did not affect the participants' Perceived adaptiveness which was moderate in both cases (mean = 3.69 SD = 0.55), or their perception of Facilitating conditions (FC), which was relatively low in both cases (mean = 3.34 SD = 0.73). We did find some interesting trends for two acceptance factors, Attitude towards technology (ATT) and Trust, as detailed in the following paragraphs.

Attitude Towards Technology (ATT). Participants of Group a Showed a More Positive Attitude Toward Technology After Customizing Their Robot. This Appears in All Three Statements Related to This Factor, as Shown in Table 2.

Table 2. The participant's agreement with ATT statements

	Group A	Group B
"I think it's a good idea to use the robot"	**Mean = 4.4 SD = 0.49**	Mean = 3.87 SD = 0.99
"The robot would make life more interesting"	**Mean = 4.0 SD = 0.5**	Mean = 3.81 SD = 0.78
"It's good to make use of the robot"	**Mean = 4.27 SD = 0.44**	Mean = 3.75 SD = 0.9
The calculated score for ATT	**Mean = 4.22 SD = 0.4**	Mean = 3.81 SD = 0.74

Trust. The Trust Level Presented by the Participants Was Relatively Low in Both Groups. Participants of Group a Showed Lower Trust. This Appears in the Two Statements Related to This Factor, as Shown in Table 3.

Table 3. The participant's agreement with trust statements.

	Group A	Group B
"I would trust the robot if it gave me advice"	Mean = 3.0 SD = 1.03	**Mean = 3.43 SD = 0.79**
"I would follow the advice the robot gives me"	Mean = 3.0 SD = 1.15	**Mean = 3.5 SD = 0.71**
The calculated score for Trust	Mean = 3.0 SD = 1.17	**Mean = 3.47 SD = 0.72**

5.2 Thematic Analysis of the One-on-One Interactions

We transcribed the discussions and behaviors of the participants during the experiment and conducted a thematic analysis [25]. Three main themes emerged from our thematic analysis: users' enjoyment, establishing human-robot relationships, and proactive interaction. For each, we determined observation measurements.

Participants in Group A showed more interest in the experimental process than Group B. They expressed joy by laughing out loud when the robot told a joke and excitement through verbal expressions such as "Wow!" and "Fantastic!" Their body language during the interaction was more open and accepting. In contrast, Group B expressed minimal interest; none laughed when the robot told a joke. Some smiled, and one replied, "This is not funny; it shouldn't tell jokes." They expressed a more closed body language.

Group A participants were omre involved in the design process and used it as an opportunity to think about and define their desired relationship with the robot. When selecting different add-ons, some of them declared their intentions out loud. For example, "I want to design a female/male robot, so I'll choose…" or "I want it to be like a butler, so I'll select…". Group B did not have the opportunity to design; hence such statements were not found. Table 4 summarizes the thematic analysis findings.

Table 4. Summary of the thematic analysis findings.

Theme	Observatory measurements	Group A	Group B
Users' enjoyment	Expressing interest	High	Low
	Laughing out loud	Yes	No
	Body language	Open	Close
	Smiling	Yes	Yes
	Verbal expressions	Yes	No
Establishing human-robot relationships	Define the desired relationship	Yes	N/A
Proactive interaction	During and between stages	Yes	No
	Saying goodbye	Yes	No

During and between the experimental stages, Group A's participants showed a higher tendency for proactive interaction (as opposed to reactive); they initiated interaction with the robot, while Group B's participants did not interact with the robot unless asked. For example, at the end of the navigation task, Temi returns autonomously to the starting point – near the participant's location. In this period, Group A tended to talk and encourage Temi by saying out loud, "Come to me!", "You are doing great!", "good job!". While group B usually waited quietly and motionless for Temi to return. In addition, participants of Group A were more likely to say goodbye to the robot at the end of the experiment; two subjects even blew the robot a kiss.

6 Discussion

This study demonstrated how allowing users to adjust the design of a personal robot by selecting predesigned add-ons can increase users' enjoyment, help define human-robot relationships and lead to proactive Interaction. Thirty-one older adult participants volunteered for this study and were invited to explore a new application for a personal robot for the elderly. Participants were divided into two groups; only the participants in group A were encouraged to select different design elements before starting the experiment with the robot: four screen frames representing different morphologies (human-like, pet-like, and a flowery frame), eight aprons with different graphics, and finally the graphic user interface (GUI) selecting from ten different options for the robot's face.

To evaluate the effect of the customization process, we used quantitative and qualitative methods; we transcribed all discussions and behaviors during the experiment and conducted a thematic analysis; in addition, the participants filled in an acceptance questionnaire after completing the interaction. Both suggested that allowing older-adult participants to adjust the design of their robots is beneficial and contributes to a more positive reaction and attitude. Observations revealed higher enjoyment expressed by verbal expressions and body gestures. This correlates with our previous study that showed that participants who customized the robot's design in an online questionnaire had shown significantly higher perceived enjoyment than the control groups [19].

In addition, customizing the design made the participant more proactive in interacting with the robot; they initiated interactions during and between stages of the experiment, either by talking to the robot or using body gestures. Making older adults more proactive is important because it can help them maintain their independence and improve their quality of life. Studies have shown that older adults who are more proactive tend to be happier and healthier than those who are not [26, 27].

The questionnaire revealed two notable trend differences between the groups; participants who customized the design showed a higher positive attitude toward using the robot; however, they rated their trust toward the robot's advice lower. One optional explanation for this finding may be in the design options we suggested in this study; the robot's morphology affected the perception of its characters and role [28–30]. Perhaps taking advice from a dog-like or a flower-like robot is not customary and does not fit the relationship users imagined.

7   Conclusion and Limitations

This study demonstrates the positive effect of allowing older adults to customize their personal robots. Together with our previous findings [19], we can conclude that mass customization can lead to higher acceptance and enjoyment, help users define and establish a relationship with the robot and encourage them to be more proactive. To make this possible, designers should consider this in the preliminary phases of the design process and suggest ways to help users adjust and personalize the robot according to their preferences. However, when designing different add-ons, designers must consider the morphology of these elements and the assumptions and perceptions that may be related to them to fit the relationship to the anticipated roles of the robot.

Limitations of this study are that the sample size was relatively small, the interaction with the robot was based on a single session, and the participants were a convenience homogenous sample. This may limit the ability to generalize the results to other populations. Additionally, the study relied on a thematic analysis of observations, which may have introduced bias into the results; behaviors may have different interpretations by other observers [25].

Acknowledgment. This research was supported by the Ministry of Innovation, Science and Technology, Israel (grant 3–15625), and by Ben-Gurion University of the Negev through the Helmsley Charitable Trust, the Agricultural, Biological and Cognitive Robotics Initiative, the W. Gunther Plaut Chair in Manufacturing Engineering and by the George Shrut Chair in Human Performance Management.

References

1. Merle, A., Chandon, J.L., Roux, E.: Understanding the perceived value of mass customization: the distinction between product value and experiential value of co-design. Rech. et Appl. en Mark. (English Edition) **23**(3), 27–50 (2008)
2. Gilmore, J.H., Pine, B.J.: The four faces of mass customization. Harv. Bus. Rev. **75**(1), 91–102 (1997)
3. Wind, J., Mahajan, V.: Issues and opportunities in new product development: An introduction to the special issue. (1997)
4. Franke, N., Schreier, M., Kaiser, U.: The I designed it myself effect in mass customization. Manage. Sci. **56**(1), 125–140 (2010)
5. Jiao, J., Ma, Q., Tseng, M.M.: Towards high value-added products and services: mass customization and beyond. Technovation **23**(10), 809–821 (2003)
6. Barco, A., Albo-Canals, J., Garriga, C.: Engagement based on a customization of an iPod-LEGO robot for a long-term interaction for an educational purpose. In: 2014 9th ACM/IEEE International Conference on Human-Robot Interaction (HRI), pp. 124–125. IEEE. (2014)
7. Guo, S., Xu, H., Thalmann, N.M., Yao, J.: Customization and fabrication of the appearance for humanoid robot. Vis. Comput. **33**(1), 63–74 (2017)
8. Sung, J., Grinter, R.E., Christensen, H.I.: Pimp my roomba designing for personalization. In: Proceedings of the SIGCHI Conference on Human Factors in Computing Systems, pp. 193–196. (2009)
9. Groom, V., Takayama, L., Ochi, P., Nass, C.: I am my robot: the impact of robot-building and robot form on operators. In: Proceedings of the 4th ACM/IEEE international conference on Human robot interaction, pp. 31–36. (2009)
10. Sun, Y., Sundar, S.S.: Psychological importance of human agency how self-assembly affects user experience of robots. In: 2016 11th ACM/IEEE International Conference on Human-Robot Interaction (HRI), pp. 189–196. IEEE. (2016)
11. Harris, M.T., Blocker, K.A., Rogers, W.A.: Older adults and smart technology: facilitators and barriers to use. Front. Comput. Sci. **4**, 835927 (2022)
12. Salichs, M.A., et al.: Mini: a new social robot for the elderly. Int. J. Soc. Robot. **12**, 1231–1249 (2020)
13. Torta, E., Cuijpers, R.H., Juola, J.F.: Design of a parametric model of personal space for robotic social navigation. Int. J. Soc. Robot. **5**(3), 357–365 (2013)
14. de Graaf, M.M.: An ethical evaluation of human–robot relationships. Int. J. Soc. Robot. **8**(4), 589–598 (2016)
15. Strohkorb, S., Huang, C.M., Ramachandran, A., Scassellati, B.: Establishing sustained, supportive human-robot relationships: Building blocks and open challenges. In 2016 AAAI Spring Symp. Ser. (2016)
16. Liberman-Pincu, E., van Grondelle, E.D., Oron-Gilad, T.: Designing Robots with the Context in Mind- One Design Does Not Fit All. In: Pablo Borja, Cosimo Della Santina, Luka Peternel, Elena Torta, (ed.) Human-Friendly Robotics 2022: HFR: 15th International Workshop on Human-Friendly Robotics, pp. 105–119. Springer International Publishing, Cham (2023). https://doi.org/10.1007/978-3-031-22731-8_8

17. Liberman-Pincu, E., Korn, O., Grund, J., van Grondelle, E. D., Oron-Gilad, T.. Designing Socially Assistive Robots: Exploring Israeli and German Designers' Perceptions. arXiv preprint (2023)arXiv:2305.00419.

18. Liberman-Pincu, E., Parmet, Y., Oron-Gilad, T.: Judging a socially assistive robot by its cover: the effect of body structure, outline, and color on users' perception. ACM Trans. Hum. -Rob. Interact. **12**(2), 1–26 (2023)

19. Liberman-Pincu, E., Oron-Gilad, T.: Exploring the effect of mass customization on user acceptance of socially assistive robots (SARs). In: 2022 17th ACM/IEEE International Conference on Human-Robot Interaction (HRI), pp. 880–884. IEEE. (2022)

20. Liberman-Pincu, E.. Audrey-Flower-like social assistive robot: taking care of older adults in times of social isolation during the Covid-19 Pandemic. In: Companion of the 2021 ACM/IEEE International Conference on Human-Robot Interaction, pp. 613–614. (2021)

21. Available online: https://www.onerobotix.co.il/ (Accessed 13 July 2023)

22. Bulgaro, A., Liberman-Pincu, E., Oron-Gilad, T.: participatory design in socially assistive robots for older adults: bridging the gap between elicitation methods and the generation of design requirements. *arXiv preprint* arXiv:2206.10990. (2022)

23. Nomura, T., Kanda, T., Suzuki, T.: Experimental investigation into influence of negative attitudes toward robots on human–robot interaction. AI & Soc. **20**(2), 138–150 (2006)

24. Heerink, M., Kröse, B., Evers, V., Wielinga, B.: Assessing acceptance of assistive social agent technology by older adults: the almere model. Int. J. Soc. Robot. **2**(4), 361–375 (2010)

25. Braun, V., Clarke, V.: Thematic analysis. In: Cooper, H., Camic, P.M., Long, D.L., Panter, A.T., Rindskopf, D., Sher, K.J. (eds.) APA handbook of research methods in psychology, Vol 2: Research designs: Quantitative, qualitative, neuropsychological, and biological., pp. 57–71. American Psychological Association, Washington (2012). https://doi.org/10.1037/13620-004

26. Leeuwen, K.M., et al.: What does quality of life mean to older adults? A th. synth. PloS one **14**(3), e0213263 (2019)

27. Kelly, M.E., et al.: The impact of social activities, social networks, social support and social relationships on the cognitive functioning of healthy older adults: a systematic review. Syst. Rev. **6**(1), 1–18 (2017)

28. Kühne, R., Peter, J.: Anthropomorphism in human–robot interactions: a multidimensional conceptualization. Commun. Theory **33**(1), 42–52 (2023)

29. Liberman-Pincu, E., & Oron-Gilad, T.: A robotic medical clown (RMC): forming a design space model. arXiv preprint arXiv:2305.05592. (2023)

30. Barco, A., de Jong, C., Peter, J., Kühne, R., van Straten, C. L.. Robot morphology and children's perception of social robots: an exploratory study. In: Companion of the 2020 ACM/IEEE International Conference on Human-Robot Interaction, pp. 125–127. (2020)

Eco-Design of a Smart Module to Provide Customizable and Effective Interaction for the Elderly

Simona D'Attanasio[⊠] [iD], Tanguy Dalléas, Dorian Le Boulc'h, and Marie Verel

Icam School of Engineering, Toulouse Campus, 75 Av. De Grande Bretagne CS 97615, 31076 Cedex 3 Toulouse, France
simona.dattanasio@icam.fr

Abstract. Social isolation and loneliness are risk factors of morbidity and mortality for the elderly, whose number will increase in the future. Smart devices can offer solutions to stimulate activities and social contact to fight these threats, on condition that the real needs, expectations and capacities of the target users are considered. Among smart devices, smart wooden furniture provides a sustainable way forward that can be easily integrated and accepted into the domestic environment. The article presents a module in a compact 3D-printed box with a smart tactile icon and visual and auditory feedback, built to be integrated in a wooden piece of furniture. A variety of simple scenarios can be programmed and the pattern of the icon can be changed according to the user's needs and preferences. Various tests to validate the design have been performed and are presented. The electronic components are accessible for repair and the aim is low consumption, according to eco-design recommendations. The module showed to be a promising simple, robust and customizable tool to promote effective interaction with the elderly.

Keywords: Social interaction · Smart wooden furniture · Customizable module

1 The Context of the Research

The ageing of the population is one of the major achievements and challenges of modern societies. In most countries, the proportion of older people will increase, from one in eight people aged 60 years or over in 2017 to one in six by 2030 and one in five by 2050 [1]. The estimate rises by at least a quarter in more than two-thirds of OECD[1] countries [2]. This demographic trend is accompanied by major social and health concerns. Older people tend to live alone more often and suffer from increased social isolation (i.e. lack of social interaction), leading to a growing feeling of loneliness, that can be defined as the gap between a person's desired and actual level of social contact [3], and there is clear evidence that these are risk factors for morbidity and mortality [4].

---

[1] Organisation for Economic Co-operation and Development.

In this context, there is an increasing interest in the potential of technologies to promote social interaction and useful functionalities to fight loneliness. In this paper, we focus on the integration of some of this technology into furniture (also referred as smart furniture), and in particular into wooden furniture. The concept of smart furniture is well-known and the state of the art is rich in examples of applications for elderly. Interesting reviews can be found in [5] and [6]. In these articles, the authors point out the importance of more strongly considering price and the target user, and of understanding and integrating cognitive and emotional needs of older adults in the design. An example of smart sensing furniture is the one provided by [7]. Sensors are hidden in furniture to monitor temperature, moisture, weight, verticality, security, and the user's spatial and temporal activities (presence and light sensors). The scope of this work is safety, prevention and healthcare. An interesting article is [8], which describes a system to connect elderly people through ICT[2] to fight loneliness. These works underline the importance of the usability of technologies and of their seamless integration to foster usage and acceptance. In addition, the introduction of digital solutions to effectively mitigate social isolation needs to consider the variability among users' skills, needs and preferences [4].

In our research, we use wood as the base material for smart furniture and in this article, we focus on a tactile sensor. The positive benefits of wood on the touch experience, its positive physiological effects and impact on stress, have already been presented in a previous work by one of the authors [9]. Wooden furniture integrates easily into the home environment and is a sustainable material. We also intend to design a person-centered solution. As pointed out in the aforementioned overview, interacting with technologies remains a challenge for the majority of older people. The use of tactile elements can be challenging and various physical disabilities can increase the difficulty of interacting with smart components [10, 11]. Contexts and personal preferences are also extremely variable. We conclude that customization is a crucial factor for the development of acceptable, useful and simple interactions that contribute effectively to fight loneliness.

The smart module presented in this article is the key element of this interaction. The module consists of an icon that can trigger a programmable scenario. The main characteristics of the module are the following:

- The design is compact and contained in a box to facilitate integration in wooden furniture.
- The module is smart. The icon can react to touch or even to the proximity of a human body part. The icon can trigger a scenario: color patterns and sounds can be generated. The module can be stand-alone or connected to an external device as an IoT (Internet of Things).
- The module is customizable to be tailored to the user. The shape of the icon can be modified with a pattern that can be inserted in the box. The lightning pattern of the icon (color, brightness, Timing) can be adjusted. The auditory feedback is programmable. The scenario is also entirely programmable.
- The design follows some of the eco-design recommendations. Issues like low power consumption and reparability of components are addressed.

---

[2] Information and Communication Technologies.

The paper is organized as follows. The next section presents the detailed design of the module and its possible integration in wooden furniture. The experimental results section presents the tests carried out to characterize the module and its performance, as well as the scenarios that have been presented to a limited set of test users. The conclusion and future work section will conclude the paper illustrating the next steps of the research.

2   The Design of the Smart Module

The smart module consists of an icon whose proximity or contact by a finger or hand can be detected. According to the programmed scenario, visual or auditory feedback can be triggered in reaction to this detection. In this section we describe the electronics integrated in the module, and the mechanical design.

2.1   The Electronic Architecture

The sensitive component of the module is a capacitive sensor. The reason for the choice of this technology is the need to detect the human touch of a surface, allowing visual feedback through the same surface that must therefore be "transparent" to light. A complete survey of capacitive sensing in human-computer interaction can be found in [11]. The sensor measures a variation in the capacitance of the capacitor, that is, two electrically isolated conductors in close proximity to one another. In this case, the human body is considered a conductor.

The sensor is a conductive pad area that is capacitively coupled to the system ground, creating a parasitic capacitance. The introduction of the user's finger then produces an increase in capacitance (by adding a parallel capacitance also coupled to the ground) that is detected by the system. In our module the conductive pad is a hexagon brass coil with a thickness of 0,150mm, a fixed inner side of 50mm, and an adjustable width, from 5 to 12mm, depending on the desired module sensitivity. This design allows an available "empty" area of $50x50mm^2$ to draw the shape of the icon, using an opaque pattern, as depicted in Fig. 1.

The sensor delta count is compared against the threshold to determine whether a touch has been detected [11]. The count value represents a change in the sensor input due to the capacitance associated with a touch and is referenced to a calibrated base "Not Touched" count value. In our setup, we used the default sensitivity 32x, which corresponds to the detection of a touch of approximately 1% of the base capacitance (or a ΔC of 100fF from a 10pF base capacitance). On the sensor, sensitivity multipliers from 1x to 128x are available.

The feedback light is obtained using addressable RGB Light Emitting Diodes (LEDs) WS2812b that are fixed at the bottom of the box. The light intensity can be adjusted by varying the number of LEDs and by adjusting the light intensity of each LED. A compromise has to be found between visual feedback and power consumption. Each LED draws approximately 50mA at 5V when it is set to full brightness. We used 3 LEDs at 1/5 of full brightness approximately (~30mA of global consumption). The module's visual feedback brightness can be improved by covering the inner sides of the box with

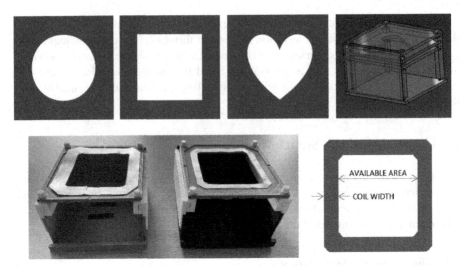

Fig. 1. The upper-left side of the figure shows three examples of pattern that can be mounted on the upper face of the box to form the icon. The design of the box allows the pattern to be easily changed. On the upper-right side, there is the 3D CAO view of the box containing a pattern. In the lower part, there is a picture of two modules, with a 10mm coil (on the left) and a 5mm coil (on the right). The external dimensions of the prototype are 88mmx83mmx51mm.

reflecting tape. An Arduino UNO R3 electronic board has been used to test three modules (see Fig. 2).

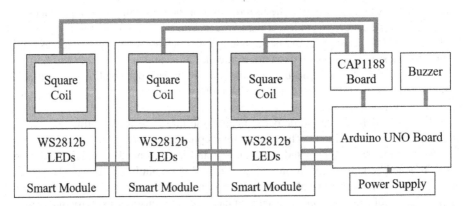

Fig. 2. Three modules, each one containing a coil and the LEDs, have been tested in an integrated system controlled by a unique Arduino board, a CAP1188 board and a buzzer. The whole electronic circuitry can be integrated into a single module. The choice of a low power consumption mode for the LEDs allowed their control without the need for an additional external power supply, as each Arduino pin can deliver a maximum current of 40mA.

The board is connected to a CAP1188 capacitive touch sensor breakout board from Adafruit and to a piezoelectric passive buzzer. The buzzer is used to produce the auditory feedback: a monophonic melody of adjustable volume can be programmed and generated. All the electronics containing the microcontroller, the sensor, the LEDs and the buzzer are easily integrable and can be placed at the bottom of the box.

2.2 The Mechanical Design

The main goal of the smart module is to provide all the functionalities in a compact design that is easily customized, mounted in the furniture, and repairable, facilitating access to the electronic components.

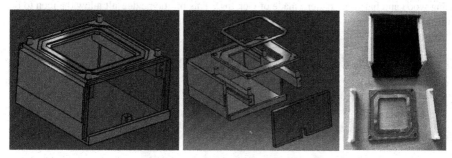

Fig. 3. The image on the left shows a CAO of the mounted box. The image in the center is an exploded view, highlighting the sliding bars. The image on the right is a picture of the prototype, made up of four removable parts.

The module is composed of a box that can be fixed to the back of the front panel of the piece of furniture. Most of the parts composing the box have been produced in rPLA (from FormFutura) using 3D printing to avoid interferences with the conductive coil. Figure 3 shows two CAO 3D views and an image of the box. Two sliding bars allow the coil to be inserted and removed. Each bar integrates two pins to allow the insertion of the pattern, which can therefore be removed and changed. The pins are long enough to allow the module to be fixed to the furniture panel without glue. A removable side cover provides access to the LEDs (and to the electronic components in the future integrated design).

The module presented in this article has been designed to be tested to determine the optimal geometry. The dimension of the icon, the sensing distance and the touch modality (using one or more fingers), as well as the visual feedback brightness, are fixed by the user's needs. Based on these constraints, the depth of the coil and its distance from the electronic components (sensor board and LEDs) will limit the sensitivity of the sensor, which can be further adjusted by programming the sensor board. Figure 4 shows a prototype integrating three modules, where the icons have been fixed.

Concerning the front panel, two other solutions have been tested. Transparent wood has already been integrated into one of the modules of the interactive counter developed by one of the authors and described in [9]. The second solution is to use a panel of Corian®, a synthetic material composed of acrylic polymer and alumina trihydrate. Corian® is non-porous, translucid, repairable and renewable. The rendering of these solutions for the smart tactile module is shown in Fig. 5.

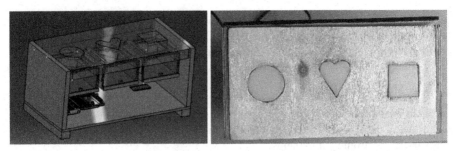

Fig. 4. On the left, the CAO view of the prototype. On the right, a picture of a prototype fabricated using wood and hardware pattern made of Corian®. This prototype doesn't allow the icon to be customized, which is possible with a front panel made from a single translucid material.

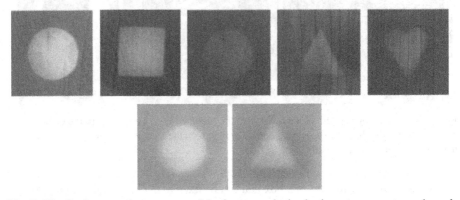

Fig. 5. The five icons on the upper part of the figure are obtained using a transparent wood panel to cover the same smart module, tested with four different patterns. The LED colors are white (two from the left), red (center) and green (two on the right). The two icons on the lower part show two icons, green and blue, obtained using a Corian® panel of a thickness of 6mm as covering material. With Corian®, borders are more faded but colors are more vivid.

3   Experimental Results

A certain number of tests have been conducted to evaluate the design of the smart module.

The first test had the objective of evaluating the influence of the human finger on the sensitivity of the module. Four different people performed several vertical movements up and down, touching the module in correspondence with the center of the coil. Figure 6 shows the sensor values obtained for an identical module setup (same coil, same distance from the point of contact to the surface of the coil of 37mm).

A variation of up to 10% of the maximum value can be observed, which is consistent with the fact that the human capacitance varies from one person to another within a range of approximately 100-200pF and depends on environmental and intrinsic factors [12]. This variation has to be considered when calibrating the module for a specific user.

A second series of measures aim to evaluate the impact of the coil width and of the coil distance from the contact surface. The image of Fig. 7 shows the frame that has

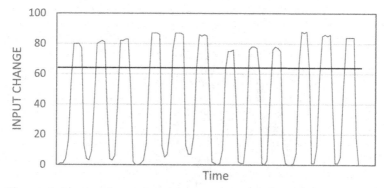

Fig. 6. The graph shows on the y-axis the sensor delta count, or input change, whose maximal value is 7Fh (127), recorded at a constant interval of 100ms (time is on the x-axis). When the value exceeds the threshold setting, a touch is detected. The threshold value used is 40h (64), shown as a straight red line.

been placed on the module, centered on the coil, allowing the recording of 17 points on an area of 10cm×10cm.

The graphs of the measures are shown in Table 1.

Table 1. In the graphs, each image represents the 16cmx16cm area centered on the wooden frame. The center of the xy plane is the center of the image. The z-axis shows the values of the sensor delta count, whose range is 0–127 (the hot colormap from matplotlib is used). The upper row shows the sensor change for a coil with a width of 5mm. The width is 10mm for the lower row graphs. From left to right, four distances (from the frame surface to the surface of the coil), obtained by piling up wooden (pine) boards are tested: 15mm, 37mm, 59mm, 81mm.

	Distance (mm)				
	15	37	59	81	
Coil width 5mm					
Coil width 10mm					

As expected, the width of the coil has an important impact on the module sensitivity. The 10mm coil shows a more uniform profile and higher stability, even at higher distances. Figure 8 highlights this tendency: the 10mm coil has an input change value approximately 35% higher.

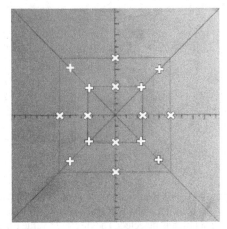

Fig. 7. A wooden frame of a thickness of 5mm has been placed on the module to provide a set of repeatable target points centered on the coil. The inner square corresponds to the inner border of the coil.

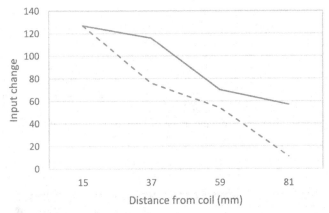

Fig. 8. In the graph, all input change values (y-axis) refer to the center of the coil. The x-axis represents the distance between the frame surface and the surface of the coil. The dotted line refers to the 5mm coil and the continuous line refers to the 10mm coil.

The final test aimed to evaluate the influence of the LEDs on the module sensitivity (three LEDs have been integrated at the base of the box). The input change is measured at a fixed finger-coil distance, while varying the LEDs-coil distance from 45 to 10mm. As expected (see Fig. 9), the proximity of conductors reduces the sensor sensitivity, but the impact is limited: input change decreases by about 8% when LEDs are inserted in the box. If the distance is shortened by up to 10mm, an additional 10% loss of sensitivity is measured.

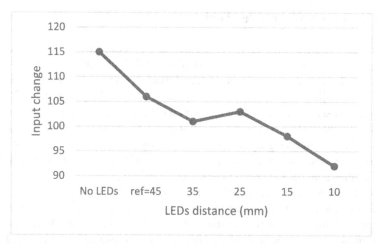

Fig. 9. The graph shows the measured input change for a fixed distance finger-10mm coil of 30mm. The "no LEDs" value is the measure recorded with no LEDs. The "ref" value corresponds to the three LEDs placed at the base of the box (at 45mm distance from the coil). The distance is then decreased from 35 to 10mm.

3.1 The Scenarios

Three different scenarios have been proposed to a limited set of test users. Scenarios are derived from a group interview conducted with about ten residents of a retirement home in France. People were asked to choose functionalities they considered useful from 48 suggestions. No structured feedback was collected but it is worth mentioning the test as an example of the diversity of application of the smart module.

Scenario 1. Your doctor recommends standing up and move 5 min once in a while during the day. The module can be programmed as a reminder of the physical activity at programmable intervals. The reminder can be both visual (flashing light) and auditory. Touching the icon starts a timer and the light remains constant until the end of the exercise.

Scenario 2. It's the end of the day and you are thinking about your family, but you don't contact them because you don't want to disturb them. Your family knows it and sends you a flashing heart icon accompanied by a jingle. As you touch it, they know that you received their message. This scenario needs the connection of the module to an external application.

Scenario 3. The house is silent. You love music and you can start one of your favorite songs by touching an icon. You simply touch again to stop the music.

The global feedback was extremely positive. The combination of touch control, visual and auditory feedback allows a rich panel of options. The main conclusion of this test is the importance of customization: each participant had different suggestions concerning the feedback modality. Most respondents suggested adding a screen to display numbers and letters to offer even more options.

4   Conclusions and Future Work

In this article we presented the design of a smart tactile module to provide an interactive icon for elderly. The module integrates visual and auditory feedback, and can be programmed to offer a variety of scenarios. It consists of a compact 3D-printed box whose geometry can be adjusted to find the best compromise of sensitivity and LED brightness, considering the user's needs (sensing modality and distance, visibility of the icon) and the module efficiency (low power consumption and robustness to electrical noise). The icon can be changed by changing the pattern on the top of the box. The design is simple, robust and entirely customizable, and allows easy and effective interactions that can be used to stimulate activity and social interaction for elderly.

Future works will address the customization issue, by adding to the module an ergonomic interface to set and adjust the parameters. The test performed on the prototype presented in this article will allow the finalization of the geometry. The integration in a piece of furniture has to be studied together with a professional woodworker. Reflective coating has to be tested to improve light intensity to lower LEDs consumption. Finally, more scenarios have to be created with final users and extensively tested in real conditions.

References

1. Decade of Healthy Ageing: Plan of Action 2021–2030. World Health Organization (WHO) UN General Assembly on 14 December 2020, Resolution **75**/131 (2020)
2. OECD: Demographic trends. In Health at a Glance 2017: OECD Indicators, OECD Publishing, Paris (2017)
3. Sandu, V., Zólyomi, E., Leichsenring, K.: Social isolation and loneliness among older people in Europe - Evidence, policies and interventions. Eur. Centre Soc. Welfare Policy Res., Vienna (2022)
4. Holt-Lunstad, J.: Loneliness and social isolation as risk factors: the power of social connection in prevention. Am. J. Lifestyle Med. **15**(5), 567–573 (2021). https://doi.org/10.1177/155982 76211009454
5. Lee, L.N., Kim M.J.: A Critical Review of Smart Residential Environments for Older Adults With a Focus on Pleasurable Experience. Frontiers in Psychology Fi:3080 (2020)
6. Frischer, R., et al.: Commercial ICT smart solutions for the elderly: state of the art and future challenges in the smart furniture sector. Electronics **9**(1), 149 (2020). https://doi.org/10.3390/electronics9010149
7. Bleda, A.L., Fernández-Luque, F.J., Rosa, A., Zapata, J., Maestre, R.: Smart sensory furniture based on WSN for ambient assisted living. In IEEE Sens. J. **17**(17), 5626–5636 (2017)
8. Herrmanny, K., Gözüyasli, L., Deja, D., Ziegler, J.: Sensor-based and tangible interaction with a TV community platform for seniors. In Proceedings of the 7th ACM SIGCHI Symposium on Engineering Interactive Computing Systems - EICS '15, pp. 180 – 189 (2015)
9. D'Attanasio, S. and Sotiropoulos, T.: Development and test of a new concept of interactive front counter designed to enhance user experience. In: Proceedings of the 4th International Conference on Computer-Human Interaction Research and Applications (CHIRA 2020), pp. 162–169 (2020)
10. Wilson, S.A., Byrne, P., Rodgers, S.E., Maden, M. A.: Systematic Review of Smartphone and Tablet Use by Older Adults With and Without Cognitive Impairment. In Innovation in Aging 6(2): igac002 (2022)

11. Clarke, H.: Closing the gap in the elderly and digital divide. Eng. Technol. Soc. **17**(8) (2022)
12. Grosse-Puppendahl, T., et al: Finding common ground: A Survey of Capacitive Sensing in Human-Computer Interaction. CHI 2017, May 06 - 11, 2017, Denver, CO, USA (2017)
13. CAP1188. 8 Channel capacitive touch sensor with 8 LED drivers. 2014 Microchip Technol. Inc. (2014)
14. Bian, S., Lukowicz, P.: A systematic study of the influence of various user specific and environmental factors on wearable human body capacitance sensing. In: Ur Rehman, M., Zoha, A. (Eds) Body Area Networks. Smart IoT and Big Data for Intelligent Health Management. BODYNETS 2021. Lecture Notes of the Institute for Computer Sciences, Social Informatics and Telecommunications Engineering, vol 420. Springer, Cham. (2022)

Technology Enhanced Mulsemedia Learning: Insights of an Evaluation

M. Mohana[1]([✉])[iD], Aleph Campos da Silveira[2,3][iD], P. Subashini[1][iD],
Celso Alberto Saibel Santos[2][iD], and Gheorghita Ghinea[3][iD]

[1] Department of Computer Science, Avinashilingam Institute, Coimbatore, India
{mohana_cs,subashini_cs}@avinuty.ac.in
[2] Department of Informatics, Federal University of Espirito Santo, Vitoria, ES, Brazil
aleph.silveira@edu.ufes.br, saibel@inf.ufes.br
[3] Department of Computer Science, Brunel University, London, UK
george.ghinea@brunel.ac.uk

Abstract. Human-Computer Interaction (HCI) is crucial in crafting effective, cost-efficient, and user-friendly e-learning systems. In the realm of e-learning, HCI focuses on creating interfaces and experiences that optimize learner engagement, interaction, and overall learning outcomes. Educators are actively pursuing initiatives to enhance student motivation, engagement, and academic achievement, particularly in Science, Technology, Engineering, and Mathematics (STEM) disciplines. However, learners often lack active engagement with electronic content when adapting and interpreting learning materials. This paper examines the Quality of Experience (QoE) in Science education content via a Technology Enhanced Multimedia Learning (TEML) Web portal featuring multisensory effects like rosemary scent, vibration, and airflow. Our ongoing research explores learners' emotional states during Mulsemedia-based learning. In this study, we present initial insights into the developed Mulsemedia test bed using IoT devices and a learning Web portal, based on self-assessed QoE questionnaires administered to 60 participants divided into experimental and control groups. The results indicate that both groups had a positive experience in the Mulsemedia-based learning environment, demonstrating its suitability for STEM subjects.

Keywords: Human-computer interaction · Mulsemedia · Multimedia · e-Learning · Quality of Experience (QoE) · STEM

1 Research Problem

In recent years, there has been a significant advancement in interactive multimedia, enabling learners to engage in dynamic and immersive learning experiences [27]. This is achieved by integrating various media elements such as audio, text, video, images, and animation. Virtual reality (VR) and augmented reality (AR) have particularly made remarkable progress in altering the educational landscape, providing learners with immersive and captivating experiences [20].

H. P. da Silva and P. Cipresso (Eds.): CHIRA 2023, CCIS 1997, pp. 24–42, 2023.
https://doi.org/10.1007/978-3-031-49368-3_3

Concurrently, e-learning or online learning has witnessed substantial growth and global adoption, with the market size projected to reach US$ 374.3 billion by 2026 [18]. In higher education, 74% of institutions in the United States now offer online or blended learning programs, and the number of students taking at least one online course has reached 6.6 million. The corporate e-learning sector is also expanding, with a projected market size of $38.09 billion. E-learning offers numerous advantages such as flexibility, cost-effectiveness, and scalability, resulting in higher retention rates and improved learning outcomes. As e-learning continues to transform education and training, it plays a crucial role in shaping the future of learning in the digital era.

Educators are currently engaged in numerous initiatives aimed at improving students' motivation, engagement, and academic performance, with a specific focus on Science Technology Engineering, and Mathematics (STEM) subjects. However, learners are not able to fully engage with e-content, when it comes to adapting and comprehending learning material and content [6,16,26]. Thankfully, advancements in multimedia technology have created opportunities for the development of innovative e-learning approaches, offering learners a diverse range of technological devices and solutions to enhance their educational experiences. As authors like [6,16,23,26] states, traditional multimedia applications in education usually only focus on two human senses, namely audio and visual, and emphasize improving the image and video quality. However, this limitation separates user and computer-based multimedia, resulting in less interaction with digital content. By incorporating a combination of audio and various other stimuli (e.g., olfactory, haptic, and gustatory), there can be increased interaction in digital content. In contemporary times, there is a growing focus on incorporating multisensory effects, including visual and audio information, haptic feedback, olfaction, and gustatory sensations, collectively known as Mulsemedia (Multisensorial Media) [13]. However, this involves exploring the integration of multiple senses to create immersive and enriched learner experiences within the e-learning environment.

In our investigation of this emerging field, we are currently evaluating a cutting-edge tool designed to enhance the learning experience through the implementation of Technology Enhanced Mulsemedia Learning (TEML). Our focus lies on the development of a web portal that serves as a comprehensive e-learning platform for STEM content. Moreover, learners' quality of experience (QoE) is analyzed through QoE self-reported questionnaires, and their emotional states have to be assessed during the learning process.

The TEML web portal extends its mission beyond mere accessibility and inclusivity by seamlessly weaving STEM concepts into its fabric, nurturing scientific literacy, and honing critical thinking skills. Within the portal's treasure trove of educational resources, with a primary focus on Biology and Physics, lie interactive simulations that explore diverse facets like airflow, olfaction, video, audio, and vibration. Meticulously crafted, the multimedia content within the Web portal serves as an indispensable tool for effortlessly grasping and comprehending complex STEM principles.

This paper presents the initial findings from the evaluation of the TEML Web Portal discussed earlier. As of now, a total of 60 participants have taken part in the subjective evaluation of this tool, providing valuable insights into both the strengths and weaknesses of the developed platform.

2   Objectives

The primary objective of this study is to gain a deeper understanding of how the TEML Web Portal can be enhanced to cater specifically to students' STEM content. To achieve this objective, we conducted an evaluation of the tool by gathering their feedback, insights, and noteworthy observations. The valuable input provided by these students will guide the iterative improvement process, resulting in a more tailored and effective learning solution for learning STEM subjects through Mulsemedia effects [3,5,12]. STEM courses might be challenging for learners. Science, technology, engineering, and mathematics encompass subjects with intricate concepts and demanding problem-solving skills. Students often find it difficult to grasp these complex ideas and apply them in practical situations. One common issue is a lack of engagement. STEM subjects can be perceived as dull or difficult, leading to a lack of interest and motivation among students, especially in e-learning [22]. This can hinder their willingness to explore the subjects further and limit their overall learning experience [24]. To address this issue, this study has to experiment with learners' experiences while using Mulsemedia effects in STEM subjects.

While biofeedback signals were not utilized in this particular study, they are planned to be incorporated in the subsequent stages of evaluation to provide a deeper understanding of participants' interactions with the system. The inclusion of both objective measures, such as cognitive and emotional response data, and subjective measures like questionnaires and interviews within a TEML Web Portal [21] is paramount for obtaining a comprehensive understanding of the listener's experience. This approach underscores the importance of multisensorial elements in fostering a positive and captivating learning environment. By capturing objective measures, such as EEG and GSR data, which offer quantifiable insights into cognitive and emotional responses [14,17], with subjective measures of QoE, a holistic assessment of the TEML Web Portal can be achieved. This comprehensive evaluation approach employed in the research facilitates a profound comprehension of the cognitive and emotional aspects of learners' responses, consequently informing further improvements and enhancements to the TEML Web Portal.

3   State of the Art

Active participation from learners plays a vital role in their academic progress and overall educational experience. When students engage actively in their learning, they shift from being passive recipients of information to becoming active participants. This transformation is essential as it influences their educational journey and contributes to a more enriching learning experience. Mulsemedia can be applied in many kinds of applications in a virtual environment [13]. The aim of previous studies is to enhance the QoE, and learner performance, and improve human-computer interaction in different environments [19].

According to Tal et al. [23], Mulsemedia-based Technology-Enhanced Learning (TEL) has demonstrated its ability to enhance the learner experience, motivation, and knowledge acquisition compared to traditional text-based learning. Mulsemedia-based TEL utilizes various media types, including text, images, video, and audio, to create an engaging and immersive learning environment. However, the design and presentation of multimedia content must be carefully considered to optimize its effectiveness. Further research is necessary to explore the optimal design principles for Mulsemedia-based TEL and its potential in different educational contexts. In a QoE study conducted by Yuan et al. [25], the impact of delivering multimedia content through multiple sensory inputs was examined. The study involved 60 participants who were exposed to various multimedia content with varying sensory inputs. The findings revealed that combining multiple sensory inputs significantly enhanced user experience and satisfaction. This study highlights the importance of incorporating multiple sensory inputs in multimedia design, with implications for e-learning, entertainment, and advertising applications.

Covaci et al. [8] conducted a study to explore users' experiences with cross-modal correspondent Mulsemedia content. The study involved 40 participants who were exposed to four different types of Mulsemedia content, each comprising three distinct types of media. The participants were then asked to evaluate their experience based on several factors, including perceived usefulness, enjoyment, engagement, and overall satisfaction. This work by Garcia-Ruiz et al. [11] introduced a virtual environment with haptic, olfactory, auditory, and visual media for the student learning process, information retrieval, and mental association process. Here, authors experimented with different kinds of scents with different various visualizations. The study reported that participants were engaged with using this device in the learning process. To analyze the learner's performance in the learning process, Ademoye and Ghinea [1] have used six kinds of olfactory-enhanced video clips in their experiments. Each video was running in the 90 s in three segments, meanwhile, the middle video was enhanced by olfactory effects. The results show that learners did not experience any negative experiences in this type of learning.

In a similar study, Alkasasbeh and Ghinea [2], which investigated the effects of the olfactory on students' learning achievement. This study included 26 students to answered five questions to test their previous knowledge of the specific topic. This experiment was conducted with and without the Mulsemedia effects of two different groups. The results showed that students were eager to use olfactory in their learning in the future. In related work, Garcia-Ruiz et al. [11] investigated the influence of olfactory in English language learning. In another similar work, Kreitlon et al. [15] delved into the concept of affective multisensorial books, which are interactive books designed to provide an immersive reading experience through the integration of various sensory inputs such as visual, auditory, and haptic feedback. The authors presented a prototype called "The Little Prince", which incorporated sensory stimuli like music, sound effects, and vibrations to enhance the emotional and affective aspects of the story. The study aimed to assess the effectiveness of affective multisensorial books in engaging readers and enhancing their emotional responses.

Zou et al. [28] also reported experiments that multimedia-based learning improves learners' experiences. The authors designed a mulsemedia test bed to play video content and synchronized it with haptic, airflow, and olfaction effects. The results showed that many learners openly suggested that mulsemedia-based learning enhanced their learning experience in the e-learning platform. Moreover, Covaci et al. [7] proposed game-based multisensorial learning using the effect of olfactory. In this study, the author investigates how fragrance improves learners learning performance, engagement, and QoE. The results showed that incorporating the olfactory smell in learning improves the learner's performance.

Several studies have focused on the development of technology-enhanced mulsemedia learning, which incorporates audio e-books, language, and video-based content to enhance the teaching and learning process. However, it is important to note that assessing the quality of learners' experiences and improving the content accordingly is essential for enhancing learner engagement in the learning process.

4   Methodology

This section presents the development and purpose of the web-based e-learning delivery system, covering its architecture and the principles governing the synchronization of Mulsemedia effects with audio and video content. The primary objective of the proposed system is to investigate the incorporation of multisensory effects into e-learning, particularly in the context of STEM-related educational material. Figure 1 provides an overview of the envisioned architecture for the Mulsemedia delivery system. This system consists of three senses namely olfactory, vibration, and airflow, which are synchronized with audio/video streaming.

4.1   Overview of Mulsemedia

Multimedia and multisensory are two related concepts that have become increasingly important in modern education. Both concepts involve the use of multiple sensory modalities to enhance learning experiences and improve learners' engagement. Multimedia refers to the use of multiple forms of media, such as text, images, audio, and video, to convey information. In education, multimedia resources are often used to provide visual and auditory cues to help students better understand complex concepts. Multisensory learning, on the other hand, refers to the use of multiple senses, such as sight, sound, touch, and even smell and taste, to enhance learning experiences. This approach can be also useful

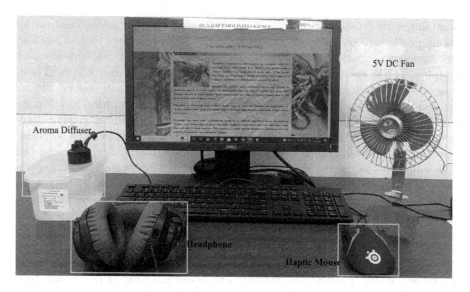

Fig. 1. Technology Enhanced Mulsemedia delivery System.

for learners with different learning styles or who have difficulty understanding complex concepts through traditional teaching methods [27]. Both multimedia and multisensory learning can be effective in promoting learner engagement and improving learning outcomes. By providing learners with multiple ways to interact with course material, teachers can create a more dynamic and engaging learning experience that caters to a wider range of learning styles and preferences of study.

TEML aims to explore the integration of affective computing and multisensory learning in e-learning, with a focus on STEM subjects. This research aims to extend the challenges faced in e-learning, such as positive and negative emotions in learning due to the over-reliance on text-based content, by utilizing the immersive and engaging aspects of multisensory learning and the personalized adaptation of affective computing. Understanding learners' involvement, motivation, and overall learning experience requires analyzing their emotional states during learning. During the learning process, emotional states have a substantial impact on learners' attitudes, behaviors, and cognitive processes. It also acknowledges the role of multimedia in enhancing the learning experience and improving student engagement.

4.2 Mulsemedia STEM Content

The proposed multisensory e-learning system incorporates multimedia technology, Internet of Things (IoT) components, and mulsemedia effects to deliver an engaging and immersive learning experience. The system features an IoT-based Mulsemedia learning platform that utilizes cost-effective components such as cooling fans, humidifiers for olfactory, and haptics to create vibration in the learning environment. It has been designed to provide learners with a realistic and immersive experience, the system incorporates rosemary and thunder and lightning STEM content, which is made up of audio and video effects. These contents are synchronized with IoT devices to stimulate multisensory effects, including olfactory, vibration, and airflow. This video clip duration is 4–5 minutes. For example, when the rosemary video begins, the humidifier triggers olfactory effects. The integration of airflow and humidifiers enhances the learners' experience by allowing them to feel and smell the environment while seeing the video content. The inclusion of haptics for olfaction enables learners to experience the scent through tactile feedback, further enhancing the immersive nature of the learning experience. The system also features synchronized audio, video, and mulsemedia effects with the airflow, olfactory, and haptic feedback provided by the IoT devices, ensuring learners have a truly immersive learning experience. Figure 2 shows the home page of the TEML web portal, and Figs. 3 and 4 show the rosemary and thunder and lightning learning material. After watching these two video content, participants requested to assess the QoE of the TEML web portal learning experience of the mulsemedia effect in STEM subjects.

Fig. 2. Home Page of TEML.

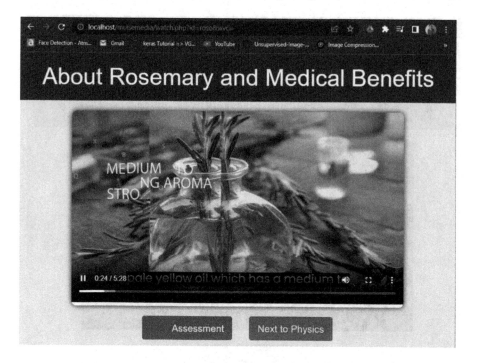

Fig. 3. Rosemary Content.

4.3 Mulsemedia Tools

To incorporate the Mulsemedia experience into e-learning, additional hardware components are required. The central processing unit of the system is the Arduino microcontroller, responsible for collecting data from sensors and controlling devices based on pre-defined rules and algorithms. Figure 1 shows the components that have been included in the TEML e-learning portal. The Arduino Microcontroller Interface plays a crucial role in connecting various devices such as cooling fans, ultrasonic humidifiers, relays, and power adapters, to the IoT system. The Cooling Fan is connected to the Arduino microcontroller via one of its digital output pins. Through the Arduino code, signals are sent to the digital output pin, enabling control over the fan's speed and direction. The ultrasonic humidifier is connected to the Arduino microcontroller using a power adapter and relay. When the code is executed, the relay sends a signal to the power adapter, activating the ultrasonic humidifier and producing mist. The relay, connected to one of the digital output pins on the Arduino, regulates the flow of electricity from the power adapter to the humidifier, allowing for on/off control. The power adapter supplies the necessary voltage to the ultrasonic humidifier, which is connected to the Arduino microcontroller through the relay. By utilizing this hardware setup, the system can integrate various sensory effects and enhance the Mulsemedia experience in e-learning.

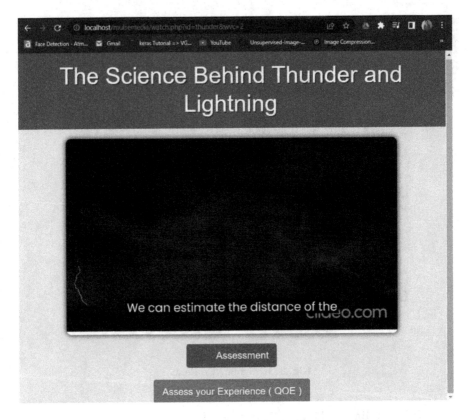

Fig. 4. Thunder and Lightning.

5   Evaluation

The experiment included a group of 60 female participants and was conducted at the Centre for Machine Learning and Intelligence, Avinashilingam University for Women (India). Their age range was 23 to 25 years old. Table 1 shows the evaluation study process. The majority of participants were undergraduate students, postgraduate students, and researchers. The test was conducted with two equal-sized groups: the experimental group and the control group. Prior to collecting the results, participants were asked to complete a consent form. The study involved approximately 20 min of watching learning content with the mulsemedia effect, and it assessed the learners' satisfaction level through a self-reported QoE questionnaire, which is presented in Table 2 in the next section. In contrast, the control group was assessed for QoE without the mulsemedia effect. This system was totally designed with Arduino-based programming to trigger the mulsemedia effects on and off at a particular time and the Web portal was designed with HTML, CSS, and PHP programs used to access the learning content based on the learner's choice of either physics or biology content first.

Table 1. Evaluation Process.

Ethical clearance	
	– Collection of self-consent form and obtained an ethical clearance certificate from Avinaishilingam Univerisity
	– Description of research study and benefits
	– Getting approval from the ethics office of Avinashilingam University
Assess learner QoE	
	– Users can see either biology or physics content based on their choice
	– Learning experience
	– Leaners satisfaction self-assessment

5.1 Questionnaire

For the evaluation, the questionnaire 2 was applied after each session. The questionnaire consists of 22 items designed to gather insights and opinions regarding the use of sensory effects and the experienced approach in e-learning. The items cover a range of factors, including olfactory effects, airflow effects, vibration effects, and the overall experience of the approach.

The first set of items (Q1-Q12) focuses on sensory effects and their impact on the sense of reality during e-learning. Participants are asked to express their views on how these effects enhance or hinder their learning experience. This includes items related to olfactory effects, such as whether they enhance the sense of reality, are distracting, annoying, or enjoyable. Similarly, items regarding airflow effects and vibration effects explore participants' perceptions of their impact on the sense of reality and their potential to be distracting or enjoyable.

The next set of items (Q13-Q22) delves into participants' evaluation of the experienced approach in e-learning. These items aim to assess the usability, effectiveness, and satisfaction with the approach. Participants are asked to provide their feedback on various aspects, including ease of use, understanding of concepts, improvement in learning, practical engagement, enjoyment, and the likelihood of recommending the approach to others. Additionally, participants are given the opportunity to express their interest in further learning with the experienced approach.

By collecting responses to this questionnaire, researchers can gain valuable insights into the subjective experiences, preferences, and perceptions of learners regarding sensory effects and the experienced approach in e-learning. The results can inform the development of instructional strategies, course design, and the integration of innovative technologies to create engaging and effective e-learning environments.

Table 2. Self-reported QoE Questions.

Item	Description
Q1	The olfactory effects enhance the sense of reality in e-learning
Q2	The olfactory effects are distracting
Q3	The olfactory effects are annoying
Q4	I enjoy e-learning with olfactory effects
Q5	The airflow effects enhance the sense of reality in e-learning
Q6	The airflow effects are distracting
Q7	The airflow effects are annoying
Q8	I enjoy e-learning with airflow effects
Q9	The vibration effects enhance the sense of reality in e-learning
Q10	The vibration effects are distracting
Q11	The vibration effects are annoying
Q12	I enjoy e-learning with vibration effects
Q13	The experienced approach was easy to use
Q14	The experienced approach was cumbersome
Q15	The experienced approach helped me better understand the concepts explained
Q16	The experienced approach did not help me learn the knowledge
Q17	The experienced approach can satisfy my learning needs
Q18	The experienced approach did not improve my learning experience
Q19	The experienced approach did not help me be more practically engaged in the learning process
Q20	I enjoyed the experienced approach
Q21	I would not recommend the experienced approach to my friends
Q22	I would like to learn more with the experienced approach

6 Results

In relation to the findings, Figs. 5 and 6 represent the participants' responses. Analysis of questions Q13 to Q22 reveals that participants highly regarded the setup and reported no discomfort.

This suggests that both groups had a positive perception of the overall experimental conditions, indicating that the setup was well-received by the participants. However, despite the positive feedback and the presence of multisensory content in the Experimental Group, there were no discernible differences were observed between the two groups. This lack of differentiation raises doubts about the actual influence of the multisensory content on the learning experience.

There are possible reasons for the absence of differences between the *Control Group* and the *Experimental Group*. One significant factor could be the homogeneity of the participants, as it is plausible that individuals in both groups

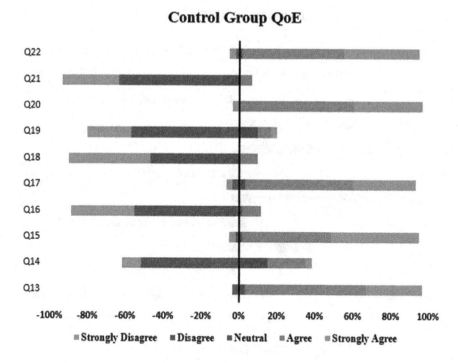

Fig. 5. Control Group QoE.

shared similar learning preferences or cognitive styles. When participants possess comparable characteristics or prior knowledge, the influence of multisensory content may not have been distinctive enough to yield noticeable distinctions.

Moreover, the learning task or materials employed in the experiment might not have posed sufficient challenge or engagement to elicit varying responses. In cases where the content was overly simplistic or if participants were already proficient in the subject matter, the impact of multisensory enhancements could have been limited in its effect. This highlights the need to explore into another aspect of the Multisensory Environment, specifically exploring ways to make multisensory elements an added value to traditional multimedia content.

6.1   One-Sample-Test

The results of the One-Sample Test presented in Table 3 provide valuable insights into the impact of olfactory, airflow, and vibration effects on the e-learning experience.

Q1: The Olfactory Effects Enhance the Sense of Reality in e-Learning. The analysis shows a significant positive mean difference of 0.933 ($p < 0.001$), indicating that participants perceived a heightened sense of reality when olfactory effects were incorporated into the e-learning environment.

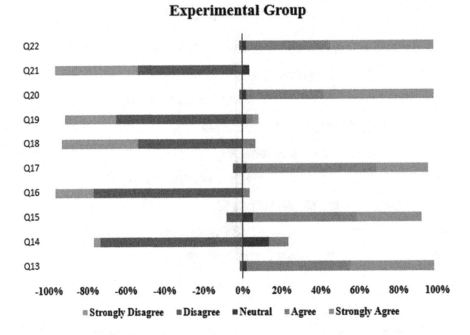

Fig. 6. Experimental Group QoE.

Q2: The Olfactory Effects Are Distracting. The analysis reveals a significant negative mean difference of -0.967 ($p < 0.001$), suggesting that participants did not find the olfactory effects to be distracting during the e-learning sessions. Regarding *Q3: The olfactory effects are annoying,* Similar to the previous question, the analysis indicates a significant negative mean difference of -1.167 ($p < 0.001$), indicating that participants did not find the olfactory effects to be annoying.

Q4: I Enjoy e-Learning with Olfactory Effects. The analysis demonstrates a significant positive mean difference of 1.533 ($p < 0.001$), indicating that participants reported enjoyment when olfactory effects were integrated into the e-learning experience.

The same pattern of analysis and significance continues for the questions related to airflow and vibration effects: Regarding *Q5: The airflow effects enhance the sense of reality in e-learning.* The analysis shows a significant positive mean difference of 0.967 ($p < 0.001$), suggesting that participants perceived an enhanced sense of reality with the incorporation of airflow effects.

Q6: The Airflow Effects Are Distracting. The analysis reveals a significant negative mean difference of -0.800 ($p < 0.001$), indicating that participants did not find the airflow effects to be distracting during e-learning sessions. Similarly to *Q7: The airflow effects are annoying* as the analysis indicates a significant negative mean difference of -0.700 ($p < 0.001$), suggesting that participants did not find the airflow effects to be annoying.

Table 3. One-Sample Test.

One-Sample Test						
Test Value = 3						
		Significance			95% Confidence Interval of the Difference	
	t	df	One-Sided p	Two-Sided p	Mean Difference	Lower	Upper
Q1	5.215	29	<.001	<.001	.933	.57	1.30
Q2	−6.227	29	<.001	<.001	−.967	−1.28	−.65
Q3	−9.143	29	<.001	<.001	−1.167	−1.43	−.91
Q4	14.699	29	<.001	<.001	1.533	1.32	1.75
Q5	5.491	29	<.001	<.001	.967	.61	1.33
Q6	−5.174	29	<.001	<.001	−.800	−1.12	−.48
Q7	−5.114	29	<.001	<.001	−.700	−.98	−.42
Q8	6.528	29	<.001	<.001	1.100	.76	1.44
Q9	3.010	29	.003	.005	.667	.21	1.12
Q10	−5.137	29	<.001	<.001	−.900	−1.26	−.54
Q11	−3.357	29	.001	.002	−.633	−1.02	−.25
Q12	5.869	29	<.001	<.001	1.033	.67	1.39

Q8: I Enjoy e-Learning with Airflow Effects. The analysis demonstrates a significant positive mean difference of 1.100 ($p < 0.001$), indicating that participants reported enjoyment when airflow effects were integrated into the e-learning experience. Q9-Q12 follow the same format, focusing on the perception of vibration effects in the e-learning environment.

These findings highlight the subjective nature of sensory effects in e-learning. Most of the participants perceive enhanced reality and enjoyment with the incorporation of olfactory, airflow, and vibration effects. These results emphasize the importance of considering individual preferences and designing flexible e-learning environments that allow users to customize their sensory experiences based on their personal preferences and learning styles.

6.2 Discussion

The results from the T-TEST reveal findings about participants' perceptions and experiences related to sensory effects in e-learning and the effectiveness of an experienced approach. The T-TEST findings indicate that the olfactory effects enhanced the sense of reality in the e-learning environment, as evidenced by a positive mean difference of 0.933 ($p < 0.001$). This suggests that participants perceived a heightened sense of immersion and realism when olfactory stimuli were integrated into the learning materials. Additionally, participants did not find the olfactory effects distracting or annoying, as indicated by the negative mean differences for both questions (Q2 and Q3).

Similar patterns were observed for the airflow effects. Participants answered that the incorporation of airflow effects helped enhance the sense of reality in e-learning, as indicated by a positive mean difference of 0.967. Similar to the olfactory effects, participants also did not find the airflow effects distracting or annoying, as suggested by the negative mean differences and significant p-values for

Q6 and Q7. Furthermore, participants reported enjoyment when airflow effects were integrated into the e-learning experience, supported by a significant positive mean difference of 1.100 ($p < 0.001$).

The findings related to vibration effects followed a similar pattern. Vibration effects significantly enhanced the sense of reality in e-learning, as indicated by positive mean differences for the relevant question. Participants did not find vibration effects distracting or annoying, as suggested by negative mean differences and significant p-values. Additionally, participants reported enjoyment when vibration effects were integrated into the e-learning experience, supported by significant positive mean differences. Most participants perceived enhanced reality and enjoyment with the incorporation of olfactory, airflow, and vibration effects. These results suggest that sensory effects can contribute positively to the e-learning experience, fostering a sense of immersion, engagement, and enjoyment.

Comparing the results, we can observe a contrast: While sensory effects demonstrated positive effects on participants' sense of reality, enjoyment, and lack of distraction or annoyance, the experienced approach did not yield significant differences in participants' responses across the analyzed dimensions. These findings suggest that incorporating sensory effects might have a more profound impact on the e-learning experience compared to the experienced approach alone.

In conclusion, these results emphasize the importance of considering individual preferences and designing flexible e-learning environments. The integration of sensory effects, such as olfactory, airflow, and vibration, can enhance the sense of reality and enjoyment in e-learning. However, the experienced approach alone might not significantly influence participants' perceptions and experiences. Future research could explore the combination of sensory effects and the experienced approach to uncover potential synergies in enhancing the overall e-learning experience.

6.3   Study Limitations

One weakness of this study is its narrow focus on female students aged 23 to 25, including undergraduate, postgraduate, and researchers from various disciplines. The restriction to this specific age range raises concerns about the generalizability of the study's findings. Research has shown that people in different age groups possess diverse life experiences and perspectives, which can influence their responses and behaviors. For instance, [9] found that olfactory perception tends to decline with age, suggesting that younger participants may have had a more heightened sense of smell compared to older individuals. This could have implications for this study's investigation of multisensory experiences and its ability to improve them. By exclusively focusing on the 23 to 25 age range, valuable insights from both older and younger individuals may have been overlooked, potentially limiting the broader applicability and relevance of the study's conclusions. On the other hand, exclusively including female subjects in the experiment could be interpreted as a deliberate effort to foster heightened motivation among women pursuing careers in STEM professions.

Another limitation of this study is its exclusive focus on female participants, which disregards the potential nuances and differences that may exist between genders. Gender and sex are known to play a significant role in shaping experiences, attitudes, and behaviors. By excluding male participants, the study fails to address an important aspect of the research question. For instance, studies such as [4] have highlighted differences in odor perception between males and females. Their research suggests that female superiority in assessing olfactory information, including odor identification, may be attributed to cognitive rather than perceptual differences in olfactory processing. Similarly, the report Doty and Cameron also discusses sex differences and the influence of reproductive hormones on human odor perception, indicating that females are more selective about odor and smells, while not males, although socio-cultural factors may also interfere in this issue. By neglecting male participants, this study overlooks valuable insights that could contribute to a more comprehensive understanding of the topic. Including both male and female participants would have allowed for a more robust exploration of potential gender-related differences in the study's findings.

Furthermore, the concentration of participants within the academic setting, specifically among students and researchers within the specified age range, presents another limitation. Although their insights and experiences are undoubtedly valuable, they may not fully represent the broader population. Including individuals from different professions and diverse backgrounds could have provided a more comprehensive understanding of the impact of multisensory content on the learning experience. This limitation calls for caution when generalizing the study's findings beyond the academic context and highlights the need for future research to incorporate a more diverse participant pool to enhance the external validity of the study.

7   Conclusion

The evaluation findings demonstrated that the use of sensory effects had a positive impact on participants' perception of reality, enjoyment, and ability to focus without distractions. This indicates that the participants responded favorably to the implementation of multisensory devices.

However, the approach based on prior experience did not result in noteworthy variances in participants' reactions to the examined aspects. These findings indicate that the integration of sensory effects may have a more substantial effect on the e-learning experience compared to relying solely on prior experience.

To gain deeper insights, future studies could explore the specific factors contributing to the differences in participants' perceptions and further investigate the relationship between these perceptions and learning outcomes. Additionally, gathering qualitative data, such as participant feedback and observations, could provide valuable context and a more comprehensive understanding of the implications of these findings in the context of e-learning.

Furthermore, regarding the participant pool, it would be beneficial to explore additional dimensions of diversity, such as socioeconomic status, cultural backgrounds, and geographic locations, to capture a wider range of perspectives and experiences. This would help to mitigate potential biases and ensure that the findings are applicable to a more diverse population.

In addition, it would be worthwhile for future studies to assess the long-term effects of incorporating sensory effects in e-learning. Tracking participants' retention of knowledge, skill acquisition, and overall learning outcomes over an extended period could provide valuable insights into the sustained benefits of multisensory approaches. Such investigations would contribute to the development of evidence-based guidelines for designing effective and engaging e-learning experiences that leverage sensory effects to optimize learning outcomes in diverse educational settings. Besides, evaluating learners' emotional states through physiological signals helps to adapt the learning content based on learners' needs and increases engagement levels.

Acknowledgement. The authors express their gratitude to the Centre for Machine Learning and Intelligence (CMLI) funded by the Department of Science and Technology (DST), India, for providing resources and support.

Celso A. S. Santos and Aleph C. Silveira also acknowledge financial support from Brazilian Agencies CNPq (National Council of Scientific and Technological Development), CAPES Foundation and, FAPES (Research Support Foundation of Espirito Santo).

Conflict of Interest. The authors declared no potential conflict of interest with respect to the publishing of this chapter.

Funding Availability. This work is supported by the Centre for Machine Learning and Intelligence funded by the Department of Science and Technology-CURIE.

References

1. Ademoye, O.A., Ghinea, G.: Information recall task impact in olfaction-enhanced multimedia. ACM Trans. Multimed. Comput. Commun. Appl. **9**(3), 1–16 (2013). https://doi.org/10.1145/2487268.2487270. Jun
2. Alkasasbeh, A.A., Ghinea, G.: Using olfactory media cues in e-learning - perspectives from an empirical investigation. Multimed. Tools Appl. **79**(27–28), 19265–19287 (2020). https://doi.org/10.1007/s11042-020-08763-3. Mar
3. Astleitner, H., Wiesner, C.: An integrated model of multimedia learning and motivation. J. Educ. Multimed. Hypermedia **13**(1), 3–21 (2004)
4. Bengtsson, S., Berglund, H., Gulyas, B., Cohen, E., Savic, I.: Brain activation during odor perception in males and females. NeuroReport **12**(9), 2027–2033 (2001)
5. Bi, T., Lyons, R., Fox, G., Muntean, G.M.: Improving student learning satisfaction by using an innovative dash-based multiple sensorial media delivery solution. IEEE Trans. Multimed. **23**, 3494–3505 (2021). https://doi.org/10.1109/TMM.2020.3025669
6. Choriev, R., Kucharov, S.: Methodology of using electronic textbooks in the field of technological education. Sci. Innov. **2**(B1), 371–373 (2023)

7. Covaci, A., Ghinea, G., Lin, C.H., Huang, S.H., Shih, J.L.: Multisensory games-based learning - lessons learnt from olfactory enhancement of a digital board game. Multimed. Tools Appl. **77**(16), 21245–21263 (2018). https://doi.org/10.1007/s11042-017-5459-2

8. Covaci, A., Zou, L., Tal, I., Muntean, G.M., Ghinea, G.: Is multimedia multisensorial? A review of mulsemedia systems. ACM Comput. Surv. (CSUR) **51**(5), 1–35 (2018)

9. Doty, R.L.: Age-related deficits in taste and smell. Otolaryngol. Clin. North Am. **51**(4), 815–825 (2018)

10. Doty, R.L., Cameron, E.L.: Sex differences and reproductive hormone influences on human odor perception. Physiol. Behav. **97**(2), 213–228 (2009)

11. Garcia-Ruiz, M., El-Seoud, S.A., Edwards, A., AL-JA'AM, J.M., Aquino-Santos, R.: Integrating the sense of smell in an educational human-computer interface. Interact. Comput. Aided Learn. (2008)

12. Ghinea, G., Thomas, J.: Quality of perception: user quality of service in multimedia presentations. IEEE Trans. Multimed. **7**(4), 786–789 (2005). https://doi.org/10.1109/TMM.2005.850960

13. Ghinea, G., Andres, F., Gulliver, S.R. (eds.): Multiple sensorial media advances and applications. IGI Global (2012). https://doi.org/10.4018/978-1-60960-821-7

14. Hussain, N., Ghinea, G.: Guidelines for evaluating wearables' quality of experience in a mulsemedia context. Multimed. Tools Appl. **81**(30), 43283–43314 (2022)

15. Kreitlon, J., Chen, L., Santos, L., Nascimento, R., Carrara, M.R., Guedes, G.P.: Affective multisensorial books. In: 2019 XIV Latin American Conference on Learning Technologies (LACLO), pp. 190–195. IEEE (2019)

16. Mortaza Mardiha, S., Alibakhshi, G., Mazloum, M., Javaheri, R.: Electronic flipped classrooms as a solution to educational problems caused by COVID-19: a case study of a research course in Iran higher education. Electron. J. e-Learn. **21**(1), 26–35 (2023)

17. Raheel, A., Majid, M., Alnowami, M., Anwar, S.M.: Physiological sensors-based emotion recognition while experiencing tactile enhanced multimedia. Sensors **20**(14), 4037 (2020)

18. ReportLinker: Global E-Learning Market to Reach $457.8 Billion by 2026 – globenewswire.com (2021). https://www.globenewswire.com/news-release/2021/07/13/2262081/0/en/Global-E-Learning-Market-

19. Richard, E., Tijou, A., Richard, P., Ferrier, J.L.: Multi-modal virtual environments for education with haptic and olfactory feedback. Virtual Real. **10**(3–4), 207–225 (2006)

20. Sanfilippo, F., Blazauskas, T., Salvietti, G., Ramos, I., Vert, S., Radianti, J., Majchrzak, T.A., Oliveira, D.A.: A perspective review on integrating VR/AR with haptics into stem education for multi-sensory learning. Robotics **11**(2) (2022). https://doi.org/10.3390/robotics11020041, https://www.mdpi.com/2218-6581/11/2/41

21. da Silveira, A.C., Santos, C.A.S.: Ongoing challenges of evaluating mulsemedia QoE. In: Proceedings of the 2nd Workshop on Multisensory Experiences-SensoryX 2022. SBC (2022)

22. Skliarova, I., Meireles, I., Martins, N., Tchemisova, T., Cação, I.: Enriching traditional higher STEM education with online teaching and learning practices: students’ perspective. Educ. Sci. **12**(11) (2022). https://doi.org/10.3390/educsci12110806

23. Tal, I., Zou, L., Covaci, A., Ibarrola, E., Bratu, M., Ghinea, G., Muntean, G.-M.: Mulsemedia in telecommunication and networking education: a novel teaching approach that improves the learning process. IEEE Commun. Mag. **57**(11), 60–66 (2019)

24. Tal, I., Zou, L., Farren, M., Muntean, G.-M.: Improving Learner experience, motivation and knowledge gain when using mulsemedia-based technology enhanced learning. In: Lane, H.C., Zvacek, S., Uhomoibhi, J. (eds.) CSEDU 2020. CCIS, vol. 1473, pp. 146–161. Springer, Cham (2021). https://doi.org/10.1007/978-3-030-86439-2_8

25. Yuan, Z., Bi, T., Muntean, G.M., Ghinea, G.: Perceived synchronization of mulsemedia services. IEEE Trans. Multimed. **17**(7), 957–966 (2015)

26. Yunusov, V., Gafarov, F., Ustin, P.: Deep learning techniques for the study of student's academic performance during distance education caused by COVID-19. In: 2023 17th International Conference on Electronics Computer and Computation (ICECCO), pp. 1–5 (2023). https://doi.org/10.1109/ICECCO58239.2023.10147143

27. Zhang, D.: Interactive multimedia-based e-learning: a study of effectiveness. Am. J. Distance Educ. **19**(3), 149–162 (2005)

28. Zou, L., Tal, I., Covaci, A., Ibarrola, E., Ghinea, G., Muntean, G.M.: Can multisensorial media improve learner experience? In: Proceedings of the 8th ACM on Multimedia Systems Conference, pp. 315–320. Association for Computing Machinery (2017). https://doi.org/10.1145/3083187.3084014

Accessible Applications to Improve the Tourist Experience

Irene De Paoli[1], Alessia M. Di Campi[2], and Flaminia L. Luccio[2]

[1] Università Ca' Foscari, Venezia, Italy
864472@stud.unive.it
[2] DAIS, Università Ca' Foscari, Venezia, Italy
{alessia.dicampi,luccio}@unive.it

Abstract. Traveling is known to improve a person's well-being and happiness, and tourism experiences should be offered to all types of tourists, including those with different disabilities. At the same time, technology is evolving and tourism applications are spreading. In this paper, we focus our attention on accessible mobile applications that can support a tourism experience. We first reviewed and classified a wide range of applications dedicated to users with visual, hearing, motor, cognitive impairments, and also others dedicated to the elderly. We have included this last category of users as they represent an interesting but at the same time specific target for the tourism industry. To understand how these dedicated apps could be better designed to improve accessibility we have then run a study collecting empirical data through questionnaires proposed to 210 users with diverse cognitive abilities, and to 50 elderly users, respectively. We have investigated and analyzed their approach to using tourist apps, also trying to understand the challenges they most commonly encounter when using them, and discussing possible improvements.

Keywords: Accessibility · Applications · Tourism

1 Introduction

The tourism experience is designed primarily for those who can participate rather than for those who, for various reasons, are excluded from participation. Equality in this context is an issue. Those excluded and neglected from the tourism experience are typically marginalized on the basis of their low socioeconomic status, ethnicity, age, gender, sexuality, ability or the intersection of these identity areas [24].

The first official interventions towards the inclusion of people with disabilities dates back to 1981 with the establishment of the International Year of Persons with Disabilities whose theme was "full participation and equality", and in 2006 with the adoption of the United Nations Convention on the Rights of Persons with Disabilities [32]. These interventions are the symptom of an awareness of the problem of the inclusion of people with disabilities in the various layers of the social fabric, including tourism.

In 2023 the World Health Organization has estimated that over 1.3 billion people, i.e., about 16% of the world's population, have some form of disability [37]. With the

H. P. da Silva and P. Cipresso (Eds.): CHIRA 2023, CCIS 1997, pp. 43–65, 2023.
https://doi.org/10.1007/978-3-031-49368-3_4

development of accessible tourism and the growing popularity of mobile devices, it is imperative to ensure that all mobile applications are accessible to every individual in their skill spectrum. Therefore, companies and developers cannot ignore the unique needs of these people and their right to participate in tourism experiences.

The constraints and limits on travel and the use of services for disabled people may vary according to the type of disability (e.g. motor, visual, hearing and cognitive disabilities), the needs of individuals, and the sectors of the tourism industry. Accessible tourism experiences involve collaborative processes between stakeholders and should offer people with different access requirements dedicated tourism products and services [28].

In this paper we focus on accessible mobile applications, noting that, poorly accessible applications can become a barrier to both users and commerce. For example, for a business, the fewer users are able to use its application, the lower its revenue stream will be. Indeed, an application that is difficult to use is often a source of stress and frustration, so it is discarded in favor of a more accessible alternative. The barrier of mobile inaccessibility therefore prevents a company from reaching its full potential. Destinations need to know how to apply the right technology to serve this audience, or else they may risk not benefiting from the economic impact this market would bring. Furthermore, it is known that in general tourist experiences improve the level of life satisfaction and well-being [23,30].

Contributions. We have first reviewed and classified, on the basis of some general characteristics (e.g., supported operating system, language, etc.), a wide range of accessible mobile applications for tourism (see Sect. 3.1). The applications considered are the most commonly used, and are very useful to support the tourist experience. Then, we have evaluated these applications on a broad spectrum of users: users with visual, hearing, motor and cognitive impairments and elderly (see Sect. 3.2 for the methodology, and Sect. 4 for the results). Our goal was to verify with real users the following: Q1) Are the tourism applications analyzed that claim to be accessible, really accessible to everyone? Q2) What features do these users consider important for an accessible tourism app?

While in general many of the applications analyzed had good feedback, users still reported limitations and suggested possible changes. Starting from the results of this evaluation, we suggest a series of recommendations that should be taken into consideration when developing new applications for accessible tourism (see Sect. 5).

2   Background and Related Work

In this section we briefly define the considered target of users, we recall known accessibility guidelines for mobile applications, and finally we discuss the related work.

2.1   Impairment Classification

A successful human-computer interaction requires the involvement of a perceptual system. This system receives sensory messages from the computer, involves a motor system that controls the actions the user takes to provide input to the computer, and uses a cognitive system to integrate the sensory input received with the appropriate actions to take [16]. When some of these systems do not interact properly, for example due to the presence of an impairment, the user may have difficulty interacting with a computer or with an application.

E.g., a user with a *visual impairment* may have a totally or partially compromised *visual perception*, due to a different sharpness of vision, i.e., *visual acuity*, or a limited *contrast sensitivity* between the brightness of the foreground and background regions of the display, or a limited *color perception*. Thus, he may not be able to decode the information on the screen correctly. People with a *hearing impairment* may suffer of a partial hearing ability, called *hypoacusia*, or a profound one, called *deafness*. They may present varying levels of language skills due to a lack of constant exposure to accessible language ever since from birth, and this may be reflected on limited reading ability, in some cases. Users with a *motor impairment* due to a missing limb, or a limited muscular control, may experience movement problems. This can limit navigation on a page, especially if there is no full keyboard support, navigational aids, text alternatives, etc. Users with a *cognitive impairment* may exhibit a neurological or a mental health disorder. They may have motor limitations, comprehension problems, etc., therefore, very complicated text or navigation contents, blinking of text and images, could compromise these users' ability to use the devices. Finally, we include in the category of *elderly people*, those who are over 65 years old. Some elderly may not have any problem at all, on the other hand others may experience several declines such as hearing loss, vision decline, physical decline, cognitive decline, or may also not be as well skilled with new technologies, or have various limitations in interacting with applications. We consider the elderly as an interesting group to study as they are a specific target for the tourism industry (see [31] and citations there mentioned). For a more detailed classification of all impairments refer to [36].

2.2 Accessibility Guidelines for Mobile Applications

W3C has promoted the Mobile Web Initiative (MWI) which has developed a series of recommendations to make Web pages suitable on mobile devices: the Mobile Web Best Practices (MWBP) [33]. These guidelines are based on the specific characteristics of the mobile Web experience and are closely related to the Web Content Accessibility Guidelines (WCAG) [35] which for mobile applications have been incorporated in the "Mobile Accessibility: How WCAG 2.0 and Other W3C/WAI Guidelines Apply to Mobile" document [34].

WCAG 2.0 outlines the guidelines for websites in three levels of compliance [35]: A, AA and AAA, where AAA is the standard of excellence and A is the minimum criterion required for a site to be considered accessible. In addition to this, there are four principles that should be followed to develop accessible mobile applications [15, 22, 29, 34]:

1) *Perceptible*, i.e., ensuring that the content is perceptible to all users, no matter which type of disability they have. To achieve this, one should minimize the amount of information on each page; provide a reasonable default size for content and touch controls; adapt the length of the link text to the width of the display area; place form fields below, rather than next to their labels.

2) *Operable*, i.e., all features should be fully usable by anyone, regardless of user limitations. To obtain this, buttons should be at least $9mm \times 9mm$, should have some empty space around, and should be placed in an accessible position; gestures should be simple; the use of external keyboards should be supported.

3) *Understandable* i.e., all users should be able to understand the meaning of the information presented. To achieve this vertical and horizontal orientation should be supported; in the layout, elements and instructions should all be simply identified; operable elements should be easily identified using special shapes, colors, etc.

4) *Robust*, i.e., the content of an app should remain accessible regardless of technological changes. To obtain this, automatic keyboard setting should be provided; the data entering should be simple; platform characteristics should be supported, e.g., the accessibility functions of Android or iOS smartphones.

2.3   Accessibile Applications for Tourism

While there is a large literature studying accessible tourism websites (see, for example, [18, 19, 25, 35]), as far as we know, much less can be found on accessible tourism applications.

Carneiro et al. in [17] propose a study on the accessibility of five mobile applications of the Portuguese public administration. While these apps are not directly dedicated to the tourism market, still this work has the general aim of raising awareness of the state of accessibility of mobile applications.

Similarly, the work of Ferreira da Silva et al. (see [21]) proposes an accessibility analysis of a mobile app called Mercado Livre, used to buy items online. The study was conducted by performing five accessibility assessment sessions on a group of visually impaired users. Although this work does not directly focus on tourism applications, it confirms how important it is for app developers to strictly follow the Web Content Accessibility Guidelines (WCAG) 2.0, in order to support accessible mobile applications, as the problems experienced by users were related to guideline violations.

Madeira et al. in [26] propose a manual and automatic approach to evaluate 14 Portuguese mobile applications of the tourism sector. Different features were evaluated w.r.t the accessibility of the applications, such as light intensity, used operating system, screen size and resolution, etc. Unlike this manual and automatic approach, in our work the evaluation of applications has been done on a wider set of applications, and not only on general technical characteristics such as operating system, language, etc., but also on different accessibility features evaluated by collecting empirical data from different categories of disabled users.

Ribeiro et al. in [31] present an overview of several mobile applications for tourism that can be used by people with different disabilities. Positive aspects and limitations are described. The authors also propose the development of a data platform for accessible tourism applications, highlighting which functionalities it should support. The main idea is to centralize the collection and updating of information, in order to simplify the distribution of data on different applications and to support and simplify the development of new ones. In our work users have tested some of the applications presented in this paper, but we have taken into consideration a much broader set of applications, and we have also tested them on users with cognitive disabilities.

Table 1. Search strategy phase: Mobile apps found for every store and search engine.

Mobile apps search engines	Number of applications
Google Play Store	30
Google Search Engine	25
Apple App Store	22

Finally, the work of Mayordomo-Martínez et al. [27] presents a new application that provides reliable accessibility information on the beaches in the Region of Murcia, Spain, for people with physical and motor disabilities.

3   Method

The aim of this work is to evaluate the current state of art of accessible applications for the tourism sector. We first conducted a review of existing accessible applications for the tourism sector in the literature and of products on the market, selecting a set works and of applications. Then, we conducted an empirical study proposing a survey to 260 users.

3.1   Classification of Accessible Applications for the Tourism Sector

Our first goal was to describe and classify the most used accessible mobile applications in the tourism sector. To find a suitable set for evaluation, a systematic review of existing applications on accessible tourism was carried out following three phases: (1) mobile apps search engines and store selection, and application of predefined search strategies, (2) application of established eligibility criteria (filtering and extraction of results with inclusion criteria), and (3) final selection of appropriate applications and their analysis.

Phase 1: Search Strategy. The product search was conducted using the Google Search Engine, the Google Play Store, the Apple App Store. During the search some keywords were used, to ensure the identification of all applications relevant to accessible tourism for people with different types of disabilities. We defined our search strings as:'tourism' AND 'app*' AND ('accessible' OR'elderly' OR'visual*' OR'motor' OR'hearing' OR'cognitive' OR'impaired users' OR'inabilitie*' OR'disabilit*'). Continuing with our search and iterating within the most relevant results, we found additional keywords and deepened our search. In Table 1 we present the list of mobile apps search engines we have used and the number of apps acquired by them (many of the apps are available on the various operating systems).

Phase 2: Study Selection Criteria. Each result extracted in Phase 1 was examined in terms of relevance and on the basis of the following selection criteria (Table 2 shows a summary):

Table 2. Summary of exclusion and inclusion criteria.

Criteria	Inclusion criteria	Exclusion criteria
App focus	For tourist experiences	Irrelevant app focus
Accessibility	Supporting disabled users/elderly	Lack of accessibility
Ongoing support	Actively maintained	Lack of ongoing support
Availability	For iOS or Android OSs	Only for other OSs
Affordability	Free or with a demo version	Costly
Time range	Up to 2022	After 2022

- The app had to be developed specifically for a tourist experience or it could be a more general application that can effectively support the tourism experience.
- The app needed to be aimed at people with disabilities and/or be an app designed for a series of critical services for the benefit not only of disabled people, but also of a wider public;
- The app had to be updated, i.e., still in use and the developers still had to support it;
- The app had to be for iOS and/or Android operating systems;
- The app had to be free, or at least had to have a demo version.
- The app had to be available before the user study (i.e., up to 2022).

Based on these criteria, 14 apps were selected.

Phase 3: Study Final App Selection and Analysis. We finally downloaded the 14 selected apps, we tested them and we analyzed their features, checking if they were compatible and interesting for the study we wanted to run. Some of these apps, useful for different types of users, have been later tested by users with different disabilities, while other specific apps for a given disability have only been tested by users belonging to the same category.

Table 3 summarizes their main features, a more detailed description of all the apps is provided in the Appendix. Links are to the official product pages, while the apps can be downloaded from Apple App Store and Google Play Store.

3.2 The Study

To be eligible to the study, participants had to be at least 18 years old and had to have some kind of disability or be an elderly person. They voluntarily gave informed consent to participate. All the questionnaires were anonymous.

Participants. To select the participants we contacted many associations located in the North-East part of Italy (for privacy reasons we omit the names), supporting people with motor, hearing, visual and cognitive disabilities. All the associations that have decided to collaborate have been very cooperative and have helped us reaching the users. The elderly users were selected among relatives and friends. Globally we were able to reach

Table 3. Accessible applications to support a tourism experience.

App Name	OS	Compatibility	Languages	Destination	Responsive	Use
Accessaloo [11]	iOS Android	Smartphone, iPad, iPod touch	37 languages	Global	Yes	Accessible toilets
AccessibItaly [8]	iOS Android	Smartphone, iPad, PC, iPod touch	Italian	Italy	Yes	Sign Language Touristic Information
BOForAll [12]	iOS Android	Smartphone, iPad, PC, iPod touch	English,French, Italian	Bologna	Yes	Cultural information
Jaccede [14]	iOS Android	Smartphone, PC	French, English, Spanish, Italian, German	France	Yes	Accessible Facilities Paris
Kimap [6]	iOS Android	Smartphone, iPad, PC, iPod touch	Italian	Tuscany	Yes	Accessible maps and itineraries
Link Cash Locator [13]	iOS Android	Smartphone, PC, iPod touch	English	UK	Yes	ATM Locator
MagnusCards [2]	iOS Android	Smartphone, iPad, PC, iPod touch	English, Spanish, French, Arabic	Global	Yes	Vacation preparation
Moovit [3]	iOS Android	Smartphone, iPad, PC, iPod touch	42 languages	Global	Yes	Assisted navigation
PerNoiAutistici [5]	iOS Android	Smartphone, iPad, PC, iPod touch	Italian	Italy	Yes	Autism friendly news, structures
Taxi Sordi [7]	iOS Android	Smartphone, PC, iPod touch	English, Italian, German	Italy	Yes	Taxi automatic reservation
TripStep [9]	iOS Android	Smartphone, iPad, iPod touch	English, Italian	Sicily	Yes	Tourist guide of Sicily
Tube Map [10]	iOS Android	Smartphone	16 languages	Different Cities	Yes	Tube and train map
TUR4All [4]	iOS Android	Smartphone, iPad, PC, iPod touch	11 languages	Different Countries	Yes	Tourist guide of different countries
WheelMap [1]	iOS Android	Smartphone, iPad, PC, iPod touch	32 languages	Global	Yes	Accessibility evaluator

260 users. 14.23% of the participants to the questionnaire were young adults with an age between 18 and 25 years, 70.77% were adults between 26 and 64 years, and 15% were over 65. Specifically, 53 users had a visual impairment, 51 users a hearing impairment, 56 users a motor impairment, 50 users a cognitive impairment, and 50 were elderly.

Most users with an age between 18 and 25 years suffered from cognitive or visual impairment. In the age group from 26 to 64 years, users mostly had motor disability and hearing impairment.

Procedure. In the first phase users had to download and install the apps, and then had to test them.

Application Download and Installation Phase. All the associations contacted helped users when necessary. However, the percentage of users who requested help at any stage was very small and therefore negligible. In particular, all users with visual and hearing disabilities were able to download, install and test the apps independently, most users with mobility disabilities were able to install the apps, and all tested them independently. Some users with cognitive disabilities needed help installing the apps, but only a few of them needed help in the testing phase. Finally, the majority of elderly users were able to install the apps independently, others were helped by one of the authors of the paper in the download phase, however all users were able to test the apps independently. The download and installation phases were not evaluated in our study. Since the percentage of individuals who received assistance in the testing phase was extremely low, this factor did not introduce bias into the data analysis.

Application Testing Phase. In the testing phase users had access to a specific set of apps targeted to their disability. The order of exposure to the apps was the order of appearance described and illustrated in the figures of Sect. 4.2. The users did not have a strict limit of time per testing an app, so not to get stressed, they had to take a break between one evaluation and the next one so not to distort the results, and in general completed the tasks of evaluating all the apps proposed for their category in at most one/two hours (w.r.t. the disability). After all users completed all app evaluation tasks, we conducted additional checks to ensure the accuracy of the data collected. We carefully reviewed all completed questionnaires to ensure that all questions were answered completely and accurately, and that the responses provided in the questionnaire were detailed and consistent, to confirm that all users had indeed completed their assigned tasks. The requested tasks were comparable, the users had to simulate a real use of the app (i.e., navigate and use the different features of the app). All users claimed that they had completed all tasks. After this, they had to fill up an on-line questionnaire that was a survey with multiple choice questions and also some open questions, which are illustrated in more details in the next section. The evaluation of the followed the WCAG principles, i.e., we asked if the app was perceivable, operable, understandable and robust and we explained this to users using a simple language.

4   Results

In this section we present and discuss the results of the evaluation of the accessible mobile applications presented in Sect. 3.1 obtained from a series of questionnaires proposed to different groups of disabled users. All the apps were evaluated on a value that ranged between 1 (very bad) and 5 (very good). The complete (translated) questionnaire is available in the Appendix.

4.1 General Questions on Mobile Apps

We do not present the entire questionnaire here but we illustrate the relevant questions. We first asked general questions on the technological abilities, expectations from any app, and from touristic apps. The questions were the following:

What is Your Skill Level in: 1) Using a Computer, 2) A Smartphone, 3) An Application, or 4) In Navigation? These were four independent questions on technological abilities. From the questionnaire it emerged that most of the participants were able to use a mobile phone (99%), run applications (96%) and navigate on the Web (92%). Not all of them were able to use a computer (only 87%).

What Does Your Satisfaction with an App Depend on? We asked user expectations from a mobile application, based on the accessibility principles of Sect. 2.2. It emerged that 76.2% of the users would like to have apps that are easy to use, 54.2% look for the services offered by the apps, 53.5% are interested in the content presented by the app, 35% expect a nice UI design, only 0.4% look for the app utility, and also other 0.4% for vocal commands.

Have You Ever Used an Accessible App? Have You Ever Used an Accessible Tourism App? From the study we conducted we found that more than half of the participants (55.4%) had already used accessible apps. This percentage decreases when the question is on the use of accessible tourism apps, only 36.2% of the users had already used one.

Can You Easily Find Information on the Accessibility of a tourist destination? About half of the participants (52.3%), declared themselves satisfied with the ease with which information on tourist accessibility can generally be found; while 23.1% of them indicated that they have never been interested in seeking information on the accessibility of a destination.

What Communication Channel Do You Use to Prepare for a Trip or Visit? When we asked how trips are organized, many participants indicated that they listen to the experiences of friends and/or relatives (56.2%); others search information on the Web (46.9%), or read comments on social networks(35.8%). Only few users indicated that they rely on travel agencies (0.8%) or directly call tourist facilities (0.8%), or read tourist magazines (0.4%). Note that, multiple answers were possible and we also left space for an open answer.

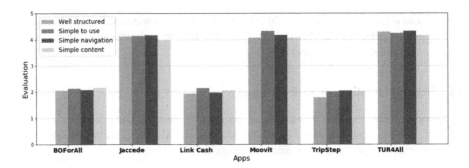

Fig. 1. Average ratings given by visually impaired users.

4.2 Evaluation Based on a Specific Disability

We now present the results of our survey broken down by specific disabilities. Each group of users had to evaluate the apps based on the following four questions:

1. Was the app you tested well structured?
2. Was the app you tested easy to use?
3. Does the app you tested have easy navigation?
4. Does the app you tested have clear and simple content?

We also left space for comments. For space limitations we are reporting different tables (one for each set of users) with the mean of the obtained values, on each of the four questions. Recall that values range between 1 (very bad) and 5 (very good). We also indicated in the text, for each app and each disability, the mean values of the results of the four questions and the standard deviation $(mean, SD)$. The resulting numbers indicate where there is most potential for improvement with the apps, and where accessibility measures vary the most. More detailed results can be found in [20].

Assessment of Applications for Users with Visual Impairments. Visual impairment applications aim to support users by providing them the ability to move independently and confidently in their surroundings and allow them to access visual or textual information. 53 users with visual impairments participated to the study, 42 out of 50 people used a device with an iOS operating system. Moreover, 8 users used assistive technologies app, including: VoiceOver, text magnification and screen magnification.

Figure 1 reports the results of the evaluation of the 6 applications. In the horizontal axis we have the evaluated app name, in the vertical axis the four evaluated features and the evaluation value (the mean) that ranges between 1 (very bad) and 5 (very good). The pink color represents "well structured", the blue color "Simple to use", the green color "Simple navigation", and finally the light blue color the "Simple content". These colors are maintained also in the next figures.

What emerges is that Jaccede, Moovit and TUR4All achieved excellent ratings, most users rated them with a score between 3 and 5, especially the value 4 was the most common choice among users. In contrast, the applications: BoForAll, Link Cash

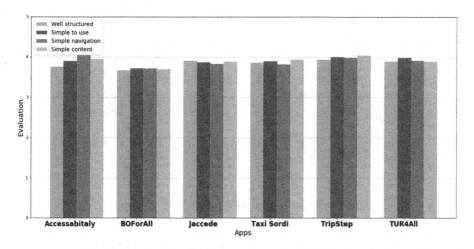

Fig. 2. Average ratings given by hearing impaired users.

Locator, and TripStep received ratings from 1 up to a maximum of 3, with the majority of users choosing a value of 2. For the apps that did not receive excellent evaluations respondents reported in the open questions the need for an explanatory tutorial on how to best use the applications since not all of them are intuitive and easy to use. Moreover, some users reported that some apps were not sufficiently described.

In summary the applications: BoForAll received a rating on the four features that ranged from 2 to 3 (excluded) (M : 2.10, SD : 0.04), Jaccede received a rating on the four features that ranged from 3 to 4 (M : 4.09, SD : 0.08), Link Cash Locator received a rating on the four features that ranged from 1 to 3 (excluded) (M : 2.03, SD : 0.09), Moovit received a rating on the four features that ranged from 4 to 5 (excluded) (M : 4.15, SD : 0.02), TripStep received a rating on the four features that ranged from 1 to 2 (M : 1.96, SD : 0.11), and TUR4All received a rating on the four features that ranged from 4 to 5 (excluded) (M : 4.24, SD : 0.06).

Assessment of Applications for Users with Hearing Impairments. For users with hearing impairments, the applications we tested make use of appropriate technologies to improve communication by implementing speech-to-text technology (that translates audio content into written words), providing subtitles, videos in sign language etc. 51 users with hearing impairments participated to the study, and more than half of the people used a device with an Android operating system.

Figure 2 reports the results of the evaluation of the 6 applications. In the horizontal axis we have the evaluated app name, in the vertical axis the four evaluated features and the evaluation value (the mean) that ranges between 1 (very bad) and 5 (very good). Participants who have tried the apps did not encounter any particular difficulties. Each application received a grade ranging from 3 to 5, and only one user indicated in rare cases a value of 2. Among the possible improvements indicated in the open questions

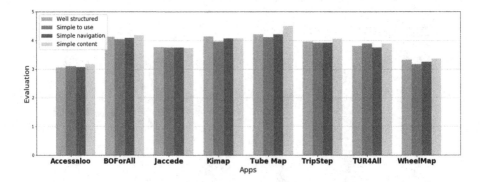

Fig. 3. Average ratings given by motor impaired users.

it emerges the request for translation from the foreign voice to a text in the native language.

In summary, applications on average received the following ratings: AccessibItaly received a rating on the four features that ranged from 3 to 5 (excluded) ($M : 3.91, SD : 0.0.18$), BoForAll received a rating on the four evaluated features that ranged from 3 to 4 (excluded) ($M : 3.70, SD : 0.02$), Jaccede received a rating on the four features that ranged from 3 to 4 (excluded) ($M : 3.90, SD : 0.05$), Taxi Sordi received a rating on the four features that ranged from 3 to 4 (excluded) ($M : 3.88, SD : 0.05$), TripStep received a rating on the four features that ranged from 3 to 5 (excluded) ($M : 3.99, SD : 0.04$), and TUR4All received a rating on the four features that ranged from 3 to 4 (excluded) ($M : 3.89, SD : 0.02$).

Assessment of Applications for Users with Motor Impairments. There are many applications that offer information support to users with motor disabilities or that allow the collaborative creation of accessibility maps. The main goal of these apps is usually to provide information on accessible facilities in public places and in transport. It is important to consider that people with motor disabilities constitute a very heterogeneous group. They can differ in physical or functional characteristics, age or transport needs. For this reason, the apps designed for these users should be aware the needs of each user to improve individual mobility skills. 56 users with motor impairments participated to the test, and 32 out of 56 used a device with an Android operating system.

Figure 3 reports the results of the evaluation of the 8 applications. In the horizontal axis we have the evaluated app name, in the vertical axis the four evaluated features and the evaluation value (the mean) that ranges between 1 (very bad) and 5 (very good). Also for this type of users, as for users with hearing disabilities, there were no problems during the app test. Moreover, each of the tested apps received very good rating, with values ranging from 3 to 5. Note that, although some applications have been rated negatively in some cases, with a score of 2, no possible improvement has been reported.

In summary, applications on average received the following ratings: Accessaloo received a rating on the four evaluated features that ranged from 3 to 4 (excluded) ($M : 3.09, SD : 0.04$), BoForAll received a rating on the four features that ranged

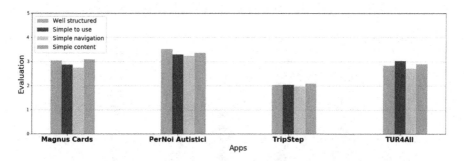

Fig. 4. Average ratings given by cognitive impaired users.

from 4 to 5 (excluded) (M : 4.10, SD : 0.05), Jaccede received a rating on the four features that ranged from 3 to 4 (excluded) (M : 3.74, SD : 0.01), Kimap received a rating on the four features that ranged from 3 to 5 (excluded) (M : 4.05, SD : 0.07), Tube Map received a rating on the four features that ranged from 4 to 5 (excluded) (M : 4.25, SD : 0.01), TripStep received a rating on the four features that ranged from 3 to 5 (M : 3.95, SD : 0.06), TUR4All received a rating on the four features that ranged from 3 to 4 (excluded) (M : 3.82, SD : 0.06), and WheelMap received a rating on the four features that ranged from 3 to 4 (excluded) (M : 3.26, SD : 0.08).

Assessment of Applications for Users with Cognitive Impairments. The market for tourism applications accessible to people with cognitive disabilities is still scarce. Most of the existing apps support everyday life, while only a smaller number include tourism applications for users with this disability. Among these, we find informative apps on places to visit in various destinations and their accessibility; few have been developed to help tourists with cognitive disabilities preparing them for new tourism experiences. 50 users with cognitive impairments participated to the test, and 46 out of 50 people used a device with an iOS operating system.

Figure 4 reports the results of the evaluation of the 4 applications. In the horizontal axis we have the evaluated app name, in the vertical axis the four evaluated features and the evaluation value (the mean) that ranges between 1 (very bad) and 5 (very good).

From the results it can be deduced that for two applications greater difficulty was encountered, the TripStep and TUR4All apps: these are very descriptive and structured applications and users found them too complicated. Above all TripStep, in all four evaluated points, received by about thirty people, therefore by more than half of the users, values between 1 and 2. The rest of the applications instead obtained an average good evaluation for each point, few users found them a bit difficult (ease of use) and assigned a value of 2, but most of the values are between 3 and 4.

In summary, applications on average received the following ratings: Magnus Card received a rating on the four evaluated features that ranged from 2 to 3 (M : 2.93, SD : 0.15), PerNoi Autistici received a rating on the four features that ranged from 3 to 4 (excluded) (M : 3.35, SD : 0.12), TripStep Map received a rating on the four features that ranged from 1 to 3 (M : 2.23, SD : 0.44), and TUR4All received a rating on the four features that ranged from 2 to 3 (M : 2.86, SD : 0.13).

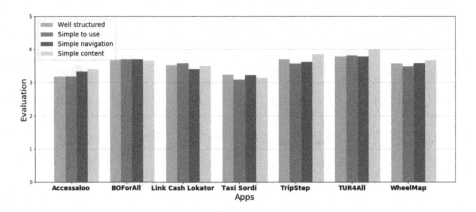

Fig. 5. Average ratings given by elderly users.

Assessment of Applications for Elderly Users. Like people with some form of disability, people entering the aging stage have special needs and interests that the tourism
industry has to meet. Indeed, sight, hearing, device use, experience with technology and
decision making are some of the characteristics that must be considered to maximize
the user experience of this group and enhance their travel experience. 50 elderly users
participated to the test, and 30 out of 50 people used a device with an Android operating
system.

Figure 5 reports the results of the evaluation of the 7 applications. In the horizontal
axis we have the evaluated app name, in the vertical axis the four evaluated features and
the evaluation value (the mean) that ranges between 1 (very bad) and 5 (very good). All
applications had an evaluation that ranged from 3 to 4 with the exception of complex
applications, such as Accessaloo, Taxi Sordi, and Link Cash Locator, that had a value
equal to 2. Even if the users liked the apps, a general comment in the open questions was
that usability would greatly improve if all these apps would be simplified. Furthermore,
when asked what is missing or what could be improved, the addition of the translation
into different native languages for the Link Cash Lokator app was indicated.

In summary, applications on average received the following ratings: Accessaloo
received a rating on the four evaluated features that ranged from 3 to 4 (excluded)
($M : 3.27, SD : 0.11$), BoForAll received a rating on the four features that ranged
from 3 to 4 (excluded) ($M : 3.68, SD : 0.01$), Link Cash Lokator received a rating on
the four features that ranged from 3 to 4 (excluded) ($M : 3.50, SD : 0.07$), TaxiSordi
Map received a rating on the four features that ranged from 3 to 4 (excluded) ($M :
3.17, SD : 0.07$), TripStep received a rating on the four features that ranged from 3 to 4
(excluded) ($M : 3.68, SD : 0.13$), TUR4All received a rating on the four features that
ranged from 3 to 4 ($M : 3.84, SD : 0.10$), finally WheelMap received a rating on the
four features that ranged from 3 to 4 (excluded) ($M : 3.57, SD : 0.08$).

General Questions and Comparisons. In addition to the specific evaluation of each
app presented above, we also asked other more general questions:

Did You Already Know or had You Already Used at Least One of the Tested Apps? First, what emerged is that many users were not aware of some/all of the existing apps. In particular, 71.1% of the visually impaired users, 54.9% of the hearing impaired, 66.1% of the motor impaired, only 12% of the cognitive impaired, and 22% of the elderly had used or were aware of at least one of the apps they have tried in the testing phase.

Do You Think Some of the Apps You Did Not Know or Did Not Use Yet Will Come in Handy? 94.3% of the visually impaired, 98% of the hearing impaired, 96.4% of the motor impaired, 72% of the cognitive impaired, and 54% of the elderly users affirmed that among the apps not yet known or not yet used, some will surely come in handy.

Finally, we focused on the statistical analysis of two elements that we consider funda-mental for this study and the most suitable ones, based on the collected data, for the statistical analysis.

To investigate whether there were differences between various groups of people in finding information about the accessibility of tourist destinations, we conducted an Anova one-way test. ANOVA, or Analysis of Variance, is a statistical test that compares the means of three or more groups to determine if there are any significant differences between them. Turkey's Honestly Significant Difference (HSD) test is a post hoc test often used after ANOVA to identify which specific groups have significantly differ-ent means from each other. Participants were asked whether they generally seek out information about accessibility when planning a trip, and their responses were used to analyze the data. The results revealed that some groups had significantly more dif-ficulty than others in finding this information, with a statistically significant result of $F(1, 4) = 24.96$ and a p-value less than 0.00001. To further explore these differences, we conducted a Post Hoc Tukey HSD analysis, which allowed us to visually compare the groups. Our findings show that cognitively impaired users and older people had dif-ferent results from the other groups, indicating that they may face greater challenges in finding information about accessibility of tourist destinations.

Finally, the apps tested by all groups were tur4All and TripStep. We performed the ANOVA test to analyze which of them was the least popular. The result was $F(1, 4) = 5.94$ with a $p - value < .05$ showing that there is a difference in the liking between the two and TripStep is the least liked app. We therefore wanted to analyze which users liked it the least and from the statistical analysis it emerged that they were the visually and cognitive impaired. We investigated, which feature of the app was problematic, and the result was that the content of the app is not presented in a simple manner (the'simple content' value received lower ratings).

5   Discussion

In this section we want to answer to the questions we initially posed.

Q1) Are the Tourism Applications Analyzed That Claim To Be Accessible, Really Accessible to Everyone? We can answer "only partially' following the results of

Table 4. Desired features.

Feature	Explanation
Informational content	Offers useful content, in-depth insights, or relevant news
Services offered	Offers a wide range of useful services or innovative features
Ease of use	Easy to navigate, user-friendly design, easy to use
Graphics	Appealing design, well-organized layout, high-quality graphics
Utilities	Offers functionalities that meet user needs or simplify tasks
Vocal commands	Interacts with the app through voice commands

Sect. 4, and from the outcome of the open questions. What emerged is that some visually impaired users did not like much some applications (lack of 'ease of use') due to the lack of an explanatory tutorial on how to use the apps, thus more detailed information on the app use should be provided. On the other hand, elderly and users with hearing disabilities have shown difficulties in using apps written in a non-native language, thus they would greatly benefit of a language text translation feature. Some cognitively impaired users also had difficulty understanding the description and layout and navigational structure of the app (e.g., the app was not "understandable", w.r.t., the four principles).

Q2) What Features Do These Users Consider Important for an Accessible Tourism App? Let us first consider the results of the questions described in Sect. 4.1. First of all, it emerges that some users were not very skilled with computers and from the data analysis we were able to identify these users with those with cognitive disabilities or the elderly. This is also confirmed by the fact that some users of both categories asked for help during the installation phase and some even during the test phase. On the other hand 96% of the users claimed to be able to use apps. Therefore, in our opinion, it is important to consider limited technological skills, but still developing mobile tourism apps could be a good choice for most users.

Table 4 summarizes the list of features that these users believe increase their satisfaction with an app, and the explanation of what each feature refers to. Dividing the results by different disabilities or by being elderly, we obtain the results shown in Table 5. We can notice that for all groups ease of use is the most important feature. From the results of the Anova test of the Sect. 4.2 it emerges for visually and cognitive impaired the lack of ease of use derived from the lack of 'simple content', so the simplicity of the content is important. Furthermore, as anticipated, users with cognitive disabilities have found some apps too descriptive and poorly structured, they got lost in navigation and did not stay focused on the indicated set of instructions. Thus, defining apps with easy navigation is a critical issue for all of them.

Recommendations. Our analysis and questionnaire results surfaced potential improvements in developing accessible tourism applications for disabled and elderly users. From our empirical study we have validated some of the standard guidelines for accessible apps, and we have also extracted new recommendations.

Table 5. Desired features for each disability. The features are described in Table 4.

Disabilitie(s)	Desired features
Visual disability	Informational content, Ease of use
Hearing disability	Services offered, Ease of use
Physical disability	Informational content, Ease of use
Cognitive disability	Services offered, Ease of use
Elderly*	Services offered, Ease of use

*We are aware that being an elderly is not a disability

First of all, companies must bear in mind that the majority of disabled and elderly users still prefer to organize a trip with a classic approach based on the experiences of friends and/or relatives. Furthermore, in some cases such as for users with cognitive disabilities, the trips are organized by others. To reach the full potential in the market, constant work is needed to advertise the apps on dedicated disability websites or social media, and contacting dedicated associations trying to reach all possible users. In particular, the two categories of cognitively disabled and elderly were very little aware not only of the existence of accessible tourism apps, but also of the possibility to search and find information about the accessibility of tourist destinations. Therefore, a targeted campaign must be launched.

Another point to be considered if which operating system to use and weather to concentrate on dedicated websites or apps. The choice of the operating system seems to be related to the disability. Most of the people with visual and cognitive impairments have claimed to use the iOs operating system, while users with hearing and motor impairments and elderly preferred the Android operating system. Depending on a specific sub-target of users this information should be kept in mind. Moreover, mobile tourism apps seem to be the better choice than standard dedicated tourism websites.

In terms of app features, it seems very important to develop tourism apps with the translation of the voice/text content in many different languages so to extend the market also to disabled users coming from other countries (so to make use of the informational content). This is very important while developing apps dedicated to users with cognitive impairments or to elderly. Another requested feature was a simple initial tutorial that briefly describes how to use the apps and which information related to the touristic experience can be found (services offered). Moreover, in our opinion, from all the observations provided by the users, the addition of a dedicated button that makes navigation more usable w.r.t. the user disability could be helpful.

Finally, some guidelines that we have validated with our study and that apply to general accessible apps are the ease of use, which was requested by all users and for visually impaired users is related to the simplicity of the content, and for cognitive impaired and elderly is related not only the simplicity of the content but also to a straightforward navigation.

We hope that pointing these recommendations out will force companies and thus app developers to take them into consideration as a must, making a tourism experience accessible to all types of users, as this is an essential key point for equality in a modern inclusive society.

6 Conclusions

In this work, we researched and analyzed a wide range of accessible applications that can be used to enhance a tourist experience and evaluated them with the help of different groups of disabled users. While a lot of work has gone into developing accessible apps, the number of apps dedicated explicitly to the accessible tourism experience is limited and, as our analysis shows, improvements can still be made. For this reason we have collected comments and ideas and provided some suggestions to improve the development of accessible (tourism) apps. In the future we intend to propose and design a tourism app that can be fully adapted, in real time, to the specific needs and disability of the user.

Acknowledgments. This work was partially supported by project SERICS (PE00000014) under the MUR National Recovery and Resilience Plan funded by the European Union - NextGenerationEU, and by "Interconnected Nord-Est Innovation Ecosystem (iNEST)" project and received funding from the European Union Next-GenerationEU - National Recovery and Resilience Plan (NRRP) - MISSION 4 COMPONENT 2, INVESTIMENT N. ECS00000043 - CUP N. H43C22000540006.

Appendix

Applications Description

- *Accessaloo* allows to find accessible toilets nearby. It provides information about the location of accessible toilets, and about their accessibility features such as wheelchair accessibility, grab bars, and changing facilities [11].
- *AccessibItaly* is an app that offers information about various Italian cities in sign language. It provides accessible and inclusive information about the culture, food, history, and other aspects of these cities, making it easier for individuals who use sign language to explore and enjoy their travel experiences [8].
- *BOForAll* is an app specifically designed for the historic center of Bologna, Italy. It helps people with visual, hearing, and motor disabilities by indicating accessible services and inclusive paths. It provides information about accessible facilities, including restaurants, shops, and attractions, to ensure a more inclusive and enjoyable experience for all visitors [12].
- *Jaccede* is an interactive platform that allows individuals to add details about accessible facilities in Paris. Users can contribute information about accessible restaurants, cafes, shops, and other establishments, creating a community-driven resource for accessibility information in the city [14].
- *Kimap* is an app that provides accessible maps and itineraries for the cities of Florence, Grosseto, and Prato in Italy. It helps users navigate these cities by offering information on accessible routes, points of interest, and services, enabling individuals with disabilities to explore and enjoy these destinations more easily [6].

- *Link Cash Locator* is an app that helps users find ATM locations and provides accessibility information. It enables individuals to locate ATMs in their vicinity and provides details about accessibility features such as wheelchair accessibility, tactile buttons, and audio assistance [13].
- *MagnusCards* is an app designed to assist travellers with cognitive problems in preparing for new vacation experiences. It provides step-by-step digital guides, including visual and auditory cues, to help individuals with cognitive challenges navigate various aspects of travel, such as airport procedures, hotel stays, and local attractions [2].
- *Moovit* is a navigation app that offers assisted navigation with notifications along the route. It provides real-time public transportation information, including bus, train, and subway schedules, helping users with disabilities plan their journeys and navigate through cities more efficiently [3].
- *PerNoiAutistici* is an app that complements the PerNoiAutistici web portal. It offers news, podcasts, and geolocation-based information on nearby autism-friendly structures. It aims to provide resources and support for individuals with autism and their families, helping them find inclusive spaces and services [5].
- *Taxi Sordi* is an app that allows users to automatically reserve a taxi using the app's geolocation feature. It caters specifically to individuals who are deaf or hard of hearing, providing a convenient and accessible way to book taxis [7].
- *Tripstep* is an accessible tourist guide of Sicily. It offers information about accessible attractions, accommodations, restaurants, and transportation options in Sicily, ensuring that individuals with disabilities can plan and enjoy their trip to the region [9].
- *TUR4All* is an accessible tourist guide available for several countries, including Spain, Portugal, Germany, India, Colombia, and Perù. It provides comprehensive information about accessible tourist attractions, accommodations, restaurants, and transportation options in these countries, promoting inclusive tourism for individuals with disabilities [4].
- *Tube Map* is an app that provides useful information on underground and railway stations, as well as their accessibility, in various cities such as London and New York. It helps users navigate the subway and railway systems, offering details about accessible entrances, elevators, and other accessibility features [10].
- *WheelMap* is an app that evaluates the accessibility of various establishments and facilities such as restaurants, cafes, toilets, shops, cinemas, parking lots, and bus stops. It allows users to contribute information about accessibility, helping individuals with mobility disabilities find places that suit their accessibility needs [1].

The Questionnaire

General Questions:

- Gender
  - Male
  - Female
  - Not specified

- Age [Free number input]
- What kind of disability/aging problem do you have?
  - Visual disability
  - Hearing disability
  - Physical disability
  - Cognitive disability
  - Aging
- How capable are you of: [Possible single answer for each: 1 (I am not capable), 2, 3, 4, 5 (I am capable)]
  - Using a PC:
  - Using a telephone
  - Using an application
  - Browsing the Web
- What does your satisfaction with an app depend on?
  - Informative content
  - Offered services
  - Ease of use
  - Graphics
  - Utility
  - Audio vocals
- Have you ever used an accessible app?
  - Yes
  - No
- Have you ever used an accessible tourism app?
  - Yes
  - No
- Can you easily find information on the accessibility of a tourist destination?
  - Yes
  - No
  - I have never been interested
- What communication channel do you use to prepare for a trip or visit?
  - Experiences of friends and/or relatives
  - Comments on social networks
  - Websites
  - Apps
  - Other [Free-text response]

For Each Group [Visual Disability; Hearing Disability; Physical Disability; Cognitive Disability; Aging] the Same Questions

- Had you already used or already knew any apps that you tested?
  - Yes
  - No
- Do you think some apps you did not know about or do not use yet could be useful to you?
  - Yes
  - No

- Do you think the apps you have tried are well structured overall? [The following answers are for each group-specific app]
  - 1(No)
  - 2
  - 3
  - 4
  - 5 (Extremely)
- Do you think the apps you have tried are easy to use? [The following answers are for each group-specific app]
  - 1(No)
  - 2
  - 3
  - 4
  - 5 (Extremely)
- Do you think the apps you have tried have easy navigation? [The following answers are for each group-specific app]
  - 1(No)
  - 2
  - 3
  - 4
  - 5 (Extremely)
- Do you think the apps you have tried have clear and simple content? [The following answers are for each group-specific app]
  - 1(No)
  - 2
  - 3
  - 4
  - 5 (Extremely)
- Is there information or content missing that you would have liked to find in the apps you tried? [Free-text answer)]
- Based on the apps you've tried, do you think they help you prepare and make the most of your trip/visit?
  - Yes
  - No
  - Only a few
  - Most of them
- What do you think is missing or could be improved? [Free-text answer)]
- To test the various applications, what type of operating system did you use?
  - iOS
  - Android
- Did you use assistive technologies to test the various apps? If yes, which ones? [Free-text answer)]

References

1. WheelMap (2010). https://wheelmap.org/. Accessed May 2023
2. MagnusCards (2011). https://magnusmode.com/products/magnuscards/. Accessed May 2023
3. Moovit (2012). https://moovitapp.com/nycnj-121/poi/it. Accessed May 2023
4. TUR4all (2012). https://www.tur4all.com/. Accessed May 2023
5. PerNoiAutistici (2015). http://www.pernoiautistici.com/. Accessed May 2023
6. Kimap (2017). https://kinoa.studio/kimap/. Accessed May 2023
7. Taxi Sordi (2017). https://2021.ens.it/servizi/83-taxi-sordi/8163-e-disponibile-l-applicazione-taxi-sordi-per-ios-e-android. Accessed May 2023
8. AccessibItaly (2018). https://www.accessibitaly.it/. Accessed May 2023
9. Tripstep (2018). https://www.tripstep.it/. Accessed May 2023
10. Tube Map (2018). https://www.mapway.com/. Accessed May 2023
11. Accessaloo (2019). https://accessaloo.com/. Accessed May 2023
12. BOForAll (2019). https://www.itcares.it/portfolio/boforall/. Accessed May 2023
13. Link Cash Locator (2019). https://www.link.co.uk/consumers/locator/. Accessed May 2023
14. Jaccede (2020). https://www.jaccede.com/. Accessed May 2023
15. Apple: Building accessible apps (2023). https://developer.apple.com/accessibility/. Accessed May 2023
16. Card, S.K., Moran, T.P., Newell, A.: The psychology of human-computer interaction (1983)
17. Carneiro, M., Branco, F., Gonçalves, R., Au-Yong-Oliveira, M., Moreira, F., Martins, J.: Accessibility in mobile applications of Portuguese public administration. In: Zaphiris, P., Ioannou, A. (eds.) HCII 2019. LNCS, vol. 11591, pp. 243–256. Springer, Cham (2019). https://doi.org/10.1007/978-3-030-21817-1_19
18. Dattolo, A., Luccio, F.L.: A review of websites and mobile applications for people with autism spectrum disorders: towards shared guidelines. In: Gaggi, O., Manzoni, P., Palazzi, C., Bujari, A., Marquez-Barja, J.M. (eds.) GOODTECHS 2016. LNICST, vol. 195, pp. 264–273. Springer, Cham (2017). https://doi.org/10.1007/978-3-319-61949-1_28
19. Dattolo, A., Luccio, F.L.: Accessible and usable websites and mobile applications for people with autism spectrum disorders: a comparative study. EAI Endorsed Trans. 4(13), e5 (2017). https://doi.org/10.4108/eai.17-5-2017.152549
20. De Paoli, I.: Le applicazioni mobili per il turismo accessibile sono realmente accessibili? Master's thesis, Faculty of Economics, Corso di Laurea magistrale in "Sviluppo intercul-turale dei sistemi turistici, University Ca' Foscari of Venice, Italy: supervisor. F.L, Luccio (2022)
21. Ferreira da Silva, C., Leal Ferreira, S.B., Sacramento, C.: Mobile application accessibility in the context of visually impaired users. In: Proceedings of the 17th Brazilian Symposium on Human Factors in Computing Systems, pp. 32:1–32:10. ACM (2018). https://doi.org/10.1145/3274192.3274224
22. Google: Accessibility (2023). https://www.google.com/accessibility/. Accessed May 2023
23. Hwang, J., Kim, J., Lee, J., Sahito, N.: How to form wellbeing perception and its outcomes in the context of elderly tourism: moderating role of tour guide services. Int. J. Environ. Res. Public Health 17(3) (2020). https://doi.org/10.3390/ijerph17031029
24. Jernsand, E.M., et al.: Tourism memories - a collaborative reflection on inclusion and exclusion. Tour. Recreat. Res., 1–11 (2023). https://doi.org/10.1080/02508281.2023.2207153
25. Luccio, F.L., Beltrame, L.: Accessible tourism for users with hearing loss. In: International Conference on Smart Objects and Technologies for Social Good, pp. 243–248. ACM (2018). https://doi.org/10.1145/3284869.3284909

26. Madeira, S., Branco, F., Gonçalves, R., Au-Yong-Oliveira, M., Moreira, F., Martins, J.: Accessibility of mobile applications for tourism-is equal access a reality? Univ. Access Inf. Soc. **20**, 555–571 (2021)
27. Mayordomo-Martínez, D., Sánchez-Aarnoutse, J.C., Carrillo-de Gea, J.M., García-Berná, J.A., Fernández-Alemán, J.L., García-Mateos, G.: Design and development of a mobile app for accessible beach tourism information for people with disabilities. Int. J. Environ. Res. Public Health **16**(12) (2019). https://www.mdpi.com/1660-4601/16/12/2131
28. Michopoulou, E., Darcy, S., Ambrose, I., Buhalis, D.: Accessible tourism futures: the world we dream to live in and the opportunities we hope to have. J. Tourism Futures **1**(3), 179–188 (2015)
29. Microsoft: Creating content for everyone (2023). https://query.prod.cms.rt.microsoft.com/cms/api/am/binary/RE4Y2lz. Accessed May 2023
30. Qiao, G., Ding, L., Zhang, L., Yan, H.: Accessible tourism: a bibliometric review (2008–2020). Tourism Rev. **77**(3) (2022). https://doi.org/10.1108/TR-12-2020-0619
31. Ribeiro, F.R., Silva, A., Barbosa, F., Silva, A.P., Metrôlho, J.C.: Mobile applications for accessible tourism: overview, challenges and a proposed platform. Info. Technol. Tourism **19**, 29–59 (2018)
32. United Nation: Department of Economic and Social Affairs, Disability (2022). https://www.un.org/development/desa/disabilities/. Accessed May 2023
33. W3C: mobile web application best practices. W3C Recommendation 14 December 2010 (2010). https://www.w3.org/TR/mwabp/. Accessed May 2023
34. W3C: Mobile accessibility: How WCAG 2.0 and other W3C/WAI guidelines apply to mobile (2015). https://www.w3.org/TR/mobile-accessibility-mapping/. Accessed May 2023, Draft 26 February 2015
35. Web Accessibility Iniziative: SO/IEC 40500:2012 Information technology - W3C Web Content Accessibility Guidelines (WCAG) 2.0. https://www.iso.org/standard/58625.html. Last reviewed and confirmed in 2019. (2019). Accessed May 2023
36. Web Accessibility Iniziative: About W3C WAI (2023). https://www.w3.org/WAI/about/
37. World Health Organization: Disability (2023). https://www.who.int/news-room/fact-sheets/detail/disability-and-health

An Augmented Reality Environment for Testing Cockpit Display Systems

Caner Potur[1,2](✉) and Gökhan İnce[2]

[1] MGEO Test and Verification Directorate, ASELSAN Inc., Ankara, Turkey
cpotur@aselsan.com.tr
[2] Faculty of Computer and Informatics Engineering, Istanbul Technical University,
Istanbul, Turkey
{potur21,gokhan.ince}@itu.edu.tr

Abstract. In the avionics industry, software test automation is a crucial component, as it plays a significant role in accelerating the development process. Since all automation systems are error-prone, the automation systems that affect flight safety should be supervised by humans as they must be reliable. In this study, an augmented reality based software verification system is designed to observe the visual verification of cockpit screens and detect possible automation errors. In the designed system, an observer can instantly see the test steps and automation results using an augmented reality headset as a hologram on the cockpit screen and can report the errors they observe in test automation. The performance of the proposed system was analyzed qualitatively and quantitatively. The experimental results demonstrated that the use of augmented reality in cockpit display verification systems accelerated the testing process, reduced users' cognitive load, and improved the system's usability.

Keywords: Augmented reality · Cockpit display systems · Test automation

1 Introduction

The use of test automation has become increasingly prevalent in software engineering due to its ability to improve testing efficiency and reduce costs. However, one of the challenges of test automation is that it can be difficult for testers to observe the testing process and identify potential issues. Augmented reality (AR) technology has the potential to address this challenge by providing a visual and interactive interface for observing test automation in real-time.

AR technology overlays digital information onto the user's physical environment, creating an immersive and interactive experience. By using AR technology to observe test automation, testers can visualize the testing process, monitor the status of test cases, and quickly identify any issues or anomalies. In this paper, we will explore the concept of observing test automation in cockpit display systems using augmented reality, its potential benefits, and its limitations. We will review existing literature on the subject, identify gaps in the current knowledge, and propose a system to investigate the use of AR in observing test automation.

H. P. da Silva and P. Cipresso (Eds.): CHIRA 2023, CCIS 1997, pp. 66–83, 2023.
https://doi.org/10.1007/978-3-031-49368-3_5

There have been many studies on AR-based applications in the literature, such as maintenance planning in production environments [1], performing surgical operations [2], military applications [3], educational environments [4], the energy industry [5], and applications in smart home environments [6]. However, in the field of avionics, no study has been found that includes AR integrated test automation applications for testing cockpit display systems.

In the traditional verification approach of cockpit display systems, a team consisting of at least two people - a test runner and an observer - manually verifies the cockpit display screens. This method carries the risk of creating a heavy workload for users and eventually triggering user errors. In a study conducted by Gungor et al. [7], a test automation system was introduced aiming to reduce the costs of this manual verification process. This system aims to alleviate the user workload in avionics software tests by enabling the tests to be executed automatically. Another study [8] discussed the features of test automation for cockpit displays, including text verification, text size verification, and color verification. Additionally, it proposed algorithms for text and color recognition. However, despite these improvements, it was concluded that the test automation system did not work without errors. Ikbal et al. [9] have stated that the Tesseract OCR algorithm can be used for validating texts in the automatic verification of cockpit display system interfaces. However, they have pointed out that this algorithm does not always work with 100% accuracy. Pal et al. [10] have presented deep learning based verification systems to detect symbols of cockpit display graphics. Their experimental results show that the mean average precision of their symbol detection systems varies between 0.59 and 0.82 for different algorithms and datasets.

Dyachenko et al. [11] proposed an avionics verification automation complex to reduce test run time and reduce errors in manual validation. Their system includes a camera and a microphone to capture the audio and visual outputs of the avionics device, and the test tool compares them to the ground truth data. Yao et al. [12] introduced an automated testing approach for validating cockpit indicators using machine vision. They highlighted that their automation system solves the challenges associated with manual testing, including wrong decision making, high workload, and inefficiency. However, while their system outperformed manual testing, it is still an error-prone system according to the experimental results. Therefore, cockpit display system tests must still be observed during testing in automation processes. This study aims to establish two separate systems fused into one integrated cockpit display verification approach: one for observing test automation through an external screen and another for observing test automation on the cockpit screen with augmented reality technology.

The first designed system aims at enabling the user to observe test automation processes through a computer screen. This system aims to track the proper functioning of test automation and detect errors early on. Since the cockpit display software operates independently from the test tools, test information cannot be directly written onto the cockpit display. Therefore, the information about the region to be validated and the results of the verification steps must be observed by looking at a secondary monitor. The second system, on the other hand, allows the observation of test automation processes through the tested cockpit display using augmented reality technology. With the use of AR, the observer has the ability to superimpose virtual information onto the physical cockpit display, allowing for real-time monitoring and evaluation of the test automation. Moreover, AR provides a significant advantage in an aircraft cockpit testing environment where there is limited space to add an extra monitor.

In this context, this study presents innovative methodologies and systems for the use of test automation, focusing on overcoming the challenges of existing testing methods and reducing user workload. Additionally, it aims to discuss the potential benefits, limitations, and potential impact of observing test automation with augmented reality on future software engineering practices.

The subsequent sections of the study will cover traditional and proposed visual verification methods of cockpit display systems in Sect. 2, experiments in Sect. 3, results and discussion in Sect. 4, and remarks in the concluding section.

2   Visual Verification Methods for Cockpit Display Systems

The cockpit display software provides critical information such as speed, altitude, engine status, and fuel level of the aircraft to the pilots during flight. Therefore, the validation and testing of cockpit display software are of vital importance to ensure that pilots can fly safely and interpret the data accurately. This section will discuss manual visual verification, which is a traditional method for validating cockpit display software, as well as the use of two proposed automated visual verification systems.

2.1   Visual Verification of Cockpit Displays

Cockpit display systems which are shown in Fig. 1 play a crucial role in aviation by presenting pilots with vital information such as aircraft's status, speed, position, altitude, engine performance, navigation data and other important parameters. The verification of cockpit screens ensures that pilots have access to up-to-date and dependable information during flight. Incorrect or deceptive data can lead to erroneous decision-making,

Fig. 1. Cockpit Display Systems.

faulty maneuvers, and potential safety hazards. As a result, visually validating the cockpit display systems is a crucial step in ensuring flight safety.

Specific standards and guidelines are available for the verification of cockpit displays. For instance, the DO-178 guidance document, published by the Radio Technical Commission for Aeronautics (RTCA), serves as a standard that guides the software testing process [8]. This standard mandates the detailed specification and support of the testing process for avionic software, including cockpit displays. Additionally, The European Union Agency for Aviation Safety (EASA) serves as the regulatory body, mandated with the principal aim of ensuring a high and consistent level of safety throughout the aviation industry [13]. Civil aviation standards established by regulatory bodies such as EASA Certification Specification (CS) CS-25 also encompass requirements for visual verification [7].

In order to test the cockpit display, test scenarios are created based on the software requirements. These scenarios include the messages sent to the cockpit system and the expected outputs to be displayed on the cockpit screen. In the traditional test execution, the verification steps are performed manually. The user reads each verification step from a test computer containing the scenarios and compares them with the displayed screen on the cockpit display. This method often leads to time waste since users have to read the test area and expected outputs from paragraphs in the test scenarios.

On the other hand, test execution with automated visual verification is achieved through the use of machine learning and image processing techniques [7,8]. In this technique, the test scenarios contain the coordinates of the test areas and the expected information. Test automation system executes the test scenarios by comparing the cockpit screen with the expected screen. This allows for test execution without the need for user intervention. However, since automation systems still have errors, they need to be monitored by a human. In the upcoming sections, we will discuss manual visual verification in depth, and then introduce two automated visual verification techniques, one without the use of augmented reality and the other with the use of augmented reality.

2.2 Manual Visual Verification

Test scenarios in manual visual verification consist of test steps that include expected values in specific areas of the cockpit display under defined conditions. The section being tested on the cockpit display can be described verbally in the test step, and some visuals specified in the requirements can also be included in the test content.

There are various communication channels between the test computer and the cockpit device, allowing the two devices to communicate with each other. This communication allows for the effective execution of tests based on the content of the test scenarios. The depicted manual visual verification environment is shown in Fig. 2.

The manual visual verification system is performed with the participation of a test runner and at least one observer. The test runner and observer read the information about the area to be visually tested from the test computer as shown in Fig. 2(a). They acknowledge the position of the section to be tested and the expected values in the test scenario by reading the test content. Subsequently, they return to the cockpit display and verify whether these expected values are indeed correctly displayed on the screen as illustrated in Fig. 2(b).

(a) Test executer and observer read test scenario.

(b) Test executer and observer check cockpit display.

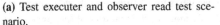

Fig. 2. Steps of manual visual verification.

2.3 Automated Visual Verification with an External Display

In the proposed system, the test execution is performed by the Automated Visual Verification (AVV) System as used in [7]. The cockpit display image is obtained digitally or through a camera placed in front of the cockpit, and it is transmitted to the test computer as shown in Fig. 3. This image is automatically compared with the expected values in the scenarios on the test computer using various image processing algorithms, and thus the test scenarios are automatically run.

The test scenarios used in the automated visual verification system include the coordinates of the areas to be tested and the expected values at these coordinates, rather than long verbal sentences. The coordinates within the tests are obtained by marking them on a reference image. The expected values can include values such as text content, text color, background color, and font size. In brief, the automated visual verification system identifies the tested area and compares it with the expected values.

Various machine learning techniques are used in automated visual verification systems, which are prone to errors. Therefore, during the test execution, at least one observer should be present in the testing environment. Since the cockpit display software should not be modified during testing, a system that directly displays test information on the cockpit screen cannot be added to the cockpit display software. As a result, it is necessary to use an external monitor to observe the test information. The observer looks at the test computer and sees the coordinate information of the visually verified region on a reference image as illustrated in Fig. 3(a). He/she also observes the results produced by the automated visual verification system on the test computer screen. The observer verifies the test result information by looking at both the cockpit display and the test computer screen as seen in the Fig. 3(b). If no issues are observed in the test results, the observer continues with the tests. However, if an error is detected, the observer reports it. This ensures the reliability of the automated visual verification system.

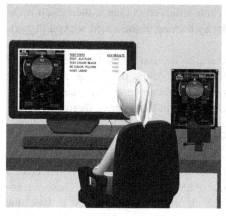 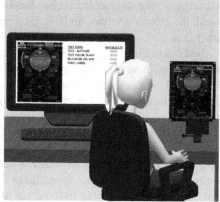

(a) Observer reads test result of AVV on the left display.   **(b)** Observer checks cockpit display on the right display.

Fig. 3. Steps of automated visual verification with multiple displays.

2.4   Automated Visual Verification with Augmented Reality

In the automated visual verification system that utilizes augmented reality for observation, the test preparation and execution phases are the same as the previous method. The test scenarios contain the coordinates of the areas tested on the cockpit display and their expected values. The test execution is performed using AVV.

In this system depicted in Fig. 4(a), the observer reads and checks the test results generated by the test automation in an augmented reality environment during the test

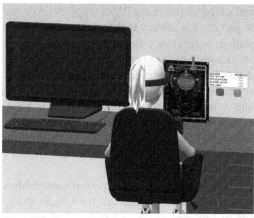 

(a) Observer reads and checks test result of the AVV with augmented reality.   **(b)** Observer uses augmented reality headset in the AVV.

Fig. 4. Steps of automated visual verification with augmented reality.

execution. Using augmented reality headset, the observer examines the region to be tested, the expected values, and the test results by looking at the tested cockpit display, rather than looking to another monitor.

Test information is sent to the augmented reality headset by the test computer, and the user sees them as holograms on and around the cockpit display as displayed in Fig. 4(b). The observer thus observes the test results in an ergonomic manner by simply looking at the cockpit screen under test. Additionally, in this system, there are buttons in the form of holograms in the augmented reality environment. If an error is detected in the test results, the observer can report the error by pressing these buttons in the augmented reality environment. Moreover, test executions can be recorded through the cameras integrated into the augmented reality headset. When an error is detected, a screenshot is captured, making it easier to analyze test automation errors. These screenshots also contribute to the training set of the algorithms used in AVV to label the misrecognized data with the proper labeling used in the machine learning processes.

3   Experiments

3.1   Design of the Experiments

Different test scenarios each consisting of 12 test steps with similar difficulty levels were created for the Manual Verification, AVV without AR (i.e., with multiple displays) and AVV with AR systems. Test steps were written to test different areas of the cockpit display. Each test step includes four sub-steps that verify the content in the region in terms of text, text color, background color, and font size.

Test scenarios consisting of 12 steps were created to include 8 PASS test steps and 4 FAIL test steps. The types of failures include Text, Color, Background Color, and Font Size errors, with one occurrence each. Participants were asked to identify the errors and specify the types of errors they found. Additionally, in the Automated Visual Verification methods, the AVV system was configured to run some PASS steps as FAIL and some FAIL steps as PASS, to assess the participants' ability to detect these errors.

Participants were requested to execute test scenarios using three different systems, generate test result reports, and fill out usability-related surveys after each test run. Test result reports were analyzed to assess quantitative values such as test execution time and the percentage of successful test runs. Surveys filled out for each system, facilitated the subjective evaluation of the systems. To ensure fair testing of the systems, the participants' order of testing the three systems was selected randomly. For instance, the first participant tested the manual testing system first, while the second participant tested the AVV without AR system, and the third participant began by testing the AVV with AR system.

In the experiments of AVV with AR, users were instructed to perform eye calibration upon wearing the AR headset to ensure optimal utilization of the system. Afterward, they were asked to open a mixed reality application to familiarize themselves with the AR environment and accomplish specific tasks. These tasks included interacting with virtual objects, moving objects from one place to another, and pressing buttons. Users were not bound by any time constraints to familiarize themselves with the AR environment, and they initiated the test scenarios once they felt comfortable and acquainted with the AR setting.

3.2 Participant Information

The experiments involved a total of 15 participants, all of whom were using the AR headset for the first time in their life. Informed consent was obtained from all participants in the study. Information such as name, age, profession, work experience, and gender were collected from the participants. The participants who took part in the experiments were software verification engineers only, with ages ranging from 23 to 36. Among the participants, 53% were female and 47% were male, with work experience varying from 0.5 to 12 years.

3.3 Experimental Setup

The experiments were conducted with a test computer in a laboratory environment. A testing tool installed on the test computer was utilized to initiate the test runs and observe the test scenarios. To simulate the cockpit display, a simulation program and a second monitor were used. The HoloLens mixed reality headset was used as the AR equipment. This device communicated with the test computer through a USB cable, ensuring that there was no delay in communication between the AR device and the test computer.

In the manual and AVV with external display methods, the test results are observed on the screen of the test computer, and the they are validated using a mouse and a keyboard. On the other hand, in the case of AR usage, the test results are observed through holograms that appear on the simulated cockpit display, and the correctness of the test results is determined by users by pressing buttons in the augmented reality environment.

To detect the cockpit display with the Hololens, Vuforia was used which provides the best balance between range and stability [14]. Two VuMark markers are placed in the corners of the cockpit screen and detected using the Vuforia library. Thus, the position of the cockpit screen is automatically detected. Mixed Reality Toolkit is used to create virtual buttons and detect user interaction with these buttons, and the AR software is developed using Unity.

3.4 Questionnaires

After Scenario Questionnaire. The After Scenario Questionnaire (ASQ) is a three-question usability satisfaction questionnaire developed by IBM, which assesses user satisfaction with the usability of a computer system [15]. The questionnaire evaluates three main aspects of usability: the ease of completing a task, the time required to complete the task, and the adequacy of support information. Due to its brevity, the questionnaire can be quickly completed by respondents, making it a practical choice for our study.

In this study, a seven-point Likert scale was utilized, with 7 points indicating "strongly agree" and 1 point indicating "strongly disagree". Participants were asked to rate each system after using them. The ASQ score is then calculated by taking the average of the responses to the three questions using the arithmetic mean.

System Usability Scale. The System Usability Scale (SUS) is an extensively utilized survey specifically crafted for the assessment of subjective perceptions regarding the usability of a system. We used the conventional configuration, which encompasses ten elements, each rated on a five-point ordinal scale, incorporating alternating positive and negative polarity [16].

The NASA Task Load Index. The NASA Task Load Index (NASA-TLX) is a prominent methodology extensively employed for assessing subjective workload. This method, which includes the dimensions of mental demand, physical demand, temporal demand, performance, effort, and frustration level is a multifaceted instrument as it encompasses six dimensions to assess various facets of mental workload over assignment execution [17].

Mental demand functions as a measure of the mental and perceptual involvement necessary for assignment execution. The dimension referred to as physical demand exhibits the extent of physical exertion necessary to successfully accomplish the task. Temporal demand pertains to the perceived magnitude of time-related pressure resulting from the task's speed. Performance denotes the perceived level of accomplishment experienced by the worker upon task conclusion. Frustration captures the degree of dissatisfaction, annoyance, and stress experienced during task performance. Lastly, effort delineates the level of mental and physical strain required to attain the desired degree of performance.

4   Results

4.1   Quantitative Results

Fifteen users have executed test scenarios on three separate systems, each consisting of 48 verification sub-steps. The test result reports were compared to a reference report to determine whether the users successfully ran the tests. Table 1 displays the average test execution times, average success rates of the tests, and the total number of errors made by all users for each of the three systems.

Table 1. Quantitative test results of the systems.

Method	Completion Time (s)	Standard Deviation (s)	Number of Errors	Success rate (%)
Manual Verification	370.6	97.13	5	99.3
AVV without AR	182.8	46.48	9	98.8
AVV with AR	148.1	60.02	8	98.9

After analyzing the test result reports of the participants, it was found that the average time for Manual Testing was 370.6 ± 97.13 s, 182.8 ± 46.48 s for AVV without AR, and 148.1 ± 60.02 s for AVV with AR. One-way Analysis of Variance (ANOVA) was applied to the completion time data, and it was observed that the p-value was significantly smaller than 0.05. It indicates that the duration of test executions is statistically different for the systems.

The completion times in Table 1 show that the manual testing system is much slower compared to the AVV systems. Moreover, considering that manual testing requires two people, it results in a labor requirement of 741.2 s. This shows that the manual testing system requires around four times more manpower compared to the AVV with AR system.

The success rates of the test runs were observed as 99.3% for Manual Testing, 98.8% for AVV without AR, and 98.9% for AVV with AR. It was observed that out of the 720 sub-steps executed for each system, testers made five errors in manual testing, nine errors in AVV without AR, and eight errors in AVV with AR. One-way ANOVA was performed on the number of error data, yielding a p-value of 0.49. This value, being significantly greater than 0.05, indicates that there is no statistical difference in error counts. These results reveal that the three systems are quite similar to each other in terms of high success rates and small error counts.

As a result, considering the shortest operation duration and high success rates, it can be concluded that AVV with AR is the most effective test running technique compared to the other methods in quantitative terms.

4.2 Qualitative Results

Results of ASQ. Participants filled out the ASQ survey after using each system. Through these surveys, they evaluated criteria such as the difficulty of the systems, the time spent on the systems, and the technical support they received. The average ASQ scores of the 15 participants in the experiments are shown in Fig. 5.

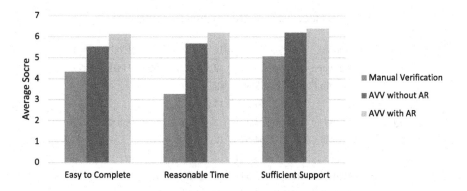

Fig. 5. ASQ scores of the systems.

The first question evaluates how easily the systems can be completed by users. According to the results, Manual Verification received a score of 4.33 ± 1.54, indicating that it was perceived as the most difficult to complete by users. On the other hand, the "AVV without AR" system received an average score of 5.53 ± 1.19, while the "AVV with AR" system obtained an average score of 6.13 ± 0.64. These results indicate that AR-enabled AVV is perceived as easier to complete by users.

The second question evaluates whether the systems can be completed within a reasonable time frame by users. According to the results, AVV without AR and AVV with AR received scores of 5.67 ± 1.29 and 6.20 ± 0.68, respectively, indicating that they can be completed within a more suitable time frame by users. Particularly, AVV with AR received the highest score, suggesting that it is perceived as capable of being completed quickly by users. Manual Verification, on the other hand, received a score of 3.27 ± 1.58, indicating that it requires more time compared to other systems.

In the final question, the adequacy of the systems in providing support to users' needs is evaluated. According to the results, Manual Verification received the lowest score of 5.07 ± 1.54, while AVV with AR received the highest score of 6.40 ± 0.74. This indicates that AVV with AR provides more support to users and better meets their needs. AVV without AR, with a score of 6.20 ± 0.56, is considered to provide a good level of support, similar to AVV with AR.

A one-way ANOVA analysis was performed to evaluate the statistical differences among systems in the ASQ results. Table 2 presents the results of this analysis, with a predefined α (alpha) value of 0.05.

The table includes the question number, the source of variation, the sum of squares (SS), degrees of freedom (df), mean squares (MS), statistical F value (F), p-value, and the critical F value (Fcrit). Each row represents the analysis results for different questions, and for each question, it includes different sources of variation: "Between Groups" and "Within Groups".

First, when examining the "Between Groups" source for Q1, the obtained total sum of squares is 25.20, with 2 degrees of freedom, resulting in a mean square value of 12.60. The computed F value is 9.00, significantly exceeding the critical F value of

Table 2. One way ANOVA results for ASQ.

Question	Source	SS	df	MS	F	p-value	Fcrit
Q1	Between Groups	25.20	2	12.60	9.00	0.001	3.22
	Within Groups	58.80	42	1.40			
	Total	84.00	44				
Q2	Between Groups	73.24	2	36.62	23.79	0.000	3.22
	Within Groups	64.67	42	1.54			
	Total	137.91	44				
Q3	Between Groups	15.51	2	7.76	7.25	0.002	3.22
	Within Groups	44.93	42	1.07			
	Total	60.44	44				
Overall	Between Groups	33.88	2	16.94	18.62	0.000	3.22
	Within Groups	38.21	42	0.91			
	Total	72.09	44				

3.22. Moreover, the p-value is less than 0.05, indicating that the results are statistically significant.

Similar analyses were conducted for Q2 and Q3 and Overall, and in all cases, the p-values were less than 0.05. These results indicate that all the questions in the ASQ and the overall outcome are statistically significant among the systems.

In conclusion, based on the ASQ results, AVV with AR obtained the most favorable results in terms of user-friendliness, timely completion, and adequate support. Manual Verification seems to need for further improvement, while AVV without AR exhibits a moderate level of performance.

Results of SUS. Participants answered the SUS questions consisting of 10 items after using the AVV without AR and AVV with AR systems. We did not apply the SUS questionnaire regarding the manual verification procedure because the participants who were indeed experts in that task were already familiar with the system for a long time. The average scores given by the 15 participants are shown in Table 3. When calculating the SUS score, as the scores for odd-numbered questions increase and the scores for even-numbered questions decrease, the usability score increases. Accordingly, the SUS scores for AVV without AR and AVV with AR systems are calculated as 81.17 ± 11.64 and 77.50 ± 8.71, respectively. Both systems receive high scores, indicating a positive user experience.

Table 3. SUS scores of the systems.

SUS Questions	AVV without AR	AVV with AR
Q1: I think that I would like to use this system frequently	4.20 ± 0.86	4.13 ± 0.92
Q2: I found the system unnecessarily complex	1.80 ± 0.86	1.93 ± 1.03
Q3: I thought the system was easy to use	4.07 ± 0.88	3.80 ± 0.94
Q4: I think that I would need the support of a technical person to be able to use this system	1.47 ± 0.64	2.47 ± 1.41
Q5: I found the various functions in this system were well integrated	4.07 ± 0.70	4.60 ± 0.63
Q6: I thought there was too much inconsistency in this system	1.60 ± 0.63	1.40 ± 0.63
Q7: I would imagine that most people would learn to use this system very quickly	4.40 ± 0.74	4.13 ± 0.92
Q8: I found the system very cumbersome to use	1.67 ± 0.62	1.73 ± 0.88
Q9: I felt very confident using the system	3.93 ± 0.96	4.07 ± 0.88
Q10: I needed to learn a lot of things before I could get going with this system.	1.67 ± 0.90	2.20 ± 1.08
SUS Score	81.17 ± 11.64	77.50 ± 8.71

In order to evaluate the statistical difference in means between the two groups, a paired two-sample t-test was performed. Table 4 displays the t-test results for the SUS scores of the AVV without AR and AVV with AR systems. In the statistical analysis, the degrees of freedom (df) used are 14, the t-statistic is 1.12, the two-tailed p-value is 0.28, and the critical t-value is calculated as 2.14. These results indicate that there was no statistically significant difference between the two systems. This indicates that there is no significant difference in terms of SUS scores between the systems.

Table 4. T-test scores for SUS evaluation.

	AVV without AR	AVV with AR
Mean	81.17	77.5
Standard Deviation	11.64	8.71
Observations	15	15
df	14	
t Stat	1.12	
P(T <= t) two-tail	0.28	
t Critical two-tail	2.14	

The t-test was separately applied to SUS questions, and a statistical difference between the systems was obtained for question 4 and question 5 with P values of 0.003 and 0.015, respectively.

The highest score in the AVV without AR system is given to question 4, while the lowest score is given to this question in the AVV with AR system. This indicates that when the AR system is not used, users do not perceive the need for technical support, but with the use of AR, they think that technical support is required to use the system. In the AVV with AR, the highest scores are given to questions 5 and 6. This implies that users believe that various functions in the AR system are well integrated, and they perceive no inconsistencies in the system.

In the system of AVV without AR, the lowest score is given to question 9. This question is related to how confident users feel while using the system. In the AVV with AR system, the question with the lowest score after question 4 is question 10. This indicates that users think they need to learn many things before transitioning to the AR system, which was an expected result because users had never used AR headset before.

Results of NASA-TLX. Participants answered the NASA-TLX survey questions after using each system. The average NASA-TLX scores and their standard deviations for the three systems, with an average of 15 users, were provided in Table 5.

As indicated in Table 5, the NASA-TLX scores for the Manual Verification, AVV without AR, and AVV with AR systems were found to be 59.86 ± 19.35, 33.70 ± 15.18, and 28.92 ± 10.59, respectively. When comparing the Manual Verification system to the AVV systems, it was observed that the use of AVV significantly reduced the NASA-TLX score. Furthermore, it was observed that the use of AR in the AVV system further

Table 5. Average NASA-TLX scores and standard deviations of the systems.

Method	Average Score	Standard Deviation
Manual Verification	59.86	19.35
AVV without AR	33.70	15.18
AVV with AR	28.92	10.59

reduced the NASA-TLX score, contributing to a decrease in mental workload for the individual.

In order to evaluate the statistical differences among the systems within the NASA TLX dataset, a one-way ANOVA analysis was carried out. Table 6 displays the findings of this study with a specified $alpha$ (alpha) value of 0.05. Based on the ANOVA results, F values and p-values were examined for both the overall assessment and individual dimensions. In the analysis of overall scores, it is found that the calculated F value, which is 17.40, exceeds the critical F value of 3.22, while the p-value falls below 0.05. It indicates the existence of statistically significant disparities among the systems in the overall NASA TLX results.

Furthermore, the ANOVA analysis conducted on the NASA TLX dataset reveals significant disparities among the systems in the dimensions of Mental Demand, Physical Demand, Temporal Demand, Effort, and Frustration, all bearing p-values below 0.05, indicating statistical significance. In contrast, the Performance dimension demonstrates no statistically significant difference between the groups, with a p-value exceeding 0.05. This outcome implies that evaluations in the Performance dimension are quite similar, and there is no statistically significant difference among the systems.

In Fig. 6, there are 6 different types of task load scores displayed for each system: Mental Demand, Physical Demand, Temporal Demand, Performance, Effort, and Frustration Level. Accordingly, the lowest workload scores for the Mental Demand, Physical Demand, Temporal Demand and Effort types were achieved in the AVV with AR system with 30.73, 35.40, 23.18, 37.2, respectively; The lowest workload scores for Performance and Frustration Level types were 15.73 and 23.13, respectively, with the AVV without AR system. Participants exerted less mental and physical effort, felt less time pressure, and completed tasks with less effort when using the AVV with AR system. On the other hand, users experienced less stress and felt more successful in terms of performance when using the AVV without AR system.

The NASA-TLX results indicate that the Manual Verification system has the highest workload across all dimensions. The score differences between the Manual Verification system and the AVV without AR system are 20.94, 21.2, 42.06, 9.67, 27.13, and 35.94 points in terms of Mental Demand, Physical Demand, Temporal Demand, Performance, Effort, and Frustration Level, respectively. Similarly, the Manual Verification system has higher mental workload scores in the same dimensions compared to the AVV with AR system, with differences of 40.54, 30.47, 49.15, 3, 28, and 33.74 points, respectively. Based on this data, the greatest score differences are observed in the dimensions of Temporal Demand, Frustration Level, and Mental Demand. This means that users

Table 6. One way ANOVA results for NASA-TLX dimensions.

Dimension	Source	SS	df	MS	F	P-value	F crit
Mental D.	Between Groups	12326.60	2	6163.30	9.67	0.000	3.22
	Within Groups	26771.20	42	637.40			
	Total	39097.80	44				
Physical D.	Between Groups	7317.60	2	3658.80	5.13	0.010	3.22
	Within Groups	29950.70	42	713.10			
	Total	37268.30	44				
Temporal D.	Between Groups	21585.60	2	10792.80	30.08	0.000	3.22
	Within Groups	15068.00	42	358.80			
	Total	36653.60	44				
Performance	Between Groups	734.40	2	367.20	1.28	0.289	3.22
	Within Groups	12064.10	42	287.20			
	Total	12798.60	44				
Effort	Between Groups	7604.80	2	3802.40	6.87	0.003	3.22
	Within Groups	23257.70	42	553.80			
	Total	30862.60	44				
Frustration	Between Groups	12169.90	2	6085.00	14.67	0.000	3.22
	Within Groups	17422.00	42	414.80			
	Total	29591.90	44				
Overall	Between Groups	8319.10	2	4159.50	17.40	0.000	3.22
	Within Groups	10039.60	42	239.00			
	Total	18358.70	44				

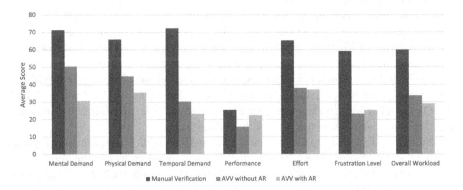

Fig. 6. NASA-TLX scores of the systems according to dimensions.

had to exert much more effort to complete tasks on time, experienced much higher levels of stress, and had to concentrate more intensely in the manual verification system.

4.3 Discussion

This study compared manual visual verification, automated visual verification, and AR-based automated visual verification methods for testing aircraft cockpit display systems. The findings indicate that manual testing takes longer and requires more effort compared to other methods. This situation highlights that the costs of test processes involving manual testing are higher. Therefore, it is important for the aviation industry to consider these results and review their testing and verification processes. Especially the increasing use of automated visual verification presents an opportunity to enhance manual testing processes and improve operational efficiency.

Furthermore, this study focuses on the usability results of AR-based AVV systems. Participants found the AVV system supported by AR to be more user-friendly and easier to use. These results suggest the potential of AR technology to simplify complex tasks, contributing to its wider adoption in the aviation industry and its use in pilot training and operational tasks.

However, this study has some limitations. For instance, users had limited exposure to the proposed test systems for a short duration, and it should be noted that prolonged use of AR devices like Hololens may lead to physical fatigue among users.

To sum up, this study represents an important step in evaluating new methods and technologies for testing aircraft cockpit display systems. Researchers can use these results to guide their efforts in developing safer and more efficient flight testing systems.

5 Conclusion

In this study, three different verification methods for cockpit display systems were examined: manual visual verification, automated visual verification, and augmented reality-based automated visual verification. In methods where AR is not used, users require a secondary screen while conducting or observing tests because the cockpit display software operates independently from the test tools and cannot be modified. Consequently, test data cannot be displayed on the cockpit screen. On the other hand, in the AR system, the test data is displayed directly on and alongside the cockpit screen, enabling users to observe the system solely by looking at the cockpit display.

Three visual verification methods were evaluated both quantitatively and qualitatively. The quantitative results have shown that participants demonstrated similar performance in the systems, but experienced significant time loss during manual test conditions. On the other hand, the use of augmented reality has revealed a time advantage in the test conditions.

Subjective surveys, namely ASQ, SUS, and NASA-TLX, were used in the study. Based on ASQ results, the augmented reality system was perceived as more user-friendly, time-efficient, and supportive compared to other systems. According to SUS scores, both AVV systems were considered successful, but the augmented reality system received a lower score due to users' concerns about technical support and the learning curve. NASA-TLX results revealed that both AVV and augmented reality usage significantly reduced mental workload, with augmented reality being particularly effective in reducing task load in various dimensions.

In conclusion, this study evaluated the usage of visual verification methods in avionic software testing. Augmented reality supported systems provide users with an ergonomic testing environment, offering advantages in terms of user-friendliness, time efficiency, and reducing mental workload.

In future studies, surveys can be diversified and applied to a larger number of users. By enhancing the software and hardware, it is possible to improve the usability scores and decrease the mental workload scores.

References

1. Runji, J.M., Lee, Y.J., Chu, C.H.: Systematic literature review on augmented reality-based maintenance applications in manufacturing centered on operator needs. Int. J. Precis. Eng. Manuf.-Green Technol. **10**(2), 567–585 (2023)
2. Lex, J.R., Koucheki, R., Toor, J., Backstein, D.: Clinical applications of augmented reality in orthopaedic surgery: a comprehensive narrative review. Int. Orthop. **47**, 375–391 (2023)
3. Livingston, M.A., et al.: Military applications of augmented reality. In: Furht, B. (eds.) Handbook of Augmented Reality, pp. 671–706. Springer, New York (2011). https://doi.org/10.1007/978-1-4614-0064-6_31
4. Pathania, M., Mantri, A., Kaur, D.P., et al.: A chronological literature review of different augmented reality approaches in education. Technol. Knowl. Learn. **28**, 329–346 (2023)
5. Cho, K., Jang, H., Park, L.W., Kim, S., Park, S.: Energy management system based on augmented reality for human-computer interaction in a Smart City. In: 2019 IEEE International Conference on Consumer Electronics (ICCE), pp. 1–3. IEEE (2019)
6. Kuyucu, M., Ince, G.: MARIoT: a framework for creating customizable IoT applications with mobile augmented reality. In: ACHI 2021, The Fourteenth International Conference on Advances in Computer-Human Interactions (2021)
7. Gungor, M.O., Ince, G.: Automated visual verification of avionics cockpit displays. In: ACHI 2022, The Fifteenth International Conference on Advances in Computer-Human Interactions (2022)
8. Karatana, A., Ekenel, H.K.: A visual verification system for aircraft cockpit display software. In: 30th Signal Processing and Communications Applications Conference (SIU), pp. 1–4. IEEE (2022)
9. Sartaj, H., Iqbal, M.Z., Khan, M.U.: Testing cockpit display systems of aircraft using a model-based approach. Softw. Syst. Model. **20**, 1977–2002 (2021)
10. Pal, D., Alladi, A., Pothireddy, Y., Koilpillai, G.: Cockpit display graphics symbol detection for software verification using deep learning. In: International Conference on Data Science and Engineering (ICDSE), pp. 1–5. IEEE (2020)
11. Dyachenko, S.A., Ilyashenko, D.M., Neretin, E.S.: Overview of automation tools for avionics verification. J. Phys. Conf. Ser. **1958**(1), 012012 (2021). IOP Publishing
12. Yao, J., Chen, R., Huang, Y.: Automatic identification system of aircraft cockpit indicators based on machine vision. In: Proceedings of the 4th International Conference on Advanced Information Science and System, pp. 1–9 (2022)
13. Fortonska, A.: Measures taken by the European Union Agency for Aviation Safety to ensure aviation safety. J. KONBiN **51**(2), 117–125 (2021)
14. Battegazzorre, E., Calandra, D., Strada, F., Bottino, A., Lamberti, F.: Evaluating the suitability of several AR devices and tools for industrial applications. In: De Paolis, L.T., Bourdot, P. (eds.) AVR 2020. LNCS, vol. 12243, pp. 248–267. Springer, Cham (2020). https://doi.org/10.1007/978-3-030-58468-9_19

15. Lewis, J.R.: IBM computer usability satisfaction questionnaires: psychometric evaluation and instructions for use. Int. J. Hum.-Comput. Interact. **7**(1), 57–78 (1995)
16. Lewis, J.R.: The system usability scale: past, present, and future. Int. J. Hum.-Comput. Interact. **34**(7), 577–590 (2018)
17. Aktas Potur, E., Toptanci, S., Kabak, M.: Mental workload assessment in construction industry with fuzzy NASA-TLX method. In: Xu, J., Altiparmak, F., Hassan, M.H.A., García Márquez, F.P., Hajiyev, A. (eds.) Proceedings of the Sixteenth International Conference on Management Science and Engineering Management – Volume 2, ICMSEM 2022. Lecture Notes on Data Engineering and Communications Technologies, vol. 145, pp. 729–742. Springer, Cham (2022). https://doi.org/10.1007/978-3-031-10385-8_52

Human-Centred Digital Sovereignty: Explorative Conceptual Model and Ways Forward

Dennis Lawo[1](✉) [iD], Thomas Neifer[1] [iD], Margarita Esau[1,2] [iD], and Gunnar Stevens[1,2] [iD]

[1] Institut für Verbraucherinformatik, Bonn-Rhein Sieg University of Applied Sciences, Sankt Augustin, Germany
dennis.lawo@verbraucherinformatik.de
[2] Verbraucherinformatik Research Group, University of Siegen, Siegen, Germany

Abstract. In recent years, both authoritarian and democratic states have started using the term *digital sovereignty* as a basis for their digital policies. Although the interpretations and resulting policies may differ, the autonomy and sovereignty of individuals and their communities are at stake. Current political discourses mainly focus on governmental and corporate actors and their aspirations to control the digital sphere. Given the importance of this term, scholars in our community have begun to engage with the discourse. However, there is still a lack of dissemination, coming with a lack of conceptual models to explain, explore, and research human-centred digital sovereignty. Inspired by claims for human-centred digital sovereignty, this paper takes up the discourse and creates an explorative conceptual model that aims to guide early research within HCI, support an understanding of the field, and helps to identify relevant cases. Moreover, we discuss key challenges and potential ways forward.

Keywords: Digital sovereignty · Human autonomy · Conceptual model

1 Introduction

"Finally, the EU is pursuing a tech industrial policy under the strategically-and morally-ambiguous heading of "digital sovereignty." Proponents of the concept toggle breezily between two definitions of "sovereignty." One is based on human-centered autonomy: each individual citizen is personally sovereign over their data, interactions with AI, etc. The other is a more Westphalian understanding of sovereignty: each state has an undisputed power monopoly within its borders." [5]

In recent years, *digital sovereignty* has become a central term in digital policy discourses [41,64]. Fueled by the increasing importance of the digital sphere, expressed in developments in artificial intelligence (AI), the Internet of Things (IoT), and ubiquitous connectivity, authoritarian and democratic states, claim sovereignty over 'their part' of the internet [26,41,64]. Depending on the intentions of the state, sovereignty comes with different perspectives, policies, and measures. The common ground, however, is

H. P. da Silva and P. Cipresso (Eds.): CHIRA 2023, CCIS 1997, pp. 84–103, 2023.
https://doi.org/10.1007/978-3-031-49368-3_6

the assertion of control over the digital sphere to prevent other states from exercising power over the network, protect their economy, and—primarily prevalent in democratic discourses—protect their citizens [41,64].

According to [66] the misconception of the digital as a territory that requires the same measures to govern it leads to a situation where the focus shifts away from the individual citizens as users and their autonomy over usage and data towards the state. However, as mentioned above, not every government is interested in decreasing its sovereignty in favour of the sovereignty and autonomy of its citizens [30]. Other governments simply lack the power to defend sovereignty, against other states, and thus are not able to share sovereignty with their citizens [3].

Given the tremendous threats and impact that digital policy discourses already have and might have on individual humans [26]—users and communities, the heart of our research community—it is surprising that the topic did not gain more attention. It is especially surprising that HCI did not start theorising about the term, nor develop definitions or conceptual models to charter research based on a common understanding. Instead current research related to the topic remains dispersed and loosely coupled [45].

Therefore, we aim to follow up on the idea of *human-centred digital sovereignty* [66] emerging from adjacent research fields and provide an overview of concepts, their relations, and challenges, as well as potential ways forward. Especially the concepts and their relations can serve as an early explorative conceptual model for understanding digital sovereignty, and as a useful reference point to explain the field to those unfamiliar with it. Furthermore, it can help structure the characteristics of cases, compare actions, actor configurations, and identify the resulting positive or negative effects on the digital sovereignty of human individuals and their communities. Such an approach of an explorative conceptual model has already been applied earlier for other emerging topics touching our research (see, e.g., [21], as they especially help guide early research by clarifying and identifying main factors and variables. Additionally, it can inspire new research and support the identification of existing knowledge and gaps.

The development of the model was guided by the following questions:

1. What are the key concepts of digital sovereignty and how are they related?
2. What can we do to strengthen a human-centred agenda for digital sovereignty?

To answer these questions and develop the conceptual model, this paper explores recent work on human-centred digital sovereignty from the ACM Digital Library, the Springer Library, the Eusset Digital Library, Scitepress and Google Scholar. The contribution of this paper is not a comprehensive review of research from privacy to digital literacy in fields relevant to the discourse. Instead, this paper introduces an explorative conceptual model and aims to initiate and guide an early discourse within our community.

2   Background

2.1   Digital Sovereignty: The Policy Discourse

"Today, sovereignty always primarily means a state's independence vis-à-vis other states (external sovereignty) as well as its supreme power to command all powers within the territory of the state (internal sovereignty)." [64]

Without the prefix *digital*, the idea of sovereignty describes the ability of the ruler, the sovereign, to execute decisions within a clearly defined territory [29,64]. In the digital sphere, there is no such clearly defined territory, even if some states, e.g., russia or china, are attempting to establish (partially) closed networks [19,69]. Thus, this characteristic of the digital sphere challenges the notion of state sovereignty from various ideological standpoints. For instance, from a cyber exceptionalism perspective, it is argued that the digital sphere is so distinct from previous objects of state control that it should be treated differently. This argument is based on the perception that states as agents in the digital sphere are too slow and inefficient in managing the fast pace [64]. Often, this perspective is associated with libertarian attitudes [39], such as those expressed in debates about cryptocurrencies [60].

Another example is the multi-stakeholder internet governance perspective, which states that the stakeholders should manage the internet on their own, resulting in a decentralised management and negotiation of best practices [16,40] among states, NGOs, and other stakeholders. However, internal disputes and a lack of coordination prevented the sustainable success of decentralised approaches. Also, many states try to exercise state sovereignty through multilateral and bilateral agreements, as well as international organisations [64].

The claim to sovereignty is not limited to states, as individuals and corporates also claim to have and to be able to exercise certain sovereignty. Resulting from these diverse claims, the digital sphere is heading towards a phase of claiming and negotiating sovereignty, with an uncertain and potentially threatening outcome. Some authors even refer to this situation as a "tech war" [17]. For example, some states' plans rely on the idea of a strong and sovereign state, which exercises sole control over its part of the internet including citizens' data [14]. Other states promote digital or surveillance capitalism in a laissez-faire approach to benefit from economic growth [6,33,37]. Again other states, mostly European states, are heading towards a third way, with a strong emphasis on the individuals as users, consumers, and citizens [26,33,41,51,64]. Some states, primarily developing countries, lack the power to claim sovereignty at all [3].

2.2 Digital Sovereignty in HCI

There is already some research within our community using the term *digital sovereignty*. For example, research on designing transparent e-Government websites [78] or smart cities [7], service switching intentions within the GDPR legal context [48], the privacy of used smart devices [9] and services [2], technology independence from monopolists [27,31,32,50], to the effect and design of social media in the context minimising user autonomy and data exploitation [67]. However, in much of this research, no clear definition of digital sovereignty is given. Luzsa et al. [48] who understand "the term 'digital sovereignty' [as the] answers to these threats and ways to increase privacy, security, and informational self-determination of individuals, economic actors, and democratic institutions". Whereby the threats for individual users, e.g., manipulation or identity theft, companies, e.g., intellectual property theft, and societies as a whole, e.g., polarisation and mistrust, are caused by fake news, hacking, and a monopolisation of services. While this definition accounts for the whole network of actors within the political discourse, other authors, such as [78], see individuals being digital sovereign when they can "act deliberate and with self-determination". Essential for this is the ability to understand which personal data is shared with which governmental or commercial actor. Quite similarly, Bernardes et al. [7] locate digital sovereignty in the discussion of privacy and control over their data. Their case is situated around smart cities in Europe that apply GDPR. The commercial line of argumentation for digital sovereignty is used by [9], who argue that sovereignty users are sovereign in the context of smart assistance when they are "able to determine which data is collected and used for which purposes".

Grohmann [31] also argues for digital sovereignty in the context of data control and ownership. But his arguments go beyond demanding transparent digital infrastructures, but for autonomously designing and maintaining own infrastructures to be independent from monopolists and their infrastructure and algorithms, which might enforce inequalities and certain ways of working. Given the context of Brazil, narratives of digital colonialism and dependence on Western countries are also picked up. In the context of smart cities, Heitlinger et al. [32] argue for software and hardware autonomy and the inclusion of citizens in the ownership, design, and maintenance of the systems to counter "the abstract digital spaces and proprietary infrastructures of neo-liberal smart cities". They also address the need for skills and literacy to enable such self-governance of a digital-common. Similarly, Marichal et al. [50] locate their work on open-source mixed-reality environments within a broader discourse of digital sovereignty. However, the dependence on monopolists is not elaborated on. Other research [27] cites digital sovereignty as one of the benefits of their recycling platform, which decreases the dependence on (foreign) resources and producers.

Schelenz et al. [67] understand digital sovereignty in the context of protecting users against the power of social media platforms and regulating these. They argue, that the service providers "minimiz[e] users' autonomy, marginaliz[e] minorities, and exploit[e] users' data for profit maximization". This critique on social media platforms also relates to the first definition, which highlighted the threat coming from fake news [48].

Although there is research picking up the term *digital sovereignty* within HCI, the discourse already covers a broad spectrum of the policy discourse. However, no paper was found that addresses digital sovereignty in such a holistic manner, e.g., by deriving a human-centred conceptual model. Besides an understanding of the term in general, such an explorative conceptual model is helpful, e.g., to guide early research by clarifying and identifying main factors and their relations. This research draws inspiration from statements [45, 66] to propose human-centered digital sovereignty. Based on those statements, we understand the concept as an enhancement of individual autonomy in the digital sphere, shifting the focus away from governments and corporations to prioritise human interests. "Human-centered" means safeguarding personal data privacy, individual agency, and designing technology for human well-being. It advocates for equitable access to digital resources and empowering individuals to shape their digital environments. Clarifying this concept is essential, as it emphasises human dignity and a fair, inclusive digital future. Thus, in the following, we aim to create a conceptual model, that supports research and design to foster such digital sovereignty.

3   Method

To identify relevant literature to serve as the basis for structuring the research field, we conducted an exploratory literature survey. This approach is inspired by the work of Bolis et al. [10]. In the following, we will provide details on the procedure.

Exploratory Survey. To create an initial corpus of literature we queried the ACM Digital Library, the Springer Library, the Eusset Digital Library as they are the primary sources for CSCW, HCI and research at the intersection of technology and societal issues. Moreover, Google Scholar and Scitepress were queried for research. Google Scholar was particularly used for information from adjacent fields and background information, e.g., from political sciences. We used the following query to retrieve the research: "digital sovereignty" AND ("individual" OR "employee" OR "user" OR "citizen" OR "consumer"). We used the second term to filter for research targeting individuals in their various roles of using technology (see e.g. [41]).

Filtering & Analysis. The discovered literature was saved for a full review if the title or abstract described terms or topics related to digital sovereignty on an individual level. This resulted in a smaller corpus of literature considered for further analysis.

The articles were fully reviewed in a concept-centric manner to deduce concepts and their relations [76]. The first iteration of analysis started with the actors (as they are already an important feature in policy research [64,73]) and application domains. The other concepts were inductively deduced from the exploration of the literature over multiple iterations.

Scope of the Survey. The goal of the literature survey and the resulting concepts and their relations to human-centred digital sovereignty is an explorative, but comprehensive, overview of this early-stage and emerging research field. It aims to guide future research by providing the means to understand the challenges of the field and to compare the cases of sovereign/non-sovereign conditions. We acknowledge that due to the exploratory character, our survey did not result in an exhaustive list of literature, but the results are a curated and representative overview of the field. From a methodological standpoint, the survey includes research that was available in the libraries on March 12th (date of the survey).

4   Human-Centred Digital Sovereignty

In this section, we dive deeper into the concepts of Human-Centred Digital Sovereignty. Figure 1 gives a high-level overview of the disparate but interwoven threads of the emerging research field. Figure 2 describes the relation between the different concepts. The illustration of the relationship is inspired by the actor-network approach of Tretter [73], who researched covid apps based on such a network.

4.1   Concept: Expressions of Sovereignty

Starting with the expressions of human-centred digital sovereignty, we aim to introduce key fields describing the degree of sovereignty from an individuals perspective.

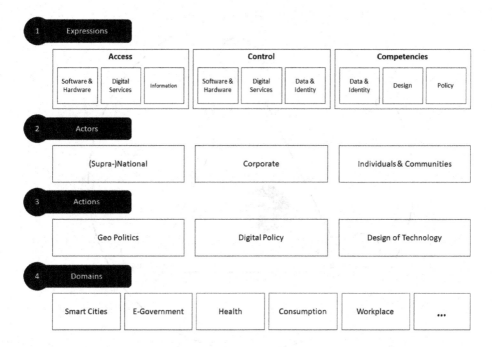

Fig. 1. Conceptual Model of Human-Centred Digital Sovereignty.

Access. An important expression of sovereignty is access to technology and the digital sphere as a prerequisite to participation in the modern information society.

Software & Hardware. Research addresses access to software and hardware as a necessity for digital sovereignty. This access is related to technology sovereignty also discussed on a (supra-)national scale [20]. However, from a human-centred perspective, it is much more related to individuals, especially marginalised individuals, and their communities gaining access to technology. For example, [74] research the access of tribal communities in the US to the internet, which has been cited as "a key factor in establishing digital sovereignty, identity, and cultural resilience in Tribal communities [52]". Moreover, resource scarcity of communities and sustainability issues play a role in establishing mechanisms to be more sovereign with technology [27]. Lastly, as the example of [50] shows, soft- and hardware of established companies come at a price, thus access might be limited for certain communities.

Digital Services. Besides soft- and hardware in the sense of technology in direct control by the individual, infrastructure alike digital services and access to these play a crucial role in human-centred digital sovereignty. Research in this field predominantly focuses on access to governmental services, such as e-petition systems [47] or administrative services [58]. However, it can also be related to other sectors, e.g., the health sector [55]. Overall, access to digital services comes with the notion of equal access, similar to the software & hardware access, as well as access in the sense of accessibility and ease of use [8].

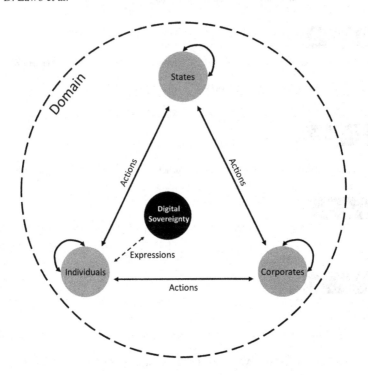

Fig. 2. Relationship of the Concepts of Human-Centred Digital Sovereignty.

Information. The example of tribal communities and their internet access, as discussed in [74], highlights the importance of having access to relevant information, particularly in the native language, as it is a crucial aspect of cultural exchange and community. However, political sanctions or attempts to create a sovereign/national internet [38], the lack of effort to bring infrastructures to marginalised communities [74], or intransparent algorithms [22] cut off individuals from the access to information, especially factual information (see the fake news discourse [15]). More positively speaking, a relevant factor for this expression of sovereignty is the access to relevant information that is shared over the internet without technical, organisational, or legal hurdles.

Control. Besides the access to technology, research cites the control over technology and algorithms as an important expression. This perspective is often strongly connected to it-security and privacy issues, but also issues of transparency and procedural control.

Software & Hardware. To be digitally sovereign control needs to be exercised over soft- and hardware in personal usage. Thereby, one factor is that both the devices and the software have it-security features that do not endanger the individuals and their data during use [58]. Moreover, control is understood in the sense that the technology does not enforce unwanted behaviours, e.g., labour law behaviours in conflict with labour law [57]. This control requires for transparency of algorithms and hardware blueprints

[22] to prevent code to overwrite the rule-of-law [65], e.g., for AI-systems [61,80]. Additionally, part of control allows the choice to not use a certain technology if, e.g., the data collection mechanisms are not in line with their preferences [73].

Digital Services. Similar to *Access* control is not limited to technology under direct control of individuals, but also extends to digital services as infrastructures. Examples cited for such control over digital services are mostly related to e-government services [79] and smart city services [23]. Therefore, it is similarly important that the underlying procedures are in line with the interest of the citizens, e.g., do not affect the city as a residential area for communities in a negative way. In this sense, it is about the democratic control over technology affecting the lives of humans [65]. Similarly, such control, for full sovereignty, is required over other technologies that heavily affect everyday life, e.g., social media as the moderator of relationships and communities [67].

Data & Identity. Besides the technology itself, the control over data [2,73] and identity within the digital sphere [9,77] are prominent features of digital sovereignty. Control over data is exercised in the sense of data portability [48,54,68] between services, regardless of whether public or private, consensual data sharing [78], and the right to access, delete, and transparently see the usage by other parties [1,2,9]. Thus, this perspective is very much related to issues around privacy and identity management.

Competencies. This perspective is only a peripheral phenomenon within the surveyed literature, but, e.g., deeply rooted in the open software movement [70]. Nonetheless, it is highly important for individuals within the digital sphere [57]. This is especially true with respect to the above-mentioned features of sovereignty *access* and *control*. This relates to **Using Software & Hardware**, where a certain level of digital competency is required to select and use technology in a sovereign way, e.g., recognising harmful algorithms in recommender systems in everyday life [44] or accessing technology by an elderly user [71].

Moreover, **Managing Data & Identity** requires certain competencies and literature to understand the potential usage, including misuse of personal data as well as opportunities and settings to protect the personal data [59].

Lastly, **Participating in Design & Policy** requires fundamental knowledge of technology and algorithms as well as political processes. For example, when articulating the need to regulate a certain technology [73] or engaging in co-design of public services and smart cities [32].

4.2 Concept: Actors

"[T]here currently is no sovereignty in the digital, but only various exercises of power through which sovereignty is claimed and the claims of others are attacked-and that when we speak of sovereignty in the digital, we are most likely describing this network of various exercises of power that are connected to different claims of sovereignty. [26]." [73]

The relationships and interactions between the actors are crucial to understand digital sovereignty. In particular, it might be interesting to compare contextual settings with their configurations of actors and distribution of power, to better conceptualise the situation of individuals and communities.

States. Given the historical connotation of sovereignty and the nation as the traditional sovereign of the last century [73], it is not surprising that the most prominent actor to claim digital sovereignty is the state or (supra-)national actors. Authoritarian and non-liberal governments see digital communication as a threat to their political systems [64], but also liberal democracies thrive for an agenda of digital sovereignty. In those contexts, the ideas of sovereignty, however, are mostly driven by security concerns, as global connectivity revealed vulnerabilities and threats to infrastructures relying on the digital sphere [41,64].

Given the traditional power distribution, this actor is also important for the digital sovereignty of individuals. For example, the state can emphasise its sovereignty over the sovereignty of other actors [66], but can also be dependent on other actors, e.g., states and corporates [79], and thus not able to claim sovereignty for itself and the citizens. For example, developing states might suffer under a new "digital colonialism" [3].

Corporates. Another actor is the corporate or economical actor [6,41,64]. Corporate actors are usually bound to the rule of law given by the economical context of the state, e.g., policy on data protection [77]. However, especially in emerging economies [3,79], but also countries without a strong digital market [22,57] there is a dependence on (foreign) corporates that provide the technology as a monopolist provider.

As the primary role of the technology provider, corporates have power through the ownership of the production resources, e.g. knowledge and facilities. Thus, they can enforce their rules [65] or misuse data [32] if other actors cannot exercise power and claim sovereignty. On the other hand, they could be a cooperative ally in the fight for sovereignty, e.g., when they take part in recycling [27] or employ privacy-by-design principles [9].

Individuals & Communities. This part of digital sovereignty is certainly most relevant to the HCI community, due to its strong focus on our groups of interest in their various life contexts. Sovereignty, here, focuses on individual self-determination in the digital sphere and the autonomy of individuals as citizens, employees, users, and consumers [41,72]. These actors are usually the ones with the smallest ability to exercise power. Thus, it is especially discussed in democratic contexts, with a certain prevalence in Europe [41,62–64]. However, especially the actions of autocratic states against their citizens resemble their fear of their citizens and their collective power [30].

Individuals and communities might be dependent on the other actors in their role of providing technologies and policies, however, as a collective, they can exercise power through political participation [23,74] or the provision of bottom-up open source technologies and infrastructures [32,50].

4.3   Concept: Actions

Within their fight for digital sovereignty, the different actors exercise various actions to support their claims of sovereignty. In the following, we will present the actions and provide examples.

Geo-Politics. Geo-Politics are primarily driven by governmental actors. States aim to bring parts of the digital sphere under their jurisdiction [41], with limited access of other actors, especially other states and corporates [64]. This can be motivated by the protection of data and the security of infrastructures, but also the increased access to data of citizens, e.g., for surveillance reasons, and potential economic benefits from closed innovation systems [14,33,53]. However, also big-tech exercise power in this field, e.g. when playing on the dependency of entire countries on their technologies [3,61,79]. This role has also resembled embassies being opened in Silicon Valley to directly negotiate with technology providers [24].

Measures within this field range from measures, such as banning certain technologies [58], nationalising the network [38], influencing other actors through technology [61,79] to collaboration on data standards [68] or forming networks to gain more power, e.g., over monopolists [79]. In summary, those measures, depending on the motivation and the goal can be both harmful and beneficial for the individual, while in some situations a ban on technology might protect consumers, in other cases, it might prevent them from free communications.

Digital Policy. Digital Policy is quite similar to Geo-Politics but comes with a stronger focus on regulation within the jurisdiction of the state. However, there is also an overlap, when it comes to forming supra-national legislation, e.g. EU-wide [77] or global standards. Thus, actors with increased power are more strongly engaging in this field of actions—corporates influencing legislation using their strong lobby or overwriting policies utilising economical power [32,57] or governments issuing complex policies to prevent communities from being sovereign [74]. However, those actions can also be beneficial for the individuals, for example when issuing policies, such as GDPR, that is cited for its positive impact on consumer/data protection [1,7,8] or the regulation of algorithms, social media, and AI through policy [67,80].

It is important to highlight that individuals and communities can also exercise a certain power in this field. Unfortunately, this is limited to certain democratic contexts. Political participation allows influencing legislation to consider the perspective of individuals and communities, such that policy is formulated in favour of their sovereignty [8,23,74].

Technology. On the technology level, this field of action involves all actors. This is primarily through the design, development, and provision of technology. Of course, most technology, including software, hardware, and digital services is provided by corporate and governmental actors, however, also individuals and communities can act to increase their sovereignty on this level, e.g., by maintaining independent infrastructures [32], contributing to open source software [50], or other forms of engagement [74]. Moreover, using the available options, e.g., privacy settings [2], to increase and strengthen their sovereignty is a technology-level action of individuals.

Supporting this engagement or employing human-centred design methods, e.g., user-centred design methods [7,8,23] or privacy-by-design [9,78], is of course also a type of action being used by states and corporates aiming to increase the sovereignty of users. On the other hand, those actors also employ malicious actions on a technology level, e.g., providing technologies that create dependencies [79,80] or primary means to collect and misuse data [7,8,32].

4.4 Concept: Research Domains

Understanding the different research domains is crucial as sovereignty varies across contexts and can be influenced by a range of factors. Each domain represents a specific area of human interaction with digital technologies, and the level of sovereignty experienced by individuals and communities can differ significantly among these domains. Here, we provide an overview of the key research domains related to digital sovereignty found during the literature research. Yet, the individual research articles did not adopt a common language, not common theory, such that comparing empirical results or design implications across contexts is inhibited.

Workplace: This domain focuses on the use of digital technologies in work environments. It explores how individuals interact with technology, data privacy in professional settings, and the influence of corporate policies on employee sovereignty. A particular example, is the use dependency on office software produced by mainly one company [57].

E-services and E-IDs: E-services involve digital interactions between citizens and governmental entities, while E-IDs refer to digital identification systems. This domain examines the level of control citizens have over their personal data when accessing e-services and the impact of digital identification on individual privacy and autonomy [1,48].

Technology/Hardware Recycling: This domain concerns the proper disposal and recycling of technology and hardware. A particular focus is on the access to technologies through recycling practices. For example [27], investigates how communities could keep technologies within a circular economy to gain access and control over distribution channels.

Internet Access: Internet access is crucial for digital participation. This domain explores how internet service providers, governments, and other actors can affect individuals' access to the internet, which can, in turn, influence their digital sovereignty [38,74]. A particular example is the fight of tribal communities which use different actions (technological/political) to access the internet in areas unconsidered by infrastructure planning [74].

Electronic Government: This domain looks at how governments leverage digital technologies to provide services to citizens. It examines the extent to which digital government services empower individuals, protect their data, and uphold their digital rights [47,58,68,77–79]. An important direction of research is presented by Wessel et al. [78], who focus on designing services that make data sharing transparent and increase the data sovereignty of citizens in their interaction with the government.

Smart Assistance: Smart assistants, such as voice-activated devices, have become prevalent in homes and workplaces. This domain investigates the implications of using smart assistants on individual privacy, data control, and the potential for abuse or surveillance [9]. A particular example, is the design of identity management mechanisms in smart environments that protect the data of users [9].

Smart Cities: Smart cities integrate various technologies to enhance urban living. This domain explores the impact of smart city infrastructure on citizens' digital sovereignty, including data collection, privacy concerns, and the potential for exclusion or discrimination [7,8,23,32,79]. In particular human communities are endangered by technologies imposed to them by monopolistic and powerful corporates working together with the governments. Heitlinger et al. [32], for example, propose "ways in which design can participate in the right to the sustainable smart city".

Health: In the digital health domain, technologies like wearables and health apps play a significant role. It examines issues related to health data ownership, consent, and the potential benefits and risks to individual sovereignty in healthcare [2,43,55]. Quite similar to e-Government interaction a main theme here is the consensual and transparent data sharing with other actors [2].

Social Media: Social media platforms are ubiquitous, and this domain delves into how these platforms handle user data, content moderation, and the implications for users' digital autonomy and freedom of expression. Especially considering the ubiquitous usage of social media, those platforms gained significant impact on everyday lives. Thus, they should also reflect human needs, e.g., for diversity and protection [67].

Artificial Intelligence: AI technologies are increasingly integrated into various aspects of life. This domain explores the implications of AI on individuals' decision-making autonomy, privacy, and potential biases affecting digital sovereignty [61,80]. Thereby, this topic particularly reflects the global nature of the discourse. AI is ubiquitously deployed, but not all humans and communities have access nor capacities to influence regulation or design and development.

5   Discussion

5.1   How to Use the Conceptual Model?

The conceptual model presented in this research enables researchers and designers to consider the relevant concepts of digital sovereignty cases during their work. It raises awareness for the different, expressions, actors, and actions present in their particular domain of engagement. Given the differences in the early stage research within HCI in general, but also the nature of the data—focusing on different domains, actors, or actions—the conceptual model is not meant to provide a domain-specific best-practice overview. Instead, it offers a tool for designers and researchers to think about digital sovereignty within their project, compare cases, and most importantly find a common language for describing the field of digital sovereignty.

Thus, there is also no fixed order in which researchers of designers should apply, research or assess the concepts. Given the relationship depicted in Fig. 2, researchers and designers can start their exploration and reflection based on any concept, depending on their own starting point, e.g., if they already identified certain actors or are aware of certain expressions of sovereignty of their users.

Also, from a methodological point of view, the model is intended to be flexible: It allows to reflect on potential configurations actors, and actions that decrease the sovereignty of users or guide empirical research and the comparison of cases by considering the key concepts. Furthermore, it is a call to action to more strongly consider digital sovereignty from a human perspective and critically engage in the discourse. We hope that individuals who apply our conceptual model find inspiration from the present viewpoint, reflect on their own work, and, consequently, design products that consider the digital sovereignty of their users.

5.2   Key Challenges and Ways Forward

Using the conceptual model as a basis for understanding the emerging topic of (human-centred) digital sovereignty, in the following, we present the key challenges and ways forward for our research community.

Researching Human-Centred Digital Sovereignty and Comparing Cases. Individuals and their communities are affected by a loss of data, loss of autonomy, or manipulation by state or economic actors not only in their role as users of a particular technology, but in all aspects of life, depending on how strongly states push their aspirations, or how strongly monopolistic economic structures succeed in bringing individual citizens and their societies into dependencies [26]. Also, increasing surveillance [42,49] and tribalisation of the internet [25] endangers the positive visions of this community [25,37]. Technology becomes a surveillance nightmare, makes dependent instead of providing support, or remains an unattainable dream due to lack of resources.

Due to this ubiquitous dimension, the network of various actors, and the dependencies of entire states, companies, and individuals, the discourse is certainly different from other trend topics. While traditional HCI primarily focuses on user participation in tool and environment design, the interpretation in this framework extends beyond mere usability and design considerations. Here, *human-centeredness* encompasses a broader perspective that incorporates the rights, interests, and agency of individuals and communities within the digital landscape and politics. This expanded definition allows for a more holistic exploration of how technology can empower users while safeguarding their digital sovereignty rights. This is important, as the narrow focus on particular technologies or design fields without the broader picture might fail to answer fundamental question about the continued existence and future of the digital sphere as we know and envision it [37].

Thus, to fully understand the network of actors and actions, its impact on digital sovereignty, as well as measures to increase the control, access, and competencies of users, it is necessary to compare cases from different application domains. This is particularly important, as communities of interest are formed around certain topics, e.g., smart cities or e-health, without constant flow of information between them. Only little research sees the full picture of the ongoing "tech war" [17]. Seeing the full picture, however, is important as we need to "pursue distributions of digital sovereignty that provide the best balance" [18], coming with a strong emphasis on individuals and communities [66,73].

Thereby, it is important to not just continue the same research with a new name, but collect and compare cases of sovereignty and non-sovereignty to understand the topic holistically. According to [18], with a reflection on different perspectives "better decisions can be made about how control of all the relevant elements of the digital should be divided". Thus, we need to find a definition of what human-centred digital sovereignty is. We are aware of the early stage nature of our explorative conceptual model, however, we see its value as a tool for dissemination of the topic, a foundation for better models, and a starting point for the comparison and research of cases.

Informing Policy & The Political Agenda. Corporate and governmental actors are usually the more powerful actors. This is particularly true when it comes to the field of politics and policy, where the state is not only sovereign in issuing a policy but an established network to inform policy exists between the public and the private economic sphere, e.g., within surveillance capitalism, [13,42]. Thus, empowering the individual cannot be solely based on research and technology design, but we need to transform knowledge into standards and norms or inform policies, that restrict state actors or corporate actors in their actions.

In the past, the HCI community has already proven that it can influence policy discourses [34]. Many examples can be found in the context of dialogue design and accessibility [34,46].

To make policy contributions, it is crucial to actively participate in policy discussions [35]. Examples of this engagement involve critically examining the implementation of policies such as GDPR [59], or uncovering dependencies, as demonstrated by [57]'s survey of Danish knowledge workers' reliance on technology monopolists.

The research of [28] and [36] highlight the importance of interdisciplinary exchange, particularly with the legal and policy communities. This exchange facilitates direct engagement with scholars at the forefront of recent developments, which can aid in achieving a shared understanding and creating new avenues for disseminating HCI contributions, such as the practical difficulties of GDPR [59]. Here, adopting terms, such as digital sovereignty, is crucial, as a common terminology facilitates the exchange [46].

Empowering Individuals & Communities Through Design and Competencies. Besides engaging in policy, an opportunity for our research community lies in elaborating positive visions for individuals and communities, e.g., in collaboration or shared sovereignty with other actors, a strong focus on software communities and free software [70], or in cases of oppression based on autonomous digital infrastructures [11].

For example, based on our research projects and design approaches, we can contribute to open-source/free software technologies to strengthen societies to reduce dependence on monopolist technology providers [3,56,70], to support individuals against their government, e.g. to bypass censorship on the internet [11] or to share and compare policy intentions under a common lens [75]. This approach might be limited by the resources of our community itself, however, there are also other chances, e.g., empowerment through competency building that helps using given rights and options [12] or collaborating/co-designing with technology providers, be it the public or private sector.

Moreover, it is certainly also important to take stock of the research within the community (see, e.g., [4]). We already have a great variety of knowledge, design approaches, and best practices on many topics ranging from open-source/free software, usable-privacy, to grass-root movements, but they are not necessarily accessible for discourse and might be worth discussing under the new outlook of ongoing fights for sovereignty. Again, the goal should be fostering the design of better technology.

5.3   Limitations

As already mentioned, the conceptual model does not provide any best-practices or guidance when it comes to "how to enhance the digital sovereignty of humans". We only provide narrow ideas by describing the expressions of such sovereignty picked up in previous research, e.g., competencies. This limitation is certainly due to the fact, that the research field as such can be considered to be in a very early stage. However, also our own focus on providing an overview of the key concepts and their relations, instead of an in-depth exploration of related concepts, e.g., human autonomy or self-determination, contributes to this limitation. Thus, this research should be seen as a charter and inspiration for HCI research on digital sovereignty in the hope that we understand digital sovereignty better, promote a positive vision of the future, and ultimately design better technologies.

6   Conclusion

While the ideas of engaging in policy discourses are not new to the HCI community, this particular exploratory paper picked up a new discourse that seems to be underrepresented so far. In particular, this paper creates an explorative conceptual model to introduce the ongoing discourse around human-centred digital sovereignty to the community, as well as guide early research by clarifying and identifying the main concepts and variables. Moreover, it should inspire new questions and help identify existing knowledge and gaps. Future research, should pick up the discourse, elaborate on a human-centred definition of digital sovereignty, engage with policy-makers and researchers, design open-source/free-software tools to support those living under non-sovereign conditions, and ultimately envision alternative futures with the individual humans and their societies as the sovereign.

References

1. Ahmadian, A.S., Jürjens, J., Strüber, D.: Extending model-based privacy analysis for the industrial data space by exploiting privacy level agreements. In: Proceedings of the 33rd Annual ACM Symposium on Applied Computing, SAC 2018, pp. 1142–1149. Association for Computing Machinery, New York, NY, USA (2018). https://doi.org/10.1145/3167132. 3167256
2. Appenzeller, A., Rode, E., Krempel, E., Beyerer, J.: Enabling data sovereignty for patients through digital consent enforcement. In: Proceedings of the 13th ACM International Conference on PErvasive Technologies Related to Assistive Environments, PETRA 2020. Association for Computing Machinery, New York, NY, USA (2020). https://doi.org/10.1145/ 3389189.3393745
3. Avila Pinto, R.: Digital sovereignty or digital colonialism. SUR-Int. J. Human Rights **27**, 15 (2018)
4. Bardzell, S.: Feminist HCI: taking stock and outlining an agenda for design. In: Proceedings of the SIGCHI Conference on Human Factors in Computing Systems, pp. 1301–1310 (2010)
5. Barker, T.: Europe can't win the tech war it just started: The European union is running in circles in pursuit of "digital sovereignty" (2020). https://foreignpolicy.com/2020/01/16/ europetechnology-sovereignty-von-der-leyen/
6. Baums, A.: Digitale Standortpolitik in der Post-Snowden-Welt. In: Digitale Souveränität, pp. 223–235. Springer, Wiesbaden (2016). https://doi.org/10.1007/978-3-658-07349-7_20
7. Bernardes, M.B., de Andrade, F.P., Novais, P.: Smart cities, data and right to privacy: a look from the Portuguese and Brazilian experience. In: Proceedings of the 11th International Conference on Theory and Practice of Electronic Governance, ICEGOV 2018, pp. 328–337. Association for Computing Machinery, New York, NY, USA (2018). https://doi.org/10.1145/ 3209415.3209451
8. Bernardes, M.B., de Andrade, F.P., Novais, P., Lopes, N.V.: Participatory governance of smart cities: a study upon Portuguese and Brazilian government portals. In: Proceedings of the 11th International Conference on Theory and Practice of Electronic Governance, ICEGOV 2018, pp. 526–536. Association for Computing Machinery, New York, NY, USA (2018). https:// doi.org/10.1145/3209415.3209464
9. Birnstill, P., Beyerer, J.: Building blocks for identity management and protection for smart environments and interactive assistance systems. In: Proceedings of the 11th PErvasive Technologies Related to Assistive Environments Conference, PETRA 2018, pp. 292–296. Association for Computing Machinery, New York, NY, USA (2018). https://doi.org/10.1145/ 3197768.3201563
10. Bolis, I., Morioka, S.N., Sznelwar, L.I.: When sustainable development risks losing its meaning. Delimiting the concept with a comprehensive literature review and a conceptual model. J. Cleaner Prod. **83**, 7–20 (2014)
11. Bradbury, D.: Routing around censorship. Netw. Secur. **2011**(5), 5–8 (2011)
12. Büchi, M., Just, N., Latzer, M.: Caring is not enough: the importance of internet skills for online privacy protection. Inf. Commun. Soc. **20**(8), 1261–1278 (2017)
13. Calacci, D., Shen, J.J., Pentland, A.: The cop in your neighbor's doorbell: Amazon ring and the spread of participatory mass surveillance. Proc. ACM Hum.-Comput. Interact. **6**(CSCW2), 1–47 (2022)
14. Chander, A., Lê, U.P.: Data nationalism. Emory LJ **64**, 677 (2014)
15. Che, X., Metaxa-Kakavouli, D., Hancock, J.T.: Fake news in the news: an analysis of partisan coverage of the fake news phenomenon. In: Companion of the 2018 ACM Conference on Computer Supported Cooperative Work and Social Computing, CSCW 2018, pp. 289–292. Association for Computing Machinery, New York, NY, USA (2018). https://doi.org/10.1145/ 3272973.3274079

16. Chenou, J.M.: From cyber-libertarianism to neoliberalism: Internet exceptionalism, multi-stakeholderism, and the institutionalisation of internet governance in the 1990s. Globalizations **11**(2), 205–223 (2014)
17. Christakis, T.: 'European digital sovereignty': successfully navigating between the 'brussels effect' and Europe's quest for strategic autonomy. Available at SSRN 3748098 (2020)
18. Conradie, N.H., Nagel, S.K.: Digital sovereignty and smart wearables: three moral calculi for the distribution of legitimate control over the digital. J. Responsible Technol. **12**, 100053 (2022)
19. Creemers, R.: The Chinese cyber-sovereignty agenda. In: Connectivity Wars: Why Migration, Finance and Trade are the Geo-Economic Battlegrounds of the Future. JSTOR (2019)
20. Crespi, F., Caravella, S., Menghini, M., Salvatori, C.: European technological sovereignty: an emerging framework for policy strategy. Intereconomics **56**(6), 348–354 (2021)
21. Entwistle, J.M., Rasmussen, M.K., Verdezoto, N., Brewer, R.S., Andersen, M.S.: Beyond the individual: the contextual wheel of practice as a research framework for sustainable HCI. In: Proceedings of the 33rd Annual ACM Conference on Human Factors in Computing Systems, pp. 1125–1134 (2015)
22. Erenli, K., Geminn, C., Pfeiffer, L.: Legal challenges of an open web index. Int. Cybersecur. Law Rev. **2**, 183–194 (2021)
23. Ertl, T., et al.: Ethical future environments: smart thinking about smart cities means engaging with its most vulnerable. In: C&T 2021: Proceedings of the 10th International Conference on Communities & Technologies - Wicked Problems in the Age of Tech, C&T 2021, pp. 340–345. Association for Computing Machinery, New York, NY, USA (2021). https://doi.org/10.1145/3461564.3468165
24. Feingold, S.: Why the european union is opening a silicon valley 'embassy' (2022). https://www.weforum.org/agenda/2022/08/why-the-european-union-is-opening-a-silicon-valley-embassy/
25. Fiebig, T., Aschenbrenner, D.: 13 propositions on an Internet for a "burning world". In: Proceedings of the ACM SIGCOMM Joint Workshops on Technologies, Applications, and Uses of a Responsible Internet and Building Greener Internet, TAURIN+BGI 2022, pp. 1–5. Association for Computing Machinery, New York, NY, USA (2022). https://doi.org/10.1145/3538395.3545312
26. Floridi, L.: The fight for digital sovereignty: what it is, and why it matters, especially for the EU. Philos. Technol. **33**(3), 369–378 (2020)
27. Franquesa, D., Navarro, L.: Devices as a commons: limits to premature recycling. In: Proceedings of the 2018 Workshop on Computing within Limits, LIMITS 2018. Association for Computing Machinery, New York, NY, USA (2018). https://doi.org/10.1145/3232617.3232624
28. von Grafenstein, M., Jakobi, T., Stevens, G.: Effective data protection by design through interdisciplinary research methods: the example of effective purpose specification by applying user-centred UX-design methods. Comput. Law Secur. Rev. **46**, 105722 (2022)
29. Grimm, D.: Sovereignty: The Origin and Future of a Political and Legal Concept. Columbia University Press, Columbia (2015)
30. Grinko, M., Qalandar, S., Randall, D., Wulf, V.: Nationalizing the Internet to break a protest movement: Internet shutdown and counter-appropriation in Iran of late 2019. Proc. ACM Hum.-Comput. Interact. **6**(CSCW2), 1–21 (2022)
31. Grohmann, R.: Beyond platform cooperativism: worker-owned platforms in Brazil. Interactions **29**(4), 87–89 (2022). https://doi.org/10.1145/3540251
32. Heitlinger, S., Bryan-Kinns, N., Comber, R.: The right to the sustainable smart city. In: Proceedings of the 2019 CHI Conference on Human Factors in Computing Systems, CHI 2019, pp. 1–13. Association for Computing Machinery, New York, NY, USA (2019). https://doi.org/10.1145/3290605.3300517

33. Hill, J.: The growth of data localization post-snowden: analysis and recommendations for US policymakers and business leaders. In: The Hague Institute for Global Justice, Conference on the Future of Cyber Governance (2014)
34. Hochheiser, H., Lazar, J.: HCI and societal issues: a framework for engagement. Int. J. Hum.-Comput. Interact. **23**(3), 339–374 (2007)
35. Jackson, S.J., Gillespie, T., Payette, S.: The policy knot: re-integrating policy, practice and design in CSCW studies of social computing. In: Proceedings of the 17th ACM Conference on Computer Supported Cooperative Work & Social Computing, pp. 588–602 (2014)
36. Jakobi, T., et al.: The role of is in the conflicting interests regarding GDPR. Bus. Inf. Syst. Eng. **62**(3), 261–272 (2020)
37. Jarvis, J.: A society relearning how to talk with itself. Digit. Gov. Res. Pract. **1**(1), 1–10 (2020)
38. Jonker, M., et al.: Where.ru? Assessing the impact of conflict on Russian domain infrastructure. In: Proceedings of the 22nd ACM Internet Measurement Conference, IMC 2022, pp. 159–165. Association for Computing Machinery, New York, NY, USA (2022). https://doi.org/10.1145/3517745.3561423
39. Keller, D., Iglesias, C.: Exception and harmonization: three theoretical debates on internet regulation (2019)
40. Klein, H.: ICANN and Internet governance: leveraging technical coordination to realize global public policy. Inf. Soc. **18**(3), 193–207 (2002)
41. Lambach, D., Oppermann, K.: Narratives of digital sovereignty in German political discourse. Governance (2022)
42. Landwehr, M., Borning, A., Wulf, V.: Problems with surveillance capitalism and possible alternatives for it infrastructure. Inf. Commun. Soc. **26**, 70–85 (2021)
43. Lauf, F., Zum Felde, H.M., Klötgen, M., Brandstädter, R., Schönborn, R.: Sovereignly donating medical data as a patient: a technical approach. In: HEALTHINF, pp. 623–630 (2022)
44. Lawo, D., Neifer, T., Esau, M., Stevens, G.: Buying the 'right' thing: designing food recommender systems with critical consumers. In: Proceedings of the 2021 CHI Conference on Human Factors in Computing Systems, pp. 1–13 (2021)
45. Lawo, D., Neifer, T., Esau-Held, M., Stevens, G.: Digital sovereignty: what it is and why it matters for HCI. In: Extended Abstracts of the 2023 CHI Conference on Human Factors in Computing Systems, pp. 1–7 (2023)
46. Lazar, J., et al.: Human-computer interaction and international public policymaking: a framework for understanding and taking future actions. Found. Trends® Hum.-Comput. Interact. **9**(2), 69–149 (2016)
47. Lips, S., Ahmed, R.K., Zulfigarzada, K., Krimmer, R., Draheim, D.: Digital sovereignty and participation in an autocratic state: designing an e-petition system for developing countries. In: DG.O 2021: The 22nd Annual International Conference on Digital Government Research, DG.O 2021, pp. 123–131. Association for Computing Machinery, New York, NY, USA (2021). https://doi.org/10.1145/3463677.3463706
48. Luzsa, R., Mayr, S., Syrmoudis, E., Grossklags, J., Kübler-Wachendorff, S., Kranz, J.: Online service switching intentions and attitudes towards data portability - the role of technology-related attitudes and privacy. In: Proceedings of Mensch Und Computer 2022, MuC 2022, pp. 1–13. Association for Computing Machinery, New York, NY, USA (2022). https://doi.org/10.1145/3543758.3543762
49. Mac Síthigh, D., Siems, M.: The Chinese social credit system: a model for other countries? Mod. Law Rev. **82**(6), 1034–1071 (2019)
50. Marichal, S., et al.: CETA: open, affordable and portable mixed-reality environment for low-cost tablets. In: Proceedings of the 19th International Conference on Human-Computer Interaction with Mobile Devices and Services, MobileHCI 2017. Association for Computing Machinery, New York, NY, USA (2017). https://doi.org/10.1145/3098279.3125435

51. Maurer, T., Skierka, I., Morgus, R., Hohmann, M.: Technological sovereignty: missing the point? In: 2015 7th International Conference on Cyber Conflict: Architectures in Cyberspace, pp. 53–68. IEEE (2015)

52. Molyneaux, H., O'Donnell, S., Kakekaspan, C., Walmark, B., Budka, P., Gibson, K.: Social media in remote first nation communities (2014)

53. Musiani, F.: Infrastructuring digital sovereignty: a research agenda for an infrastructure-based sociology of digital self-determination practices. Inf. Commun. Soc. 1–16 (2022)

54. Neifer, T., Lawo, D., Bossauer, P., Gadatsch, A., et al.: Decoding IPaaS: investigation of user requirements for integration platforms as a service. In: ICE-B, pp. 47–55 (2021)

55. Nielsen, M.M.: Digitising a small island state: a lesson in Faroese. In: Proceedings of the 9th International Conference on Theory and Practice of Electronic Governance, ICEGOV 2015–2016, pp. 54–59. Association for Computing Machinery, New York, NY, USA (2016). https://doi.org/10.1145/2910019.2910042

56. Nordhaug, L.M., Harris, L.: Digital public goods: enablers of digital sovereignty (2021)

57. Nouwens, M., Klokmose, C.N.: A survey of digital working conditions of Danish knowledge workers. In: Proceedings of 19th European Conference on Computer-Supported Cooperative Work. European Society for Socially Embedded Technologies (EUSSET) (2021). https://doi.org/10.18420/ecscw2021_. No. 24

58. Pavlyutenkova, M., Ksenz, P.: New conditions of electronic government in Russia. In: Proceedings of the 2015 2nd International Conference on Electronic Governance and Open Society: Challenges in Eurasia, EGOSE 2015, pp. 77–81. Association for Computing Machinery, New York, NY, USA (2015). https://doi.org/10.1145/2846012.2846027

59. Pins, D., Jakobi, T., Stevens, G., Alizadeh, F., Krüger, J.: Finding, getting and understanding: the user journey for the GDPR's right to access. Behav. Inf. Technol. **41**, 1–27 (2022)

60. Pistor, K.: Statehood in the digital age 1. Constellations **27**(1), 3–18 (2020)

61. Png, M.T.: At the tensions of south and north: critical roles of global south stakeholders in AI governance. In: 2022 ACM Conference on Fairness, Accountability, and Transparency, FAccT 2022, pp. 1434–1445. Association for Computing Machinery, New York, NY, USA (2022). https://doi.org/10.1145/3531146.3533200

62. Pohle, J.: Digital sovereignty. A new key concept of digital policy in Germany and Europe (2020)

63. Pohle, J.: Digitale souveränität. Handbuch Digitalisierung in Staat und Verwaltung, pp. 1–13 (2020)

64. Pohle, J., Thiel, T., et al.: Digital sovereignty. In: Practicing Sovereignty: Digital Involvement in Times of Crises, pp. 47–67 (2021)

65. Rosengrün, S.: Why AI is a threat to the rule of law. Digit. Soc. **1**(2), 10 (2022)

66. Ruohonen, J.: The treachery of images in the digital sovereignty debate. Mind. Mach. **31**(3), 439–456 (2021)

67. Schelenz, L., et al.: The theory, practice, and ethical challenges of designing a diversity-aware platform for social relations. In: Proceedings of the 2021 AAAI/ACM Conference on AI, Ethics, and Society, AIES 2021, pp. 905–915. Association for Computing Machinery, New York, NY, USA (2021). https://doi.org/10.1145/3461702.3462595

68. Siapera, M., Douloudis, K., Prentza, A.: A common data model for once-only cross-border data exchanges in Europe. In: Proceedings of the 14th International Conference on Theory and Practice of Electronic Governance, ICEGOV 2021, pp. 223–230. Association for Computing Machinery, New York, NY, USA (2022). https://doi.org/10.1145/3494193.3494224

69. Stadnik, I.: Internet governance in Russia-sovereign basics for independent Runet. In: TPRC47: The 47th Research Conference on Communication, Information and Internet Policy (2019)

70. Stallman, R.: Viewpoint why "open source" misses the point of free software. Commun. ACM **52**(6), 31–33 (2009)

71. Stein, M., Meurer, J., Boden, A., Wulf, V.: Mobility in later life: appropriation of an integrated transportation platform. In: Proceedings of the 2017 CHI Conference on Human Factors in Computing Systems, CHI 2017, pp. 5716–5729. Association for Computing Machinery, New York, NY, USA (2017). https://doi.org/10.1145/3025453.3025672

72. Stevens, G., Boden, A., Winterberg, L., Gómez, J.M., Bala, C.: Digitaler konsum: Herausforderungen und chancen der verbraucherinformatik (2019)

73. Tretter, M.: Sovereignty in the digital and contact tracing apps. Digit. Soc. 2(1), 2 (2023)

74. Vigil, M., Rantanen, M., Belding, E.: A first look at tribal web traffic. In: Proceedings of the 24th International Conference on World Wide Web, WWW 2015, pp. 1155–1165. International World Wide Web Conferences Steering Committee, Republic and Canton of Geneva, CHE (2015). https://doi.org/10.1145/2736277.2741645

75. Waller, A.: Public policy issues in augmentative and alternative communication technologies a comparison of the UK and the US. Interactions 20(3), 68–75 (2013)

76. Webster, J., Watson, R.T.: Analyzing the past to prepare for the future: writing a literature review. MIS Q. xiii–xxiii (2002)

77. Weigl, L., Amard, A., Codagnone, C., Fridgen, G.: The EU's digital identity policy: tracing policy punctuations. In: Proceedings of the 15th International Conference on Theory and Practice of Electronic Governance, ICEGOV 2022, pp. 74–81. Association for Computing Machinery, New York, NY, USA (2022). https://doi.org/10.1145/3560107.3560121

78. Wessel, D., et al.: Prototypes for e-government websites to support the digital sovereignty of citizens. In: Proceedings of Mensch Und Computer 2022, MuC 2022, pp. 615–617. Association for Computing Machinery, New York, NY, USA (2022). https://doi.org/10.1145/3543758.3547514

79. Zakiyeva, Z.: Problems and perspectives of digital silk road in central Asia. In: Proceedings of the 6th International Conference on Engineering & MIS 2020. ICEMIS 2020. Association for Computing Machinery, New York, NY, USA (2020). https://doi.org/10.1145/3410352.3410741

80. Zambrano, R., Sanchez-Torres, J.M.: AI public policies in Latin America: disruption or more of the same? In: Proceedings of the 14th International Conference on Theory and Practice of Electronic Governance, ICEGOV 2021, pp. 25–33. Association for Computing Machinery, New York, NY, USA (2022). https://doi.org/10.1145/3494193.3494294

MAS4Games: A Reinforced Learning-Based Multi-agent System to Improve Player Retention in Virtual Reality Video Games

Natalia Maury-Castañeda, Sergio Villarruel-Vasquez, and Willy Ugarte[✉][iD]

Universidad Peruana de Ciencias Aplicadas, Lima, Peru
{U201816996,U201714083}@upc.edu.pe, willy.ugarte@upc.pe

Abstract. In this paper, we present a Q-learning-based multi-agent system designed for Dynamic Difficulty Adjustment (DDA) in a 3D fighting game. Our primary goal is to enhance the player's gaming experience through dynamic game difficulty adjustments based on their performance. We leverage the Unity game development platform and the ML-Agents framework to implement the Q-learning algorithm, training intelligent agents to adapt the game's difficulty. Our findings underscore the efficacy of Q-learning and multi-agent systems in improving DDA for video games. In the conclusion section, we discuss potential implications and future directions for our research.

Keywords: Dynamic difficulty adjustment · Q-learning · Multi-agent systems · Unity 3D · Virtual reality · Gaming experience · Game development · ML-agents framework · Video games · Artificial intelligence · Player performance · Difficulty level adaptation · Intelligent agent Training

1 Introduction

Even though more and more people are playing video games in the last few years, in 2022 there was a decrease of 20.9% in people playing and ordering Virtual Reality (VR) devices throughout the years[1]. Despite the fact that Meta has sold around 20 million units of VR devices, user retention is a main issue. Meta executives have declared that they need to be better at retention and the resurrection of their user base[2]. This is caused by multiple factors, such as being a new device, lack of games, new competition from established companies such as Sony or Apple, etc. Because of this, our main objective is to increase player retention in VR games using multi-agent systems with Reinforcement Learning (RL).

This is important because the gaming industry has been growing over the years, reaching its peak growth in the third quarter of 2020, producing over 11.2 billion dollars, a 24% increase compared to the previous year. There have been more people playing

---

[1] Global Shipments of AR/VR Headsets Decline Sharply in 2022 Following the Prior Year's Strong Results - IDC - https://www.idc.com/getdoc.jsp?containerId=prUS50467723.

[2] This is Meta's AR/VR hardware roadmap for the next four years - The Verge - https://www.theverge.com/2023/2/28/23619730/meta-vr-oculus-ar-glasses-smartwatch-plans.

© The Author(s), under exclusive license to Springer Nature Switzerland AG 2023
H. P. da Silva and P. Cipresso (Eds.): CHIRA 2023, CCIS 1997, pp. 104–120, 2023.
https://doi.org/10.1007/978-3-031-49368-3_7

with more gaming devices, such as Nintendo Switch, Playstation, Xbox, etc. The best performing games were Among Us, Super Mario Odyssey, Animal Crossing, Minecraft, Call of Duty: Modern Warfare, Fortnite, etc.[3]

While developing games, the main challenge is to ensure gaming balance, which directly affects the player's experience and interactions with the game. This is achieved by having a good learning curve that maintains the game's complexity in perfect balance: not too hard to be frustrating, and not too easy to be boring. Various techniques are employed to achieve this balance. For example, Sony is actively investing in technologies to enhance the gaming experience. It has established a subsidiary dedicated to exploring Artificial Intelligence (AI) techniques such as reinforcement learning and multi-agent systems for use in their future games[4]. These endeavors reflect the industry's commitment to delivering the best possible gaming experiences.

The dynamic adjustment for game difficulty is more complex to achieve in a virtual reality environment due to the many different sorts of actions and inputs that the player can execute. In a regular video game, the player owns a discrete quantity of possible actions in possible scenarios based on the limitations of the game. In VR, players have the freedom to move their body, their arms, and their position, which could lead to fooling classic AI-enemies. To validate the unique challenges of VR games, we conducted a test by playing Resident Evil 4 for Meta Quest, comparing it to its non-VR version on Playstation 2. This hands-on testing process provided insights into the complexities involved. For this reason, user-agents must be trained with real data and simulations to learn from human behavior, which will certainly be a challenge to reproduce.

There have been other related works that apply multi-agents in games, but they have different purposes (all of the mentioned methods will be further explained in the related works section). In [8] the authors use an agent to regulate the game difficulty based on a Machine Learning (ML) model and introduces it into the Monte-Carlo Tree Searching Algorithm to detect the player's state (Competence, Valence, Challenge, Flow, etc.). Based on the obtained result, the agent will adjust the difficulty of the game to ensure the best experience. Another approach uses machine learning with Artificial Intelligence to build a model based on massively multiplayer online role-playing games (MMORPG) with the most common actions made by players over a 6 month period. With this information, they train generative models that create agents that will recreate the most common actions, helping the testing process by finding the most common bugs with the agents [10]. Finally, the research of Reis et al. uses multi-agent in meta games to adjust the difficulty of the other agents in the game so it maintains its equilibrium in difficulty [11]. What all of these works have in common is that all of them use agents in games. However, the aim is to implement agent-based technologies in a different way. For example, Moon's research regulates the difficulty based on state not player ability, Pfau's work uses multi-agents for testing and debugging the game, Reis uses them for maintaining the game flow. The approach with multi-agents will be using

---

[3] Third Quarter 2020 U.S. Consumer Spend on Video Game Products Shattered Previous Record Highs - NPD - https://www.npd.com/news/press-releases/2020/the-npd-group-third-quarter-2020.

[4] Sony Research Inc - https://ai.sony/projects/gaming_ai/.

the player's abilities, and we will adapt the game difficulty using QLearning Algorithm in VR games [2, 10, 13].

In order to do this research, there are key components that will lead to achieving its objective. First, for the purpose of increasing player retention in VR games, this work will apply multi-agent systems using reinforcement learning with Q-Learning to the enemies of the game. These agents will learn based on the abilities and behavior of the player, so it's neither too easy nor too hard, making it the perfect challenge for the player's capabilities. However, due to time constraints, the agents won't communicate with each other or cooperate to defeat the player. In the next phase of work, the goal is to make the agents work together by sharing information and making joint decisions. This will help them achieve their common objective of defeating the player.

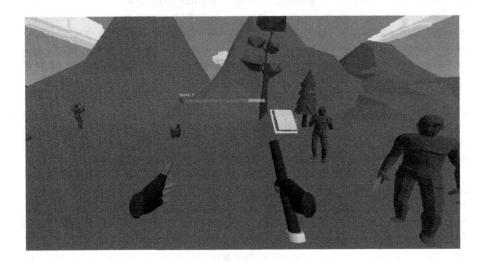

Fig. 1. Adapted Game for VR.

To achieve this, a game that has the player in constant confrontation with enemies was needed. A game repository title "3rd-person-fighting" developed in Unity by Vyshnovka, available at https://github.com/vyshnovka/3rd-person-fighting was found and used as the foundation for the project. Once the base-code of the game was obtained, improvements had to made and add more features like the enemy hordes, convert the game to VR-capable, add more weapons, update the game mechanics, and implement the agents for Dynamic Difficulty Adjustment, as can be seen in Fig. 1. Finally, a VR device was needed to test the game, so the goal was to build the game for Meta Quest 2.

This research makes three primary contributions. Firstly, the implementation of a multi-agent system specifically designed for DDA allows for dynamic game difficulty adjustments based on user performance. Secondly, the open-source game has been modified, integrating our multi-agent system to create an immersive gaming experience. Lastly, a comparative analysis of different approaches is conducted to validate their effectiveness in enhancing user retention.

This paper is structured as follows: it begins by reviewing related works on Dynamic Difficulty Adjustment and its impact on the player's game experience. Following that, the paper delves into the relevant concepts and theories associated with the research background. Subsequently, we detail the procedures performed and the experiments conducted during our research. Finally, we conclude the paper by summarizing our findings and providing recommendations for future research endeavors.

2   Related Works

There are many algorithms, methods, and techniques that are used to regulate the game difficulty and improve the player experience. In this section, we will further explain the five most important and relevant papers for our paper research, the previous papers mentioned in the introduction will be explained to a bigger extent.

In [8] uses dynamic difficulty adjustment integrating it with Monte-Carlo Tree Search algorithm to regulate the game difficulty. The researchers focus their investigation on DDA with multi agent systems (MAS). However, instead of using the player's abilities, they use the player's affective states to regulate the difficulty to ensure that they have the most enjoyment while playing. To archive this, they use Monte-Carlo tree search (MCTS) with Machine Learning models referencing the game features in order to effectively predict the player's affective state. There are four player states that the MCTS uses: valence (VA), flow (FL), challenge (CH) and competence (CO), and there are four ML, one for each state. In other words, the game difficulty is determined by the player's state so that they don't feel like the game doesn't have enough action, etc. The results show that the approach Moon et al. took enhanced the players' game experience [8].

The main difference between this paper and the one we are doing is that they regulate the difficulty of the game based on the state of the player and not on their skills. Another difference is that they use a different technique, the Monte Carlo Tree Search Algorithm, which is very effective in getting the state of the player accurately, and we plan on using Q-Learning. Because of that, our work is different than the one made by Moon et al.

In [9], a new reinforcement learning technique combined with deep learning is proposed to create Artificial Intelligence agents that can compete in real-time fighting games.

The researchers designed and implemented the neural network with LSTM architecture, in the game "Blade & Soul", a two-dimensional fighting game. They made use of the autoplay function to face the agents against each other in order to train them, and they programmed three different agent styles (aggressive, balanced, and defensive) so that the model can achieve better efficiency. These agents were created through the reward configuration. In addition, data-skipping techniques are suggested to further improve data efficiency [9].

The trained AI agents competed against five professional players and achieved a 62% win rate. The results demonstrate that the proposed reinforcement learning technique can be applied to other fighting games and could be useful in game development and automatic level balancing [9].

While our project shares similarities with the research paper about trying to get the best experience for the players, the main difference is that we plan to train our model using data from human players, whereas the authors of the paper trained their agents against other agents.

Another paper [5] employs meta and deep reinforcement learning algorithms to create a set of trained agents that subsequently train other agents through reinforcement learning. In this setup, a primary trainer, referred to as the meta learner, is responsible for instructing inner learners, preparing them for various scenarios. In this manner, the meta agent's role is to produce agents (inner learners) capable of effectively addressing the given problem and acting as exemplars for further learning [5].

A flexible end-to-end framework was implemented. The upper layer of this framework receives the input of the deep learning algorithms to be used; here the meta learner and the inner learners are defined, and the internal environment with the problem to be solved. The conversion layer receives the previous information and processes it to create a personalized external environment, defining the rewards and punishments for it. With this reinforcement learning algorithm, the meta learner will try to solve the problem by interacting with the external environment. The meta agent receives information from the external environment based on rewards and punishments in order to learn; this parameter is the state space. The state space is the difference between the weights of two neural networks, where the neural networks are constructed by the inner learners. The reward parameter is the average of the rewards of the inner learners; this information is received by the meta learner and is vital for the correct functioning of the algorithm [5].

With all this information, the meta learner will generate other agents (inner learners), where they will be tested in the internal environment. With the results obtained from the interactions of the environment, it will know which features to ignore and which to use to improve the agents. Once the meta learner has finished learning, a Randomized Batch Vector (RBV) will be used where a random number of samples are used and the meta learner is left to adjust the weights of the vector with the agents (inner learners) it created to solve the problem. The goal of RBV is to reduce the number of parameters that the meta learner has to monitor and thus have a better result [5].

The key differentiator between this paper and our project is the training methodology employed. While the paper uses meta and deep reinforcement learning algorithms to train a sample of agents, which will then train other agents, our project is focused on training agents using Q-learning against human players. Additionally, the paper's framework involves a meta agent generating inner learners that solve the problem appropriately, whereas our approach focuses on using a multi-agent system to dynamically regulate the difficulty of VR games and improve player retention. In summary, our project aims to directly address the issue of player retention in virtual reality games by training agents to adapt to individual players, while the paper focuses on a more complex training methodology to generate agents that can solve problems in a general sense.

To determine the impact that difficulty pacing has on the player's motivation, [3] reviews the state of the art and literature of the curve difficulty in order to develop the one that best enhances and impacts the player's motivation in a game. To achieve this, the authors, Rao Fernandes, William; Levieux, Guillaume, used the dynamic difficulty adjustment model to regulate the curve based on the player's ability, base lines, and peak difficulty points. The DDA allows them to see the trace of the difficulty curve, see the base lines and peak points throughout the gameplay, and adjust the difficulty based on the parameters in which the model is configured. Rao Fernandes et al. developed four different curve difficulties to test them in a simulation and determine which curve the players prefer and motivates them to keep playing. After doing that, the authors implemented an enemy that was controlled by artificial intelligence, and this AI would be regulated by the dynamic difficulty adjustment model. The results obtained prove that players prefer curves with peaks rather than ones that are flat [3].

This paper shares a similar objective with our work, with the primary difference lying in the techniques employed to achieve the goal. Rao Fernandes et al. utilize a Data Model, while our approach involves implementing Agents, a form of Artificial Intelligence, in the enemies to regulate difficulty and maintain player engagement.

In [1], they use reinforcement learning, which is also used to implement Dynamic Difficulty Adaptation as a Meta Game to achieve automatic game balance, so the game is neither too hard nor too easy, by using RL to train the DDA algorithm. The reason why the balance task was chosen to be made like a Meta Game is because in Meta Games, actions change the rules of another base game. The technique consists of giving the agents different roles so they work like a meta game. There are two main roles: game master and training agent. The agent that will assume the role of game master is in charge of learning the optimal policy of the meta game by playing it. The other agents are in charge of training the game master with reinforcement learning so that the game master regulates the game difficulty based on the input it is receiving. To test this, they put the agents in a grid and made the game master agent play, showing that the agent was able to balance the difficulty based on the information provided by the other agents [1].

This paper aims to regulate the difficulty using dynamic difficulty adjustment algorithms by mixing them with reinforcement learning and multi agent systems. The main difference between our paper is in the way we both use the MAS technique. Reis et al. use it so they have a game master who will be in charge of regulating the difficulty based on the input it receive from the other agents. We plan to use the agents on the enemies so that the training of the agents and their behavior are trained by the player itself. This further proves that the use of multi agent systems is a good approach to regulate the game difficulty in order to obtain balance.

3 Contribution

3.1 Preliminary Concepts

In this section, the main concepts used in our work are presented. We aim to train agents using the reinforcement learning technique QLearning to regulate the game difficulty so that it adapts to the player's ability. We believe that by using this technique, the player will be more motivated to finish the game and keep on playing.

The Difficulty Curve, illustrated in Fig. 2, plays a critical role in shaping the game's challenge level from start to finish. It ensures that players experience varying levels of difficulty during gameplay, creating an engaging and satisfying experience. Game

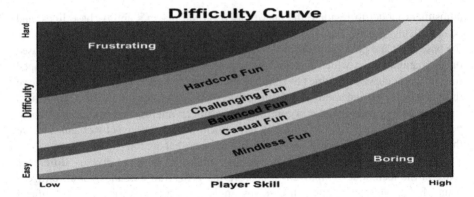

Fig. 2. Difficulty Curve.

designers employ diverse strategies when crafting these curves. Some opt for a curve that begins with ease, escalates to a climax of intensity, and then eases off to let players savor their victories. Others prefer a gradual, steady rise in difficulty as the game progresses. These approaches are important as they directly influence player retention, influencing whether players complete the game [3].

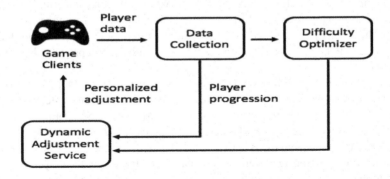

Fig. 3. Dynamic Difficulty Adjustment diagram.

Dynamic Difficulty Adjustment, as depicted in Fig. 3, is a method to regulate the game difficulty with different mechanisms. One way is to use game parameter tuning, where the algorithm adjusts the difficulty using a timer depending on the player's skill. Another one is to use in-game manipulation, where DDA uses the user's inventory to measure the item drop rate and the damage patterns, based on the assumption that the player's skill is represented by these measurements. Finally, the use of game agents that mixes artificial intelligence and Reinforcement Learning to regulate the complexity of the game based on metrics established by the game developer. In order to measure the player's ability, most dynamic DDA algorithms use heuristic score functions specified by game developers, but the downside of using them is their inconsistency [8].

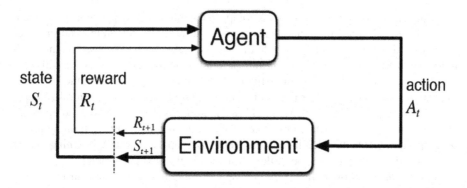

Fig. 4. Reinforcement Learning diagram.

Reinforcement Learning, as shown in Fig. 4, is a type of ML approach that imitates the way how brain gains knowledge through applied mathematics and statistics. A RL problem is usually formulated as a Markov Decision Process (MDP), where an agent interacts with an external environment at discrete time steps. Each step, the agent observes a state and chooses an action according to its policy, using a probability distribution from states to actions. From the action taken, the agent receives a reward, and the environment changes to a new state. This process is repeated until a terminal state is reached [1].

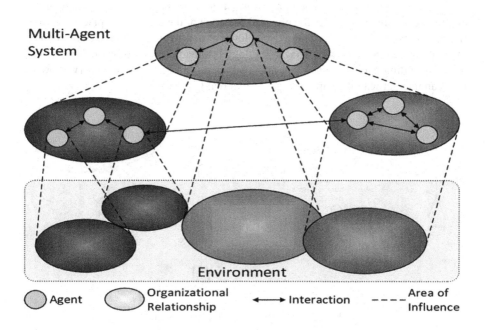

Fig. 5. Multi Agent Systems diagram.

Multi Agent Systems, a are systems composed of mutually independent agents inter-acting with each other in a shared environment to achieve their individual or group objectives, this is represented in Fig. 5. Each agent makes decisions based on the infor-mation they receive from their environment and the information they share with each other. Because they are a type of Artificial Intelligence, they can be trained by tech-niques like reinforcement learning with central approach and with decentralized app-roach. The major difference between the two methods is that the centralized approach uses real-time policies obtained by expensive calculations to an offline training proce-dure for training. On the other hand, the decentralized approach uses QLearning to train its agents; this technique will be further explained in the next paragraph [7].

Q-learning is an off policy reinforcement learning algorithm that can learn from actions taken according to a different policy. This algorithm uses backpropagation and loss function to learn the parameters using Q-Function and V-Function as approximators to denote their values. The obtained value is the action value, which shows the quality of the action made by the agent for a specific state, often denoted as Q-Value. With the knowledge obtained, a new state is reached, and the consequences of the action taken are stored in the experience replay transition table, which is denoted as Q-Tables. Combined with the loss function and Bellman equation, the algorithm uses the distribution of Q-Tables to determine the best optimal state. The main disadvantage of this technique is that it requires multiple iterations to achieve its optimal state. The main reason for this is that the rewards given only have a direct effect on the value state-action that triggered them. As consequence, the other state-action pairs are affected indirectly by them with the updated Q-Value [1].

Virtual Reality is a technology that allows users to immerse themselves in a virtual-environment, which simulates the physical presence of the user in that place. VR expe-riences can be designed to be interactive, allowing users to engage with the environment in a natural and intuitive way. This technology has the potential to revolutionize many fields, including gaming, education, and healthcare. In Fig. 6 we can observe how the user can interact with the game using a virtual reality device.

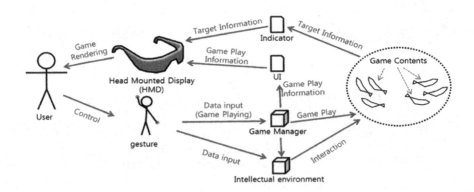

Fig. 6. Virtual Reality interaction diagram.

Our hypothesis is that the implementation of a multi-agent system based on the Q-learning algorithm will effectively regulate the difficulty of virtual reality games, resulting in an enhanced player experience and an increased player retention rate. By dynamically adjusting the game difficulty based on the performance of the player, the system will provide a more engaging and challenging experience while preventing frustration and boredom. Furthermore, the system's ability to learn and adapt to different game scenarios and player profiles will lead to more personalized and satisfying gameplay.

3.2   Method

In this section, we describe the method used to implement a Q-learning-based multi-agent system for a video game developed in Unity. We explain the architecture of the system and its two main contributions: the integration of Q-Learning for decision-making and the implementation of agents. As it was previously mentioned, due to time constraints, we couldn't implement the agents to be cooperative, but they are still competitive because each of them wants to defeat the player. We provide step-by-step details of the experimental setup and present the outcomes in figures and tables to convey our story.

The objective was to implement the agents as shown in Fig. 7. In order to accomplish this, we would need to implement a Joint-QTable that has all the QTables from each agent combined and a super Agent so that it controls the training. The agents

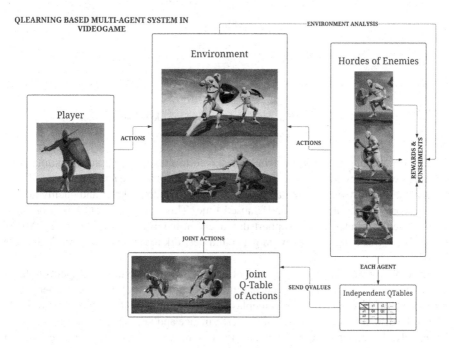

Fig. 7. Qlearning Based Multi-Agent System in videogame diagram.

would communicate with each other through the Joint-QTable before making a decision while also considering their own experience (their own QTable). Because of the complexity and time required, we are committed to continue our investigation and plan to implement this in a future paper research.

Architecture. To address the first contribution, we implement the QLearning algorithm for the agents, as shown in Fig. 8, which allows for the creation of intelligent agents capable of learning from their past experiences and adapting their actions accordingly.

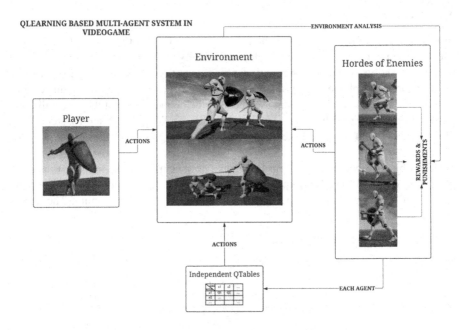

Fig. 8. Agents implement with Qlearning in videogame diagram.

The Q-Learning algorithm has been designed to maximize the agent's cumulative reward over time by identifying the most suitable actions for each game state. These optimal actions rely on current game state metrics, including player and enemy health, player score, enemy accuracy, and elapsed time. This approach results in more efficient gameplay strategies. To support this decision-making process, the Unity MLA-gents library was employed, providing a neural network to estimate the agent's discrete actions.

In summary, our multi-agent system utilizing Q-Learning empowers agents to learn and adjust their behavior by considering the game state and their previous experiences. As a result, players can enjoy the gameplay experience more, as the system dynamically adapts the difficulty level to match their performance and keeps the challenge for them. Ultimately, this enhancement contributes to an improved player retention rate, making the game enjoyable for a longer period of time.

Implementation. For the implementation, as mentioned before, Unity was chosen for game development. As for the agents and QLearning implementation, we leveraged the MLAgents library from Unity, which comes with an already implemented Agent-System Framework. Our focus was on developing the custom QLearning algorithm, refining the reward function, and configuring the agent training iterations.

The reward function utilizes statistics recovered from both the player and the enemy to regulate its parameters. The metrics used for the rewards are the player's and enemy's health, the time of death for both the enemy and the player, the enemy's accuracy, and the player's score. The reward function utilizes these observations to determine the most appropriate rewards, enabling the agents to adapt to the player's abilities. This reward and punishment function is designed to encourage more favorable behaviors while discouraging undesirable ones. In Table 1, the reward and punishment system is shown as it was implemented.

Table 1. Rewards and punishments for enemy agents in a q-learning based multi-agent system.

Input/Observation	Reward	Punishment
Distance to player	Reward if close to the player	Punishment if it is far away from the player
Health of player	Reward for reducing the player health	–
Health of enemy	–	Punishment for receiving damage
Enemy hit accuracy	Reward for hitting the player	Reward for failing the attack
Enemy's death time	–	Punishment for dying too early
Enemy position	Higher rewards as being closer to player	Punishment for getting through the mountains

To make sure that the agent learns effectively, we had to take certain steps. Firstly, we adjusted the reward values so that the QTable could be updated to provide the agent with new QValues. To update these values, we used the reward for a specific action applying the discounting factor; therefore, the impact of long term rewards is reduced. The rewards are designed to favour and encourage desired behavior like chasing the player, attacking it successfully, etc., and disencourage undesired behaviour like going anywhere else but not towards the player, attacking all the time, etc. These penalties have a high impact to ensure that the agent knows that it shouldn't take these actions and improves over time. This iterative process continued until the completion of the training episode for every action that the agent took.

Overall, our implementation uses game statistics for reward and punishment functions so that the agent learns to maximize their progress and performance in the game. The additional adjustments we made to the rewards ensure that the agent learns effectively and converges to an optimal policy in the game.

4   Experiments

In order to test our hypothesis, we will see the training results obtained through multiple iterations. As it has already been stated, due to a time constraint, we couldn't train the model for a longer time, meaning that if we add the model to the actual game, it will give poor results that will not reflect the actual potential of the algorithm. Because of this, we are just testing the results obtained after a short training period.

However, before we started training the model, we had to finish the improvements to the game and ensure the correct setup for the reward and punishment system in the algorithm so the training could give expected results like chasing the players, attacking, etc.

Once the game was ready, we started the training of the agents for 24 h straight through multiple episodes. Finally, when the training is finished, we check the cumulative rewards obtained at the end of the training and see its improvements made throughout time.

4.1 Experimental Protocol

To run this experiment, the following configuration requirements must be met:

- A PC with a VR-compatible graphics card.
- At least 16 GB of RAM and an SSD for optimal performance.
- An Intel Core i5 or AMD Ryzen 5 processor.
- Unity Hub installed, with Unity version 2021.3.21f1 selected as the active version.
- The Oculus Link Software installed, which serves as the driver for the Meta Quest 2 headset.
- Python 3.9 installed, along with the MLAgents library, which should be updated to the latest version.
- The ONNX library should also be installed and updated.

Once all the necessary setup is completed, follow these steps to run the project:

1. Open the Unity project and navigate to the gameplay scene.
2. Add the desired number of agents to the scene.
3. Open a command prompt or terminal and run the following command on python:
   ```
   mlagents-learn --run-id=T1
   ```
4. In the Unity Editor, enter Play Mode to start the game.

By following these steps, the project will be executed, the agents will be trained, and you can observe and evaluate their performance in the game environment in real-time.

To run the project in its non-AI version, simply enable the enemy spawner script and disable the agent in the Unity game inspector. This will allow you to experience the game without the AI-controlled agents, providing a different gameplay experience. This can be useful for comparison purposes or when evaluating the difference in gameplay with and without AI agents.

The source code can be found in this Github repository.

4.2 Training Trials

To train the model, several steps were followed. Firstly, the number of enemies/agents in the scene was configured. Next, the training process was initiated by running the game for multiple hours. During this training period, numerous episodes took place, each with a maximum duration of 5 min. An episode concluded under the following conditions: if the player died, if the enemy died, if the enemy left the battleground, or if the simulation had been ongoing for 5 min and the player isn't dead.

At the end of each episode, the main variables for training were reset. These variables included the player's and enemy's health, character positions, health bars for both the player and enemies, episode time, and character statistics. By resetting these variables, the training process was able to progress with fresh data for each new episode.

During the initial training hours, we allowed the agent to learn the fundamental task of locating the player. It was only after the agent demonstrated proficiency in locating the player that we introduced dynamic movement and combat training for the enemies.

Once the training period ended, we saw the statistics of the accumulative reward to see how well the agents did. If the result was negative or too low, we trained them again. If the result was positive and high, we finished the training and exported the trained model.

4.3   Results

The results on the accumulative reward score that we obtained over every checkpoint in 1 h training process are the following:

Table 2. MLAgents based model results

Training Step	Time Elapsed (seconds)	Mean Reward
50,000	400	−71,488.846
100,000	720	−96,191.720
150,000	1,030	−86,629.965
200,000	1,350	−70,140.864
250,000	1,670	−52,870.763
300,000	1,990	−21,410.757
350,000	2,320	−24,754.569
400,000	2,640	−8,355.116
450,000	2,964	13,746.567
500,000	3,600	13,372.431

As seen from Table 2, the algorithm starts with a negative reward, but overall, as time goes by, it shows improvement and eventually finishes with a positive reward.

This is also clearly shown in Fig. 9, a graph that reflects the agent's learning process. At the beginning, the graph shows negative rewards, because the agent performed poorly and would randomly attack and move away from the battlefield to the mountains. However, as the training progressed, the agent learned to stay within the battlefield limits, as they got punished everytime they got closer to it. It then started adopting movement patterns that brought it closer to the player's position. Over time, the agent reduced the frequency of consecutive attacks and introduced longer intervals between each attack. At a certain point during the 24 h training, it stopped repeatedly attacking and only struck when the player was nearby, although it remained outside the range to cause damage. Despite rarely being able to approach the player and eliminate them during this training phase, the agent successfully maintained proximity and improved its attack rate as the reward system was developed to encourage this behaviour. This shows that the agents are learning based on the rewards they are receiving and the algorithm is working.

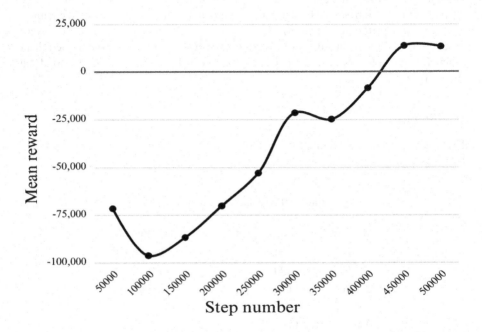

Fig. 9. Mean Reward Progression Over Training Steps.

5   Discussion

In this section, we engage in a comprehensive discussion of our study's findings and their implications, addressing the following key components:

5.1   Interpreting Results

Our primary objective was to investigate the efficacy of our approach in improving player retention by dynamically adjusting the game difficulty in VR video games. As highlighted in the abstract, we have successfully implemented a Multi-Agent System based on the Q-Learning algorithm to dynamically adjust the game's difficulty.

Our findings, as presented in the results section, indicate a trend of improvement in the agent's performance over time, reflected in the accumulative reward scores. We have systematically analyzed the training process and the associated agent behaviors, concluding that the agent exhibits a capacity to adapt to the game environment and player behavior. Furthermore, the initial negative rewards during early training stages, as explained in the results section, are interpreted as a part of the learning process as the agent's strategy evolves.

5.2 The Impact of Training Time

As demonstrated by the accumulative reward scores presented in Table 2, underscore the significance of training time. The agent's performance considerably improved with extended training duration. This implies that a more extended training period can produce more accurate models, ultimately resulting in improved adaptation to player behavior and enhanced difficulty adjustments. This point is vital for our discussion, as it showcases the direct impact of training time on the effectiveness of our approach. Training time plays a primary role in the success of our model, emphasizing the need for longer training durations to attain optimal results.

5.3 Comparison with Related Work

In discussing our study's findings and implications, we draw comparisons with related work. The main points of comparison include the differentiation between our skill-based difficulty adaptation approach and affective state-based approaches found in other research [8]. Additionally, we contrast our methodology, which involves Q-Learning against human players, with the practice of training agents against each other, as witnessed in a different study [9]. We also distinguish our use of a multi-agent system tailored for DDA from the flexible end-to-end framework presented in another paper [5]. These comparisons highlight the unique aspects of our study and its contributions to the field.

5.4 Future Directions

We aim to explore techniques such as the Joint QTable to enable communication between agents for cooperative behaviors, as discussed in the conclusion section. Additionally, we propose investigating alternative Q-Learning methods to reduce training time while maintaining model effectiveness. By dedicating more time and resources to future research, we aim to refine our models and explore techniques to overcome training time limitations. These future research directions emphasize the ongoing relevance and importance of our work.

6 Conclusions

In conclusion, our research has shown the promising potential of Q-Learning in dynamically adjusting the difficulty of enemies in real-time within virtual reality gaming environments. Despite the limitations imposed by the duration of our training sessions, we've unveiled the substantial impact that extended training times can have on the performance of the AI agents. These findings emphasize the crucial role of time in shaping the capabilities of our agents.

Looking ahead, our focus will be on discovering and implementing more efficient Q-Learning methods that can significantly reduce the time required for training while maintaining the quality of the models. We are determined to tackle the challenge of limited training periods, making it possible to develop sophisticated models that adapt to the unique behaviors of individual players and offer finely tuned adjustments to the game's difficulty levels, similar to soft constraints [12].

The implications of our work, rooted in Q-Learning and multi-agent systems, opens up new avenues for developers to craft immersive and engaging virtual reality gaming experiences, such as [4]. By affording players a more personalized and challenging journey, our research contributes to the ongoing advancement of game development, ensuring that users' abilities and expectations are met to the fullest, and it may be applied to other media [6].

References

1. Asperti, A., Cortesi, D., Pieri, C.D., Pedrini, G., Sovrano, F.: Crawling in rogue's dungeons with deep reinforcement techniques. IEEE Trans. Games **12**(2), 177–186 (2020)
2. Bojanić, M., Bojanić, G.: Self-learning mechanism for mobile game adjustment towards a player. Appl. Sci. **11**, 4412 (2021)
3. Fernandes, W.R., Levieux, G.: Difficulty pacing impact on player motivation. In: Göbl, B., van der Spek, E., Baalsrud Hauge, J., McCall, R. (eds.) ICEC. LNCS, vol. 13477, pp. 140–153. Springer, Cham (2022). https://doi.org/10.1007/978-3-031-20212-4_11
4. Fernández-Samillán, D., Guizado-Díaz, C., Ugarte, W.: Story creation algorithm using Q-learning in a 2D action RPG video game. In: IEEE FRUCT, pp. 111–117 (2021)
5. Lazaridis, A., Vlahavas, I.P.: REIN-2: giving birth to prepared reinforcement learning agents using reinforcement learning agents. Neurocomputing **497**, 86–93 (2022)
6. Leon-Urbano, C., Ugarte, W.: End-to-end electroencephalogram (EEG) motor imagery classification with long short-term. In: IEEE SSCI, pp. 2814–2820 (2020)
7. Li, Y., et al.: Learning adversarial policy in multiple scenes environment via multi-agent reinforcement learning. Connect. Sci. **33**(3), 407–426 (2021)
8. Moon, J., Choi, Y., Park, T., Choi, J., Hong, J., Kim, K.: Diversifying dynamic difficulty adjustment agent by integrating player state models into Monte-Carlo tree search. Expert Syst. Appl. **205**, 117677 (2022)
9. Oh, I., Rho, S., Moon, S., Son, S., Lee, H., Chung, J.: Creating pro-level AI for a real-time fighting game using deep reinforcement learning. IEEE Trans. Games **14**(2), 212–220 (2022)
10. Pfau, J., Liapis, A., Yannakakis, G.N., Malaka, R.: Dungeons & replicants II: automated game balancing across multiple difficulty dimensions via deep player behavior modeling. IEEE Trans. Games **15**(2), 217–227 (2023)
11. Reis, S., Reis, L.P., Lau, N.: Game adaptation by using reinforcement learning over meta games. Group Decis. Negot. **30**(2), 321–340 (2021)
12. Ugarte, W., Boizumault, P., Loudni, S., Crémilleux, B., Lepailleur, A.: Soft constraints for pattern mining. J. Intell. Inf. Syst. **44**(2), 193–221 (2015)
13. Zhang, Y., Goh, W.: Personalized task difficulty adaptation based on reinforcement learning. User Model. User Adapt. Interact. **31**(4), 753–784 (2021)

Human-Centered AI Goals for Speech Therapy Tools

Chinmoy Deka⬤, Abhishek Shrivastava^(✉)⬤, Saurabh Nautiyal⬤,
and Praveen Chauhan⬤

Indian Institute of Technology Guwahati, Guwahati, Assam, India
`shri@iitg.ac.in`

Abstract. With the advent of improved Artificial Intelligence (AI) algorithms and the availability of large datasets, researchers worldwide are developing numerous AI-based applications to replicate human capabilities. One such application is automating the task of Speech Language Pathologists (SLPs) and building automated speech therapy tools for children with Speech Sound Disorder (SSD). However, this development of AI focused on imitating human capabilities brings concerns such as algorithmic discrimination or biased algorithms, job displacements, and privacy issues. To address these challenges, researchers advocate for Human-Centered AI (HCAI) and have proposed various frameworks for AI-based systems. Although the proposed frameworks were developed for generalized AI application, it is not clear about its relevance in specialized AI application such as speech therapy. This study aims to establish HCAI goals and a goal hierarchy specific to an HCAI-based Speech Therapy Tool (HCAI-STT) designed for children with SSD. Through an Affinity Mapping exercise, we identify seven top-level goals and sub-goals, which include fairness, responsibility and accountability, human-centered empowerment, trustworthiness, privacy, unbiased funding, and security. Our findings highlight the importance of considering not only the technical capabilities of AI systems, but also their ethical and social implications. By prioritizing these goals, we can help ensure that AI-based speech therapy tools are developed and deployed in a responsible and ethical manner that aligns with the needs and values of their users. Our findings have broader implications for the development and deployment of AI systems across domains, and future research can build on our findings by exploring how the goal hierarchy we developed can be operationalized in practice.

Keywords: Human-centerered AI · AI-based speech therapy tool · HCAI-based speech therapy

1 Introduction

The use of Artificial Intelligence (AI) in healthcare has been increasing rapidly in recent years, with the potential to revolutionize the way healthcare is delivered. Speech therapy is one area where AI has the potential to make a significant impact, especially for children with Speech Sound Disorder (SSD). SSD refers to any difficulty or combination of difficulties with perception, motor production, and phonological representation of speech sounds, and speech segments [3]. A person with SSD may have difficulty producing or using certain sounds correctly. In various studies, the estimated prevalence of

H. P. da Silva and P. Cipresso (Eds.): CHIRA 2023, CCIS 1997, pp. 121–136, 2023.
https://doi.org/10.1007/978-3-031-49368-3_8

SSD in school-aged children ranged from 1.06% to 13.4% [11,17,20,33]. In a 2012 survey by the National Center for Health Statistics (NCHS), it was found that 48.1% of children aged 3 to 10 and 24.44% of those aged 11 to 17 had speech sound problems [6]. Speech Language Pathologists (SLPs) play a vital role in screening, assessing, diagnosing, and treating individuals with such speech impairments. Personalized speech therapy, overseen by SLPs, can significantly enhance speech skill development [32]. However, despite the importance of SLPs in these interventions, there have been reports of shortages of SLPs [12,19]. Additionally, speech therapy requires prolonged interactions and multiple sessions with SLPs, rendering it costly and inaccessible for individuals residing in impoverished or rural areas.

In response to the challenges posed by limited accessibility and high costs of traditional speech therapy, several researchers have explored AI-based solutions to address these issues [8]. These innovative tools offer automated assessment, diagnosis, and treatment capabilities for patients, streamlining the therapeutic process. With the advancements in Automatic Speech Recognition (ASR) tools, the availability of impaired speech data, and the integration of AI-based techniques, building autonomous tools for speech therapy is now more feasible than ever before. For instance, Desolda et al. developed a web application that enables SLPs to assign speech therapy exercises remotely to children with SSD, benefiting both children and their caregivers [9]. Additionally, various technologies such as tablet-based speech therapy game [16], computer-based prosody teaching system [23], robotic assistants [24,26], and augmented reality system [5] have been proposed and integrated into the field. Many of these tools leverage ASR technology, an advanced AI-powered technology that transforms spoken language into written text, among other AI techniques. These technologies offer a range of capabilities, including automated assessment, diagnosis, and treatment. For instance, they can provide valuable automatic pronunciation feedback, significantly enhancing the efficiency and effectiveness of speech therapy interventions. However, with the potential benefits of such AI-based tools, it brings multiple concerns such as algorithmic discrimination (biased pronunciation feedback), job displacement of SLPs, and privacy issues of speech/behavioral data of end users [7]. One possible way to address these issues is by adopting Human-Centered AI (HCAI) principles. Leading AI researchers and scientists increasingly recognize the necessity of HCAI for effectively designing, developing, and deploying AI-based applications [29].

HCAI is an approach that prioritizes human experiences, satisfaction, and needs, aiming to enhance human performance and make AI systems reliable, safe, and trustworthy [29]. The core focus of HCAI development lies in understanding and addressing human needs and perspectives when designing AI applications. Therefore, designing such HCAI application requires a clear understanding of the goals and needs of the end-users and the stakeholders. With this in mind, we envisage the development of an HCAI-based Speech Therapy Tool (HCAI-STT) for children with SSD based on the principles of HCAI. In this context, we define the HCAI-STT for children with SSD as:

"The HCAI-STT for children with SSD is an AI-based speech therapy application that prioritizes experiences, satisfaction and needs of the stakeholders, aiming to enhance their performance while upholding HCAI principles."

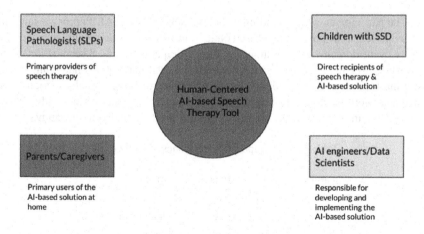

Fig. 1. Stakeholders of the HCAI-based Speech Therapy Tool (HCAI-STT).

Figure 1 presents an illustration of the key stakeholders involved in the HCAI-STT. The aim of this study is to engage one of the crucial stakeholders, namely data scientists/AI engineers, to actively participate in developing HCAI goals for the HCAI-STT and create a goal hierarchy. The goal hierarchy is a method of organizing goals into a hierarchical structure that reveals the relationships between them [15]. Higher-order goals exhibit an abstract nature, while lower-order sub-goals are characterized by their specificity and concreteness. Operationalizing the associated sub-goals allows for the attainment of the higher-level goals. Consequently, the goal hierarchy will serve as a guiding framework, informing the development of the HCAI-STT by effectively organizing and prioritizing goals. Furthermore, the insights derived from utilizing the goal hierarchy will provide a valuable resource for future researchers and designers in the field.

The rest of the paper is organized as follows: Sect. 2 outlines the Methodology, Sect. 3 presents the Results, Sect. 4 provides the Discussion, and Sect. 5 concludes the paper.

2 Methodology

2.1 Study Design

The study employed a qualitative research design using Affinity Diagramming [28] to explore the goals and ideas of data scientists/AI engineers regarding the development of the HCAI-STT for children with SSD. Affinity Diagramming is a collaborative technique adapted from the KJ diagramming method which is used to organize and categorize large amounts of information or ideas into meaningful groups.

2.2 Participants

The study recruited 5 participants who were data scientists/AI engineers having prior experience in speech technology and have worked with disordered speech data such as

SSD. The participants were attending a summer school on HCAI. Purposive sampling was used to select the participants based on their professional background and expertise in the relevant domain. The mean age of the participants was 34.8 years (SD=11.39). There were three male and two female participants. All participants had completed at least a master's degree and had an average of 9 years of professional experience. All participants were proficient in English, which was the language of the study. Table 1 presents the demographic information of the participants included in the study.

Table 1. Demographic Characteristics of Participants.

Participant	Age	Experience	Country
P1	25 years	2 years	Turkey
P2	28 years	5 years	United Kingdom
P3	32 years	6 years	Czech Republic
P4	35 years	8 years	Indonesia
P5	54 years	25 years	Honduras

2.3 Procedure

The following procedure was followed to conduct the study.

1. **Introduction:** The participants were provided with an explanation of the HCAI-STT for children with SSD to be developed.
2. **Idea Generation:** The participants were asked to write down their ideas and goals on sticky notes. Each idea or goal was written on a separate sticky note, which were pasted on a whiteboard.
3. **Grouping:** The sticky notes were then grouped together based on their similarity. The participants were instructed to move the sticky notes around and place them next to other sticky notes that they felt were similar. The facilitator monitored this process and assisted if needed.
4. **Labeling:** Once the sticky notes were grouped, a label was created for each group. The label described the common theme or idea that the group represented. The participants were asked to suggest labels and the facilitator assisted in finalizing the labels.
5. **Sub-Grouping:** The groups were then further sub-grouped based on more specific themes or ideas within each group. This process was repeated until a clear and useful representation of the ideas and themes was achieved.
6. **Hierarchy Creation:** The sub-groups were organized into a hierarchy, with the more general groups at the top and the more specific sub-groups at the bottom. The participants were asked to suggest the hierarchy and the facilitator assisted in finalizing the hierarchy.
7. **Refining:** The Affinity Diagramming process was repeated to refine the groupings and hierarchy until a clear and useful representation of the ideas and themes is achieved.

8. **Analysis:** The resulting clusters, labels, and hierarchy were used to identify patterns, themes, and insights that informed decisions related to the development of the HCAI Goals presented in this study.

Figure 2 shows participants engaging in discussion while working on the Affinity Diagramming process.

Fig. 2. Participants discussing goal hierarchy clusters.

2.4 Ethical Considerations

Informed consent was obtained from all participants prior to their participation in the study, and the study was conducted in accordance with ethical guidelines. The data collected was kept confidential, and all identifying information was removed to ensure anonymity.

3 Results

In this section, we present the results of our goal hierarchy analysis (see Fig. 3), which aimed to identify and prioritize the key goals that can guide the development of the HCAI-STT for children with SSD. The goal hierarchy diagram provides a visual representation of the interrelationships among the different goals and their subgoals, and serves as a useful tool for guiding the design and evaluation of such tool.

3.1 Goal 1: Fairness

The first goal of the HCAI-STT is "Fairness". The goal of fairness aims to ensure that the HCAI-STT is developed and deployed without any biases or discrimination. For instance, the pronunciation feedback system integrated into the tool must be designed to avoid any form of discrimination against individuals from marginalized communities, acknowledging that they may speak the target language with different accents. The goal of fairness can be achieved by reducing algorithmic bias.

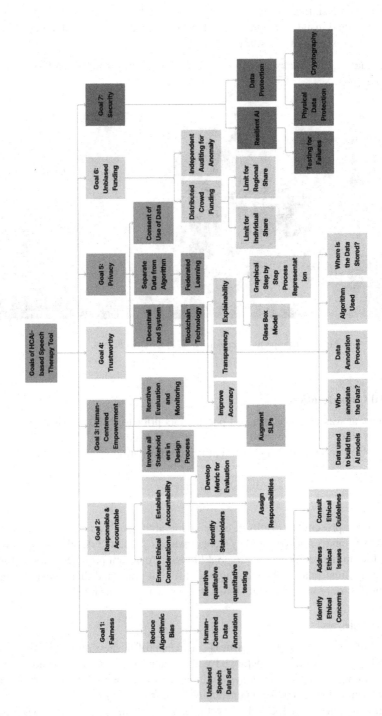

Fig. 3. Goal Hierarchy for Developing HCAI-based Speech Therapy Tool (HCAI-STT).

Reduce Algorithmic Bias: This subgoal seeks to reduce biases in the HCAI-STT by using a) Unbiased Speech Data Set, applying b) Human-Centered Data Annotation, and conducting c) Iterative qualitative and quantitative testing.

- **Unbiased Speech Data Set:** This subgoal aims to ensure that the speech data set used to train the HCAI-STT is diverse and representative of the targeted population.
- **Human-Centered Data Annotation:** This subgoal suggest involving expert SLPs in the data annotation process, to ensure that the data set is labeled accurately and without any biases. To achieve high-quality annotations, a multi-tiered approach shall be adopted, with expert SLPs providing multiple levels of annotation. Moreover, inter-rater reliability assessments shall be conducted to measure the agreement among annotators, ensuring consistent and reliable labeling throughout the dataset.
- **Iterative Qualitative and Quantitative Testing:** This subgoal involves regularly testing and evaluating the HCAI-STT, both qualitatively and quantitatively, to identify any biases and to ensure that the tool is fair.

3.2   Goal 2: Responsible and Accountable

This goal aims to ensure that the HCAI-STT is developed and used in a responsible and accountable manner. The goal can be achieved through subgoals such as a) Ensures Ethical Consideration and b) Establish Accountability.

Ensure Ethical Considerations: Ensuring ethical considerations is an essential component of building responsible and accountable HCAI-STT for children with SSD. Ethical considerations ensure that the design and implementation of these tools are in compliance with ethical principles and guidelines, and do not cause any harm or discrimination to any group or individual. In the context of speech therapy, ethical considerations are particularly important as the tools are intended to improve the quality of life of children with SSD. It can help ensure that the tools are designed and implemented in a way that is inclusive and respectful of the needs and values of all stakeholders involved in the therapy process. Therefore, it is crucial to identify and address any ethical concerns that may arise during the development and deployment of the tools.

- **Identify Ethical Concerns:** To ensure ethical considerations, the first subgoal is to identify ethical concerns that may arise during the development and deployment of the HCAI-STT.
- **Address Ethical Issues:** Once ethical concerns are identified, the next subgoal is to address them appropriately. This may involve modifying the algorithms, changing the training data, or adjusting the evaluation metrics.
- **Consult Ethical Guidelines:** Consulting ethical guidelines is an important step to ensure that the HCAI-STT is developed and deployed in an ethical manner.

Establish Accountability: The second subgoal of the "Responsible and Accountable" goal is "Establish Accountability". The development and deployment of HCAI-STT pose complex ethical, legal, and social implications. Establishing accountability within the system is necessary to ensure that the system operates in compliance with relevant regulations and standards.

- **Identify Stakeholders:** Identifying stakeholders is a crucial subgoal under the Establish Accountability goal in creating a responsible and accountable HCAI-STT for children with SSD. These stakeholders include the children with SSD, their parents or guardians, SLPs, and the data scientists/AI engineers developing the tool. Identifying these stakeholders helps in understanding their interests, concerns, and expectations.
- **Assign Responsibilities:** Assigning responsibilities involves identifying the individuals or teams responsible for various tasks and activities throughout the project lifecycle.
- **Develop Metric For Evaluation:** Identifying stakeholders and assigning responsibilities is incomplete without developing appropriate metrics to measure the effectiveness of the efforts toward accountability. Metrics should be designed in a way that helps to assess the success of the established processes and to identify areas that need improvement. They should be measurable, relevant, and aligned with the project's objectives. They can be used to evaluate the performance of the stakeholders and the effectiveness of the accountability measures in place. Additionally, they can provide feedback to stakeholders and adjust the accountability measures if necessary. Overall, developing appropriate metrics for evaluation is an essential step in ensuring that the project is on track to achieving its objectives and stakeholders are held accountable for their responsibilities.

3.3   Goal 3: Human-Centered Empowerment

The third goal of the HCAI-STT for children with SSD is "Human-Centered Empowerment". This goal focuses on creating a tool that is designed with inputs from all stakeholders and empowers them to use it effectively. The subgoals under this goal are as follows:

Involve All Stakeholders in the Design Process: This subgoal involves engaging all stakeholders, including children with SSD, their families, SLPs, data scientists/AI engineers and other stakeholders in the design process. By involving all stakeholders, the tool can be designed to meet the specific needs of the children with SSD and their families, while also being compatible with the existing practices and workflows of SLPs.

Augment SLPs: This subgoal involves augmenting the work of SLPs involved in the speech therapy process, rather than replacing them with automation. By providing tools and resources that support the work of SLPs, the tool can help improve the efficiency and effectiveness of speech therapy, while also reducing the workload on SLPs and enabling them to provide better care for their patients.

Iterative Evaluation and Monitoring: This subgoal involves continuously evaluating and monitoring the tool's performance and effectiveness through feedback from all stakeholders. By collecting feedback and making improvements based on that feedback, the tool can continue to evolve and improve over time, ensuring it remains effective and relevant.

3.4   Goal 4: Trustworthy

The fourth goal in the HCAI-STT development is "Trustworthy". This goal is crucial in building and deploying the AI-based tool as it ensures that the tool is reliable and its outcomes can be trusted. To achieve this goal, the subgoals "Transparency", "Explainability", and "Improve Accuracy" are identified.

Transparency: "Transparency" is crucial for establishing trust in the tool, and it involves providing information about the data used to build the tool, data annotators, data annotation process, the model used to build the AI tool, and the site of data stored.

Explainability: "Explainability" is essential for ensuring trust in the tool, and it has subgoals such as glass box model and graphical step-by-step process representation to make the tool's functioning and decision-making process understandable to the stakeholders.

Improve Accuracy: Improving accuracy is a critical subgoal for developing an effective speech therapy tool, and it involves continuously working on improving the tool's performance by using various techniques like refining the model and ensuring the quality of the data used for training.

3.5   Goal 5: Privacy

The fifth goal of the HCAI-STT for children with SSD is to ensure privacy. To achieve this, the following subgoals were identified:

Decentralized System: A decentralized system is proposed to ensure the privacy of the data. The use of blockchain technology can help achieve this by making the system transparent and tamper-proof.

Separate Data from Algorithm: Separating data from the algorithm is crucial for ensuring privacy. Federated learning is a proposed method that can achieve this by training the algorithm locally on user devices without transmitting their data to a centralized server.

Consent of Use of Data: Obtaining the consent of users before collecting and using their data is essential for ensuring privacy. The tool must provide clear and understandable information about the purpose of data collection and how it will be used. Users should have the right to revoke their consent at any time.

3.6   Goal 6: Unbiased Funding

The goal of "Unbiased Funding" is to ensure that the funding for the development of the HCAI-STT is fair and unbiased. To achieve this goal, two subgoals have been identified: "Distributed Crowd Funding" and "Independent Auditing for Anomaly".

Distributed Crowd Funding: Under "Distributed Crowd Funding", the focus is on ensuring that the funding is not dominated by a small number of individuals or a particular region. To achieve this, limits are needed to be set on the individual share of funding and the regional share of funding. This will ensure that a diverse range of individuals and regions have the opportunity to contribute to the funding of the project.

Independent Auditing for Anomaly: The second subgoal, "Independent Auditing for Anomaly", is focused on ensuring that the funding is used appropriately and there is no misuse of funds. To achieve this, independent auditing needs to be conducted regularly to identify any anomalies in the funding and to take corrective action where necessary. This will help to ensure that the funding for the project is used ethically and in accordance with the intended purpose.

3.7   Goal 7: Security

To ensure the security of the HCAI-STT for children with SSD, the development team needs to take various measures.

Resilient AI: The AI models shall be designed to be resilient and able to withstand unexpected failures. Extensive testing should be conducted to identify potential failures and ensure the AI models can respond appropriately.

Data Protection: Additionally, physical data protection measures needs to be implemented to secure data storage and prevent unauthorized access. The data shall be encrypted using advanced cryptography to further enhance its security. These security measures provide confidence in the safety and protection of the sensitive data used in the speech therapy tools.

4   Discussion

The presented results of our goal hierarchy analysis provide valuable insights into the development of the HCAI-STT for children with SSD. The goal hierarchy illustrates the interrelationships among different goals and their corresponding subgoals, which are essential for guiding the design and evaluation of the tool. In this discussion, we will analyze and interpret the significance of these results, addressing their implications for the development and deployment of the HCAI-STT. The identified goals and subgoals align with the key principles of HCAI frameworks in the literature. For instance, Xu's HCAI framework proposed an "ethically aligned design" component that aims to create AI solutions that avoid discrimination, maintain fairness and justice, and do not replace humans [34]. Similarly, the "Fairness" goal strives to avoid algorithmic discrimination, and the "Human-Centered Empowerment" goal reflects the importance of augmenting SLPs rather than replacing them. The goal of augmenting human capabilities has been advocated by different HCAI frameworks [29]. Moreover, researchers are exploring these goals through different subfields such as algorithmic fairness [18], responsible AI [2,27], explainable AI [25], and ethical AI [31]. The goals of "Privacy" and "Security" emphasize the significance of the user's data and its application. Privacy and security have been emphasized in multiple HCAI frameworks. For instance, Microsoft's principles for ethical AI emphasize privacy and security along with other goals [30]. Similarly, Google's Responsible AI practices recommend fairness, interpretability, privacy, and safety [1].

4.1 Goal 1: Fairness

The first goal, "Fairness," is of paramount importance when developing an AI-based tool for children with SSD. Ensuring fairness in AI systems has been recognized as a critical aspect of building equitable and inclusive technologies [21]. The subgoal of "Reduce Algorithmic Bias" emphasizes the need to mitigate potential biases that may exist within the HCAI-STT. The incorporation of an "Unbiased Speech Data Set" is vital to ensure diverse and representative training data, free from discriminatory elements. Additionally, involving expert SLPs in "Human-Centered Data Annotation" can ensure accurate labeling without biases, further enhancing the fairness of the tool. However, this will require effective annotation methods and techniques such as data statements [4] and model cards [22]. Regular "Iterative qualitative and quantitative testing" is essential to identify and rectify any biases that may emerge during the development process. Ensuring fairness in the HCAI-STT contributes to equitable support for all children with SSD, irrespective of their background or linguistic variation.

4.2 Goal 2: Responsible and Accountable

The second goal, "Responsible & Accountable," focuses on building and using the HCAI-STT in an ethical manner. Ethical considerations have been highlighted as crucial in the development of AI technologies [14]. By "Ensuring Ethical Consideration," the development team acknowledges the ethical implications of their work and commits to compliance with ethical principles and guidelines. Identifying and addressing ethical concerns during the development process is crucial to ensure that the tool aligns with the values and needs of all stakeholders involved. By involving stakeholders such as children with SSD, their families, SLPs, and data scientists/AI engineers in the decision-making process, the tool can be designed to meet specific needs and foster inclusivity. The subgoal of "Establish Accountability" reinforces the need for transparency and adherence to regulations and standards. Assigning responsibilities, involving stakeholders in decision-making, and developing appropriate evaluation metrics are essential components of accountability. These measures enable the team to monitor the progress of the project, identify areas for improvement, and ensure that the tool's objectives are met responsibly.

4.3 Goal 3: Human-Centered Empowerment

The third goal, "Human-Centered Empowerment," is in line with the principles of human-computer interaction and participatory design. Engaging all stakeholders, including children with SSD, their families, SLPs, and data scientists/AI engineers, reflects the user-centered design approach advocated in HCI research [10]. Augmenting the work of SLPs through the tool's resources can enhance the effectiveness and efficiency of speech therapy while maintaining a human-centered approach. The "Iterative Evaluation and Monitoring" subgoal ensures continuous improvement of the tool by incorporating feedback from stakeholders. This iterative process allows for the tool's continuous evolution, ensuring its relevance and effectiveness over time.

4.4   Goal 4: Trustworthy

The fourth goal, "Trustworthy," is fundamental for building confidence in the HCAI-STT's outcomes. Transparency and explainability have been identified as key factors in establishing trust in AI technologies [13]. The subgoal of "Transparency" involves providing comprehensive information about the tool's development, data used, and model employed. Transparency instills trust by offering stakeholders a clear understanding of how the tool functions and makes decisions. "Explainability" further reinforces trust by making the tool's decision-making process understandable through a techniques such as glass box model and graphical representation. Improving the tool's accuracy through "Improve Accuracy" ensures that the HCAI-STT delivers reliable and precise results. Continuous efforts to refine the model and validate data quality are crucial for maintaining the tool's accuracy, thereby building trust among users.

4.5   Goal 5: Privacy

The fifth goal, "Privacy," addresses the critical need to protect sensitive data while using the HCAI-STT. A "Decentralized System" and "Separate Data from Algorithm" approach safeguard user privacy by minimizing the exposure of personal data and preventing unauthorized access. Separating data from the algorithm is a recognized privacy-preserving technique. Federated learning, for example, allows training models locally on user devices without sharing raw data with a central server [35]. This approach reduces the exposure of sensitive data while still benefiting from a collective model's knowledge. Obtaining the "Consent of Use of Data" is essential to ensure transparency and respect users' autonomy. By adopting these privacy measures, the HCAI-STT respects the confidentiality of user data and builds trust among stakeholders, thereby encouraging wider adoption and usage of the tool.

4.6   Goal 6: Unbiased Funding

The sixth goal, "Unbiased Funding," highlights the importance of equitable distribution of resources for the development of the HCAI-STT. "Distributed Crowd Funding" ensures that the funding base is diverse, reducing the dominance of specific individuals or regions. By involving a broader range of contributors, the project becomes more inclusive and reflects a wider array of perspectives. "Independent Auditing for Anomaly" strengthens the integrity of the funding process, preventing misuse and ensuring that resources are used effectively and ethically. An independent audit fosters accountability and reinforces the credibility of the project.

4.7   Goal 7: Security

The seventh goal, "Security," addresses the need to protect the HCAI-STT from potential failures and unauthorized access. Designing AI models to be "Resilient AI" ensures that the tool can handle unexpected failures, enhancing its reliability. Implementing "Data Protection" measures, including advanced encryption techniques, bolsters data security and prevents potential breaches. By incorporating robust security measures, the HCAI-STT protects sensitive information and ensures the safety of users' data, fostering trust in the tool's reliability.

4.8   Limitations and Future Work

It is important to note that the study had several limitations. One notable limitation of this study is the small sample size of data scientists/AI engineers recruited for the Affinity Mapping exercise. While the exercise provided valuable insights into goal identification, the limited number of participants might restrict the diversity of perspectives and the generalizability of the identified goals and sub-goals to a broader population of data scientists. Additionally, the study primarily focused on data scientists, potentially overlooking crucial insights from other stakeholders involved in the development and usage of the HCAI-STT, such as children with SSD, their families, speech-language pathologists (SLPs), and other experts. Engaging a more diverse range of participants in future research could enhance the comprehensiveness and inclusivity of the identified goals.

To address the limitations and further enrich the study's outcomes, future research will consider expanding the participant pool to include a more diverse group of stakeholders. Involving children with SSD, their families, SLPs, and other relevant experts would provide a broader perspective on the goals and sub-goals essential for the HCAI-STT's development. Additionally, empirical evaluations of the HCAI-STT will be conducted to validate the identified goals and sub-goals in real-world scenarios. Such evaluations could assess the tool's effectiveness, usability, and impact on speech therapy outcomes for children with SSD. Furthermore, investigating the applicability of the identified goals in different linguistic, cultural, and regional contexts would enhance the tool's adaptability and relevance across diverse populations. Addressing these avenues of future work will contribute to a more comprehensive and informed approach to developing a human-centered and effective HCAI-based speech therapy tool.

5   Conclusion

In this study, our primary objective was to develop HCAI goals and a goal hierarchy specifically tailored for an HCAI-STT designed for children with SSD. Employing the Affinity Mapping method with a focused group of five participants, we successfully identified and prioritized seven top-level goals and corresponding subgoals. These goals encompassed crucial aspects such as "Fairness," "Responsibility & Accountability," "Human-Centered Empowerment," "Trustworthiness," "Privacy," "Unbiased Funding," and "Security." By centering these goals, we aim to ensure that the HCAI-STT is responsibly and ethically deployed, catering to the unique needs and values of its users. It is important to note that while our study specifically focused on a speech therapy tool, the broader implications of our results extend to the development of AI systems in diverse domains. Incorporating a human-centered approach, which emphasizes collaboration, user involvement, and iterative development, is essential to ensure AI systems align with user preferences while minimizing potential risks and adverse consequences. In our pursuit of further research, we plan to seek feedback and reviews from a broader range of stakeholders, including children with SSD, their families, SLPs, and other relevant experts. By incorporating diverse perspectives, we aim to refine and validate the identified HCAI goals and the goal hierarchy. Additionally, our goal is to leverage this comprehensive framework of HCAI Goals and the goal hierarchy to develop the HCAI-STT, ensuring its efficacy, usability, and alignment with the identified goals. By undertaking this iterative and inclusive process, we envision creating a truly impactful and human-centered tool that addresses the specific needs and challenges of children with SSD, fostering positive outcomes in speech therapy and contributing to the advancement of HCAI.

Acknowledgement.. We would like to express our heartfelt gratitude to all the participants who generously dedicated their time and cooperation to be a part of this study. Informed consent was obtained from each participant, and ethical guidelines and protocols were rigorously adhered to in our research. We would like to affirm that there are no conflicts of interest.

References

1. Responsible AI practices - google AI. https://ai.google/responsibilities/responsible-ai-practices/ (2019). Accessed 28 Feb 2023
2. Arrieta, A.B., et al.: Explainable artificial intelligence (XAI): concepts, taxonomies, opportunities and challenges toward responsible AI. Inf. Fusion **58**, 82–115 (2020)
3. ASHA: Speech sound disorders: Articulation and phonology. (practice portal). www.asha.org/Practice-Portal/Clinical-Topics/Articulation-and-Phonology/ (2022). Accessed 28 Feb 2022
4. Bender, E.M., Friedman, B.: Data statements for natural language processing: toward mitigating system bias and enabling better science. Trans. Assoc. Comput. Linguist. **6**, 587–604 (2018)
5. Bílková, Z., et al.: Human computer interface based on tongue and lips movements and its application for speech therapy system. Electron. Imaging **32**, 1–5 (2020)
6. Black, L.I., Vahratian, A., Hoffman, H.J.: Communication disorders and use of intervention services among children aged 3–17 years: United states, 2012. NCHS data brief. number 205. Centers for Disease Control and Prevention (2015)
7. Cave, S., ÓhÉigeartaigh, S.S.: Bridging near-and long-term concerns about AI. Nat. Mach. Intell. **1**(1), 5–6 (2019)
8. Chen, Y.P.P., et al.: Systematic review of virtual speech therapists for speech disorders. Comput. Speech Lang. **37**, 98–128 (2016)
9. Desolda, G., Lanzilotti, R., Piccinno, A., Rossano, V.: A system to support children in speech therapies at home. In: CHItaly 2021: 14th Biannual Conference of the Italian SIGCHI Chapter, pp. 1–5 (2021)
10. Draper, S.W., Norman, D.A.: User Centered System Design: New Perspectives on Human-Computer Interaction. L. Erlbaum Associates, Hillsdale, NJ (1986)

11. Eadie, P., Morgan, A., Ukoumunne, O.C., Ttofari Eecen, K., Wake, M., Reilly, S.: Speech sound disorder at 4 years: prevalence, comorbidities, and predictors in a community cohort of children. Dev. Med. Child Neurol. **57**(6), 578–584 (2015)
12. Edgar, D.L., Rosa-Lugo, L.I.: The critical shortage of speech-language pathologists in the public school setting: features of the work environment that affect recruitment and retention. Lang. Speech Hear. Serv. Sch. **38**(1), 31–46 (2007)
13. Floridi, L.: Establishing the rules for building trustworthy AI. Nat. Mach. Intell. **1**(6), 261–262 (2019)
14. Floridi, L., et al.: An ethical framework for a good AI society: opportunities, risks, principles, and recommendations. In: Floridi, L. (ed.) Ethics, Governance, and Policies in Artificial Intelligence. PSS, vol. 144, pp. 19–39. Springer, Cham (2021). https://doi.org/10.1007/978-3-030-81907-1_3
15. Guide, P.: Project management body of knowledge. Project Management Institute. 5ª Edição. Versão em português (2000)
16. Hair, A., Monroe, P., Ahmed, B., Ballard, K.J., Gutierrez-Osuna, R.: Apraxia world: a speech therapy game for children with speech sound disorders. In: Proceedings of the 17th ACM Conference on Interaction Design and Children, pp. 119–131 (2018)
17. Karbasi, S.A., Fallah, R., Golestan, M.: The prevalence of speech disorder in primary school students in yazd-iran. Acta Medica Iranica, pp. 33–37 (2011)
18. Kleinberg, J., Ludwig, J., Mullainathan, S., Rambachan, A.: Algorithmic fairness. In: AEA papers and proceedings. vol. 108, pp. 22–27 (2018)
19. Mashima, P.A., Doarn, C.R.: Overview of telehealth activities in speech-language pathology. Telemedicine e-Health **14**(10), 1101–1117 (2008)
20. McKinnon, D.H., McLeod, S., Reilly, S.: The prevalence of stuttering, voice, and speech-sound disorders in primary school students in Australia. Lang. Speech Hear. Serv. Schools **38**(1), 5–15 (2007)
21. Mehrabi, N., Morstatter, F., Saxena, N., Lerman, K., Galstyan, A.: A survey on bias and fairness in machine learning. ACM Comput. Surv. (CSUR) **54**(6), 1–35 (2021)
22. Mitchell, M., et al.: Model cards for model reporting. In: Proceedings of the Conference on Fairness, Accountability, and Transparency, pp. 220–229 (2019)
23. Ng, S.I., Tao, D., Wang, J., Jiang, Y., Ng, W.Y., Lee, T.: An automated assessment tool for child speech disorders. In: 2018 11th International Symposium on Chinese Spoken Language Processing (ISCSLP), pp. 493–494. IEEE (2018)
24. Ramamurthy, P., Li, T.: Buddy: a speech therapy robot companion for children with cleft lip and palate (CL/P) disorder. In: Companion of the 2018 ACM/IEEE International Conference on Human-Robot Interaction, pp. 359–360 (2018)
25. Ras, G., van Gerven, M., Haselager, P.: Explanation methods in deep learning: users, values, concerns and challenges. In: Escalante, H.J., et al. (eds.) Explainable and Interpretable Models in Computer Vision and Machine Learning. TSSCML, pp. 19–36. Springer, Cham (2018). https://doi.org/10.1007/978-3-319-98131-4_2
26. Robles-Bykbaev, V., et al.: Onto-SPELTRA: a robotic assistant based on ontologies and agglomerative clustering to support speech-language therapy for children with disabilities. In: Solano, A., Ordoñez, H. (eds.) CCC 2017. CCIS, vol. 735, pp. 343–357. Springer, Cham (2017). https://doi.org/10.1007/978-3-319-66562-7_25
27. Sambasivan, N., Holbrook, J.: Toward responsible AI for the next billion users. Interactions **26**(1), 68–71 (2018)
28. Scupin, R.: The KJ method: a technique for analyzing data derived from Japanese ethnology. Hum. Organ. **56**(2), 233–237 (1997)
29. Shneiderman, B.: Human-Centered AI. Oxford University Press (2022)
30. Smith, B., Shum, H.: The Future Computed. Artificial Intelligence and its Role in Society (2018)

31. Torresen, J.: A review of future and ethical perspectives of robotics and AI. Front. Robot. AI **4**, 75 (2018)
32. Wren, Y., Harding, S., Goldbart, J., Roulstone, S.: A systematic review and classification of interventions for speech-sound disorder in preschool children. Int. J. Lang. Commun. Disord. **53**(3), 446–467 (2018)
33. Wren, Y., Miller, L.L., Peters, T.J., Emond, A., Roulstone, S.: Prevalence and predictors of persistent speech sound disorder at eight years old: Findings from a population cohort study. J. Speech Lang. Hear. Res. **59**(4), 647–673 (2016)
34. Xu, W.: Toward human-centered AI: a perspective from human-computer interaction. Interactions **26**(4), 42–46 (2019)
35. Yang, Q., Liu, Y., Chen, T., Tong, Y.: Federated machine learning: concept and applications. ACM Trans. Intell. Syst. Technol. (TIST) **10**(2), 1–19 (2019)

Designing a WhatsApp Inspired Healthcare Application for Older Adults: A Focus on Ease of Use

Saurabh Nautiyal⬥ and Abhishek Shrivastava(✉)⬥

Indian Institute of Technology Guwahati, Guwahati, Assam, India
`shri@iitg.ac.in`

Abstract. The increasing ageing population in any country necessitates high-quality healthcare services. Smartphone-based healthcare applications can play a pivotal role in meeting this requirement. Previous studies indicated that older adults exhibit lower acceptance of smartphone-based healthcare applications. In contrast, older adults popularly use smartphone applications for social interaction. WhatsApp is one such popular application used by older adults for social interaction. This study aims to enhance the ease of use of a dedicated healthcare application among older adults by incorporating WhatsApp's user interface design attributes. The present study comprises three phases. In the first phase, we assessed the usability of WhatsApp and observed its good usability characteristics for older adults. In the second phase, we identified the design attributes of WhatsApp's user interface by employing the affinity mapping method. In the third phase, we applied the identified design attributes to develop a prototype of a healthcare application and tested it with older adults. We found that the developed prototype of the healthcare application is easy to use among older adults. This study recommends developing a WhatsApp-inspired dedicated healthcare application for older adults. The study demonstrates how older adults perceive a new healthcare application as user-friendly, inspired by a familiar user interface. This research will aid designers and developers in creating dedicated healthcare applications tailored to the needs of older adults. Consequently, it will enhance the adoption of digital healthcare applications among the ageing population.

Keywords: Ageing population · Digital healthcare · Healthcare application · User Interface (UI) design · WhatsApp · Older adults

1 Introduction

The advancements in the healthcare system have facilitated an increase in global life expectancy. The trend of longer life span is evident across all the countries, as the size and proportion of older individuals in the population are rising [1]. The changes in the age structure of a population, such that there is an increase in the proportion of older persons, is termed population ageing [2]. As per WHO, population ageing started in high-income countries, and now low- and middle-income countries are experiencing it [3].

H. P. da Silva and P. Cipresso (Eds.): CHIRA 2023, CCIS 1997, pp. 137–159, 2023.
https://doi.org/10.1007/978-3-031-49368-3_9

For the ageing population, healthcare is paramount and requires the utmost attention. The growing proportion of older people will be needed adequate healthcare facilities to fulfil the goal of healthy ageing. Digital healthcare technologies can play an important role in this regard. These technologies aim to boost health and well-being or to improve health systems [4]. It includes healthcare-related smartphone applications, standalone software, wearable devices (such as step trackers), and platforms that provide remote healthcare (telehealth) [5]. Particularly, smartphones, equipped with internet connectivity, provide ideal platforms for utilising various healthcare-related applications (apps). The smartphone comprises multiple sensors such as a gyroscope, fingerprint, microphones, cameras, gyroscopes, and touch-screen fingerprinting. Further, it is compatible with other external sensors, medical devices, and wearable devices. It allows for directly acquiring physiological/biomedical data, which can be processed and analysed by smartphone applications [6].

Most people use smartphones for various purposes, and users are steadily increasing. It can be the most convenient and affordable medium to connect people with digital healthcare facilities. Nonetheless, many older adults exhibit limited receptiveness when it comes to embracing smartphone-based healthcare applications [7–10]. Some reports suggest that this population has shown good interest in social media and entertainment applications [11]. Specifically, WhatsApp [12] is the most popular application among older adults [13, 14]. There is a widespread use of WhatsApp among older adults as they easily connect with family members and friends [15, 16].

Moreover, older adults have shown a positive inclination towards utilizing WhatsApp to seek medical consultations [17, 18]. A user-friendly interface is one of the contributing factors to WhatsApp's popularity among its users, including older adults [19–21]. This research focussed on the attributes of the user interface design of the WhatsApp application.

In this research, we considered that WhatsApp is already a popular and easy to use application among older adults. Moreover, older adults' users can use it for healthcare-related communication. Thus, we aimed to develop a dedicated healthcare application inspired by WhatsApp's user interface (UI). We assume that "Applying the design attributes of WhatsApp's user interface in new healthcare applications will make it easier to use among older adults since they are already familiar with it".

This study aims to enhance the ease of use of a dedicated healthcare application among older adults by incorporating WhatsApp's user interface design attributes.

The objectives of the present study are as follows:

1. To evaluate the usability of WhatsApp features relevant to healthcare communication among older adults.
2. To identify the attributes of WhatsApp's user interface (UI) design that can be incorporated into dedicated healthcare applications to improve user-friendliness for older adults.
3. To design the user interface of a dedicated healthcare application by incorporating the attributes of WhatsApp UI design.

We divided these three objectives into three phases of the present study. In the first phase, we planned to conduct a usability test to know whether WhatsApp is easy to use among older adults. We performed the usability testing of WhatsApp with older adults based on three-task related to healthcare communication. In the second phase, we conducted the affinity mapping method to identify attributes of WhatsApp in terms of UI design and proposed design recommendations. In the third phase, we developed the user interface for a dedicated healthcare application based on the findings from the second phase.

This study is organised as follows: Sect. 2 describes the research methodology used in this study. Section 3 describes the findings of the study, and Sect. 4 discusses the interpretation of findings, recommendations, and limitations. Finally, Sect. 5 conclude the study.

2 Research Methodology

This section explains the research methodology of the overall study. This study was conducted in three phases, as shown in Fig. 1. The corresponding details of each phase is described as follows:

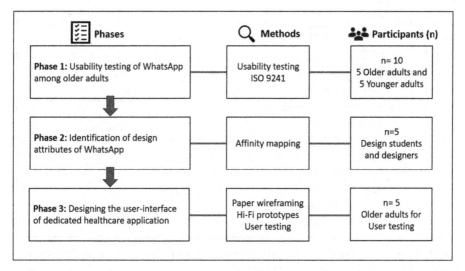

Fig. 1. Research Methodology implement to conduct the study.

2.1 Phase-1 Study

In this phase, we wanted to know the ease of using WhatsApp for healthcare communication among older adults. The objective was to evaluate the usability of WhatsApp for older adults to conduct healthcare communication. In addition, we involved younger adults to assess whether older adults have the same level of proficiency in using WhatsApp as younger adults.

Method. We used the ISO 9241–11 standard to conduct the usability testing of the WhatsApp application. This standard provides guidelines for assessing the usability of interactive systems, including mobile applications. The ISO 9241–11 standard refers to Part-11 of ISO 9241, "Guidance on usability". It defines usability as "[The] extent to which specified users can accomplish specified goals with effectiveness, efficiency, and satisfaction, within a defined context of use, is known as usability for a system, product, or service" [22, 23]. Effectiveness refers to how accurately and completely the users can achieve their intended goals. Efficiency is the measure of resources expended concerning how accurately and completely users achieve their goals. Satisfaction refers to freedom from discomfort and a favourable attitude towards product use [24]. Figure 2 shows the guidance on usability in the context of using WhatsApp for healthcare communication.

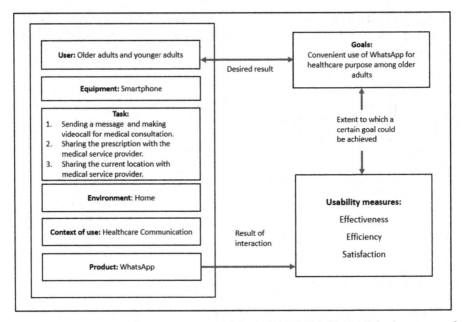

Fig. 2. Guidance on usability (ISO9241–11:2018 - NEN-EN-ISO 9241–11) in the context of using WhatsApp for healthcare communication.

Participants. This phase involved a total of ten participants recruited through convenience sampling. We categorised the participants into two groups. One was the older adults' group (includes participants 60 years old or older), and the other was younger adults (includes participants 18 to 59 years old). Prior research suggested that a mere group of five individuals would be sufficient to detect approximately 85% of the usability issues [25]. Therefore, primarily we recruited five participants for each user group. There were three female and two male participants in the younger age group and three male and two female participants in the older age group. All the participants have more than two years of experience using smartphones. Table 1 shows the Phase-1 study participants details.

Table 1. Participants Details of Phase-1 Study.

Participant Group	Participant ID	Age (in Years)	Gender	Experience of using smartphone
Younger Adults	YP1	27	Female	More than 10 years
	YP2	31	Female	More than 10 years
	YP3	28	Male	More than 10 years
	YP4	24	Male	6 to 10 years
	YP5	32	Female	More than 10 years
Older adults	OP1	62	Male	6 to 10 years
	OP2	63	Male	2 to 6 years
	OP3	61	Female	2 to 6 years
	OP4	60	Female	6 to 10 years
	OP5	61	Male	More the 10 years
Total (n)	10			

Study Procedure. We conducted the usability testing as per convenience and the preferred location of participants. At first, we introduced the study and its objectives, followed by the testing instrument, procedure, scenarios, and tasks. Before starting the test, we obtained informed consent from the participants. A research facilitator (one author) asked participants to complete the three tasks in the WhatsApp application. These tasks were based on real-life communication between healthcare service providers and patients. A facilitator provided a task sheet to the participants for each task and verbally explained the task and scenario. Table 2 shows the test scenario and tasks.

Table 2. Scenario and Tasks for participants.

S. No.	Scenario	Task
1	Consider that you are feeling the cough related problem and you want to consult doctor using WhatsApp	Task1: Sending the message and using the feature of videocall for medical consultation using WhatsApp
2	You already have a prescription that you want to share with medical service provider	Task 2: Click and Send the Prescription using the WhatsApp Camera
3	You need to share your current location for the delivery of medicines at your place	Task 3: Share your current location with medical service provider

We used quantitative measures to evaluate the usability attributes. These were effectiveness, efficiency, and satisfaction. Figure 3 shows the experiment setup with participants. The findings of this experiment (Phase-1 study) are reported in the results section.

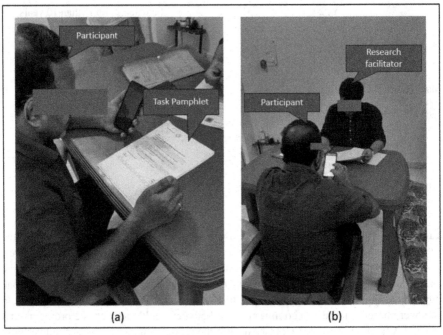

Fig. 3. The complete setup of the experiment: (a) Participant reading the task before experiment; (b) participant performing the task on smartphone.

2.2 Phase-2 Study

In this phase, we wanted to know the qualities of WhatsApp in terms of design perspective that make it appealing to users of all ages, specifically older adults. This phase's objective was to identify the attributes of WhatsApp in terms of UI design that can be incorporated into a dedicated healthcare application.

Method. We conducted the affinity mapping session with a group of design students. This method involved two main steps: generating the ideas on sticky notes and organising the notes in categories [26].

Participants. This study involved five participants (see Table 3). Research facilitator invited the participants via mail for the affinity mapping activity. Two participants were user experience designers and other three were PhD students enrolled in design department.

Table 3. Participants Details of Phase-2 Study.

Participant ID	Designation	Age (in Years)	Qualification	Experience in Human computer Interaction (HCI) field
P1	UX Designer	22	Bachelor of Design	1 Year
P2	PhD Student	29	Masters of Design	5 Years
P3	PhD Student	27	Master of Design	4.5 Years
P4	PhD Student	35	Master of Technology	5 Years
P5	UX designer	29	Master of Design	2 Years

Study Procedure. The phase-2 study was conducted in lab environment of the institute. Research facilitator introduced about the present study and collected the participation consent from the participants. Figure 4 shows the affinity mapping activity conducted with the student participants. Each distinct colour of a sticky note represents an individual participation in the affinity mapping activity.

The affinity mapping involved the following steps:

1. The research facilitator introduced the activity and research context to the participants.
2. Participants were asked to collect specific colour sticky notes from the research facilitator.
3. The WhatsApp task sheets related to healthcare communication were provided to participants for reference.
4. Participants were asked to write each attribute of WhatsApp in terms of UI design on a separate sticky note.
5. After writing, sticky notes were pasted on the board by each participant.
6. Participants were asked to group the sticky notes based on similarities or relatedness.
7. Participants were asked to look for common themes and patterns and categorise them into one.
8. Participants prioritised the attributes after the discussion and consentient.
9. Participants finalised the list of attributes of WhatsApp UI design.
10. The research facilitator ended the affinity mapping session with a vote of thanks to the participants.

The final list of identified attributes of WhatsApp UI design are described in the result section. After completing the affinity mapping session, we created a list of recommendation that can be implemented while deigning a dedicated healthcare application for older adults (described in discussion section).

Fig. 4. Affinity mapping activity with participants: (a) Uncategorised sticky notes by individual participants; (b) Participants grouping the sticky notes; (c) Categorised sticky notes.

2.3 Phase-3 Study

In this phase we ideated and developed the user interface design for a dedicated healthcare application. The objective of this phase was to design the user-interface of dedicated healthcare application by incorporating the design attributes of WhatsApp.

Method. This phase involved conceptualisation, paper wireframing and high-fidelity prototyping. We used the Figma platform [27] to develop the high-fidelity prototype. After development of the prototype, we tested it with five older adults.

Procedure. In this phase, we first shortlisted some of the UI design attributes from phase-2 of the study. Concerning these attributes, we brainstormed design ideas with fellow researchers. We initially performed design iteration using the paper wireframing (see Fig. 5). Subsequently, we concluded a user flow, paper wireframe and developed a high-fidelity prototype in the Figma platform. In the entire development phase, our goal was to create an application that provides a familiar user interface like WhatsApp. The developed user interface for the dedicated healthcare application is explained in the result section.

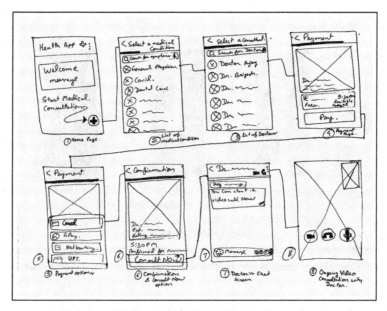

Fig. 5. Paper wireframing for the healthcare application.

3 Results

This section presents the findings of each phase involved in the complete study.

3.1 Results of Phase-1 Study

This subsection presents the result of usability testing conducted with older adults. We additionally conducted usability testing with younger adults for the comparison. The results derive from three usability attributes: Effectiveness, Efficiency, and Satisfaction. We have done all the mathematical calculation at backend by recording the task time, task status and response of each participant. This subsection, uses graphs to show the usability testing results.

Effectiveness. We used task completion rate to measure the effectiveness of WhatsApp among younger adults and older adults. We assigned a binary value of '1', if the participant successfully completed a task and a value of '0', if the participant failed to complete the task. We labelled the task as a failure when the participant spent time beyond the two minutes for a task. At first, we performed the task with younger adults and then with older adults. The research facilitator provided them with a task pamphlet for each task and verbally explained the task. The facilitator recorded each concerning task's response with task completion status.

The formula used to calculate the effectiveness as follow:

$$\text{Effectiveness } \% = \frac{\text{No. of successful task}}{\text{Total no. of users who undertaken the task}} * 100 \qquad (1)$$

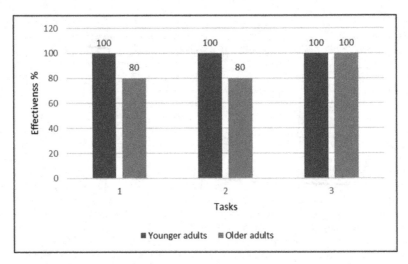

Fig. 6. Effectiveness comparison between younger adults and older adults.

During the experiment, younger adults completed all three tasks successfully. Therefore, we found 100% effectiveness of each task of WhatsApp for younger adults. For older adults we found that they successfully completed the third task, however, some of the older adults were not able to complete Task 1 and Task 2. Therefore, we found 80% effectiveness for the first two tasks and 100% for the third. Figure 6 shows the comparison of effectiveness between younger adults and older adults. We found the WhatsApp mean effectiveness for younger adults was 100%, and for older adults was 93.34%.

Efficiency. For this study, we calculated the time-based efficiency. It helps measure the time spent by the user to complete the task. It is also referred to as the speed of work or time on task.

The time-based efficiency is calculated using following formula:

$$\text{Time based Efficiency} = \frac{\left(\sum_{j=1}^{R} \sum_{i=1}^{N} \frac{n_{ij}}{t_{ij}} \right)}{NR} \tag{2}$$

where,

N = Total no. of tasks.

R = Total no. of participants.

n_{ij} = The result of the task i by user j; if the participant successfully completes the task, then n_{ij} = 1, if not, then n_{ij} = 0.

t_{ij} = The time spent by user j to complete task i. If the task is not successfully completed, then time is measured till the moment the user quits the task.

As per the results, the third task had the highest efficiency, 7.1340 goals/min (For younger adults) and 2.6316 goals/min (for older adults); it indicates that the third task was simple for the participants. The second task had medium efficiency, 4.5270 goals/min (For younger adults) and 1.4952 goals/minute (for older adults). It indicates the second task was a little complicated task for the participants. The first task was the most challenging task for both participant groups. It had the lowest efficiency, 1.6404 goals/min (For younger adults) and 0.8934 goals/min (For older adults). Figure 7 shows the time-based efficiency comparison between younger adults and older adults.

We found that the mean time-based efficiency for younger adults was 4.43 goals/min and 1.6734 goals/minute for older adults.

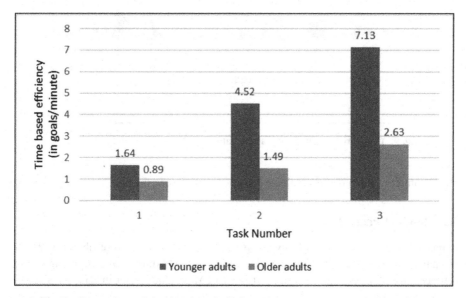

Fig. 7. Comparison of the time-based efficiency between younger and older adults.

Satisfaction. In this study, we used Single Ease Questionnaire (SEQ) [28] to measure the task level satisfaction as it was convenient for participants. As our one user category was older adults, it was easy for them to answer the task satisfaction-related questionnaire SEQ (see Fig. 8) just after task completion. Figure 9 shows comparison the mean value of task satisfaction between younger and older adults.

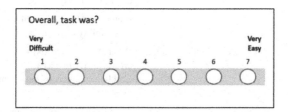

Fig. 8. Single Ease Question (SEQ) scale to measure the task satisfaction.

We found that younger adults rated each task above 6.8 on the SEQ scale, whereas older adults rated each task above 6.2 on the SEQ scale.

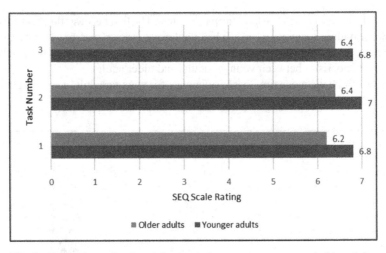

Fig. 9. Comparison of task satisfaction rating among younger and older adults.

The interpretation of the results is discussed in the Sect. 4.

3.2 Result of Phase-2 Study

In phase 2, we conducted an affinity mapping session to identify the attributes of Whats-App in terms of UI design. This subsection presents the findings of the affinity mapping activity. Table 4 shows the identified attributes of WhatsApp's user interface design.

Table 4. Identified attributes of WhatsApp's user interface design.

S. No.	Attribute	Description
1	Simple and Intuitive navigation	WhatsApp's interface is simple, minimal, and easy to navigate. All tabs & links on the top bar. Separate tabs for chat, status, calls
2	Clean and legitimate typography	The font size and type in WhatsApp are big enough and easy to read
3	Easy to use Emojis	It enhances the understanding and accessibility of the user
4	Easily accessible voice and video calling:	WhatsApp's voice and video calling features are very easy to access for all users Call button on each chat to contact individuals or groups
5	Chronological Chat listing	The recent conversation appears on top and older ones are appears below. It helps to access the frequent conversations

(continued)

Table 4. (*continued*)

S. No.	Attribute	Description
6	Simplified and large icons	User can easily recognize and click on the icons to perform a particular task
7	Instant messaging	WhatsApp promptly facilitate the user with its primary function of messaging It has instant messaging functionality, readily available on its first screen
8	Easily accessible payment option	It simplified the transactions and made it convenient for users to send and receive money directly within the chat screen
9	Instant location sharing	User can quickly share the location with others using easily accessible location share option within the chat screen
10	Quick access to share media	User can send images, voice notes, short videos, and documents quickly
11	Profile picture are clickable	The clickable profile pictures work as button. It also helps the user to look for other options related to user profile of self or others
12	Easily accessible camera	The camera feature is inbuilt in the WhatsApp User can easily click and send the images to end user
13	Pin to top feature	User can prioritize the conversions by using pin to top feature
14	Customization Notification Sound	User can customize the notifications sounds for alerts or messages
15	WhatsApp group feature	User can create or join the groups in WhatsApp. To receive and send information to a group of people

3.3 Result of Phase-3 Study

This subsection presents the developed user interface of a dedicated healthcare application inspired by WhatsApp. We finalise the paper wireframe and user flow for the healthcare application. Figure 10 shows the final user flow of the healthcare application.

We developed the user interface of the healthcare application as per the user flow. The following steps explains the user flow and corresponding user interface of the healthcare application:

- Step 1: The interaction with the healthcare application starts with selecting a language for the application. For the user registration, first-time user needs to enter the basic details such as name, gender, and user location. Figure 11 shows the launch screen, language selection screen and user registration screen of the application.

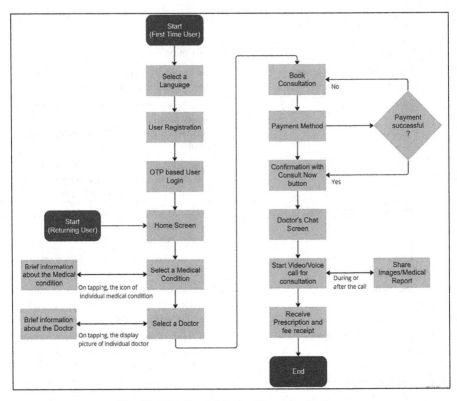

Fig. 10. User flow of the healthcare application.

- Step 2: After the registration, a OTP (One time password) based login screen appears and asks to enter the mobile phone number. The OTP verification launches the home screen with a welcome message. Figure 12 shows the login screen and home screen of the developed healthcare application. The home screen provides instant access to connect with the doctor for medical consultation by tapping the plus sign button.

- Step 3: On tapping the plus sign button opens the list of options to select a medical condition for the consultation. The list includes medical conditions such as General health, cough, fever, Eye disease, stomach pain, skin disease etc. The health conditions appear with a graphical icon to represent the medical condition. Tapping on a specific graphic icon provides more elaborative details of that medical condition. Figure 13 shows the list of medical conditions, and shows a brief description of a specific medical condition.

- Step 4: After selecting a medical condition, a list of doctors appears on the screen. Users can select the doctor for the consultation based on their years of experience, rating, and time of availability. In addition, the user can see the brief introduction of the doctor by tapping on the profile picture of the doctor (See Fig. 14).

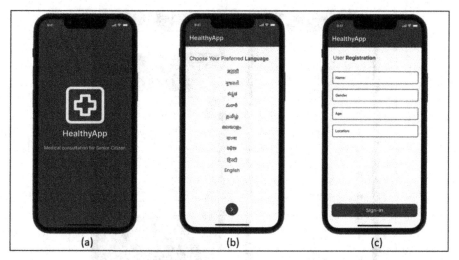

Fig. 11. Developed user interface of healthcare application: (a) Launch Screen; (b) Language selection; (c) User registration.

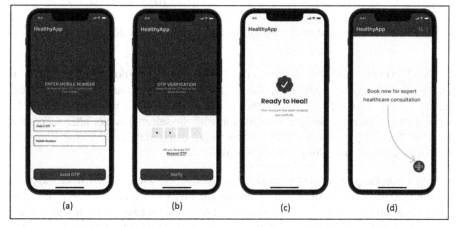

Fig. 12. User login procedure: (a) OTP login screen; (b) OTP verification; (c) confirmation of account registration; (d) Home screen.

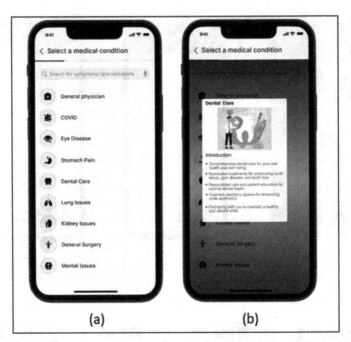

Fig. 13. (a) List of medical conditions; (b) Brief description of selected medical condition[1].

Step 5: After the doctor's selection, a brief introduction of the doctor and consultation fee details with payment options appear on the screen. On tapping the "Pay" button, the application asks for payment methods such as cards, UPI, net banking etc. The application confirms the medical consultation with the selected doctor after successful payment. The screen provides a "Consult Now" option to start the consultation. Figure 15 shows the payment procedure of the application.

- Step 8: On tapping on the "Consult Now" button, the doctor's chat screen appears with the video/voice call option. From here, the user can start a video/voice call to the doctor for the consultation. The application provides easy access to video/voice call. During the call user can switch on/off the mic and video. The user can end the call by tapping the hangup red button on the screen. Figure 16 shows the consultation procedure with the doctor.

- Step 10: A User can share medical reports, prescriptions, images, and other healthcare-related documents with the doctor during or after the call. The application interaction ends with ending the call with the doctor and receiving the medical prescription.

For a returning user (who is using the application second time), the application starts with the home screen, showing the previously consulted medical condition. It also has the plus sign to initiate the new consultation. If the user selects the previously consulted medical condition, the application prioritizes the previously consulted doctors

---

[1] 'Dental care' illustration by Freepik.com.

Fig. 14. (a) List of doctors under a selected medical condition; (b) Brief introduction of doctor[2].

Fig. 15. Payment procedure: (a) Consultation fee payment; (b) Payment methods; (c) Confirmation of payment.

---

[2] 'Doctor sitting at workplace and using laptop' image by Freepik.com.

Fig. 16. Consultation procedure: (a) Doctor's chat screen (b) Video consultation with doctor[3].

on the doctor's list. Thus, the application prioritizes the previous preference of the returning user. It makes the user flow convenient for older adults. Figure 17 shows the user preference attributes of the application.

After developing the screens of the healthcare application, we connected the screens(frames) to prototype the interactions. We have corrected some flaws that occurred during the application interaction. To use the application prototype on a smartphone, we downloaded the Figma mobile application.

User Testing. After developing the high-fidelity prototype on the Figma platform, we tested it with five older adults (same set of older adults who participated in the Phase-1 study). All five participants had more than two years of smartphone experience. We asked them to consult the doctor for dental-related problems using the application. After completing the task, we asked the participants to rate the application on a Single-Ease Questionnaire (SEQ) scale[28]. Three out of five participants rated the application interface as 6 on a 7-point scale. Two participants rated the application interface as 7 on a 7-point scale.

---

[3] 'Smiley doctor at desk' image by Freepik.com.

Fig. 17. User prior preference in the healthcare application: (a) Previously consulted medical conditions; (b) Previously consulted doctor in priority.

4 Discussion

This section discusses the implications of the results, recommendations, and limitations of the present study.

4.1 Implications and Recommendations

In the phase-1 study, we tested the WhatsApp application's usability among younger and older adults. The task performed in the usability testing were related to healthcare communication on WhatsApp applications.

We found that the effectiveness in terms of the task completion rate by younger and older adults was 100% and 93.34%, respectively. As per prior studies task completion rate above 78% is considered good in terms of usability [29]. It means WhatsApp's effectiveness in task completion rate is good for both user groups. However, we found the time-based efficiency higher for younger adults. It means younger adults performed each task faster than the older group on WhatsApp. Regarding task satisfaction, both groups rated above 6 on a 7-point scale for each task. It indicates that it was perceived to be usable by both user groups. Overall, the phase-1 study revealed that the WhatsApp application has good usability characteristics for younger and older adults. From older adults' perspective, it indicates they found it easy to perform tasks on the WhatsApp application.

Thus, to improve the usability and adoption of healthcare applications among older adults, we recommend incorporating WhatsApp's UI design attributes in dedicated healthcare applications.

In the phase-2 study, we identified the attributes of WhatsApp's UI design. Thus, based on identified attributes, we recommend the following points:

- We recommended adopting a simple and intuitive interface design in healthcare applications for older adults.
- Text in healthcare applications should also be clear and easy to read to avoid confusion and misunderstanding.
- In healthcare applications, emojis can represent symptoms and medical procedures, making it easier for older adults to understand and use.
- Healthcare applications should incorporate voice and video calling features that are easily accessible to older users.
- Healthcare applications should prioritise user preferences. For example, Application can prioritise the previously consulted medical condition or medical consultant.
- Icons or symbols in healthcare applications should be easily recognisable to the user.
- The main task of healthcare application should be available on its first screen to perform it instantly.
- The healthcare application should provide instantly accessible payment and Media (Medical related Image, audio, video) sharing options.
- The healthcare application should provide customisation of notification sound for appointment alerts, medication reminders or receiving medical reports etc.

In phase-3 of the study, we implemented some of the important UI design attributes of the WhatsApp application. We developed a prototype of a healthcare application for online medical consultation. We tested the developed prototype application among older adults. We received high satisfaction ratings on the SEQ scale. We successfully addressed the potential usability concerns and developed an application that accommodates older users' needs and preferences. It suggests that to enhance the ease of use of new healthcare applications among older adults, designers can take inspiration from what is already popular among them. It will reduce the burden, of operating a new application as they would be already familiar with its user interface.

4.2 Limitation of the Study

The present study has several limitations, as follows:

- The sample size of older adults who participated in this study is less to validate the findings statistically. In addition, the participants only belong to the younger old group (60–69 years), and results may vary for the middle old group (70–79 years) and oldest old group (80 years or older). Future researchers can use the present study on a larger sample size for more accurate results encompassing all categories of old age groups.

- Participants of the present study are smartphone users who use the WhatsApp application. Therefore, the findings of the study may vary for the non-users of the smartphone and the WhatsApp application.

5 Conclusion

The prior studies suggested that most older adults do not use dedicated healthcare applications for various reasons. We identified the WhatsApp, among all other applications, that is popular among all age groups and can be used for healthcare purposes. We found that the WhatsApp application has good usability characteristics for younger and older adults. It indicates that it was perceived to be usable by both age groups. Therefore, we identified the user interface (UI) design attributes that made WhatsApp easily usable among all age groups. With the help of identified attributes, we developed a prototype of a healthcare application. We tested the developed prototype among older adults, who found it easy to use. Hence, we conclude that incorporating WhatsApp's UI design attributes in a dedicated healthcare application can improve the ease of use among older adults. Moreover, it will enhance the adoption of dedicated healthcare applications in future among older adults and connect them with digital healthcare. For the future work, more UI design attributes of WhatsApp or other popular applications can be used to enhance the adoption of digital healthcare applications among older adults.

Acknowledgements. The Authors would like to thank all the participants, involved in the study. All procedures performed in studies involving human participants were in accordance with the ethical standards. This study was approved by the Institute Human Ethics Committee of Indian Institute of Technology Guwahati, India (Reference No. IHEC/2022/AS/10, Approval Date: 26 August 2022). An Informed consent was obtained from all individual participants included in the study. The authors declare that they have no competing interests.

References

1. Ageing. https://www.who.int/health-topics/ageing#tab=tab_1, Accessed 22 May 2023
2. Land, K.C., Lamb, V.L.: Demography of Aging. Presented at the (2008). https://doi.org/10.1016/B978-012373960-5.00205-7
3. Ageing and health. https://www.who.int/news-room/fact-sheets/detail/ageing-and-health, Accessed 29 May 2023
4. Hoskin, L.: What is digital health technology and what can it do for me?. https://evidence.nihr.ac.uk/collection/what-is-digital-health-technology/, Accessed 1 June 2023
5. Evidence standards framework for digital health technologies | Guidance | NICE (2018). https://www.nice.org.uk/corporate/ecd7/chapter/section-a-technologies-suitable-for-evaluation-using-the-evidence-standards-framework,
6. Faezipour, M., Faezipour, M.: Sustainable Smartphone-Based Healthcare Systems: A Systems Engineering Approach to Assess the Efficacy of Respiratory Monitoring Apps (2020). https://doi.org/10.3390/su12125061
7. Jokisch, M.R., Schmidt, L.I., Doh, M.: Acceptance of digital health services among older adults: Findings on perceived usefulness, self-efficacy, privacy concerns, ICT knowledge, and support seeking (2022). https://www.frontiersin.org/articles/,https://doi.org/10.3389/fpubh.2022.1073756,

8. Frishammar, J., Essén, A., Bergström, F., Ekman, T.: Digital health platforms for the elderly? Key adoption and usage barriers and ways to address them. Technol. Forecast. Soc. Change. **189**, 122319 (2023). https://doi.org/10.1016/j.techfore.2023.122319

9. Panagopoulos, C., Menychtas, A., Tsanakas, P., Maglogiannis, I.: Increasing Usability of Homecare Applications for Older Adults: A Case Study (2019). https://doi.org/10.3390/des igns3020023

10. Nautiyal, S., Shrivastava, A., Deka, C., Chauhan, P.: Role of digital healthcare in the well-being of elderly people: a systematic review. In: Proceedings of the 13th Indian Conference on Human-Computer Interaction. pp. 30–41. Association for Computing Machinery, New York (2023). https://doi.org/10.1145/3570211.3570214

11. Busch, P.A., Hausvik, G.I., Ropstad, O.K., Pettersen, D.: Smartphone usage among older adults. Comput. Human Behav. **121**, 106783 (2021). https://doi.org/10.1016/j.chb.2021. 106783

12. WhatsApp: WhatsApp. https://www.whatsapp.com/, Accessed 15 May 2023

13. Hämmerle, V., Braundwalder, R., Pauli, C., Misoch, S.: Shaping social relationships digitally: whatsapp's influence on social relationships of older adults BT - HCI International 2020 - Posters. Presented at the (2020)

14. Desai, K.: Why grandmom is always on WhatsApp. https://timesofindia.indiatimes.com/ home/sunday-times/why-grandmom-is-always-on-whatsapp/articleshow/64407228.cms, Accessed 5 June 2023

15. Nimrod, G.: Technostress in a hostile world: older internet users before and during the COVID-19 pandemic. Aging Ment. Health **26**, 526–533 (2022). https://doi.org/10.1080/13607863. 2020.1861213

16. Dixit, P.: Older Indians Drive Millennials Crazy On WhatsApp. This Is Why They're Obsessed. https://www.buzzfeednews.com/article/pranavdixit/older-indians-drive-millennials-crazy-on-whatsapp-this-is, Accessed 3 June 2023

17. Sixsmith, A., Horst, B.R., Simeonov, D., Mihailidis, A.: Older people's use of digital technology during the COVID-19 pandemic. Bull. Sci. Technol. Soc. **42**, 19–24 (2022). https:// doi.org/10.1177/02704676221094731

18. Sousa, L., Freitas, J., Pinto, M., Lemos, D., Tavares, J.: Influence of social media use among older adults in Portugal. Act. Adapt. Aging. 1–17 (2023). https://doi.org/10.1080/01924788. 2023.2219518

19. DH Web Desk: WhatsApp: Simple steps on how to block spams on messenger app, https://www.deccanherald.com/technology/whatsapp-simple-steps-on-how-to-block-spams-on-messenger-app-1208213.html, Accessed 19 Sep 2023

20. Tech, H.: Senior citizens are not averse to technology, it's time to teach them to use it for security. https://tech.hindustantimes.com/tech/news/senior-citizens-are-not-averse-to-techno logy-it-s-time-to-teach-them-to-use-it-for-security-71610109246084.html, Accessed 19 Sep 2023

21. Desk, T.: WhatsApp guide for your parents: How to get started and connect with loved ones. https://indianexpress.com/article/technology/techook/whatsapp-guide-for-elderly-peo ple-6397217/, Accessed 21 Sep 2023

22. ISO 9241–11:2018(en) Ergonomics of human-system interaction — Part 11: Usability: Definitions and concepts. https://www.iso.org/obp/ui/#iso:std:iso:9241:-11:ed-2:v1:en, Accessed 1 June 2023

23. Moumane, K., Idri, A., Abran, A.: Usability evaluation of mobile applications using ISO 9241 and ISO 25062 standards. Springerplus **5**, 548 (2016). https://doi.org/10.1186/s40064-016-2171-z

24. Franzreb, P.: Setting Standards for Usability Testing. https://www.uxbooth.com/articles/set ting-standards-for-usability-testing/, Accessed 6 June 2023

25. Nielsen, J.: Why You Only Need to Test with 5 Users. https://www.nngroup.com/articles/why-you-only-need-to-test-with-5-users/, Accessed 19 May 2023

26. Pernice, K.: Affinity Diagramming: Collaboratively Sort UX Findings & Design Ideas. https://www.nngroup.com/articles/affinity-diagram/, Accessed 10 June 2023

27. Figma: Figma: the collaborative interface design tool. https://www.figma.com/, Accessed 19 June 2023

28. Sauro, J.: 10 Things To Know About The Single Ease Question (SEQ) – MeasuringU, Accessed 20 Sep 2023

29. Sauro, J.: MeasuringU: What Is A Good Task-Completion Rate?. https://measuringu.com/task-completion/, Accessed 20 Sep 2023

Understanding Adoption of Last Mile Electric Micromobility in Rural Areas: A Structural Equation Modeling Approach

Thomas Neifer[1,2,3(✉)], Ariane Stöbitsch[2,3], Kalvin Kroth[2,3], Caroline Baja[3],
Dennis Lawo[2], Lukas Böhm[2,3], Paul Bossauer[2,3], and Alexander Boden[2,3]

[1] Information Systems, University of Siegen, Siegen, Germany
thomas.neifer@uni-siegen.de
[2] Institut für Verbraucherinformatik, Bonn-Rhein-Sieg University of Applied Sciences, Sankt
Augustin, Germany
[3] Management Sciences, Bonn-Rhein-Sieg University of Applied Sciences, Sankt Augustin,
Germany

Abstract. Electric micromobility is a promising part of the transition towards
more sustainable and ecologic transportation systems – especially as a complement to public transportation on the last mile. However, so far adoption of such
services is still not ideal, especially in rural areas. By means of a quantitative
study with 137 users, our work-in-progress paper investigates user acceptance in
urban and rural areas. Based on a structural equation model, our research shows
that rural municipalities and providers should especially consider aspects that
address the performance expectation and the perceived collective environmental
impact of potential users, as these have been found to be especially relevant for
the intention to use. Our study thus contributes to the theoretical understanding
of e-micromobility, which has so far been mostly investigated in urban areas.

Keywords: Electric micromobility · Last mile problem · Public transport ·
Adoption

1 Introduction

Current mobility patterns are not aligned with widely accepted sustainability and car-
bon reduction goals [38]. In particular, the dominance of private motorized transport
in the modal split [9] is considered problematic. Private vehicles contribute to traffic
congestion and noise in densely populated regions, as well as air pollution on a local
and global level [46].

Electric Micromobility (E-Micromobility) has emerged as a promising solution to
address these challenges. Electrically powered micro-vehicles, such as kick scooters
and e-bikes [39], are considered especially effective in short-distance transportation,
such as the "first and last mile" before or after using public transportation (PT) [26].
This refers to overcoming the distance between the starting or ending point of a trip and
the nearest stop, which often discourages people from using PT [16]. By bridging these
gaps, e-micromobility has the potential to promote more sustainable mobility patterns
by supporting the adoption of PT [1].

© The Author(s), under exclusive license to Springer Nature Switzerland AG 2023
H. P. da Silva and P. Cipresso (Eds.): CHIRA 2023, CCIS 1997, pp. 160–175, 2023.
https://doi.org/10.1007/978-3-031-49368-3_10

In many cities, e-micromobility is being introduced as part of shared mobility services that allow consumers to temporarily on-demand access these vehicles via a mobile app [42]. However, the mere availability of these services is not enough to ensure a more sustainable mode of transportation. To fully realize the potential of e-micromobility, it is crucial that these services are adopted and used together with PT [28]. Several studies have already examined citizen adoption of e-micromobility [7,10,20]. However, these studies focus mainly on urban areas. For rural areas with their unique challenges of dispersed settlements and less frequent PT research, there is little insight or knowledge about the adoption of e-micromobility.

Therefore, this work aims to investigate the adoption of e-micromobility as a complementary solution of PT for the first and last mile in rural regions. The adoption of the service can be measured by the intention to use, an item from the technology acceptance model [6]. In particular, for this study, we adopted the TAUSM research model (Theory for the Acceptance and Use of Smart Mobility). This is an extension of UTAUT2 (Unified Theory of Acceptance and Use of Technology), which was developed specifically to measure smart mobility acceptance [18].

We focus mainly on students and young adults, as representatives of the younger generation, exhibiting a greater tendency towards using alternative mobility solutions [52], and becoming early adopters [21]. Furthermore, students and young adults are the potential car owners of tomorrow and, thus, are able to decide between starting the ownership of a private motorized vehicle or using PT [23]. Especially for students and young adults, who live in rural regions, this is a central decision, as their lives are influenced by an often poor PT connection [3]. Furthermore, students and young adults are potentially future residents of rural areas, e.g., when they start a family [3,5], which is why we build up a scenario-based approach - also for city-living students.

The study aims to achieve two main objectives: First, it is intended to provide a complementary study to the existing works on urban areas, thereby contributing to the theoretical understanding of mobility research. Second, the results should provide practical insights for rural municipalities or sharing service providers seeking to establish similar services in rural communities.

2   E-Micromobility and First and Last Mile Problems

The first and last mile problem in PT refers to the accessibility difficulties commuters face when reaching or leaving PT stops [16]. Research has shown that lack of connections to and from PT stops forces people to rely more heavily on private motorized transportation to meet their mobility needs. In contrast, transit systems that feature robust connectivity and accessibility evidence greater use of public transit as well as alternative modes such as walking and bicycling [34].

Existing studies shed light on the acceptance of e-micromobility as a complement to PT. For example, surveys on the impact of stationless scooter systems in Paris have found that users of these services often combine e-scooter travel with PT. For a considerable proportion of trips, PT was the main mode of transport for the majority of the journey, with e-scooters playing a crucial role in bridging the first or last mile [20].

A survey conducted in Oslo, found that about 57% of respondents combined several modes of transport on their last trip. Different modes of PT were mentioned, with 24% combining trips with the subway, 22% with buses, 12% with trains, and 9% with streetcars. However, the quantitative survey data do not provide conclusive evidence on whether scooters were used specifically for the first or last mile of these trips [10].

Three Polish cities (Gdansk, Gdynia, and Sopot) were studied by conducting a survey to investigate the differences in the behavior of users of e-scooter services and e-bike services. Unlike the above-mentioned studies, this work distinguished between different forms of e-mobility in order to identify differences between these transportation modes. The results show that nearly 72% of e-bike sharing service users use the service to bridge the first or last mile of their trips. In contrast, the percentage was lower for e-scooter users, with about 33% using the service for the same purpose. While the study does not explicitly address the reasons for these discrepancies, it makes clear that there may indeed be differences between the diverse types of e-micromobility vehicles [4].

E-micromobility also became a topic of interest in HCI, within the broader attempt to promote more sustainable transportation [2,24]. The focus of this research was on user experience issues, accessibility, or safety. While other HCI research highlights the importance of infrastructures especially in synchronization with the needs of (rural) users [23,25], there is little knowledge about the infrastructure of e-micromobility in rural areas and its adoption. This adds to the general need for studies focusing on rural areas, especially as the infrastructures differences in rural and urban areas are an important topic when designing systems to support sustainable mobility [25].

3   Research Model

The mentioned studies provide valuable insights into the acceptance of e-micromobility as a complement to PT, as they were able to collect data on the actual use of these services. However, there are very few e-mobility services in rural areas, making it difficult to collect usage data specifically for these areas. To overcome this data limitation, one approach of measuring adoption is the use of acceptance models. Models such as the Technology Acceptance Model (TAM) [6] or the Unified Theory of Acceptance and Use of Technology (UTAUT or UTAUT2) allow the study of people's intentions to use technology. These models are based on the fundamental assumption that a person's intention to use a technology strongly predicts his or her actual use [6,48]. Therefore, a quantitative survey that assesses the intention to use a particular technology can be used to gain insight into the potential adoption of the technology, even in the absence of actual use at the time of the study.

The TAUSM model, which was developed as an extension of the UTAUT2 as part of a study to investigate the acceptance of smart mobility, is suitable for the present situation [18]. Figure 1 shows the research model with the included constructs, the respective impact paths between them, and the resulting hypotheses. The variables and hypotheses are adopted from the original paper. It was originally developed in the context of smart mobility. However, a transfer to the area of e-micromobility is justified for two reasons. First, the TAUSM is a supplement to the UTAUT2. In the literature, the UTAUT2 has already been successfully used several times to investigate the acceptance of e-micromobility [30,33]. The two supplements from [18] (perceived risk and collective environmental impact) are both latent constructs that also play a role in the acceptance of e-micromobility, even though they have not yet been taken into account in the UTAUT2 [51].

A transfer of the TAUSM can be justified by the fact that the terms smart mobility, shared mobility and e-micromobility have a close, hierarchical relationship to each other. Shared mobility is considered in the literature as a subfield of smart mobility, and e-micromobility in turn is offered within the framework of shared mobility [17].

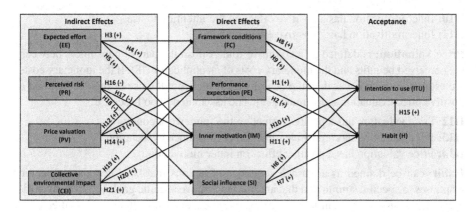

Fig. 1. Research Model [18].

The TAUSM includes the following variables and hypotheses, which were translated from German to English:

Performance expectation provides information about how strongly a person believes that using technology will help him or her improve his or her own performance [48].

H1: Performance expectation has a positive effect on the intention to use.
H2: Performance expectation has a positive effect on habit.

Expected Effort. Effort expectancy, or perceived ease of use, expresses the subjectively perceived ease associated with using technology [48]. The related hypotheses are:
H3: Expected effort has a positive effect on the framework conditions.
H4: Expected effort has a positive effect on performance expectation.
H5: Expected effort has a positive effect on inner motivation.

Social Influence: is defined as the degree to which an individual perceives that other individuals significant to that person believe that he or she should use the new system. Assessments of the opinion of society also play a role here [48]. The associated hypotheses are:

H6: Social influence has a positive effect on the intention to use.
H7: Social influence has a positive effect on habit.

Framework Conditions: are defined as the extent to which a person assumes that an organizational and technical infrastructure exists that supports the use of the system. This also includes the question of the compatibility of the technology in question with corresponding other technologies [48]. The associated hypotheses are:

H8: The framework conditions have a positive effect on the intention to use.
H9: The framework conditions have a positive effect on habit.

Inner Motivation. (or hedonic motivation) refers to the fun or pleasure a person feels when using a certain technology [49]. It has already been shown in the past that hedonic motivation is one of the most important motivators for the use of (e-)micromobility [31]. The associated hypotheses are:

H10: Inner motivation has a positive effect on the intention to use.
H11: Inner motivation has a positive effect on habit.

Price Valuation: is defined as a cognitive trade-off on the part of consumers between the perceived benefits and the monetary costs of an application [8]. If the monetary costs are estimated to be lower than the benefits resulting from the use of this technology, a positive price evaluation is assumed [49]. The associated hypotheses are:

H12: Price valuation has a positive effect on the framework conditions.
H13: Price valuation has a positive effect on performance expectation.
H14: Price valuation has a positive effect on inner motivation.

Habit: can be defined as a learned sequence of actions that have become automatic responses to specific stimuli and that are used to achieve specific goals [32,50]. Accordingly, a person's habits can have a strong influence on one's intentions. Studies have shown that the choice of the means of transport may partly depend on existing habits [45]. The associated hypothesis is:

H15: Habit has a positive effect on the intention to use.

Perceived Risk, as a counterpart to inner motivation, reflects all the fears of loss associated with the use of technology. In the mobility domain, for example, these include fears of loss related to one's freedom, safety, time, and comfort [18,43]. The associated hypotheses are:

H16: Perceived risk has a negative effect on performance expectation.
H17: Perceived risk has a negative effect on inner motivation.
H18: Perceived risk has a negative effect on social influence.

Collective Environmental Impact: is defined as the degree to which a person believes that he or she, as part of a collective, can bring about an actual change for the environment [18]. Especially in the field of mobility, it is assumed that such sustainability aspects can have a relevant influence on the acceptance of technologies or means of transport [51]. The associated hypotheses are:

H19: Collective environmental impact has a positive effect on performance expectation.
H20: Collective environmental impact has a positive effect on inner motivation.
H21: Collective environmental impact has a positive effect on social influence.

Intention to Use: expresses the extent to which a person intends to use technology. In the literature, this construct is considered a central predictor of whether a technology in question is actually used [6,48].

4   Data Analysis and Results

The existing items from [18] were used to operationalize the constructs with a seven-point Likert scale with (1) strongly disagree and (7) strongly agree; accordingly, the reliability of the measurement instruments did not need to be tested beforehand. The questions were adapted to the acceptance of e-micromobility as a supplement to PT. Since the focus of this study is on rural areas, a scenario description was included in the developed questionnaire to ensure that respondents, when answering the individual questions, put themselves in a scenario in which they could use e-scooters and e-bikes to cover the last mile in a rural area. In addition, the questionnaire asked whether the respondent lives in a rural area or not.

Google Forms was used to collect the data. The survey was conducted between November 2022 and January 2023 in Germany. After data collection, outliers were removed according to the recommendations of [11], leaving 137 completed questionnaires. This is a comparatively small sample size. However, the present model was evaluated using Partial Least Squares-Structural Equation Modeling (PLS-SEM), which can also work with such sample sizes [12]. Descriptive analyses were conducted with Pingouin, an open-source statistical package written in Python 3 [47]. Calculations of the Structural Equation Model were conducted with SmartPLS v4 [36] according to the proposed procedure of [37].

4.1   Demographics and Descriptive Results

Out of the total 137 participants, 53.2% (73) were female and 46.8% (64) were male, with an average age of 24.84 years. The majority of respondents, 67.9% (93), resided in urban areas, while 32.1% (44) lived in rural areas. In addition, 82.4% (113) of participants were students. A comprehensive overview of participant demographics can be found in Table 1, and detailed statistics on the means and standard deviations of the model constructs can be found in Table 2.

Table 1. Demographics.

Characteristic	Specification	n	Characteristic	Specification	n
Gender	Female	73	Education	School graduation	75
	Male	64		Apprenticeship	21
Age	<21	24		University	41
	21–30	98	Residence	Urban	93
	>30	15		Rural	44
Occupation	Student	113	Net income	<1,000	79
	Employee	18		1,000–2,000	49
	Other	6		>2,000	9

4.2   Measurement Model

Since we have used a reflective operationalization, we first examine both the reliability and validity of the measurement model as part of the evaluation of the external model.

Table 2. Means and Standard Deviations of the Constructs.

Characteristic	Specification	ITU	PE	EE	FC	SI	IM	H	PV	PR	CEI
Gender	Female	3.6	4.4	4.6	5.0	3.6	3.7	2.0	3.3	3.9	5.0
	Male	3.6	4.4	5.0	5.6	3.6	4.0	2.4	3.1	3.3	5.0
Age	<21	3.7	4.7	5.2	5.3	4.0	4.3	2.6	3.4	3.4	5.3
	21–30	3.6	4.4	4.8	5.3	3.5	3.8	2.1	3.3	3.6	4.9
	>30	3.8	4.3	4.3	5.1	3.3	3.5	2.2	2.7	3.6	5.0
Residency	Urban	3.8	4.6	4.9	5.4	3.7	4.0	2.4	3.3	3.5	5.1
	Rural	3.2	4.0	4.6	5.1	3.4	3.7	1.8	3.2	3.7	4.7
Occupation	Student	3.5	4.3	4.6	5.2	3.5	3.8	2.1	3.2	3.7	4.9
	Employee	4.4	5.1	5.8	5.7	4.0	4.2	2.9	3.5	2.9	5.2
	Other	4.7	4.2	4.6	5.0	3.6	3.2	2.2	3.5	3.3	4.8
Net Income	<1,000	3.5	4.3	4.6	5.2	3.6	3.8	2.1	3.2	3.6	5.0
	1,000–2,000	4.1	4.9	5.1	5.6	3.4	4.0	2.8	3.1	3.3	5.0
	>2,000	4.5	4.9	5.8	5.7	3.9	4.3	2.5	3.9	2.9	5.5
Education	School graduation	3.6	4.6	4.8	5.4	3.7	3.9	2.3	3.2	3.5	5.0
	Apprenticeship	3.3	4.2	4.9	5.2	3.6	3.8	2.2	3.4	3.5	5.0
	University	3.8	4.2	4.6	5.1	3.3	3.7	2.0	3.0	3.9	4.9
Family status	Unmarried	3.6	4.3	4.7	5.3	3.6	3.8	2.2	3.3	3.6	5.0
	Married	3.5	4.9	5.3	5.4	3.6	4.1	2.2	2.7	3.4	4.9
Total	**Mean**	**3.6**	**4.4**	**4.8**	**5.3**	**3.6**	**3.9**	**2.2**	**3.2**	**3.6**	**5.0**
	Standard deviation	**1.9**	**1.9**	**1.7**	**1.3**	**1.4**	**1.6**	**1.4**	**1.3**	**1.4**	**1.3**

Indicator reliability provides information on the relationship between an indicator and the underlying construct. More precisely, it describes the proportion of variance of the indicator that can be described by the superordinate construct. Factor loadings can be used to make statements about indicator reliability, whereby a value close to 0.708 is assumed to explain more than 50% of the variance and thus to provide a sufficient degree of reliability [37]. Of the 40 factor loadings, nine were below this threshold. Here, it is recommended to first check whether removing the corresponding items has a positive effect on the construct's validity and reliability. Accordingly, six of the nine items were removed (see Table 3).

To ensure the reliability of the scales utilized, it is crucial to estimate the internal consistency. This can be achieved by calculating Cronbach's alpha, as suggested by [41]. In general, values between 0.70 and 0.90 are considered acceptable [44]. Table 3 shows Cronbach's alpha values for all constructs discussed. Only the value for the construct "framework conditions" is just below the value of 0.70 at 0.692. The remaining values are above this value.

In Sarstedt's procedure model, the next step is to assess the validity of the measurement model [37]. Validity refers to the accuracy with which a procedure measures its intended target [35]. The first aspect to be examined is convergence validity, which

Table 3. Validity and Reliability of the Measurement Model.

Construct	Items	Validity (factor loadings)	Reliability (Cronbach's alpha)
Intention to Use	ITU1	0.913	0.930
	ITU2	0.886	
	ITU3	0.956	
	ITU4	0.884	
Performance Expectation	PE1	0.877	0.928
	PE2	0.900	
	PE3	0.914	
	PE4	0.938	
Expected Effort	EE1	0.882	0.909
	EE2	0.892	
	EE3	0.900	
	EE4	0.871	
Social Influence	SI1	removed	0.843
	SI2	0.877	
	SI3	0.852	
	SI4	0.887	
Framework Conditions	FC1	9.665	0.692
	FC2	0.744	
	FC3	0.773	
	FC4	0.677	
Inner Motivation	IM1	0.861	0.868
	IM2	0.923	
	IM3	0.847	
	IM4	0.752	
Habit	H1	0.887	0.792
	H2	0.913	
	H3	9.702	
Price Valuation	PV1	0.900	0.841
	PV2	removed	
	PV3	0.953	
Perceived Risk	RISK1	9.765	0.763
	RISK2	0.828	
	RISK3	0.869	
	RISK4	removed	
	RISK5	removed	
Collective Environmental Impact	CEI1	0.468	0.723
	CEI2	0.928	
	CEI3	removed	
	CEI4	0.915	
	CEI5	removed	

examines the extent to which the individual indicators of a construct are strongly correlated with each other. Ideally, these indicators should measure the same underlying construct. One way to assess convergence validity is to calculate the Average Variance Extracted (AVE), where the threshold is usually 0.50 [37]. In this case, the framework construct has the lowest AVE value, but still exceeds the threshold at 0.513. The AVE values for the other constructs range from 0.639 to 0.859.

Besides convergence validity, discriminant validity is also an important aspect, assessing how clearly each construct differs from others in terms of empirical differences and the clarity with which the indicators represent only that particular construct. For this purpose, the heterotrait-monotrait (HTMT) matrix is commonly used, with values ideally below 0.90 [37]. Regarding our model, no value exceeds this threshold, indicating acceptable discriminant validity.

Since the measurement model used consists exclusively of reflectively operationalized constructs, the corresponding procedures for formatively measured variables can be omitted. This concludes the evaluation of the measurement model and the structural model can be examined in more detail [37].

4.3   Structural Model

As part of the evaluation of the structural model, we first check whether there are collinearity problems between the individual constructs that may distort or falsify the regression results. This can be determined using the VIF (Variance Inflation Factor) of each construct. All values are below the threshold of 3.0. Accordingly, there is no multicollinearity between the latent variables [37]. In the next step, the path coefficients of the inner model are examined with respect to their relevance and significance. For this purpose, bootstrapping with 5,000 repetitions was performed. Table 4 shows the direct effect and the total effect on the intention to use as well as the significance (represented by the p-values) for all constructs.

Table 4. Direct and Total Effects on Intention to Use.

Construct	Direct Effect on ITU	Significance	Total Effect on ITU	Significance
Intention to Use	–	–	–	–
Performance Expectation	0.597	0.000	0.666	0.000
Expected Effort	–	–	0.244	0.000
Social Influence	0.251	0.001	0.273	0.001
Framework Conditions	0.005	0.925	−0.011	0.834
Inner Motivation	−0.131	0.079	−0.064	0.416
Habit	0.223	0.003	0.223	0.003
Price Valuation	–	–	−0.013	0.725
Perceived Risk	–	–	−0.169	0.004
Collective Environmental Impact	–	–	0.341	0.000

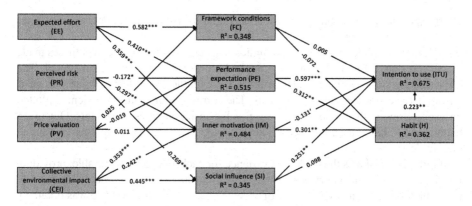

Fig. 2. Inner model with path coefficients, p-values (***<0.001, **<0.01, *<0.05, '<0.10), and explained variances.

Table 5. Acceptance/Rejection of Hypotheses.

Hypothesis	Acceptance/Rejection
H1: Performance expectation has a positive effect on the intention to use.	Accept
H2: Performance expectation has a positive effect on habit.	Accept
H3: Expected effort has a positive effect on the framework conditions.	Accept
H4: Expected effort has a positive effect on performance expectation.	Accept
H5: Expected effort has a positive effect on inner motivation.	Accept
H6: Social influence has a positive effect on the intention to use.	Accept
H7: Social influence has a positive effect on habit.	Reject
H8: The framework conditions have a positive effect on the intention to use.	Reject
H9: The framework conditions have a positive effect on habit.	Reject
H10: Inner motivation has a positive effect on the intention to use.	Reject
H11: Inner motivation has a positive effect on habit.	Accept
H12: Price valuation has a positive effect on the framework conditions.	Reject
H13: Price valuation has a positive effect on performance expectation.	Reject
H14: Price valuation has a positive effect on inner motivation.	Reject
H15: Habit has a positive effect on the intention to use.	Accept
H16: Perceived risk has a negative effect on performance expectation.	Accept
H17: Perceived risk has a negative effect on inner motivation.	Accept
H18: Perceived risk has a negative effect on social influence.	Accept
H19: Collective environmental impact has a positive effect on performance expectation.	Accept
H20: Collective environmental impact has a positive effect on inner motivation.	Accept
H21: Collective environmental impact has a positive effect on social influence.	Accept

Except for the direct and total effects of the constructs framework conditions and internal motivation on the intention to use, as well as the total effect of price valuation, all effects can be considered significant. Performance expectancy has the strongest effects on intention to use, followed by environmental impact and social influence, effort expectancy, and habit. All these effects are positive in nature. Perceived risk has a small, negative effect.

The path coefficients and p-values indicate the extent to which the hypotheses made must be rejected. Figure 2 shows a graphical representation of the inner model. The constructs are shown as blue circles, whereas the hypothesized effect paths are shown as arrows between the respective constructs. The corresponding path coefficient is plotted on each arrow, with the corresponding p-value in parentheses to the left. Out of 21 hypotheses, 7 have to be rejected because no significant relationship could be found (see Table 5).

Figure 2 also shows the explained variance for each endogenous variable, providing insight into the "explanatory power" of the current model. In the case of intention to use, which serves as a key predictor of acceptance, an R^2 value of 0.675 was obtained. This means that about 68% of the variability of this variable can be explained by the exogenous variables influencing it. As a general guideline, values of 0.75, 0.50, and 0.25 are usually considered significant, moderate, and weak, respectively [12, 13].

To evaluate the predictive ability of the model, the "PLSpredict procedure" introduced by [40] is used. This procedure uses k-fold cross-validation, where the entire dataset is divided into k subsets of equal size. Each subset is then predicted using the remaining k minus 1 subsets. The results provide information on the predictive power of the model, focusing on the $R^2_{predict}$ values for both manifest and latent variables. According to [37], the focus should be on the key latent constructs of the model, with positive values above 0 indicating strong predictive power. In the present study, 10 subgroups were created, and $R^2_{predict}$ values for all endogenous constructs ranged from 0.263 to 0.482.

In addition, the influence of the control variables on the intention to use was investigated. For this purpose, dummy variables were formed and bootstrapped in order to be able to make statements about the relevance and significance of the respective relationships to the intention to use. No significant effects were found for the control variables age, gender, experience with e-micromobility, marital status, number of children, personal monthly net income, and employment situation. Only the level of education had a significant effect on the intention to use. According to the present model, the fact that people have a college or university degree has a positive influence on the intention to use the PT.

5 Discussion

The analysis of the collected data shows the acceptance structure of e-mobility as a supplement to PT in rural areas. In particular, the latent variable of performance expectation shows a significant effect on intention to use as a key endogenous construct. The direct effect is measured as 0.597, while the overall effect is 0.666. These results are consistent with similar studies that have investigated the adoption of mobility technologies using similar models. For example, Kopplin et al. (2021) examined the acceptability of shared e-scooters for short-distance trips in urban areas using the UTAUT framework [19]. In their study, performance expectancy was also found to be the most influential factor in usage intention. The results suggest that individuals are primarily motivated to use vehicles such as e-scooters and e-bikes because of their efficiency and convenience for personal transportation. Actors who want to introduce corresponding offers for better connection to PT in rural areas should take this aspect into account.

Collective environmental efficacy has the second largest effect on intention to use, with a total effect of 0.341. This reinforces Zhang and Kamargianni's (2022) [51] statement that sustainability aspects as latent variables have an influence on the acceptance and use of (e-)micromobility. In addition, collective environmental impact influences performance expectancy, as well as social influence, both of which exert a significant effect on usage intention. Sustainability aspects will continue to gain importance in the future [46], so it can be expected that the influence of collective environmental impact will continue to grow in the future.

The expected effort, i.e., expected user-friendliness, has a moderate total effect. It also has the most relevant effect of all endogenous constructs that affect performance expectations, with a path coefficient of 0.410, and is therefore not negligible. Empirical studies show that consumers already perceive the use of e-scooters via shared mobility services as simple and user-friendly [14]. When establishing corresponding services in rural areas, there is therefore no need to focus additionally on creating such usability.

Social influence and habit show a moderate influence on the intention to use. When looking at the mean values for the construct habit in Table 2, it is noticeable that relatively low values are achieved. This is consistent with the data on current experiences with e-scooters and similar micro-vehicles.

As expected, perceived risk has a negative total influence on the intention to use. However, this is small with a path coefficient of -0.169. Additionally, the construct has a negative influence on performance expectancy, intrinsic motivation, and social influence. Safety concerns are a frequently addressed e-micromobility issue. Concerns about traffic and road safety [14], as well as health consequences [15, 27], are often the subject of current research and should be considered when developing rural offerings.

No significant results can be found with regard to the control variables discussed in the model. Only the education of the respondents has a significant influence on the intention to use, insofar as people with a college or university degree have a higher intention to use. This is (at least partially) in line with empirical studies on the acceptance of (e-)micromobility. Here, it has been found that highly educated, young, male persons in particular are among the active users of this form of mobility [22].

The inner motivation has no significant influence on the intention to use. When interpreting this fact, however, it must be taken into account that most respondents from both rural and urban areas stated that they had little or no experience with the use of e-micromobility. Accordingly, it is questionable to what extent hedonistic aspects can be neglected when establishing offers in rural areas. The same applies to the price valuation and framework conditions. The interviewees may have had too little experience with this mobility technology to be able to assess the price-performance ratio of e-mobility for bridging the first and last mile, as well as the existing framework conditions.

But not only the results for the internal motivation, the framework conditions, and the price evaluation have to be considered critically. The original goal of this work was to gain insights into the acceptance of e-micromobility as a supplement to PT in rural areas. However, looking at the descriptive description of the sample, it is noticeable that the majority of the respondents live in the city. Although the participants were asked to imagine a scenario in the rural areas when answering the items, this alone cannot provide any meaningful values about the actual situation in less densely populated areas.

The results should therefore be continued and further confirmed by further research with an even stronger focus on the rural areas. Also to be considered is the fact that the sample consists mainly of students and young adults. Accordingly, other socio-demographic groups, such as persons of higher age or persons with a higher income and a different employment situation, are underrepresented.

6 Conclusion

The modal split in many European countries is dominated by private motorized transport [9], which has a negative impact on the environment [46]. E-micromobility has the potential to solve the first and last mile problem of PT and thus promote a more sustainable mobility behavior [26]. However, for this potential to be unleashed, e-micromobility needs to be accepted and used as a complement to PT. There are already a number of studies that address the study of acceptance, but these focus mainly on urban areas [7,10,20]. Given that the first and last mile problem seems particularly severe in rural areas due to low settlement density [29], the question arises as to how the acceptance structure is set up here. With the help of technology acceptance models such as UTAUT2 [49], this question can be answered without the need for concrete offers to exist in rural areas at the present time. Therefore, a quantitative survey using the TAUSM model was conducted as part of this work.

From our results, we can derive recommendations for rural municipalities or providers of e-micromobility and PT services that want to introduce and establish corresponding services in rural areas. Thus, due to the high relevance for the intention to use, aspects that address the performance expectation and the perceived collective environmental impact of potential users of these offers should be considered in particular. Since a large part of the participants put themselves into a theoretical scenario without actually living in rural areas, the results are limited thereby. In order to be able to confirm the statements of this work, further studies must be conducted.

References

1. Abduljabbar, R.L., Liyanage, S., Dia, H.: The role of micro-mobility in shaping sustainable cities: a systematic literature review. Transp. Res. Part D: Transp. Environ. **92**, 102734 (2021)
2. Bennett, C., Ackerman, E., Fan, B., Bigham, J., Carrington, P., Fox, S.: Accessibility and the crowded sidewalk: Micromobility's impact on public space. In: Designing Interactive Systems Conference 2021, pp. 365–380 (2021)
3. Berg, J., Ihlström, J.: The importance of public transport for mobility and everyday activities among rural residents. Soc. Sci. **8**(2), 58 (2019)
4. Bieliński, T., Ważna, A.: Electric scooter sharing and bike sharing user behaviour and characteristics. Sustainability **12**(22), 9640 (2020)
5. Buchenrieder, G., Dufhues, T., Möllers, J., Runschke, D., Sagyndykova, G.: Return to the countryside: the return intentions of highly educated young people in the Akmola province of northern Kazakhstan. Popul. Space Place **26**(2), e2273 (2020)

6. Davis, F.D.: Perceived usefulness, perceived ease of use, and user acceptance of information technology. MIS Q. **13**(3), 319–340 (1989)
7. Dean, M.D., Zuniga-Garcia, N.: Shared e-scooter trajectory analysis during the COVID-19 pandemic in Austin, Texas. Transp. Res. Rec. **2677**(4), 432–447 (2023)
8. Dodds, W.B., Monroe, K.B., Grewal, D.: Effects of price, brand, and store information on buyers product evaluations. J. Mark. Res. **28**(3), 307–319 (1991)
9. Eisenmann, C., Köhler, K., Schulz, A., Seiffert, I., Gaus, D., Link, H.: Verkehr in zahlen 2022/2023 (2022)
10. Fearnley, N., Johnsson, E., Berge, S.H.: Patterns of E-Scooter use in Combination with Public Transport. Findings (2020)
11. Hair, J., Hult, G.T.M., Ringle, C.M., Sarstedt, M.: A Primer on Partial Least Squares Structural Equation Modeling (PLS-SEM), 2nd edn. SAGE Publications, Thousand Oaks, CA (2016). May
12. Hair, J.F., Ringle, C.M., Sarstedt, M.: PLS-SEM: Indeed a silver bullet. J. Mark. Theor. Pract. **19**(2), 139–152 (2011)
13. Henseler, J., Ringle, C.M., Sinkovics, R.R.: The use of partial least squares path modeling in international marketing. In: New challenges to international marketing. Emerald Group Publishing Limited (2009)
14. Huang, F.H.: User behavioral intentions toward a scooter-sharing service: an empirical study. Sustainability **13**(23), 13153 (2021)
15. Kappagantu, A., Yaremchuk, K., Tam, S.: Head and neck injuries and electronic scooter use in the united states. Laryngoscope **131**(11), E2784–E2789 (2021)
16. Kåresdotter, E., Page, J., Mörtberg, U., Näsström, H., Kalantari, Z.: First mile/last mile problems in smart and sustainable cities: a case study in Stockholm county. J. Urban Technol. **29**(2), 115–137 (2022)
17. Karlı, R.G.Ö., Çelikyay, S.: Current trends in smart cities: shared micromobility. In: Ben Ahmed, M., Boudhir, A.A., Karas, I.R., Jain, V., Mellouli, S. (eds.) SCA 2021. LNNS, vol. 393, pp. 187–198. Springer, Cham (2022). https://doi.org/10.1007/978-3-030-94191-8_15
18. Kauschke, L.: Akzeptanzstudie Smart Mobility. htw saar Forschungsgruppe Verkehrstelematik (2020). https://kosmos-project.eu/wp-content/uploads/2020/05/Akzeptanzstudie-Smart-Mobility_2.pdf
19. Kopplin, C.S., Brand, B.M., Reichenberger, Y.: Consumer acceptance of shared E-scooters for urban and short-distance mobility. Transp. Res. Part D: Transp. Environ. **91**, 102680 (2021)
20. Krier, C., Chrétien, J., Lagadic, M., Louvet, N.: How do shared Dockless E-scooter services affect mobility practices in Paris? A survey-based estimation of modal shift. Transp. Res. Rec. **2675**(11), 291–304 (2021)
21. Kriswardhana, W., Esztergár-Kiss, D.: Exploring the aspects of MaaS adoption based on college students preferences. Transp. Policy **136**, 113–125 (2023)
22. Laa, B., Leth, U.: Survey of E-scooter users in Vienna: who they are and how they ride. J. Transp. Geogr. **89**, 102874 (2020)
23. Lawo, D., Böhm, L., Flügge, A.K., Pakusch, C., Stevens, G.: Going car-free: investigating mobility practice transformations and the role of ICT. In: Proceedings of the 5th International Conference on Computer-Human Interaction Research and Applications (CHIRA 2021), October 28-29, 2021, pp. 36–47. SciTePress, Science and Technology Publications (2021)
24. Matviienko, A., et al.: E-scootar: exploring unimodal warnings for E-scooter riders in augmented reality. In: CHI Conference on Human Factors in Computing Systems Extended Abstracts, pp. 1–7 (2022)

25. Meurer, J., Lawo, D., Pakusch, C., Tolmie, P., Wulf, V.: Opportunities for sustainable mobility: re-thinking eco-feedback from a citizen's perspective. In: Proceedings of the 9th International Conference on Communities & Technologies-Transforming Communities, pp. 102–113 (2019)

26. Nigro, M., et al.: Investigating potential electric micromobility demand in the city of Rome, Italy. Transp. Res. Procedia **62**, 401–407 (2022)

27. Nisson, P.L., Ley, E., Chu, R.: Electric scooters: case reports indicate a growing public health concern (2020)

28. Oeschger, G., Carroll, P., Caulfield, B.: Micromobility and public transport integration: the current state of knowledge. Transp. Res. Part D: Transp. Environ. **89**, 102628 (2020)

29. Oswalt, P., Meyer, L., Rettich, S., Böker, F., Roost, F., Jeckel, E.: Bauen für die neue mobilität im ländlichen raum: Anpassung der baulichen strukturen von dörfern und kleinstädten im zuge der digitalisierung des verkehrs (2021)

30. Öztaş Karlı, R.G., Karlı, H., Çelikyay, H.S.: Investigating the acceptance of shared E-scooters: empirical evidence from turkey. Case Stud. Transp. Policy **10**(2), 1058–1068 (2022)

31. Pimentel, R.W., Lowry, M.B., Consortium, P.N.T., et al.: If you provide, will they ride? motivators and deterrents to shared micro-mobility. Tech. rep., Pacific Northwest Transportation Consortium (PacTrans)(UTC) (2020)

32. Polites, G.L.: The duality of habit in information technology acceptance. Ph.D. thesis, University of Georgia (2009)

33. Putri, B.A.I., Atha, F., Rizka, F., Amalia, R., Husna, S.: Factors affecting E-scooter sharing purchase intention: an analysis using unified theory of acceptance and use of technology 2 (UTAUT2). Int. J. Creative Bus. Manag. **1**(2), 58–73 (2021)

34. Quadrifoglio, L., Chandra, S., et al.: Evaluating the Effect of Street Network Connectivity on First/Last Mile Transit Performance. Southwest Region University Transportation Center (US), Tech. rep. (2011)

35. Rammstedt, B.: Reliabilität, validität, objektivität. Handbuch der sozialwissenschaftlichen Datenanalyse, pp. 239–258 (2010)

36. Ringle, C.M., Wende, S., Becker, J.M.: Smartpls 4. oststeinbek: SmartPLS GmbH (2022)

37. Sarstedt, M., Ringle, C.M., Hair, J.F.: Partial least squares structural equation modeling. In: Homburg, C., Klarmann, M., Vomberg, A.E. (eds.) Handbook of Market Research. Springer, Cham (2021). https://doi.org/10.1007/978-3-319-05542-8_15-2

38. Schmidt, J.A., Hellali-Milani, S.: Herausforderung für die stadtplanung: Mobilität findet stadt–neue intermodale urbane mobilität mit neuen nutzer-und nutzungsansprüchen. Elektrofahrzeuge für die Städte von morgen: Interdisziplinärer Entwurf und Test im DesignStudio NRW, pp. 19–25 (2016)

39. Şengül, B., Mostofi, H.: Impacts of E-micromobility on the sustainability of urban Transportationa systematic review. Appl. Sci. **11**(13), 5851 (2021)

40. Shmueli, G., Ray, S., Estrada, J.M.V., Chatla, S.B.: The elephant in the room: predictive performance of pls models. J. Bus. Res. **69**(10), 4552–4564 (2016)

41. Shultz, K.S., Whitney, D.J., Zickar, M.J.: Measurement Theory in Action: Case Studies and Exercises. Routledge (2020)

42. Stocker, A., Shaheen, S.: Shared automated mobility: early exploration and potential impacts. In: Meyer, G., Beiker, S. (eds.) Road Vehicle Automation 4, pp. 125–139. Springer International Publishing, Cham (2018). https://doi.org/10.1007/978-3-319-60934-8_12

43. Stone, R.N., Winter, F.W.: Risk: is it still uncertainty times consequences. In: Proceedings of the American Marketing Association. vol. 1, pp. 261–265. Winter Educators Conference Chicago, IL (1987)

44. Tavakol, M., Dennick, R.: Making sense of Cronbach's alpha. Int. J. Med. Educ. **2**, 53–55 (2011). https://doi.org/10.5116/ijme.4dfb.8dfd

45. Thøgersen, J., Møller, B.: Breaking car use habits: the effectiveness of a free one-month travelcard. Transportation **35**(3), 329–345 (2008). https://doi.org/10.1007/s11116-008-9160-1
46. Umweltbundesamt, U.: Umweltbelastungen durch verkehr. Link: https://www. umweltbundesamt.de/daten/verkehr/umweltbelastungen-durch-verkehr. Letzter Zugriff **28**, 2022 (2022)
47. Vallat, R.: Pingouin: statistics in python. J. Open Source Softw. **3**(31), 1026 (2018)
48. Venkatesh, V., Morris, M.G., Davis, G.B., Davis, F.D.: User acceptance of information technology: toward a unified view. MIS Q. **27**(3), 425–478 (2003)
49. Venkatesh, V., Thong, J.Y., Xu, X.: Consumer acceptance and use of information technology: extending the unified theory of acceptance and use of technology. MIS Q. **36**(1), 157–178 (2012)
50. Verplanken, B., Aarts, H.: Habit, attitude, and planned behaviour: is habit an empty construct or an interesting case of goal-directed automaticity? Eur. Rev. Soc. Psychol. **10**(1), 101–134 (1999)
51. Zhang, Y., Kamargianni, M.: A review on the factors influencing the adoption of new mobility technologies and services: autonomous vehicle, drone, micromobility and mobility as a service. Transp. Rev. **43**(3), 407–429 (2023)
52. Zijlstra, T., Durand, A., Hoogendoorn-Lanser, S., Harms, L.: Early adopters of mobility-as-a-service in the Netherlands. Transp. Policy **97**, 197–209 (2020)

Participative Development of a Learning Dashboard for Online Students Using Traditional Design Concepts

Gilbert Drzyzga$^{(\boxtimes)}$, Thorleif Harder , and Monique Janneck

Institute for Interactive Systems, Technische Hochschule Lübeck, Lübeck, Germany
{gilbert.drzyzga,thorleif.harder,monique.janneck}@th-luebeck.de

Abstract. In order to improve online learning outcomes, a Learning Dashboard (LD) for online students is being developed as a plugin for the learning management system Moodle to support self-regulation. The project itself focuses on the factors that lead to success and failure in online learning. Using a user-centered design approach, the LD will provide students with feedback and functional elements through different cards. 24 online students completed a three-part term paper in which they examined the elements of two wireframes of the LD in relation to Wertheimer's Gestalt Laws and in terms of factual and interaction problems. We also received 11 card designs from them as a voluntary bonus assignment. Assignments 1 & 2 had to be completed successfully in order to be admitted to the exam. The study was designed to encourage student participation and improve accessibility by taking into account their expertise. The results showed that clearer overviews, clarification of how content elements fit together, more compact solutions, and intuitive controls improved clarity and usability.

Keywords: Digital degree programs · Dropout rates · Self-regulation · User-centered design · Gestalt laws · Factual and interaction problems · Learning analytics

1 Introduction

In recent years, digital degree programs have become increasingly important, in part because they allow students to customize their learning process [11] However, such programs have higher dropout rates [22, 4, 5]. In order to successfully complete such programs, self-regulation skills are important [1, 21]. A research project within a university network is currently working on the development of a dashboard using machine learning (ML) methods for the learning management system (LMS) Moodle[1] [13]. This learning dashboard (LD) is intended to help students better monitor their learning progress and process, so that they can learn effectively and self-directedly in a digital environment [8]. For this purpose, ML models are used to support learning through personalized feedback based on learning analytics. The content and functional elements provided in

---

[1] https://www.moodle.org

© The Author(s), under exclusive license to Springer Nature Switzerland AG 2023
H. P. da Silva and P. Cipresso (Eds.): CHIRA 2023, CCIS 1997, pp. 176–191, 2023.
https://doi.org/10.1007/978-3-031-49368-3_11

the dashboard will be explored in terms of their importance for self-regulation [7]. The LD to be developed is divided into different areas called cards. They provide different information or allow interactions, e.g., the creation of personal learning goals [7]. The study focused on the research questions (RQ) of designing content elements to comply with the Gestalt Laws and factual and interaction problems, identifying issues in the current implementation of the wireframes, and exploring alternative design solutions to improve the user experience (UX) [16, 25], which is part of a design study [6]. The theory of Gestalt Laws, developed in the early 20th century [26], focuses on how people organize and interpret environmental information into a single whole, or gestalt. The theory can be linked to interaction issues in the development of a self-regulation dashboard for students, as it highlights the importance of contextual factors in shaping perception. For example, Gestalt principles suggest that people tend to perceive objects or stimuli as part of a larger whole, rather than as individual elements. In the context of developing a self-regulation dashboard, this means that students may be more likely to engage with the platform if they see it as an integrated system rather than a collection of separate features. These tools are often designed for professionals, so the study looked at the issues that students or professionals might face when visualizing data for such an audience, as they are more likely to be casual users [3, 9, 10].

(1) RQ1. What are the most effective ways to design content elements that comply with Gestalt Laws?
(2) RQ2. How can factual problems in current implementations of wireframes be identified and addressed?
(3) RQ3. Can alternative design solutions improve the UX, and if so, how can they be effectively explored and implemented?

2 Background

The involvement of the students, who are the main target group of the LD, in the development gives us the opportunity to understand their needs or expectations, to support the development process with their professional expertise on the one hand, and on the personal level (gaining understanding to prepare personal feedback) on the other. By examining the Gestalt Laws and also by reviewing possible factual and interaction problems, we obtain additional information for the further development of the LD from the perspective of the student.

2.1 The Gestalt Laws

The Gestalt Laws are a set of principles that describe how humans perceive visual patterns. These Laws help us understand how our brains organize information into groups, based on factors such as proximity, similarity, closure, continuation, and form [12, 23, 26]. The Gestalt Law of Proximity states that elements that are close together tend to be grouped together. This means that we naturally group objects or shapes that are physically near each other in our field of vision. Similarly, the Gestalt Law of Similarity suggests that similar things tend to be grouped together. Our brains have a natural tendency to categorize and organize items based on their shared characteristics.

The Gestalt Law of Closure states that elements that are close together tend to be grouped together. This means that our brain fills in missing pieces or gaps in visual patterns, creating a sense of completion or closure. The Gestalt Law of Good Continuation suggests that elements should be visually connected to each other. Our brains have an innate tendency to connect lines and shapes that are close together, forming continuous paths or trajectories. Finally, the Gestalt Law of Good Form states that elements should be visually appealing and easy to understand. This means that our brain naturally prefers patterns and designs that are simple, symmetrical, and well-balanced. Overall, these principles help us better understand how we perceive visual information and can inform design decisions in fields such as graphic design.

2.2 Factual and Interaction Problems

Factual problems occur when users encounter incorrect or incomplete information that hinders their ability to complete a task successfully. This can include errors in the content itself (e.g., wrong facts, outdated information), inconsistencies between different parts of the interface, or missing information that is necessary for understanding and using the system effectively [2, 24].

Interaction problems occur when users have difficulty interacting with the system due to poor design choices or implementation problems. This can include confusing or unintuitive interfaces (e.g., unclear labels, inconsistent navigation), slow response times or performance problems, or inaccessible features that prevent users from completing their tasks successfully [2, 24].

Both factual and interaction problems can negatively impact the UX and make it difficult for users to achieve their goals with the system. Addressing these types of usability problems is crucial for improving overall user satisfaction and ensuring that users are able to effectively use and interact with a product or service [15, 17, 19, 20].

3 Method

In a wireframe evaluation, 24 students analyzed two wireframe designs for an LD in relation to Wertheimer's Gestalt Laws [26] and in terms of factual and interaction problems (the task used the German term "Sachprobleme", which in the context of this paper is used to mean "factual problems" or "technical problems") [6].

The purpose of the study was to apply a user-centered design approach to examine the elements of the dashboard in relation to Wertheimer's Gestalt Laws [26] and the model of Streitz (1985) [24] in Fig. 1. This model provides a comprehensive framework for system design and emphasizes the integration of four central components: User, Task, System, and Context. It sees conception not as a linear, but as a cyclical and interactive process in which all components are interrelated and influence the factual and interaction problems [6].

The participants were enrolled in an online media computer science program and were studying human-computer interaction as part of their degree program. They were given readings and weekly web conferences led by a university instructor to prepare them for the assignments. Successful completion of the assignments was required for

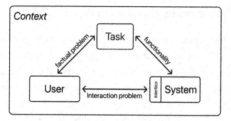

Fig. 1. Streitz model for representation of factual and interaction problems (based on Streitz (1985) [24]).

admission to the final exam [6]. The first versions of the two LD wireframes were slightly different (e.g., different icon language). One view showed a view that might be used in the content area of the LMS (Fig. 2, translated from German), the second view showed a view that might be used in the right sidebar of the LMS (Fig. 3, translated from German). Both are intended to help students stay organized and on track throughout their studies.

3.1 Wireframe for the Learning Dashboard in the Content Area

The wireframe LD for the content area of the LMS is designed to provide students with an intuitive interface for navigating their coursework. Key navigation features such as the complete program, term, and course overviews are prominently displayed at the top of the LD. In addition, cards with various elements such as exercises, course completion, learning goals, current term activities, and a "chance of success" score are included to provide students with an overview of their progress and upcoming assignments.

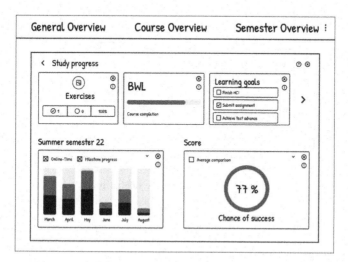

Fig. 2. Wireframe for the content area.

3.2 Wireframe for the Learning Dashboard in the Sidebar

The LD wireframe for the right sidebar area of the LMS is also designed to provide students with access to important information and resources in their learning process. The main navigation features, access to the complete study, semester and course overviews are displayed in a dropdown list at the top of the page. Below this are cards with various elements, such as a calendar with upcoming events, "learning activities", "learning organization" with possible learning partners, and a student progress indicator, to give students a comprehensive view of their schedule and progress [6].

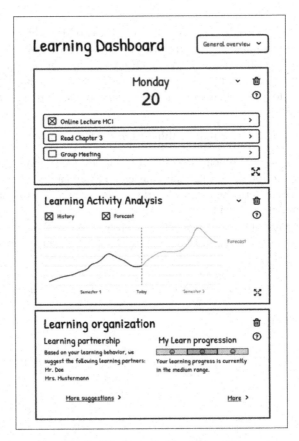

Fig. 3. Wireframe for the sidebar [6].

3.3 The Scope of the Study

1. **Evaluating the Gestalt Laws.** The first part of the task was to evaluate the Gestalt Laws mentioned above by asking them to list positive or negative examples of the current implementation of the elements. The Gestalt Laws to be examined were

proximity, similarity, closure, continuity, and good form. These were to be verified using the two wireframes provided [6].

2. **Identifying Factual and Interaction Problems.** In the second part of the task, the online students were asked to identify and validate the factual and interaction problems of the LD using the Streitz model (1985) [24]. For this purpose, the study participants were familiarized with the Streitz model. This theoretical model distinguishes between factual and interactional problems. Factual problems refer to the challenges that arise in performing a particular task, while interaction problems refer to the difficulties that users may experience when interacting with a system [2]. After being introduced to the Streitz model, participants were instructed to use the LD wireframes continuously throughout the task. They were encouraged to collect both quantitative and qualitative data. This included specific examples of problems they experienced as well as their thoughts and feelings while analyzing the wireframes. The data collected was then used as the basis for a detailed analysis of the factual and interaction problems associated with the current LD designs [6].

3. **Creating an Alternative Solution of a Card.** The third part was an optional bonus assignment. The students had to come up with an alternative solution for a card of their choice using the Gestalt Law of Proximity [6].

Scope of the Elaborations. As a result of this comprehensive analysis, a sizeable amount of student work was compiled into a 75-page (ISO 216 A4 specification) document of anonymized results. These findings, interpretations, and recommendations are a valuable resource for further research and improvement of the LD [6].

4   Results

The students' results were analyzed according to the topics of Gestalt Laws and factual and interaction problems. The different results of the Gestalt Laws are summarized and the factual and the interaction problems are grouped into appropriate categories. Finally, we show the students' drafts of how they would design and see a card in an LD for their online learning based on a Gestalt Law.

4.1   Evaluating the Gestalt Laws of the Content Area Wireframe (Fig. 2)

Gestalt Law of Proximity. The distance between cards is in different sizes. The positioning of the label "Course completion" cannot be assigned unambiguously and is therefore not clear and thus violates this Gestalt Law. Headings are not assignable, which does not allow an immediate order of titles. In addition, they are unevenly sized, which also violates the Gestalt Law of Proximity. The coloring of the headings in the overall, course, and semester views should be helpful in assigning each heading to its corresponding content according to this Gestalt Law and also the Gestalt Law of Closure. Arrows are perceived as a group and represent progress based on the Gestalt Law of Proximity. They are divided into areas that can be sorted into groups, but they do not follow horizontal lines on a line according to the Gestalt Law of Proximity.

Gestalt Law of Similarity. There were six things that the students noted about this rule, including inconsistent orientation and headings, different sizes of headings, inconsistent use of circles and curves for diagrams, and unclear labeling of elements. In particular, the last card in the first row ends before those in the second row. It is not clear which gray belongs to which element. Headings are also inconsistently implemented - sometimes they appear within the cards, sometimes they are missing (e.g., "BWL"). The captions vary in size, with some elements having larger or smaller captions than others. It is also mentioned that cards with similar shapes should be used for elements that have a similar structure or symbolism. The use of circles and curves as diagrams is inconsistent. The "Exercises" and "Learning Objectives" sections should also have a consistent layout, although a horizontal layout for "Exercises" and a vertical layout for "Learning Objectives" might be better.

Gestalt Law of Closure. It is suggested that the captions be integrated into the cards or displayed in separate sections for better clarity. Using color for the overarching navigation would help create a sense of unity and coherence. Headings could be integrated into the cards or displayed in their own sections so that they do not get lost on the page.

Gestalt Law of Good Continuation. The size of the cards is different and this can cause confusion in the grouping of the elements. It is suggested that the cards have a consistent size for better clarity. In the "Summer semester 22" card, there is a problem with the order of the elements, as the online time and milestone progress are not grouped correctly.

Gestalt Law of Good Form. In the "Score" card, a filled circle suggests 100% completion, when in fact it is only 77%. It is suggested that a simple circle be used instead. In addition, the "BWL" progress bar is unclear as to how the number of exams passed is calculated. The "Chance of Success" card should also include information about what it refers to.

4.2 Evaluating the Gestalt Laws of the Sidebar Wireframe (Fig. 3)

Gestalt Law of Proximity. There are three interaction elements (in the calendar card), but the arrow buttons are too far away from the text. There is also a problem with the "Learning organization" card, where there is no good spatial separation between longer texts and potential learning partners. The Calendar and Current Dates elements are perceived as separate entities because they are presented as separate sections, even though they are thematically related to the calendar. It's also unclear what the "more" link belongs to, whether it's for the entire element or just the arrow button.

Gestalt Law of Similarity. As in wireframe 1, headings are implemented inconsistently - sometimes they appear inside cards, sometimes they are missing (e.g., "Monday").

Gestalt Law of Closure. The "Learning organization" sections are not clearly separated from each other, and there is no clear structure or unity in the presentation of information. It is also mentioned here that it is important to have a clear separation between the text on the left and right (for ease of reading) by using a vertical line or other visual cue. If there are multiple learners, bullet points can be used instead of long text.

Gestalt Law of Good Continuation. In this area of the Gestalt Laws, it appears that the date is in the center of the card, with other information on the left. This can make it difficult for users to quickly understand the layout and find the information they are looking for. Consideration could be given to placing important elements, such as dates or headings, in a more prominent position and using visual cues, such as arrows or lines, to guide the user's eye through the layout. In addition, consider using clear and descriptive labels for each element to help users understand its purpose.

Gestalt Law of Good Form. Here, there may be some confusion about the order of events due to the centrally located icon for the current date. This could lead users to believe that this is the center of their studies, rather than simply a visual representation of the current day. To improve this, it could be considered to use different icons or colors to represent different dates and events, and to arrange them in chronological order to avoid confusion. Adding labels or captions to each icon could provide additional context and clarity for users.

4.3 Factual Problems

This assignment identified the following factual problems that affect the understandability and presentation of information. These challenges could be categorized into the four main categories listed below. This should help to better understand each of the problem areas and to develop targeted approaches to solving them:

Self-Assessment and Progress Tracking. Participants identified fundamental problems with self-assessment of progress. In particular, the unclear markings on the x-axis in the content area, such as "semester 1 and 3" and "today" for the "Learning Activity Analysis" card, contributed to confusion and affected the understanding of one's own learning progress. The interpretation of the "chance of success" card in the sidebar was also perceived as problematic, as at least one participant could not clearly determine which specific chance of success it referred to.

Visual Presentation and Information Structure. The visual design and information structure of various elements in the content area, such as the daily tasks and the to-do list, was another problem. A lack of month and year information in the daily tasks made it difficult to classify the tasks in terms of time. The daily structure of the to-do list was perceived as problematic as it could put pressure on the student to complete tasks on a daily basis. One participant suggested using a more neutral term such as "Next upcoming to-dos" to address this challenge.

Task Management and Information Preparation. This category includes the difficulties in using and displaying the "Tasks" card in the content area. In particular, it was unclear whether the display referred to a day, a week, or a semester. The lack of a temporal component confused the participants and prevented them from interpreting the meaning correctly. In addition, the placeholder graphic above the "Task" label led to confusion and information gaps because no specific function could be assigned to it.

Interpretation of Diagrams. There were also issues with interpreting and differentiating the diagrams in the two wireframes. These challenges resulted from a lack of color coding and unclear meaning of highlighted elements within the bar charts. Insufficient differentiation of the graphs and missing information on the y-axis was a significant barrier to understanding and correctly attributing the data presented.

4.4 Interaction Problems

The research also identified the following interaction problems that could affect usability [17]. These challenges range from difficulties with problems with the clarity and comprehensibility of features and information, to navigation and design issues, to usability on mobile devices. These four categories are explored in more detail below:

Clarity and Understandability of Features and Information. Participants expressed difficulty in identifying which view they were in. As a result, participants suggested that the current context - especially in the sidebar - be better highlighted to help users better understand their position within the application. Another issue was the lack of clarity about the different elements and their relationship to each other. For example, in the Content section, it was unclear to users how the "Tasks", "BWL", and "Learning Goals" cards related to each other and whether they belonged in the "Study Progress" section. Students also questioned whether the elements on the cards were interactive or just for information.

Navigation Issues. Orientation within the main navigation of both areas is a challenge. It is not always clear to the users which area of the application they are in. Participants suggested that the currently selected area should be better highlighted to help users navigate.

Design Issues There are certain design choices that created challenges for the students. In particular, the similarity of the cross and trash can icons and the question and question mark icons caused confusion. The similarity of the icons suggested to users that they had similar functions, which was not the case. In addition, the "Chance of Success" card caused confusion. It was unclear what the specific "chance of success" was supposed to represent. Secondly, the use of the term "score" and the lack of clarity about its origin and calculation posed an additional challenge.

Usability on Mobile Devices. While it was not the primary goal of the study to test the design for mobile usability, some students provided valuable information. It was noted that icons in a mobile view, both in the content area and in the sidebar, may be too small for comfortable use. This could lead to inaccurate input during touch interactions, which has a significant impact on the UX. The students recommended that the size of the icons be reviewed to ensure that they are visible and easy to use on mobile devices.

4.5 Bonus Task: Students Create an Alternative Solution to a Card of Their Choice Using the Gestalt Law of Proximity

Participants were asked to think of an alternative solution to a card based on the Gestalt Law of Proximity that they could imagine within the LD. 11 of the 24 individuals completed this additional task. Because some of the content was repetitive or did not show sufficient progress, some designs were excluded from further development. The selection criteria used to select the student designs are shown in Table 1.

Table 1. Inclusion and exclusion criteria for selecting student design submissions.

#	Inclusion Criteria	Exclusion Criteria
1	Significant improvement to existing design	No significant change in design
2	Concepts are not mixed together	Mixing two concepts (not goal-oriented)
3	No other Gestalt Laws broken	Other Gestalt Laws violated
4	Clarity in construction exists	Lack of clarity (e.g., listed contents are unclear)
5	New concept introduced	Repetition of approaches from other design concepts
6	Orientation on the implementation of the concept in the sense of wireframes	Advanced design (no wireframe)
7	New information provided	No new information
8	An existing wireframe was similar, but the design was significantly improved	Current design maintained

The resulting selection of student designs is shown in Table 2, which illustrates students' perceptions of such functionality, the elements and information included, and what aspects are important to them. These cards were designed by students for students to help them keep track of their progress and tasks using various visual elements such as calendars, to-do lists, buttons, and progress bars. The first design (Fig. 4) provides a calendar view of today's date and any relevant schedule or task information, while the second design (Fig. 5) places certain items in boxes to make them more visible as buttons and arranges them for better organization. The third design (Fig. 6) provides an overview of learning progress in a course, with each item displayed individually with a progress bar, a checkbox for comparison to the average, and a summary of all. This approach to the implementation of LD elements not only involved students in the design process, but also illustrates the benefits of involving students in the creation of rich, student-centered outcomes.

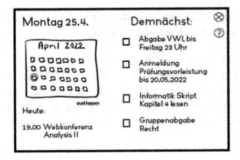

Fig. 4. Alternative solution 1.

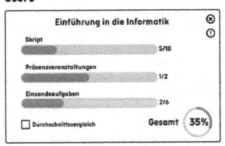

Fig. 5. Alternative solution 2.

Fig. 6. Alternative solution 3.

Table 2. A selection of student designs for an alternative solution to a card based on the Gestalt Law of Proximity.

#	Alternative solution	Short description
1	**Translation:** **Left column:** *Monday 25.4* *fold out* *Today:* *19.00 Analysis II web conference* **Right column:** *Upcoming:* *- VWL submission until Friday 11 p.m* *- Registration for exam until 20.05.2022* *- Read computer science script chapter 4* *- Group task law*	1. A short, time-oriented view using a calendar and a to-do list (a short, time-oriented view of the schedule and tasks) 2. Calendar view to enter appointments (a way to add today's date and any other relevant information about the schedule or tasks) 4. To-Do list for upcoming tasks 5. To-Do list structuring by priority or importance (ability to organize the list based on urgency)
2	**Translation (both cards):** *Pass HCI* *Obtain preliminary exam results* *Submit homework* **Button left:** *Add entry* **Button right:** *Delete entry*	The student's modification involves placing certain items in boxes to make them more visible as buttons, and arranging the boxes for better organization and clarity. It should increase clarity when checked and unchecked items are next to each other. Controls for intuitive use. Displayed in boxes to make items visible as buttons. Placed close together
3	**Translation:** *Introduction to Computer Science* *Script* *Face-to-face events* Submissions *Average comparison* *Total*	This design by a student shows an overview of the learning progress in a course. Each item that appears in the study is displayed individually with a progress bar. In this view the student can also see the total number of points for each of the sections "Script", "Face-to-face events" and "Submissions". A checkbox has been added for comparison to the average. At the bottom right, the progress of each item to date is totaled and displayed as a percentage. Progress is indicated by the amount of the darker colored edge of the circle. The percentage achieved is displayed inside the circle

5 Summary

The students analyzed two wireframes (Figs. 2 & 3) for possible violations of Gestalt laws, including proximity, similarity, closure and continuity, as well as factual and interactional problems. For Wireframe 1, the analysis of this evaluation identifies the following nine problems with the layout and labelling of elements in the wireframe, including inconsistent alignment, varying sizes of headings, unclear labeling. There should be a use of color to create unity and coherence, and a consistent use of circles and curves as diagrams. It also suggests that similar things should be grouped together and that elements should have consistent structures or symbolism to improve the overall design of the system. It also points out the Gestalt Law of closure, which states that elements that are close together tend to be grouped together, and suggests that labels be integrated into the cards for better clarity. For wireframe 2, these include elements that are too far apart or not clearly grouped, a lack of clear structure or unity, difficulty creating a logical flow, unclear labels for each element, and potential user confusion about the order of events.

For the factual and interaction problems, the results show that participants identified different challenges in the use of the dashboard. The difficulties identified can be primarily attributed to content deficiencies (factual problems) and user interaction challenges (interaction problems). The factual and interaction problems could be categorized into four categories. For the factual problems, these are: self-assessment and tracking progress, visual presentation and information structure, task management and information preparation, interpretation of diagrams, and for the interaction problems, these are: usability on mobile devices, clarity and understandability of features and information, navigation issues, design issues.

6 Discussion

The results show that the application of the Gestalt Laws [26] has brought up a number of points which are discussed below. With Fig. 2 in mind, a certain notion of how to improve the wireframe design and adhere to the perception of the LD can be made:

1. Proximity: To address proximity issues, elements should be placed closer together or properly aligned to create clear groups. This could include adjusting the layout of cards and labels to ensure that similar items are grouped together.
2. Similarity: To improve similarity, elements within the design system should have consistent visual relationships. This could include using a consistent size and shape for headings, aligning elements horizontally or vertically, and ensuring that symbols and structures are used consistently throughout the wireframe.
3. Closure: To address closure issues, elements that are close together should be grouped together. This could include incorporating labels into the cards or displaying them in separate cards for clarity. In addition, using color to create a sense of unity and coherence can help improve the overall design.
4. Continuity: To improve continuity, elements should be visually connected. This can include ensuring that card sizes are consistent and that items are grouped together in an intuitive manner. In addition, adjusting the layout or adding more visual cues such as arrows can help create a sense of flow and connection between different parts of the wireframe.
5. Good form: To improve good form, elements should be visually appealing and easy to understand. This might include using simple shapes and symbols that are easy to recognize, avoiding ambiguity in labeling, and ensuring that progress bars and other visual cues are clear and intuitive. In addition, providing more information about what certain elements represent can help improve understanding and clarity for the user.

With Fig. 3 in mind, considerations might include placing important elements in more prominent locations, using visual cues to guide the user's eye through the layout [25], using different icons or colors to represent dates and events, adding captions or labels to provide additional context, and organizing information chronologically to avoid confusion. Clearer overviews, clarification of how content elements fit together, space-saving solutions, and intuitive controls should improve clarity and usability [17]. Color differentiation and the separation of time spent online from progress, for example, contribute to the clarity and comprehension of the information presented.

The results of the bonus assignment presented three alternative designs for a card that supports self-regulation in online learning. Each design has its own unique features and benefits. The first design includes a calendar view that displays today's date and any relevant schedule or task information. This feature is useful for students who need to keep track of their assignments and deadlines. The second design places certain items in boxes to make them more visible as buttons. Organizing items in this way can help students better understand and navigate their learning materials. In addition, displaying these items prominently on a card can serve as a helpful reminder for students to stay on track with their studies. Finally, the third design provides an overview of progress within a course. Each item is displayed individually with its own progress bar, allowing students to easily monitor their progress and identify areas where they may need additional support or resources. The inclusion of a checkbox for comparison to the average can also be helpful in identifying potential gaps or weaknesses in a student's understanding of the material. Overall, these three designs offer different approaches that could support self-regulation in online learning. Each has its own strengths and may be more appropriate depending on the individual needs and preferences of each student.

The analysis identified critical aspects that have an impact on the UX and the comprehensibility of the application under study in the main problem areas of the factual problems and the interaction problems. Among the factual problems, it was found that users had difficulties in evaluating their progress and success. This underlines the need to make progress and success indicators more transparent and intuitive. In addition, the visual presentation and information structure was found to be confusing and non-intuitive, indicating a need for better explanation and standardization of illustrations. In addition, problems were identified with task management, information presentation, and chart interpretation. These findings suggest that the use of clear timing, better defined color coding and markings, and consistent presentation standards could improve the comprehensibility and usability of the application.

In terms of interaction problems, the potential usability on mobile devices was identified as critical. To optimize the UX on these devices, icon sizes could be adjusted to minimize input errors [14]. In addition, problems related to the clarity and comprehensibility of functions and information were identified. Improved visual highlighting of the current context and clearer representations of the relationships between different elements could help improve user comprehension and orientation [18]. It was also noted that the navigational structure could be improved to facilitate orientation and optimize the UX. Finally, design issues were identified that point to potential misunderstandings regarding the use of symbols and icons. Revising these elements could contribute to a more intuitive UX.

At this early stage in the development of the LD, it was identified that there were key issues with the wireframe design. These issues were discovered through the eyes, understanding, and sometimes feelings of the users who would be using the dashboard in the future. This gave us valuable insight into how to deal with the LD we were developing. The additional design sketches involved the students in the design process. We gained an understanding of how students would like to see the cards of an LD designed to meet their needs. This allows us to develop an LD that will be adopted and used.

Overall, our findings suggest that targeted revisions to both the visual and interactive aspects of the application could significantly improve the UX and comprehensibility. However, these revisions should always take into account the specific needs and preferences of the target audience.

References

1. Beard, L.A., Harper, C.: Student perceptions of online versus on campus instruction. Education **122**, 658–663 (2002)
2. Benda, H.V.: Sachproblem, Interaktionsproblem und die Rolle des Benutzers. Kognitive Aspekte der Mensch-Computer-Interaktion (1984)
3. Chang, D., Dooley, L., Tuovinen, J.E.: Gestalt theory in visual screen design—a new look at an old subject (2002)
4. De Silva, L.M.H., Chounta, I.A., Rodríguez-Triana, M.J., Roa, E.R., Gramberg, A., Valk, A.: Toward an Institutional analytics agenda for addressing student dropout in higher education: an academic stakeholders' perspective. J. Learn. Anal. **9**(2), 179–201 (2022)
5. Diaz, D.P.: Online drop rate revisited. Extending Pedagogy Threaded-Topic Disc. **2002**(1) (2002). https://www.learntechlib.org/p/96381/. Accessed 8 May 2023
6. Drzyzga, G., Harder, T.: Student-centered development of an online software tool to provide learning support feedback: a design-study approach (2022)
7. Drzyzga, G., Harder, T., Janneck, M.: Cognitive effort in interaction with software systems for self-regulation - an eye-tracking study. In: Harris, D., Li, WC. (eds.) Engineering Psychology and Cognitive Ergonomics. HCII 2023. Lecture Notes in Computer Science, vol. 14017. Springer, Cham (2023). https://doi.org/10.1007/978-3-031-35392-5_3
8. Farahmand, A., Dewan, M.A.A., Lin, F.: Student-facing educational dashboard design for online learners, pp. 345–349 (2020). https://doi.org/10.1109/DASC-PICom-CBDCom-Cyb erSciTech49142.2020.00067
9. Fernandez Nieto, G.M., Kitto, K., Buckingham Shum, S., Martínez-Maldonado, R.: Beyond the learning analytics dashboard: alternative ways to communicate student data insights combining visualisation, narrative and storytelling. In: LAK22: 12th International Learning Analytics and Knowledge Conference, pp. 219–229 (2022)
10. Few, S.: Information Dashboard Design: Displaying Data for At-a-Glance Monitoring, vol. 5. Analytics Press, Burlingame (2013)
11. Getto, B., Hintze, P., Kerres, M.: (Wie) Kann Digitalisierung zur Hochschulentwicklung beitragen?, pp. 13–25 (2018). https://doi.org/10.25656/01:16983
12. Graham, L.: Gestalt theory in interactive media design. J. Humanities Social Sci. **2**(1) (2008)
13. Janneck, M., Merceron, A., Sauer, P.: In Companion Proceedings of the 11th Learning Analytics and Knowledge Conference (LAK 2021), Workshop on Addressing Dropout Rates in Higher Education, Online – Everywhere, pp. 261–269 (2021)
14. Lindberg, T., Näsänen, R.: The effect of icon spacing and size on the speed of icon processing in the human visual system. Displays **24**(3), 111–120 (2003). https://doi.org/10.1016/S0141-9382(03)00035-0

15. Marcus, A., Abromowitz, S., Abulkhair, M.F.: Design, User Experience, and Usability. Springer, Heidelberg (2013)
16. Mazumder, F.K., Das, U.K.: Usability guidelines for usable user interface. Int. J. Res. Eng. Technol. 3(9), 79–82 (2014). https://doi.org/10.15623/ijret.2014.0309011
17. Nielsen, J.: Usability inspection methods. In: Conference Companion on Human Factors in Computing Systems, pp. 413–414 (1994)
18. Norman, D.A.: The Design of Everyday Things (Revised and Expanded Edition). Basic Books, New York (2013)
19. Notess, M.: Usability, user experience, and learner experience. Elearn 2001(8), 3 (2001)
20. Petrie, H., Bevan, N.: The evaluation of accessibility, usability, and user experience. Univ. Access Handbook 1, 1–16 (2009)
21. Pintrich, P.R.: The role of goal orientation in self-regulated learning. In Handbook of Self-Regulation, pp. 451–502. Academic Press (2000). https://doi.org/10.1016/B978-012109890-2/50043-3
22. Prenkaj, B., Velardi, P., Stilo, G., Distante, D., Faralli, S.: A survey of machine learning approaches for student dropout prediction in online courses. ACM Comput. Surv. (CSUR) 53(3), 1–34 (2020)
23. Rock, I., Palmer, S.: The legacy of gestalt psychology. Sci. Am. 263(6), 84–91 (1990)
24. Streitz, N.: Die Rolle von mentalen und konzeptuellen Modellen in der Mensch-Computer-Interaktion: Konsequenzen für die Software-Ergonomie? Software-Erqonomie 85, 280–292 (1985). ISBN: 3-519-02443-8
25. Watzman, S.: Visual design principles for usable interfaces. In: The Human-Computer Interaction Handbook: Fundamentals, Evolving Technologies and Emerging Applications, pp. 263–285 (2003)
26. Wertheimer, M.: Untersuchungen zur lehre von der Gestalt. Psychologische Forschung 1(1), 47–58 (1922). https://doi.org/10.1007/BF00410385

Easy Induction: A Serious Game Using Participatory Design

Yuwen Li, Yue Li(✉), Jiachen Liang, and Hai-Ning Liang

School of Advanced Technology, Xi'an Jiaotong-Liverpool University, 111 Ren'ai Road,
Suzhou, China
{yuwen.li17,jiachen.liang21}@student.xjtlu.edu.cn,
{yue.li,haining.liang}@xjtlu.edu.cn

Abstract. College freshmen often face difficulties adjusting to the new academic and social environment of university life. It is critical to help them adapt to academic and personal life, while also improving their sense of belonging and engagement with the university. In this paper, we focus on the context of an international joint venture university, Xi'an Jiaotong-Liverpool University (XJTLU), and present a participatory design approach to identify potential solutions collaboratively. We conducted three participatory design workshops with freshmen in undergraduate and postgraduate studies, where we discovered specific challenges, developed serious game content and design alternatives, and delivered a board game that supports academic and social integration at XJTLU. To evaluate the effectiveness of the board game, we collected both quantitative and qualitative data. The quantitative analysis revealed that the board game is effective in improving freshmen's knowledge acquisition of academic affairs, increasing their familiarity with the environment and resources, and enhancing their ability to access information and resources. The board game also received high scores in system usability and user experience. The qualitative analysis indicated that the board game was engaging, interesting, and well-received by students. They found the board game helpful in their academic and social integration and expressed a desire to play it again in the future. Our participatory design approach and the resulting board game provide a promising avenue for universities to support freshmen's transition to university life.

Keywords: Serious games · Participatory design · Interaction design

1 Introduction

Getting adapted to university life is a significant process for freshmen and closely relates to their overall experience and learning in the university. However, many college freshmen struggle to adjust to their first-year life at university during the transition from high school to college, finding it hard to adapt themselves to the new environment [24]. It has been proven that a stronger sense of presence and engagement in the university can positively impact academic achievement and self-identity, as well as reduce problematic behavior [21]. Therefore, it is essential to help college freshmen adapt to the new environment and improve their campus engagement to increase their campus experience and

ⓒ The Author(s), under exclusive license to Springer Nature Switzerland AG 2023
H. P. da Silva and P. Cipresso (Eds.): CHIRA 2023, CCIS 1997, pp. 192–211, 2023.
https://doi.org/10.1007/978-3-031-49368-3_12

personal achievement. This study focuses on an international joint venture university, Xi'an Jiaotong-Liverpool University (XJTLU) and aims to understand freshmen's campus experience and the issues that they are encountering. XJTLU has executed many online and offline activities, such as information sessions for freshmen, campus tours, an E-journey system, and social media engagement, etc. Despite the variety, some freshmen are not motivated to attend the activities and are still unfamiliar with the university resources. Therefore, this study aims to create a more effective and engaging induction system or product to support freshmen to fit into the university environment.

Initial research was conducted by studying related works and interviewing stakeholders, including freshmen students, senior students, and university advisors. Four general problems were identified: 1) unfamiliarity with the university environment and places; 2) unfamiliarity with academic affairs; 3) lack of ability to search and filter information; 4) lack of engagement in social activities. To address the aforementioned issues, we need to identify an effective and engaging approach to help freshmen learn about the campus environment and academic affairs, the ways to search for information, and increase social interaction. Tabibian et al. [27] found that spaced repetition is a successful technique to enhance memorization efficiency and strengthen long-term memory. A repetitive activity with an engaging and interactive format could be a potential solution for freshmen to adapt better to college life. Serious games, designed for educational purposes and behavior modification, have been used for knowledge learning and skill training [20]. Thus, developing a serious game will provide an entertaining way for freshmen to learn about XJTLU and improve their sense of campus engagement. With a high degree of acceptance among college students, multiplayer board games are a popular form of serious games and can be played in various settings such as class meetings, round table discussions, or small gatherings of friends. Playing board games is also a social activity in nature. Therefore, a serious board game is a suitable approach for freshmen to acquire university related knowledge while having fun. Some gamification mechanisms, such as team competitions and the discussion of game strategies, can increase communication and interaction among players while improving their understanding of the university and their sense of belonging.

In this paper, we present a serious game design that facilitates freshmen in their transition to university life and enhances students' sense of engagement and belonging. To achieve this goal, we conducted participatory design workshops to understand user requirements at an early stage of the design process. The results of this research showed the efficiency of our serious game design, Easy Induction, in supporting students to learn about the university environment, academic affairs, and information access. The evaluation also showed a satisfying usability and user experience of the system. Our research promotes further exploration and innovation in the domain of education and entertainment, contributing to the future design for knowledge acquisition and engaging user experiences.

2   Background and Related Work

2.1   Adaption Challenges for University Freshmen

In the context of university education, the transition from high school to college represents a critical period for freshmen to adapt to their new academic and social environments. Despite its importance, previous research suggested that many college freshmen experience difficulties adjusting to university life [1,5,24]. Challenges encountered by new students include increased academic demands, greater freedom, and reduced academic structure. As such, adjusting to the new environment is often the most common problem encountered by freshman students. Marshall et al. [16] identified a range of factors that can influence the transition from high school to university, including academic, social, and emotional components. Students' sense of belonging in the academic environment has also been found to be a significant factor contributing to their overall experience and success [9]. Midgley et al. [18] suggested that positive outcomes result when changes in students' needs are aligned with changes in opportunities, whereas negative consequences may arise when this alignment is lacking. Similarly, Tinto [29] proposed that managing both the social and academic aspects of the new environment is crucial for freshmen to adjust successfully to college. However, since freshmen enrollment conditions vary from university to university, it is hard to obtain a universal solution. Therefore, investigating specific adjusting methods of freshmen at a university is of significant importance.

2.2   Participatory Design

Participatory design is a process and strategy that involves users and customers in the design process, enabling stakeholders, designers, and end-users to contribute to the design process, ensuring that the final product meets the users' requirements [12,25]. Participatory design considers co-research and co-design as crucial elements of the process [22], where the researcher or designer draws conclusions together with the user. In participatory design workshops, the participants will be encouraged to think about opportunities or situations where they feel things might be different, using a journey map [3]. Through the co-design process of the designer and participants, hidden opportunities and potential design value can be discovered [15]. Case studies had shown that insights into problems can be found through participatory design and participatory research [8]. Despite the effectiveness of the participatory design workshop as a research and co-design method, few studies have focused on university students. This study intends to employ the participatory design method by facilitating participatory design workshops with stakeholders to explore the possibilities of freshmen induction.

2.3   Serious Game Design

Serious games have become increasingly popular in recent years due to their potential to educate while entertaining [26]. These games are designed with a specific educational purpose in mind, whether it be to teach students about history, science, math, or any other subject [30]. In the field of education, serious games have been used to make difficult or boring topics more engaging for students and to help them better retain information [7]. One of the key factors in creating a successful serious game is finding the right balance between game elements and educational content. This means that the game must be both entertaining and educational in order to be effective [11,31]. In other words, the game should be fun enough to keep players engaged, while also conveying important information or teaching them new skills.

Players were rarely consulted in early stage game designs, but a growing number of game designers have begun to combine participatory design workshops with game design sessions [10]. For example, Tan et al. [28] designed a serious game for children to develop their social skills. When children were invited to play an early prototype, they provided a wealth of information used to improve the game. Similarly, Mazzone et al. [17] invited young people to participate in the design of a game for improving the emotional intelligence of adolescents. Danielsson and Wiberg [6] were inspired by this modality to design a learning game for adolescents on gender identity. Lukosch et al. [14] developed an immersive virtual training environment to improve users' situational awareness skills. Based on the game feedback, the participatory design approach resulted in a meaningful experience for the users.

Thus, by developing a serious game in collaboration with participants in participatory design workshops, it may be possible to create an engaging and effective solution for helping freshmen adapt to university life. The game could be designed to address a variety of challenges, such as managing time, navigating campus, developing study habits, and building social connections. By involving stakeholders, designers, and end-users in the design process, the final product can be tailored to meet the specific needs of freshmen and help them succeed in their academic and personal lives.

3   Methodology

Based on the preliminary research, the study attempts to address four design goals (DGs). Achieving these design goals will facilitate freshmen's adaptation to the university.

DG1: To help freshmen get familiar with the campus environment and places.

DG2: To help with freshmen's knowledge acquisition about the university academic affairs.

DG3: To help freshmen develop a sense of well-being and belonging.

DG4: To help improve freshmen's abilities to access information and resources.

3.1   Double Diamond Model

The Double Diamond Model provides a framework for our design process. The model's essence is to solve problems and find solutions in the design structure, which is applicable to our serious game design. Its main focus is to *"design the right thing"* and *"design things right"* [4]. The model has four stages: Discover, Define, Develop, and Deliver. These stages can serve as a map for designers to organize their ideas and improve the creative design process.

In the first stage, *Discover*, preliminary online research and stakeholder interviews were conducted to gain insights into general problems faced by university freshmen during their adaptation process. The obtained data was then filtered in the second stage, *Define*, to identify the core contradictions underlying the phenomenon. The first participatory design workshop was held to achieve this goal. In the third stage, *Develop*, the actual design process began and the second participatory design workshop was conducted to generate potential solutions by co-designing with stakeholders based on the findings from the first two stages. In the final stage, *Deliver*, the third participatory design workshop was conducted to evaluate and select the most suitable solution through a process of design, testing, evaluation, and iteration conducted over three rounds.

3.2 Participatory Design Workshop

We conducted three participatory design workshops, run by a primary researcher and a facilitator. The first workshop serves to verify the initial research findings and to gain deeper insights into user requirements. The workshop took the form of a focus group, where participants discussed four workshop questions related to the four design goals. We gathered qualitative data on freshmen's behaviors, feelings, and attitudes toward XJTLU and filtered these requirements into specific design goals.

In the second workshop, we focused on ideation and development. Participants and researchers brainstormed and co-designed initial concepts, created rough prototypes, and worked on several possible solutions while considering their respective advantages and disadvantages. Low-fidelity prototypes were evaluated in the workshop, and participants voted for the most suitable concept.

The third workshop aimed to deliver the concept into a real product and to test, evaluate, and iterate the design. Through the three rounds of participatory design workshops, a final product was produced and delivered.

4   Participatory Design of the Serious Game

We present the design process of the serious game in this section, structured by the three participatory design workshops in sequential order. Each workshop will detail the study design, participants, procedures, and results. The aim is to provide a comprehensive overview of the design process and illustrate how the project progressed through active involvement and collaboration with the users. Since the researcher could influence users' engagement level in the design process [13], the participatory design workshops were held in an organized way, following a clear procedure structure and prepared scripts.

4.1   First Participatory Design Workshop: Discover and Define

Study Design. The first participatory design workshop aimed to identify the challenges faced by freshmen during their adaptation process and explore potential solutions through intense brainstorming and discussions. Based on the focus group methodology, this workshop utilized a qualitative research approach to uncover insights into the adaptation process of freshmen. We followed the focus group guidelines [19] to define the purpose, select participants, facilitate a conversation, and summarize the findings.

Participants. Given the project's objective of improving the adapting experience of XJTLU freshmen, the workshop participants comprised Year 1 undergraduate and postgraduate students. We sent out recruitment flyers online via social media, which ran for a week, and a total of 20 volunteers (8 undergraduate students and 12 master students) signed up for the activity. The undergraduates aged between 18 and 19 (M = 18.25, SD = 0.21). The postgraduate aged between 21 and 26 (M = 23.08, SD = 1.90). We thus had two groups of four undergraduate students and two groups of six postgraduate students.

Procedure. The workshop lasted about 60 min and was divided into four sections.
(1) Introduction and Warm-up. The first section involved a 5-min warm-up, where the researcher welcomed the participants, explained the workshop's purpose and procedures, and collected informed consent.
(2) Brainstorming. The second section was a 20-min brainstorming activity. The researcher proposed four questions[1] about the participants' experiences at XJTLU, from the general to the specific.

The researchers wrote the questions on a whiteboard to cultivate an active brainstorming atmosphere and encourage more ideas. Participants were given 3 min and encouraged to write down their answers on sticky notes, after which the researchers then collected the notes and moved on to the next question. To keep the focus group organized and clear, a script was prepared to guide the brainstorming session, emphasizing that participants were free to share all their ideas without judgments or comments. All verbal instructions were given by the primary researcher in a consistent way.
(3) Classification. After the brainstorming session, the participants and the researcher spent 15 min working together to put the sticky notes onto the whiteboard under their respective categories. We encouraged them to group similar keywords together to identify recurring trends.
(4) Discussion. Once the sticky notes were classified, the participants engaged in a 20-min open discussion about the four brainstorming questions.

Results. We transcribed the texts on sticky notes and used Excel to categorize the problems and determine their frequency. The outcomes confirmed the validity of our

---

[1] Workshop questions:

Q1: Generally, how do you feel about your academic and social life at XJTLU?
Q2: Did you encounter any issues when adapting to the campus environment (DG1), academic affairs (DG2), and social life (DG3)? Can you give some examples?
Q3: Are there any happy moments that you can think of at XJTLU? Can you give some examples (DG3)?
Q4: Where do you seek information about the university? How do you use university resources (DG4)?

four design goals and offered valuable insights into the design solutions. The workshop helped us gain a better understanding of the difficulties that freshmen face when adapting to college life, and several potential solutions have been identified. We summarize the key lessons learned from this workshop in response to the four design goals.

1. Introduce maps and buildings to help freshmen navigate the campus. Participants (N = 9) found the abbreviated names of buildings difficult to memorize and recognize.
2. Survival guides (e.g. late submission penalty calculation) (N = 5) and tips about academic affairs (e.g. how to book a discussion room) (N = 10) are useful and needed, but largely unknown.
3. The happy moments are related to the participation in social activities (e.g. board game) (N = 7), campus activities (e.g. buddy programme) (N = 5), student club activities (e.g. arts and sports) (N = 13), awards and achievements (e.g. winning a scholarship or championship) (N = 8), and their time spent with their friends and classmates (N = 9).
4. Many freshmen were not aware of some official accounts on social media that provide easy access to university information (N = 11), and did not realize the importance of checking their university E-mail.

4.2   Second Participatory Design Workshop: Develop

Study Design. During the second participatory design workshop, we transitioned from the initial requirements phase to the design phase. We invited five freshmen (3 males and 2 females), aged between 18 and 19 (M = 18.40, SD = 0.30) to engage in cooperative design for potential solutions based on the data collected in previous workshops.

Procedure. The second workshop lasted about 90 min and was divided into three sections: (1) Introduction, (2) Map Drawing, and (3) Discussion.
(1) Introduction. During this section, we introduced the results from the first workshop to the participants. In addition, the researcher explained the purpose and procedures of this workshop, and collected informed consent. This part lasted for around 10 min.
(2) Map Drawing. To clearly understand the actions and patterns of freshmen and to spot similar activities and events, we arranged a 10-min session for participants to map out their daily routes on the XJTLU campus map (see Fig. 1a–c). Then, we invited them to describe their daily lives based on their routes and locations for around 25 min.
(3) Discussion. The discussion lasted for 45 min. We superimposed the potential solutions proposed in the first workshop onto the map and invited participants to add more ideas related to the map in terms of the physical environment, academic affairs, social activities, and information access of XJTLU. Finally, we categorized different kinds of events with color codes, and summarized different forms of game solutions (see Fig. 1d–e).

Results. After the Map Drawing section, we gained some information about the participants' campus life. For example, most of the participants had lectures to attend in

Fig. 1. Second participatory design workshop. Participants (a) drawing routes on the university map, (b) discussing their daily lives based on the routes and locations, (c) routes drawn by participants, (d) notes of questions, events, and tips about the physical environment, academic affairs, and (e) exploration on various forms of game solutions.

the Foundation Building (FB) and the Science Building (SA, SB, SC, SD) (as shown in Fig. 1c). This information could be considered in the subsequent game design. Moreover, participants confirmed the importance of the WeChat official account to provide tips on accessing information, the necessity for students to use email, and the feasibility of using board games as a medium to deliver faculty information—WeChat is the most popular instant messaging and social media network application. Participants agreed that board games promote engagement and communication among players. Thus, we ultimately chose to use a board game to better help students be familiar with the campus environment, including building locations and facility usage.

During the Discussion section, we explored two map design alternatives for connecting buildings and creating game routes. We compared two forms of routes and spots and ultimately chose the second form, as it was reported to reflect the events on the map in a visually simplistic way, allowing the placement of activities and questions next to the relevant buildings with more flexibility and regularity. We also explored two ways of game control: spinning a wheel and rolling a dice. Compared to spinning a wheel, participants preferred to move to points set up on the route by rolling a dice. This allowed users to have interactions around the buildings and maintain a sense of uncertainty.

The mechanics setup for this game was based on the possible solutions from the first workshop and was supplemented in the second workshop. The specific extension process of the game mechanics has been demonstrated in Fig. 2. The events and activities identified by participants were grouped into *Question* and *Event* on the map, highlighted in green and orange, respectively. In addition, the discussion showed that the happy moments and survival guides can be categorized by their emotion states, where the positive events (e.g. winning a scholarship) were included in the *Chance* cards, and the negative events (losing the student ID card) were included in the *Accident* cards. Based on the above results, we came up with the initial design of the board game, Easy Induction: XJTLU Adventure for Freshmen. The format of the game is similar to the *Monopoly*[2], where 3–8 players will be divided into two groups, each group will work together to gain or lose credits and building cards via various actions throughout the game. The first group to collect all the building cards wins.

Overall, the second participatory workshop allowed us to define the problems and develop an initial design to solve the problems. It yielded results in following:

---

[2] https://en.wikipedia.org/wiki/Monopoly-(game).

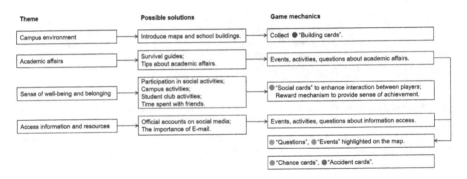

Fig. 2. Game mechanics extended from possible solutions of design goals.

1. Since participants agreed that board games could promote their engagement, we decided to incorporate a board game into XJTLU.
2. Building on the results of the first workshop, we expanded the related content about academic affairs, social activities, and information access, and developed the game mechanics.
3. Based on the information added by the participants, we finalized the map and route design, and identified three types of cards (*Social*, *Chance*, and *Accident*) and two types of activities (*Event* and *Question*).
4. A low-fidelity prototype was created based on the results obtained so far.

4.3   Third Participatory Design Workshop: Deliver

In the third participatory design workshop, we focused on testing, evaluating, and iterating the game design, with a specific emphasis on delivery. This workshop included a series of short discussions with stakeholders, who evaluated the prototype design and provided suggestions.

Evaluating the Low-Fidelity Prototype. We invited four participants (3 males, 1 female, aged between 18–22, M = 19.25, SD = 3.58) to test a low-fidelity prototype produced by the second workshop. Participants suggested that the annotations on the map appeared disorganized (P1, P2, P3, P4), and the annotations reduced the sense of surprise and randomness of the game (P2, P4). Therefore, we decided to move the annotations to a script held by the game host.

Improving the Low-Fidelity Prototype. According to the user feedback, we proposed two types of map spots with accompanying scripts. Map spots of different colors trigger different actions. The blue, red, orange, and green spots represent the drawing of a *Chance* card and an *Accident* card, and the encountering of an *Event* and a *Question*, respectively. The white spots do not trigger any action. In *Type A*, each spot was assigned a unique number. As for *Type B*, on the other hand, we only assigned numbers to spots of *Event* and *Question*, and mapped them to the host scripts.

Evaluating the Improved Low-Fidelity Prototype. For the two types of spot and script forms, we invited six participants (3 male, 3 female, aged between 18–21, M = 18.83, SD = 1.34) to conduct another user test. The results showed that *Type B* was preferred because of its simplicity and clarity. The cluttered numbers in *Type A* confused participants, who tended to follow the numbers consecutively, even though they could move in any direction. However, participants were also confused when they saw identical numbers in different colors in *Type B*. To address this issue, we replaced the numbers on the *Question* spots with letters to distinguish them from the *Event* spots.

Developing the Mid-Fidelity Prototype. Based on the results from the two workshops and the participant feedback in the iterative evaluations, we improved the design and produced a mid-fidelity prototype with enhanced game content, including cards, events, and extended maps. 5 participants (3 male, 2 female, aged between 18–21, M = 18.80, SD = 1.70) evaluated the mid-fidelity prototype and confirmed that the content in the game design was clear and easy to understand. They only suggested that the visual appearance of the map and the cards need to be improved.

5 Design Outcome: Easy Induction

5.1 Game Presentations

The final map design was optimized for visual appeal (see Fig. 3a) The visual effects of the mid-fidelity prototype's cards were also optimized (see Fig. 3b–d). Graphical design in a flat style was also utilized for the buildings (see Fig. 3e). The final prototype of game board, cards, and accessories brought visual aesthetic experience to users (see Fig. 3f–i). The game board was made of KT board, with a size of 841 mm × 594 mm. The building pieces were made of wood. The total cost of the board game was around 20 USD.

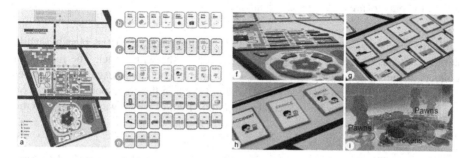

Fig. 3. Digital graphics view of the (a) map, (b) social cards, (c) accident cards, (d) chance cards. Photos of physical prototype showing the (e) building cards, (f) game board with accessories, (g) building cards, (h) Accident, Chance, and Social cards, and (i) pawns and tokens.

Some participants gave suggestions that it would be more cheering if there was a celebration session at the end of the game, using emerging technology such as

Augmented Reality (AR). Therefore, we combined AR at the end of our game. Upon completion of the game, players who collect all building cards can exchange their paper cards for wooden building pieces and place them in their corresponding locations on the map. They can then use their smartphones to scan the map and view the celebratory AR effects (see Fig. 4).

Fig. 4. AR celebration at the end of the game could provide a sense of achievement and a celebratory game atmosphere.

5.2 Rules of Easy Induction

Players. The game can include 3–8 players. Every player receives 10 tokens at the beginning. One player can act as the host to lead the game and give instructions. The rest of the players are divided into 2 teams.

Objective. Players' objective is to collect all building cards as fast as possible while earning tokens. If anyone loses all the tokens, he or she will be out. The team who collects all building cards first will win. The winning team could exchange the paper cards of the buildings on wooden boards and put them in the corresponding places on the map. This will trigger the AR celebration, the effect of which was unknown to the players.

Equipment. The equipment consists of a board, a dice, several pawns and tokens (see Fig. 3i). There are 7 Chance cards, 7 Accident cards, 8 Social (interaction) cards, and 19 Building cards.

Preparation. Place the board on a table and put the Chance cards, Accident cards, and Social cards face down on their allotted spaces on the board. Each player chooses one pawn to represent them and move on the board.

Rules. On each turn, the active player rolls the dice and moves their pawns to the same number of spots. When there is more than one way to go, the player can choose the direction freely.

Building. Players can gain the building cards when they stop in buildings.

Event. When they stop on orange spots, the host will read the instruction according to the script, in which the player may gain or lose tokens depending on the event.

Question. When players stop on green spots, they have to answer the question, if correct, they can win one token; otherwise, they will lose one token.

Chance. When players stop on blue spots, they should draw a Chance card. The player may collect extra tokens or win a building card. For example, *"Gained scholarship, +3 tokens"*; *"Participated in club activity, +1 token"*; and *"Lucky guy, you can win a building card"*.

Accident. When players stop on red spots, they should draw an Accident card. The player may lose their tokens or get a penalty. For example, *"You lost your ID card, –1 token"*; and *"You got lost in the building, pause for one turn"*.

Social. When two or more players stop at the same spot, they should draw a Social card and discuss the given topic. For example, *"Talk about your favorite sport/ music/ book"*.

6 Evaluating Easy Induction

6.1 Study Design

We evaluate the serious game in three aspects: knowledge acquisition, usability, and user experience. Pretest and post-test questionnaires were applied to measure participants' knowledge acquisition. The System Usability Scale (SUS) [2] was applied to measure the system usability of the game. The User Experience Questionnaire (UEQ) [23] was applied to measure user experience from six dimensions: attractiveness, perspicuity, efficiency, dependability, stimulation, and novelty. A total of 14 students from XJTLU (9 males and 5 females) participated in the user evaluation and we coded them from P1 to P14, including 6 freshmen and 8 junior students. Their ages are ranged from 18 to 25 ($M = 20.29$, $SD = 4.68$).

6.2 Experimental Procedure

The evaluation procedure starts with the study briefing and a pretest questionnaire, followed by a gameplay session with instructions from the researcher, and a post-test questionnaire and debriefing. Participants were encouraged to provide their comments and suggestions during the post-tests. The experiment lasted for about 50 min on average.

6.3 Measures and Scoring

Pre-Test and Post-Test. The pre-test consisted of 15 questions. There were 5 questions related to the university's physical environment (e.g. *"Where is the university museum?"*); 5 questions related to academic affairs (e.g. *"What will happen if you submit your coursework late?"*), and 5 questions related to information access (e.g. *"How to make an appointment for counseling service?"*). The same questions were asked again after the gameplay in the post-test. For each question, participants scored 2 marks if correct, 1 mark if partially correct, and 0 marks if they did not know the answer or provided a wrong answer.

System Usability Scale (SUS). The SUS includes ten questions rated on a 5-point Likert scale, ranging from 1 (Strongly Disagree) to 5 (Strongly Agree). Following the scoring procedure suggested in [2], we get a score ranging from 0–100, where a SUS score above 68 is considered above average, and anything below 68 is below average.

User Experience Questionnaire (UEQ). The UEQ measures the user experience of a system or product's attractiveness, pragmatic quality (efficiency, perspicuity, and dependability), and hedonic quality (stimulation and novelty). It includes 26 items, rated from –3 (horribly bad) to 3 (extremely good). Values between –0.8 and 0.8 represent a neural evaluation of the corresponding scale, values greater than 0.8 represent a positive evaluation, and values smaller than –0.8 represent a negative evaluation.

7   Results

Data collected from the evaluation study was analyzed in this section. It comprises three parts: participants' knowledge acquisition before and after the experiment, the system usability scale, and the user experience questionnaire.

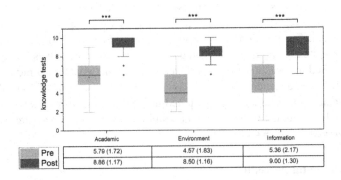

Fig. 5. Box plots and means (with standard deviations) for the comparison of pre-test and post-test. $***p < 0.001$.

7.1 Knowledge Acquisition

We calculated participants' scores on knowledge tests related to the physical environment, academic affairs, information access, and the total scores before and after playing the board game. We conducted Shapiro-Wilk tests to assess the normal distribution of data. For normally distributed data, paired-samples T-tests were conducted to identify significant differences (see Fig. 5).

Physical Environment. Results from the Shapiro-Wilk test indicated that both environment pre-test ($W = 0.920, p > 0.05$) and environment post-test ($W = 0.909, p > 0.05$) were normally distributed. Paired-samples tests demonstrated a significant improvement in participants' knowledge acquisition of the environment before and after playing the board game ($t(13) = -6.577, p < 0.05$), with a higher mean score in the post-test. These findings suggest that the serious board game significantly enhanced freshmen's familiarity with the environment and locations of XJTLU.

Academic Affairs. Shapiro-Wilk test revealed that academic pre-test ($W = 0.944, p > 0.05$) conformed to the normal distribution. However, the data of academic post-test ($W = 0.801, p < 0.05$) was not normally distributed. Thus, related-samples Wilcoxon signed rank test was used to analyze the data. The results in Fig. 5 showed a significant difference in the participants' knowledge acquisition of academic affairs between before and after playing the board game ($z = 3.190, p = 0.001$). Moreover, the mean of post-test was significantly higher than the pre-test. The results indicate that the serious board game effectively enhanced freshmen's understanding of XJTLU's academic affairs.

Information Access. The normality test indicated that the data of information pre-test ($W = 0.916, p > 0.05$) conformed to normal distribution, whereas the data of information post-test ($W = 0.790, p < 0.05$) did not. Therefore, a related-samples Wilcoxon signed rank test was conducted, and the results showed a significant difference in the participants' knowledge acquisition of information access before and after playing the board game ($z = 3.194, p = 0.001$). These findings suggest that the board game enhanced freshmen's abilities to access information and utilize resources at the university.

Overall Performance. The Shapiro-Wilk test showed that both the total pre-test ($W = 0.958, p > 0.05$) and total post-test ($W = 0.925, p > 0.05$) data conformed to the normal distribution. Paired-samples t-test showed a significant improvement in participants' total knowledge about XJTLU, including physical environment, academic affairs, and information access, before and after playing the board game ($t(13) = -9.427, p < 0.05$). The post-test mean was also significantly higher than the pre-test mean. These results demonstrate that the serious board game effectively helped freshmen familiarize themselves with the campus and its resources.

7.2   System Usability Scale

The SUS was utilized to assess the system usability of the board game. Figure 6 presents the scores for the ten SUS questions from the 14 participants. The mean value of the SUS score was 73.6, which surpassed the average SUS score of 68, indicating that the board game performed well in terms of system usability, with potential for further improvement.

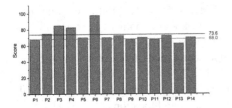

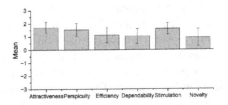

Fig. 6. The SUS scores provided by all participants. The blue line is the mean value of our SUS score (73.6), and the red line is the SUS reference score (68). (Color figure online)

Fig. 7. The means of scale of attractiveness, perspicuity, efficiency, dependability, stimulation and novelty.

7.3   User Experience

The UEQ data analysis toolkit was employed to obtain analysis results. The results of the user experience evaluation demonstrated a positive evaluation on all scales (see Fig. 7b). An initial analysis indicates that the values of attractiveness (1.70), stimulation (1.61), and perspicuity (1.54) exceeded 1.5, nearly double the value of 0.8, suggesting that the serious game performed well in these aspects. In contrast, the values of novelty (0.93), dependability (1.04), and efficiency (1.13) were around 1, slightly higher than 0.8, indicating that the product has potential for improvement in these areas.

In order to get a better picture on the quality of a product, the measured user experience of the game was compared with the results of other established products, from a benchmark data set offered by UEQ, which contains the data of 452 product evaluations with the UEQ. In terms of attractiveness and stimulation, our product performed well, ranking the top 25% to 10%. Perspicuity, efficiency, and novelty were above average, ranking the top 50% to 25%. However, dependability was below average, with 50% of results being better and 25% of results being worse. In summary, our product performed well in attractiveness and stimulation, and above average in perspicuity, efficiency, and novelty. The only area that requires improvement is dependability, which suggests a need to enhance users' sense of control during interaction with the product.

Based on the evaluation experiment and quantitative data analysis, it was found that the serious board game effectively addresses the design goals. Specifically, the game assists freshmen in becoming familiar with the environment and locations of XJTLU, enhancing their knowledge acquisition of XJTLU's academic affairs and improving their ability to access and use university resources. Moreover, the overall user experience and system usability showed positive results. While the game was found to be attractive, stimulating, and clear, there is room for improvement in terms of novelty, dependability, and efficiency.

8 Discussion

8.1 Summary of Findings

Knowledge Acquisition, Usability, and User Experience. Our serious game board design was found to have significantly improved students' learning about the university's physical environment, academic affairs, and information access. They also enjoyed the social activities during the gameplay, showing that the four design goals were satisfied. The system usability was above the suggested threshold value, indicating good usability. The user experience questionnaire showed that our game performed well except for dependability, and we could find some reasons from participants' comments in the post-test. P1 mentioned that *"When I play the game, I am not sure what will happen next. The game events are a bit random"*. P2 also mentioned that *"The game is not that predictable, but this increases the sense of surprise"*. Other participants also commented that randomness is an acceptable property for a board game. Combing the feedback, we will enhance users' sense of control in the future, such as adding icons to suggest related events on the map.

Perceived Value of the Serious Board Game. During the gameplay, we observed joyfulness and positive emotions from participants. At the end of the evaluation study, they also expressed happiness and a sense of competition and cooperation while playing the board game. Participants reported that they tried their best to step into the buildings to get the building cards, which required them to weigh several paths and different directions. They also expressed that the events were just like real events that happened in their daily life. Playing the board game can trigger their empathy, especially when moving on the map, and encountering some events or activities also reminds them of their memories. Participants found the board game valuable since they learned lots of knowledge and tips about XJTLU through the questions. This was not only supported by the freshmen, but also the senior students. When players were not sure about the question they met, their teammates would always think together and try to give some hints. The process was found engaging and can improve the interaction between players. At the end of the experiment, one participant even asked if he can get a copy of the question scripts, because he thought these tips and answers were really helpful. We thus conclude that the board game is useful and meaningful for not only freshmen, but also senior university students.

Game Duration. In the experiments, it was found that the game duration and pace are related to the number of players. For example, when there were only 2 players, they collected all the building cards in 20 min, while in another test with 6 players, the increased time in rolling dice, encountering events and questions, and social card activities have slowed down the game pace. If there are more players, they may step on the same spot, so they have the chance to draw a Social card to interact and communicate with each other about their hobbies, which will take longer time and slow down the game pace. Further experimentation is needed to identify the most appropriate time limitation and game mechanics in the future.

8.2 Research Implications

The research methods employed in this study can be extended to other universities, educational institutions, and other groups and organizations. As the issue of induction is prevalent in universities worldwide, participatory design workshops that involve stakeholders such as freshmen, senior students, and teaching fellows can be organized to discover and define problems, develop solutions together, and deliver them. The evaluation and testing of the serious board game in this study demonstrated its potential to enhance students' knowledge about the environment (DG1), academic affairs (DG2), and information access (DG4) while also promoting a sense of well-being and belonging through communication and interaction with peers (DG3). Therefore, our research implicate that serious board games have huge potential to contribute to student engagement in other educational institutions and facilitate learning through play.

8.3 Limitations and Future Work

First, the workshop series' limited sample size and participant number may have resulted in incomplete data collection. The workshops included mainly freshmen students, considering that they are the main target users. However, our results suggested that the game design was also perceived as valuable by senior students. To improve this, future workshops should consider increasing the sample size and involving more senior students and teaching fellows in the co-design process to offer more beneficial suggestions and tips for freshmen. Additionally, administering questionnaires or directly requesting freshmen to provide written feedback on university-related issues could enhance the efficiency of data collection. Second, a participant (P5) from the design school, who paid special attention to the color code, suggested that the colors of "Events" and "Social cards" were very similar, which was rarely noticed but may cause confusion to some rigorous players. The color of "Social cards" could be changed to distinguish it from other components, such as purple or pink. Third, participants reported that the AR celebration is an interesting and novel mode, which provided them with a cheering feeling after they collected all the building cards. It provided them with a sense of achievement. However, they suggested that the content and form of the AR celebration could be improved. Currently, the game can only be completed by scanning the entire map with a phone after placing all building blocks on their corresponding locations, which can be difficult to achieve within a limited time frame. To address this issue, additional AR features can be incorporated into the game, such as allowing players to scan building cards and trigger 3D models of the buildings when they enter a building on the map. They also suggested the AR collection of 3D building models as a game mechanic. This could give players a better understanding of the physical environment of XJTLU. Future improvements in the AR content and form can also be explored.

9   Conclusion

In this paper, we present the development and evaluation of a serious board game, Easy Induction, aimed at facilitating freshmen's adaptation to the academic and social life at XJTLU. The game was designed through a participatory design process that involved stakeholders from the university, in a total of three workshops. The purpose of the game was to enhance freshmen's sense of well-being and belonging, and the level of engagement with the university, by providing a fun and interactive tool for learning about the university physical environment, academic affairs, and information access. To evaluate the effectiveness of the game, we conducted both quantitative and qualitative analyses. Specifically, we compared participants' knowledge acquisition before and after playing the game, and gathered feedback through the system usability scale and the user experience questionnaire. The results indicated that the game significantly improved freshmen's understanding of the university's academic affairs, enhanced their abilities to access information and resources, and helped them become more familiar with the campus environment and facilities. Overall, the findings of this study contribute to the growing body of research on gamification and serious games in educational contexts, and provide valuable insights for designing and implementing effective interventions for supporting students' academic and social integration in universities. We hope that this work will inspire further exploration and innovation in this area, ultimately leading to enhanced student experiences and success.

Acknowledgments. We would like to thank our participants for their time and valuable comments. This work is supported by the National Natural Science Foundation of China (62207022), Natural Science Foundation of the Jiangsu Higher Education Institutions of China (22KJB520038), and the Xi'an Jiaotong-Liverpool University (RDF-20-02-47).

References

1. Belay Ababu, G., Belete Yigzaw, A., Dinku Besene, Y., Getinet Alemu, W., et al.: Prevalence of adjustment problem and its predictors among first-year undergraduate students in Ethiopian university: a cross-sectional institution based study. Psychiat. J. **2018** (2018)
2. Brooke, J.: Sus: a "quick and dirty' usability. Usabil. Eva. Ind. **189**(3), 189–194 (1996)
3. Chang, W.L., Shao, Y.C.: Co-creating user journey map-a systematic approach to exploring users' day-to-day experience in participatory design workshops. In: Kurosu, M., Hashizume, A. (eds.) International Conference on Human-Computer Interaction, pp. 3–17. Springer, Heidelberg (2023). https://doi.org/10.1007/978-3-031-35596-7_1
4. Council, B.D.: The double diamond: 15 years on (2019). https://www.designcouncil.org.uk/our-resources/archive/articles/double-diamond-15-years
5. Credé, M., Niehorster, S.: Adjustment to college as measured by the student adaptation to college questionnaire: a quantitative review of its structure and relationships with correlates and consequences. Educ. Psychol. Rev. **24**, 133–165 (2012)
6. Danielsson, K., Wiberg, C.: Participatory design of learning media: designing educational computer games with and for teenagers. Interact. Technol. Smart Educ. **3**(4), 275–291 (2006)

7. De Freitas, S.: Are games effective learning tools? a review of educational games. J. Educ. Technol. Soc. **21**(2), 74–84 (2018)

8. Duarte, A.M.B., Brendel, N., Degbelo, A., Kray, C.: Participatory design and participatory research: an HCI case study with young forced migrants. ACM Trans. Comput.-Human Interact. (TOCHI) **25**(1), 1–39 (2018)

9. Freeman, T.M., Anderman, L.H., Jensen, J.M.: Sense of belonging in college freshmen at the classroom and campus levels. J. Exp. Educ. **75**(3), 203–220 (2007)

10. Khaled, R., Vasalou, A.: Bridging serious games and participatory design. Int. J. Child-Comput. Interact. **2**(2), 93–100 (2014)

11. Kiili, K., De Freitas, S., Arnab, S., Lainema, T.: The design principles for flow experience in educational games. Procedia Comput. Sci. **15**, 78–91 (2012)

12. Kuhn, S., Muller, M.J.: Participatory design. Commun. ACM **36**(6), 24–29 (1993)

13. Luck, R.: Learning to talk to users in participatory design situations. Des. Stud. **28**(3), 217–242 (2007)

14. Lukosch, H., van Ruijven, T., Verbraeck, A.: The participatory design of a simulation training game. In: Proceedings of the 2012 Winter Simulation Conference (WSC), pp. 1–11 (2012). https://doi.org/10.1109/WSC.2012.6465218

15. Lupton, D.: Digital health now and in the future: findings from a participatory design stakeholder workshop. Dig. Health **3**, 2055207617740018 (2017)

16. Marshall, S., Zhou, M., Gervan, T., Wiebe, S.: Sense of belonging and first-year academic literacy. Can. J. High. Educ. **43**(3), 116–142 (2012)

17. Mazzone, E., Read, J.C., Beale, R.: Design with and for disaffected teenagers. In: Proceedings of the 5th Nordic Conference on Human-Computer Interaction: Building Bridges, NordiCHI 2008, pp. 290–297. Association for Computing Machinery, New York (2008). https://doi.org/10.1145/1463160.1463192

18. Midgley, C., Middleton, M.J., Gheen, M.H., Kumar, R.: Stage-environment fit revisited: a goal theory approach to examining school transitions. In: Goals, Goal Structures, and Patterns of Adaptive Learning, pp. 109–142 (2002)

19. Morgan, D.L., Krueger, R.A., King, J.A.: The Focus Group Guidebook. Sage, Thousands Oaks (1998)

20. Nazry, N.N.M., Romano, D.M.: Mood and learning in navigation-based serious games. Comput. Hum. Behav. **73**, 596–604 (2017)

21. Pittman, L.D., Richmond, A.: University belonging, friendship quality, and psychological adjustment during the transition to college. J. Exp. Educ. **76**(4), 343–362 (2008)

22. Scariot, C.A., Heemann, A., Padovani, S.: Understanding the collaborative-participatory design. Work **41**(Supplement 1), 2701–2705 (2012)

23. Schrepp, M., Hinderks, A., Thomaschewski, J.: Applying the user experience questionnaire (UEQ) in different evaluation scenarios. In: Marcus, A. (ed.) DUXU 2014. LNCS, vol. 8517, pp. 383–392. Springer, Cham (2014). https://doi.org/10.1007/978-3-319-07668-3_37

24. Scott, H., Donovan, E.: Student adaptation to college survey: the role of self-compassion in college adjustment. Psi Chi J. Psychol. Res. **26**(2), 101–112 (2021)

25. Spinuzzi, C.: The methodology of participatory design. Techn. Commun. **52**(2), 163–174 (2005)

26. Susi, T., Johannesson, M., Backlund, P.: Serious Games: An Overview. Technical report, Institutionen för kommunikation och information (2007)

27. Tabibian, B., Upadhyay, U., De, A., Zarezade, A., Schölkopf, B., Gomez-Rodriguez, M.: Enhancing human learning via spaced repetition optimization. Proc. Natl. Acad. Sci. **116**(10), 3988–3993 (2019)

28. Tan, J.L., Goh, D.H.L., Ang, R.P., Huan, V.S.: Child-centered interaction in the design of a game for social skills intervention. Comput. Entertain. (CIE) **9**(1), 1–17 (2011)

29. Tinto, V.: Leaving College: Rethinking the Causes and Cures of Student Attrition. University of Chicago press, Chicago (2012)
30. Wouters, P., Van der Spek, E.D., Van Oostendorp, H.: Current practices in serious game research: a review from a learning outcomes perspective. In: Games-Based Learning Advancements for Multi-Sensory Human Computer Interfaces: Techniques and Effective Practices, pp. 232–250 (2009)
31. Ye, L., Zhou, X., Yang, S., Hang, Y.: Serious game design and learning effect verification supporting traditional pattern learning. Interact. Learn. Environ. 1–15 (2022)

Creating StoryLines: Participatory Design with Power Grid Operators

Wissal Sahel[1,2(✉)], Wendy E. Mackay[1], and Antoine Marot[3]

[1] Université Paris-Saclay, CNRS, Inria Saclay, Gif-sur-Yvette, France
`wissal.sahel,wendy.mackay}@inria.fr`
[2] IRT SystemX, Palaiseau, France
`wissal.sahel@irt-systemx.fr`
[3] RTE, Paris, France
`antoine.marot@rte-france.com`

Abstract. Designing interactive technology to support safety-critical systems poses multiple challenges with respect to security, access to operators and the proprietary nature of the data. We conducted a two-year participatory design project with French power grid operators to both understand their specific needs and to collaborate on the design of a novel collaborative tool called *StoryLines*. Our primary objective was to capture detailed, in-context data about operators' work practices as part of a larger project designed to provide bi-directional assistance between an intelligent agent and human operator. We targeted handovers between shifts to take advantage of the operators' existing practice of articulating the current status of the grid and expected future events. We use information that would otherwise be lost to gather valuable information about the operator's decision rationale and decision-making patterns. This paper describes how we combined a bottom-up participatory design approach with a top-down generative theory approach to design *StoryLines*, an interactive timeline that helps operators collect information from diverse tools, record reminders and share relevant information with the next shift's operator. We conclude with a discussion of the challenges of working with users in safety-critical environments and directions for future research.

Keywords: Collaborative work · Generative theories of interaction · Participatory design · Power grid operation · Safety critical systems

1 Introduction

The *Cockpit and Bidirectional Assistant CAB)* project is exploring how to take advantage of the increasing capabilities of artificial intelligence to assist operators of safety-critical systems. Rather than deskilling them or replacing them with new technology, we seek to design tools that enhance each operator's capabilities over time. This requires new forms of co-adaptive [20] interaction where the system learns from the user as the user learns from the system. To be effective, users need to benefit from the system without it disrupting their work.

Achieving this requires a shift from traditional intelligent assistant design that prioritizes creating more efficient algorithms to focusing instead on designing the interaction

© The Author(s), under exclusive license to Springer Nature Switzerland AG 2023
H. P. da Silva and P. Cipresso (Eds.): CHIRA 2023, CCIS 1997, pp. 212–230, 2023.
https://doi.org/10.1007/978-3-031-49368-3_13

from the user's perspective in what we call a human-computer partnership [23]. This in turn requires a detailed understanding of the operator's real-world work practices, not only how they monitor the system to build situation awareness but also how they capture, interpret and communicate information under both normal and crisis situations.

This paper describes our approach for capturing the day-to-day activities and decisions of control room operators at RTE (Réseau de Transport d'Electricité), the French national power grid. Our immediate goal is to provide better support for their current activities, with a longer term goal of capturing in-context data about how and when they made their decisions to inform an intelligent agent. This is particularly important since the operator's decisions are judgment calls that balance a variety of trade-offs, only some of which are captured by the system. Instead of assuming an intelligent agent can capture the "ground truth" to define an optimal solution, we need to take advantage of the best characteristics of human common sense and system data management, where the combination of the two is more effective than either alone.

Developing such a system requires understanding operators' work context and the challenges they face when making decisions, which requires access to them and their work environment. We describe our participatory design [13, 22] approach to meeting our first objective: to ensure that the resulting system fits seamlessly into their current and future work practices without increasing their workload. A secondary objective is to collect relevant information that will inform a future intelligent agent that provides recommendations based on detected patterns of behavior. We thus hope to create a virtuous cycle where operators in the course of their daily work feed information to the agent that feeds it back to them in a form that lets them develop a more sophisticated understanding of the system, thus increasing their skills.

We wanted to take advantage of our work on generative theory [4] to design the interaction with the new system. Generative theories of interaction are inspired by established theory in the natural and social sciences but are transformed into concepts and actionable principles that inform design. We describe how we combined bottom-up participatory design methods with a more top-down theoretical approach based on *Instrumental Interaction* [2, 5] to develop a novel system we call *StoryLines*.

We began by asking two research questions:

- *RQ1*: How can we gather in-context information from operators without increasing their workload?
- *RQ2*: How can we take advantage of a generative theory to design an interactive tool that supports light-weight data gathering?

The paper begins with a review of related literature on information management for safety critical systems, especially control rooms. We then describe the results of a preliminary study with control room operators from the French power grid. Next, we describe how generative theories of interaction [4] offer new insights into the design of interactive tools and how we applied the principle of *reification* [5] from the theory of *Instrumental Interaction* [2] to our design. We then describe the series of workshops we conducted with control room operators to design and assess *StoryLines*, a timeline-based tool for capturing information and transmitting it to the next shift operator. We conclude with a discussion of the benefits and limitations of combining theory-driven and participatory design approaches when developing tools for safety critical systems.

2   Related Work

Control rooms are highly complex safety-critical environments. Operators must ensure normal operation and resolve breakdowns by managing technologies that help them interpret and manage large amounts of information. Researchers have investigated various aspects of control room management, including identifying advantages and costs of shifting to automated systems; examining how users manage information to maintain situated awareness and designing interactive technology that supports control room operators.

2.1   Adapting to Control Room Modernization

The goal of automating control rooms is usually framed in terms of reducing human error and operator workload. However new systems also risk reducing the operator's situation awareness and the skills they need to successfully perform automated tasks [37]. They may significantly change the operator's role [28] and, if poorly designed, may actually increase the operator's workload. For example, Mackay [20] showed that air traffic controllers' interactions with physical paper flight strips can be safer than using screens.

Early transitions from analog to digital control systems often affected how operators accessed, perceived, and processed information. For example, Dai et al. [9] showed that interacting with monitors rather than physical control panels in nuclear power plants decreased the operator's access to information, required additional information management tasks and required operators to rely on the computer system rather than their own memory, thus diminishing their skills over time. In these control rooms, Porthin et al. [37] observed that increasing the number of systems that provide information involves a corresponding increase in the number of interface management tasks. Kluge et al. [18] showed how introducing more advanced technology increased the operator's physical and cognitive workload by forcing them to collect additional information and build more complex mental models to understand cause-and-effect relationships across system elements.

Salo et al. [43] argue that control room modernization often requires additional training and skill to master multiple systems and resolve inconsistencies. Operators must constantly calibrate their trust in the technology and often lack a clear overview of the current state of the system. They may have difficulty acquiring and maintaining knowledge of rare events and must continuously adapt to the increasing complexity of the technology.

Of course, some of the challenges operators face are due to problems unique to the particular type of control room. For example, radio astronomy control rooms require extensive screen real estate which makes it difficult for operators to access relevant information and increases their cognitive overload [36]. Similarly, maritime surveillance displays are often insufficient for effective situation awareness [32]. By contrast, Han et al.'s study [15] of a steel manufacturing control room highlighted the inefficiency of warnings about irregular situations and the lack of systematic classification and overviews of abnormal work conditions. Walker et al.'s study of oil production platform control rooms [45] described how operators lacked support for diagnosing and resolving non-routine conditions and found that the system's alarms were excessive, not timely, irrelevant or inappropriately prioritized. Operators also suffered from the lack of history logs, which made it difficult for them to identify trends and determine the causes of specific incidents.

Power grid systems often fail to provide operators with an effective overview, which forces them to constantly search for and integrate information from different screens [29]. Prevost et al. [38] show how the excessive number of display pages, missing information about equipment status and maintenance requests prevent operators from effectively synthesizing relevant information. Baranovic et al.'s study of four power grid control centers [1] showed that the SCADA system generates more information than operators can easily handle, especially when multiple faults appear in the grid at the same time. Militello et al. [30] highlight the coordination problems emergency room operators face due to asymmetric knowledge and experience, barriers to maintaining mutual awareness, uneven workload distribution and disruptions in communication.

These studies suggest that control room operators would benefit from better tools for synthesizing an overview of the current state of the system, recording a history of incidents to highlight trends, controlling alarms and reminders for future maintenance activities and supporting collaboration across operators with asymmetric knowledge.

2.2   Operator Strategies for Managing Information

In order to make informed decisions, control room operators develop information management strategies including closely monitoring system components, building a mental model of the current state and developing situation awareness. Vicente et al. [44] describe how operators build and maintain specific situation models using knowledge-driven monitoring strategies [44], while Roth et al. [42] show that operators enhance situation awareness by doubting the accuracy of the system: They check for problems and pursue unlikely findings, seeking additional information to confirm their expectations. Pilots are sometimes confused by inconsistencies between their expectations, the aircraft's behavior and the auto-flight system [10], which they resolve by turning off the autopilot and fly under manual control.

Hutchin's classic study of "distributed cognition" on the bridge of a naval ship [16] showed how operators take advantage of physical artifacts and other people to expand their cognitive capabilities, both to remember information and trigger future actions. Similarly, Mumaw et al. [31] showed how nuclear power plant operators offload cognitive demands by creating external reminders and collaborating with other operators. They recommend reducing noise, augmenting signals and documenting baselines or trends to enhance operators' ability to extract information.

Walker et al. [46] emphasize the importance of communication in the control room, both to facilitate collective sense-making and ensure timely and effective action during a crisis. They describe the phenomenon of "talking to the room" where an operator shares information with the entire room as opposed to conversing with specific individuals. This non-directed talk helps teams interpret and explain ambiguous information and facilitates shared understanding and coordinated action. Similarly, Carvalho et al.'s studies of a nuclear power plant control room [6] found that operators use informal talk to maintain continuous verbal interaction with each other, not only enhancing mutual awareness but also helping operators anticipate and prevent errors.

These studies illustrate the importance of supporting operators' natural strategies for trying to understand the system. Operators need help resolving conflicts between their intuitions and the system, lightweight methods for extracting information, either from the system or other operators, and low-effort tools for creating reminders and triggering future action.

2.3   Information Management Tools

Researchers have developed various technologies for helping control room operators manage information. Although some systems reduce the overall quantity of information, others use information visualization techniques to highlight relevant information. Other tools focus on facilitating inter-operator collaboration or provide decision support.

Kang & Park [17] argue that improving information visualization is critical for transforming massive quantities of data into useful information. Zhu et al. [47] proposed a data-driven interactive visualization approach for reducing cognitive load and increasing situation awareness for power systems. They proposed powerful data manipulation algorithms to generate visualizations of empirically and mathematically derived data. Pertl et al. [35] also proposed a method that summarizes the current state of a control room so that operators can anticipate and take appropriate preventative measures. However neither of these systems were evaluated with operators. Romero and Diez [41] went further with their *Alarm Trend Catcher* which filters and prioritizes alarms and projects future power grid states, providing operators with additional operational insights. Baranovic et al. [1] proposed an intelligent alarm monitor that not only selected 98% fewer alarms than the existing *SCADA* system but also correctly analyzed and represented the root cause of the corresponding faults.

Systems that require collaboration among operators usually incorporate large displays to facilitate data sharing, increase situation awareness and encourage inter-operator communication [39]. Conversy et al.'s interactive tabletop for Air Traffic Controllers [8] enabled operators to communicate more effectively, both orally and with deictic gestures. They emphasized the need for "feedthrough" to help controllers maintain awareness their colleagues' actions. Another study of power grid operators [29] identified problems that arise in rooms where operators must shift between a general overview and specific details related to each alarm. Their prototype supports coordinated views with interactive visual filtering and parallel coordinates and helps operators transition between focus and context views.

Of course control rooms are not static and must change to adapt to changing needs. Marot et al. [28] proposed guidelines for updating power grid control rooms that include redefining the operator's role to enhance communication and facilitate complex decision making, centralizing information through a common interface and structured decision-making framework and integrating artificial intelligence technology to detect patterns and make informed recommendations.

In summary, the research literature shows that, despite the benefits of introducing automation into control rooms, operators often suffer from increased workload, reduced system awareness and lack of trust in the system. They have developed multiple strategies for improving their ability to make informed decisions and resolve conflicts between their intuitions and the information displayed on the screen. This suggests that future system designs should explicitly support their coping strategies. Finally, future research should take advantage of advances in data visualization research and artificial intelligence to help operators adapt to increasingly complex control rooms.

3   Preliminary Study: Identifying Operators' Needs

The above research literature shows that increased automation in the control room can increase operator workload while reducing system awareness and trust in the system. It suggests that new technologies should provide lightweight ways of extracting information and better synthetic overviews of the different components of the system, with tools for resolving conflicts between their intuitions and what is displayed on the screen. Operators would benefit from interactive incident logs that highlight trends and reminders for future action, both for themselves and others. Finally, they need better support for collaboration and communication with other operators.

We are working with the French national electricity distributor *RTE* (Réseau de Transport d'Électricité), which is responsible for managing the power grid across France and to other European countries. The current system is complex and becoming more so, with recent spikes in demand due to climate change and the war in Ukraine. At the same time, France is transitioning from its former reliance on nuclear power to other, less predictable forms of "green" energy, such as solar and wind power. By 2022, only 62.7% of electricity came from nuclear power, compared to 70–80% in previous decades.

RTE is a member of the *CAB (Cockpit and Bidirectional Assistant)* project whose long-term goal is to take advantage of recent advances in artificial intelligence to provide a bidirectional virtual assistant that augments the real-time capabilities of control room operators. One of the key challenges in creating such an intelligent assistant is to develop the "ground truth" that will serve as the foundation for making effective decisions in a complex, ever-changing environment. However, although the rules and procedures for handling problems are well established, little of the operators' reasoning about trade-offs and choices is captured. This makes it challenging to design an effective intelligent system that considers the nuances and complexities of different situations.

Initial Interviews. Although we were committed to using a participatory design process [21, 22] with RTE operators, the project began in the midst of the COVID-19 pandemic, which prevented face-to-face contact with operators or access to their control rooms. Even virtual meetings were initially difficult, given their reaction to previous project interviews that emphasized abstract discussions of the tasks they perform. We later learned that operators who had heard of those interviews viewed them as a waste of time, making them reluctant to talk to us.

After we explained our interview approach, which emphasizes concrete personal experiences over abstractions, we were granted an initial video interview with a junior operator. In order to establish trust, we explained that interviews would not be recorded (although we did take notes) and nothing they said would be reported to their employer.

We first asked the operator to prepare by remembering recent, memorable incidents of breakdowns or problems he had experienced. We then conducted a "story interview" [22,24] that gathers details about their recent experiences, especially breakdowns, workarounds and innovations.[1] He enjoyed this interview and encouraged a senior operator to participate as well. The two interviews resulted in multiple specific stories about recent breakdowns that formed the basis for future design activities.

We were gratified by their positive reaction to story interviews and the focus on their actual, lived experience. The senior operator appreciated our grounded interview approach:[2] *"I really see the work we can do together from a concrete usage perspective... I am really satisfied since this really makes things concrete for me... I am excited to continue!"* The junior operator agreed: *"This allows us to really make the things we talk about concrete and to clearly show you the problems that we encounter every day, whether they are simple problems or profound problems in the organization we have today. I want to wish you bravo since, despite the frustration of the fact that we can't be in the same room and interact with even just our hands, you have managed to find tools that are practical enough for us to feel like we are making progress, even if we can't be together physically."* Our focus on their perspective about their experiences rather than forcing them to adopt a system-oriented design perspective gave us access to a very scarce resource — the operator's time — and provided a solid foundation for understanding their work practices and generating ideas for improvements.

Control Room Visit. Despite their highly restricted schedules, within less than three months, the two operators each granted us seven hours of contact time and asked other operators to provide additional input. They also invited us to observe their control room in Nantes (although only through an observation platform due to COVID-19 restrictions).

Workshop 1. The first workshop was conducted in person, in our lab in Paris. The goal was to identify breakdowns faced by operators in the control room. We first sent the operators an explanatory video that explained the five workshop activities with examples of what we expected. We also asked all participants, both operators and researchers, to prepare a one-minute video that illustrated a specific breakdown that they had recently encountered at work. Finally, we asked them to have blank sheets of paper and pens to support paper prototyping. Each participant explained their video and we probed for more details about what actually happened. The goal was to avoid generalized descriptions of what usually happens and instead, capture the nuances of what happened that particular time.

We then conducted an online brainstorming session to collect additional breakdowns, including: retrieval problems due to information scattered across multiple tools, the mismatch between information displays and their mental models, the disruptive effect of interruptions that caused them to forget important information, information overload due to excessive numbers of software tools, paper documents that are hard to

---

[1] The *Story interview* method was inspired by the *Critical Incident Technique* [11] but adapted to support interaction design.

[2] Quotations are translated from French.

Preliminary design workshop results

Information mismatch
- Paper and screen-based views out of sync
- Paper and electronic systems are not linked
- No shared view when collaborating with someone
- Display not adapted to current operation, risks confusion
- Lack of real-time visualization overview
- Cannot access views of adjacent sectors

Interruptions
- Phone calls interrupt work flow
- Distracted from a document and forget where I was
- Switching from tool on one screen to another

Risk of forgetting
- Need to update the schema (paper map) after each maneuver
- When busy, easy to forget information for the handover

Wasted time
- Always have to search for options
- Instructions are complex, confusing and not adapted for real-time operation
- System should propose actions relevant to the current alarm

Fig. 1. Preliminary workshop results include issues with information mismatch, interruptions, risk of forgetting and wasted time.

manage and often out of sync and system features that waste their time (Fig. 1 summarizes these findings.) We concluded with a debriefing to gather feedback and gauge the operators' interest in continuing to collaborate with us.

Workshop 2. The first workshop was extremely well received by the operators who not only recruited an additional operator, but also invited us to visit them at the control room in Nantes for a day-long workshop. This launched the second, participatory design phase of the project, described in Sect. 5. However, in parallel, we also began working on a more theoretically driven design process, described in Sect. 4.

4 Inspirations from Generative Theories of Interaction

The long-term goal of the CAB (Bi-directional Cockpit) project is to design an intelligent assistant that learns from and augments the operator's skills. However, before we can accomplish this, we first need to collect detailed, in-context data about how operators currently perform complex operations and make difficult judgments. We need to balance two potentially conflicting goals:

1. Capture a large quantity of detailed in-context data from operators, including characteristics of normal and unusual incidents, specific actions the operators performed, which decisions were made and how effective those decisions were.
2. Ensure that the act of collecting this data is not viewed as an additional, cumbersome task that increases the operator's workload, but rather as a tool that saves them time and makes them more effective.

We thus prioritized our design goals to begin with the user's perspective so that the resulting system offers them concrete benefits, and only secondarily focusing on capturing the most detailed relevant data possible. Based on our observations and discussions with the operators, we decided to focus on the handover between operators at the end of every shift. We can take advantage of the fact that all operators already prepare information notes for themselves that summarize the current state of the power grid, any upcoming actions or expected critical events, and the results of any research the operator conducted to solve current or projected incidents.

We decided to address the needs identified in the preliminary study (Sect. 3) using the strategy outlined in [4] for applying a *generative theory of interaction* to a real-world design problem. This strategy combines bottom-up analyses of current work practices with top-down concepts and principles derived from theories of human behavior. We were particularly influenced by *instrumental interaction* [2,5], which builds upon theories of affordances [12] and human tool use [33,34,40] from experimental psychology. In particular, we explored the principle of *reification*, which transforms an otherwise ephemeral action into a persistent interactive tool.

For example, the design of *StickyLines* [7] was inspired by studies of designers who spend an inordinate amount of time aligning graphical objects. Users must select the objects to be aligned, navigate via a pull-down menu, and choose the appropriate form of alignment. Any future adjustments of any of these objects breaks the alignment and requires further realignment. By contrast, *StickyLines* "reify" the alignment command into an interactive object that makes the alignment persistent. It acts as a magnetic guideline to which shapes can be attached so that moving the guideline also moves the attached objects. *StickyLines* can align to any shape, such as a circle, and create multiple, interconnected alignments, such as an easily adjustable grid.

When we examined the results of the preliminary study, we saw the opportunity for reifying sequences of incidents and corresponding actions into a persistent, interactive object that we call *StoryLines*. Each operator can collect personally meaningful sequences of events, either automatically or intentionally, to create coherent "stories" that capture relevant information and actions associated with different tools. They can also set reminders or trigger future events. *StoryLines* are designed to replace operators' hand-written notes but should save time by avoiding duplicate information and providing real-time links back to relevant information on a global timeline that would otherwise require time to search. *StoryLines* should also filter information to give an easy-to-scan overview of current incidents, actions and upcoming events.

The current environment used by operators is an example of what Beaudouin-Lafon [3] calls "walled gardens and information silos", with no easy mechanisms for transferring information across non-interoperable systems. The design of *StoryLines* is also inspired by systems such as *Passages* [14], which let users create a common representation for transferring information from one tool to another.

The design of the *StoryLines* involved a number of challenging design questions: Do operators want a single *StoryLine* composed of multiple incidents or multiple *StoryLines*? Are *StoryLines* associated with a single operator during a single shift or are they transferred from one shift to another? What is the relationship between individual *StoryLines* and the overall history of events? What is the best way to visualize

StoryLines and what information should they prioritize? In order to address these and other design questions, we engaged in what turned out to be a two-year participatory design project that involved a series of remote and in-person workshops and activities with operators and members of the research team.

5   Participatory Design of *StoryLines*

We wanted to combine our theoretical work (see Sect. 4) with a participatory design approach. The traditional "user-centered" approach to designing interactive systems can be oversimplified as first conducting a user study to determine users' needs, then exploring a new design and finally testing it with target users. By contrast, participatory design [13,21,22] actively involves users throughout the design process. While this has proven to be highly successful in a few safety-critical settings, such as that described by Mackay [20,26] with air traffic controllers, it is relatively rare due to security restrictions, limited physical access to users and their work environments, and the confidential or proprietary nature of the technologies and associated data.

We also cannot risk losing participants' interest by forcing them to adopt our theoretical stance. Instead, we need to let them express their experiences and needs in their own terms while contributing concrete examples of design ideas inspired by our theories which they can interpret and evaluate as they like.

We followed the participatory design approach outlined in [21,22] and [24], beginning with story interviews that capture detailed examples of recent, memorable incidents, especially breakdowns, workarounds and user innovations. We transformed these into scenarios in which personas who represent actual controllers encounter a series of events that highlight the issues that must be resolved. We brainstormed ideas, first verbally then as short video clips that illustrate the interaction [27] and then collaborated on creating various types of prototypes [25], ranging from paper to Figma to working software. We ran different types of qualitative evaluations to advance the design, and iterated with additional interviews, brainstorming, design sessions and evaluations. Participants found this approach highly engaging, since all the activities were designed to emphasize their perspective, with concrete activities that let them express their needs and ideas, as well as react to our ideas, in an enjoyable, non-threatening format.

These participatory design activities were conducted over a two-year period with delays due to the COVID-19 pandemic, changes in personnel and scheduling challenges, as well as requiring time to digest the results of each workshop and to develop prototypes, which evolved significantly across the different workshops and design sessions.

Participants: We recruited a total of four active participants who contributed to multiple activities over several months and three additional operators who contributed to specific events. One very senior operator participated throughout the entire design process. The junior operator who participated in the first series of activities left RTE after the first year. He was replaced by a junior and a senior operator who were actively involved in later activities. Three other operators participated in individual workshops and others contributed information or joined discussions at various points in the process.

RTE Control Room Organization: Four researchers visited the RTE control center which began with a "virtual" guided tour from the senior operator. The main control room is designed to support four operators: three who supervise a particular zone (east, west and south) and a senior manager who oversees the others. During busy times, a fifth operator may also be included. Operators are trained on all three zones and spend approximately seven weeks in one zone before shifting to another. The manager supervises all three zones.

The three operator desks were positioned to face a wall-sized display on the back wall with a huge map that displayed the entire energy grid.[3] The manager's desk is positioned behind them, with a view of all three desks. Each operator has a large U-shaped desk with an interior approximately three meters wide. We counted about a dozen "stations" for different tools and information sources, including multiple screens, a printer, two telephone stations and areas for other devices. One set of three screens is operated with a single mouse and keyboard, whereas other tools have dedicated keyboards or control panels. Some tools provide overviews and details about the current status of the energy grid, some sound and monitor alarms while others help operators research re-routing solutions to current failures, expected maintenance or other projected problems. The size of the desk area requires them to use rolling chairs to transition from one station to another.

Software Tools. Energy grid operators are trained on over 50 different software tools that gather information, sound alarms and suggest solutions. These tools have been introduced over several decades with correspondingly different, often incompatible user interfaces. Operators must collect information scattered across their work area and they struggle to form a coherent overview of the power grid. Most information is presented as raw data that rarely matches the operators' mental models. Worse, some information is cumbersome or difficult to retrieve in real-time and junior operators reported that instructions and guidelines were often difficult to understand.

Paper-Based Tools. Operators also use multiple paper-based tools. An A0-sized paper map of the energy grid, reprinted monthly, is used to note current breakdowns which they must remember to erase when the problem is solved. Although this paper map provides a concise overview of the grid, it is usually out of date since it is not linked to any online software tools. Other paper-based supports include a large ring binder, exchanged monthly, with hand-annotated printouts of specific "incidents", an A3-sized log sheet for recording completed maneuvers and "floating sheets" for informally recording notes, reminders and information for the shift handover.

We were particularly interested in the fact that all operators took paper notes that they used to keep track of ongoing activities and manually transfer information from one system to another (which they view as a waste of time). They also create reminders for future actions and list key items to communicate to the next shift's operator during the handover. We were also struck by the level of oral communication between operators, not only during shift handovers but also across zones and with the manager. Operators

---

[3] This wall has since been removed as part of a major renovation that will consolidate multiple control rooms.

were often interrupted by phone calls from clients and other stakeholders. From the perspective of the CAB project, this is extremely valuable information that is lost and unavailable to the system.

Participatory Design Workshops: After the preliminary study, we conducted a series of participatory design workshops between July 2021 and June 2023. Figure 2 shows this sequence of activities with operators, both in person and online, as well as the evolution of the *StoryLines* prototype from paper mock-ups to working software.

Workshop 2. The success of workshop 1 (see Sect. 3) led to an invitation to visit the RTE control center in Nantes. Workshop 2 was an all-day event with seven participants (three controllers and four researchers). Six were physically present and one controller joined via video from the control room. The controllers gave us a virtual tour of the control room (described above) after which we brainstormed ideas for how to address the breakdowns specified in the scenarios from workshop 1. Next, we paired controllers with researchers to draw a short "interaction snippet" or storyboard to illustrate each idea. Finally, each pair created paper mock-ups and shot short video clips where the controllers demonstrated how they would interact with each idea. The operators especially liked the video brainstorming activity because it gave them a concrete way to communicate both the problem and the solution. The workshop resulted in 10 interaction snippets and five video prototypes, all of which highlighted the need for centralizing information.

Workshop 3. The third workshop was also conducted in person, in Nantes and focused on situating the breakdowns identified earlier in a realistic context. We began with a visit to the observation deck above the actual control room, which allowed us to observe the operators in action. Next, we ran a design session that involved creating realistic personas based on the operators involved in the project and a "current scenario" to illustrate the breakdowns in a realistic context. The operators drew from their experiences to adjust the scenarios, especially with respect to the ways in which small errors, particularly in communication, can cause problems or complicate the situation.

The workshop resulted in scenarios related to two personas: Charles and Julie. Charles is a senior operator with 12 years of experience and Julie is a junior operator who just finished training. The scenario includes three main situations: a busy morning for Charles who just returned from vacation; a rushed and poorly prepared handover to Julie and an afternoon filled with complex problems for Julie.

Workshop 4. The fourth workshop was conducted in our labs with five researchers and two operators. We developed a "future scenario" based on the scenario created in workshop 3 that explored potential solutions. We supplied prototyping materials and simulated their environment with paperboard "screens". We then created paper mock-ups of the different tools and created video prototypes of various solutions proposed by the operators and researchers. The results included four specific solutions designed to improve communication with the planning team, visualize cognitive load and visualize failures as they evolve over time.

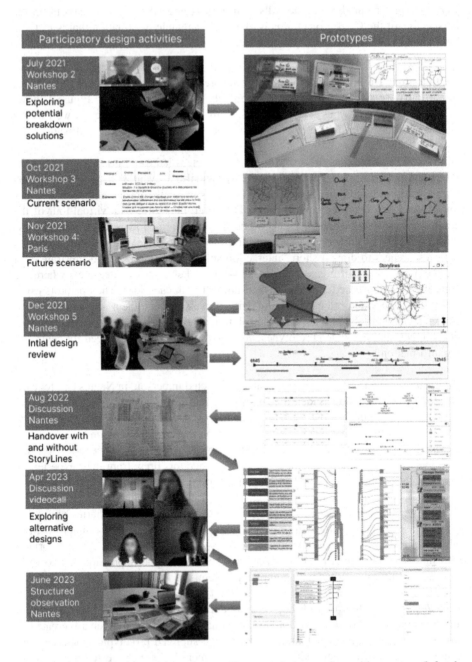

Fig. 2. Participatory design activities alternated between design sessions with operators (left column) and prototypes created by operators and researchers (right column) over a period of approximately two years.

Workshop 5. The fifth workshop was conducted at the RTE control center with three researchers and one operator physically present as well as one remote senior operator. The goal of the workshop was to use a generative walk-through [19] to evaluate the scenarios and ideas from workshop 4. We played the video prototypes and discussed how to improve the proposed solutions, including incorporating new information as a situation evolves, automatic update of other information and tasks, tracking and comparing solutions and taking into account the "last time to decide" (LLTD). This workshop highlighted how much critical information is lost, either because it was transmitted orally or it was never captured in the first place.

Workshop 6. The sixth workshop was also conducted at the RTE control center with four researchers and five operators. Our goal was to present the operators with a working prototype of *StoryLines* and obtain their feedback, suggestions and ideas. We worked with pairs of operators who followed two scenarios, one extremely busy with multiple overlapping events and the other relatively calm. They performed tasks, interacted with *StoryLines*, took notes and prepared for the handover to the other operator, after which they continued with the second scenario. Half of the operators first performed the "busy" scenario, followed by the "calm" one. The other half performed the "calm" scenario first. We conducted two sessions with two operators each and then ran a debriefing session with the operators who participated plus another senior controller.

6 *StoryLines*

We designed *StoryLines* to provide operators with a personal, interactive history and overview of their past, current and upcoming activities. It serves as a shareable repository of relevant information where they can take notes, register reminders and ensure they have access to all the information they need to handle the handover. Figure 3 shows the final working prototype that we tested in workshop 6 with operators at the RTE control center.

This prototype includes five panels. The toolbar includes buttons for adding stories, events and reminders. The event panel provides a chronological list of events, including alarms, telephone calls, simulations and actions performed on the grid. The reminder list includes reminders, with the ability to trigger notifications based on time or events. The story timeline includes the series of stories, each with a title, status (completed, ongoing or predicted) and access to events, which can be included with the + button. The Event details panel appears when the operator clicks on an event and lets them inspect its time, type, story, and any associated notes or other annotations.

StoryLines offer a lightweight, central location for the information collected from different tools and is fully configurable by the operator. Operators can link relevant information together into "stories" to describe important events. *StoryLines* preserve the provenance of system-supplied information, which facilitates future retrieval of additional details and captures the context in which various decisions were made. *StoryLines* can facilitate record-keeping by providing templates for common tasks and help operators track their previous decisions for future reference. Finally, *StoryLines* support sharing information between operators, not only during shift handovers but also with managers and other stakeholders during the shift.

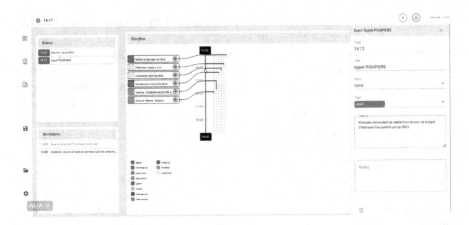

Fig. 3. The working *StoryLines* prototype includes five panels (from left to right): toolbar for adding stories, events and reminders; chronological event list; reminder list; story timeline and the panel for displaying event details.

Reactions to StoryLines. The focus of this prototype was how to provide a concise interactive visualization of the events that make up a story, including the events that occurred and the actions performed. The second-to-last panel of Fig. 2 shows an alternative approach, with various strategies for expanding and contracting the level of information displayed. We plan to continue working on the design to further simplify the interface.

The operators found the visualization effective, but shifted their attention to the keyboard-based method of capturing information. They viewed this as "yet-another-keyboard" and were far more interested in a tablet or paper-based interface that more closely matched their current note-taking methods. They also wanted the ability to use templates for commonly occurring types of events with pre-filled elements and the ability to add additional annotations.

7 Conclusion

We are interested in designing tools for control room operators that enhance their skills instead of deskilling them. This requires shifting the focus from the design of intelligent algorithms to the design of effective interaction with those algorithms in real-world contexts. We conducted a two-year participatory design project with operators from the RTE French power grid, with two key research questions:

– *RQ1*: How can we gather in-context information from operators without increasing their workload?
– *RQ2*: How can we take advantage of a generative theory to design an interactive tool that supports light-weight data gathering?

We examined the research literature and found that increased automation in the control room can increase operator workload while reducing system awareness and trust in the system. Previous work suggests that new technologies should provide lightweight ways of extracting information and better synthetic overviews of the different components of the system, with tools from resolving conflicts between the operators' intuitions and what is displayed on the screen. Operators would benefit from interactive incident logs that can be augmented to highlight trends and the ability to register reminders of future actions, both for themselves and others. Finally, they need better support for collaboration and communication with other operators.

The results of our studies with operators echo these findings and provide specific examples of challenges faced by users. They also suggest a key opportunity for design, i.e. targeting the operators' existing use of informal notes to support the handover to the next shift.

We combined participatory design methods with design inspiration from *Instrumental Interaction* to create *StoryLines*, an interactive timeline that helps operators collect information from diverse tools, record reminders and share relevant information with the next shift's operator. *StoryLines* illustrate a successful application of the principle of "reification" by transforming a series of ephemeral events into a persistent, interactive timeline that serves as a repository for key information during the operator's shift. We also show the evolution and refinement of the concept through multiple design iterations and discussions with operators.

We are now exploring how to enhance data capture by providing tablet-based interaction, and are working with members of the CAB project to integrate *StoryLines* with the new software system that they are developing. This will enable us to conduct evaluations of *StoryLines* in a realistic setting.

Our work shows that participatory design is an effective way of engaging operators of safety-critical systems in productive design activities, and that combining participatory design with a theoretically based approach can lead to a simple yet effective user-centered design. At a time where artificial intelligence and automation risk deskilling and disenfranchising users, we hope to see this approach applied to other contexts, safety-critical or not, to create socio-technical systems where machines empower rather replace or enslave users.

Acknowledgments. This work has been supported by the French government under the "France 2030" program, as part of the SystemX Technological Research Institute within the CAB project.

References

1. Baranovic, N., Andersson, P., Ivankovic, I., Zubrinic-Kostovic, K., Peharda, D., Larsson, J.E.: Experiences from intelligent alarm processing and decision support tools in smart grid transmission control centers. In: Cigre Session, vol. 46, pp. 21–26 (2016)
2. Beaudouin-Lafon, M.: Instrumental interaction: an interaction model for designing post-wimp user interfaces. In: Proceedings of the SIGCHI Conference on Human Factors in Computing Systems, CHI 2000, pp. 446–453. ACM, New York (2000). https://doi.org/10.1145/332040.332473
3. Beaudouin-Lafon, M.: Towards unified principles of interaction. In: Proceedings of Advanced Visual Interfaces (AVI'17), CHItaly 2017. Association for Computing Machinery, New York (2017). https://doi.org/10.1145/3125571.3125602
4. Beaudouin-Lafon, M., Bødker, S., Mackay, W.E.: Generative theories of interaction. ACM Trans. Comput.-Human Interact. (TOCHI) **28**(6), 1–54 (2021)

5. Beaudouin-Lafon, M., Mackay, W.E.: Reification, polymorphism and reuse: Three principles for designing visual interfaces. In: Proceedings of the Working Conference on Advanced Visual Interfaces, AVI 2000, pp. 102–109. ACM, New York (2000). https://doi.org/10.1145/345513.345267

6. Carvalho, P.V., Vidal, M.C., de Carvalho, E.F.: Nuclear power plant communications in normative and actual practice: a field study of control room operators' communications. Human Fact. Ergon. Manuf. Serv. Ind. **17**(1), 43–78 (2007)

7. Ciolfi Felice, M., Maudet, N., Mackay, W.E., Beaudouin-Lafon, M.: Beyond snapping: persistent, tweakable alignment and distribution with stickylines. In: Proceedings of the 29th Annual Symposium on User Interface Software and Technology, UIST 2016, pp. 133–144. Association for Computing Machinery, New York (2016). https://doi.org/10.1145/2984511.2984577

8. Conversy, S., Gaspard-Boulinc, H., Chatty, S., Valès, S., Dupré, C., Ollagnon, C.: Supporting air traffic control collaboration with a tabletop system. In: Proceedings of the ACM 2011 conference on Computer supported cooperative work, CSCW 2011, pp. 425–434. Association for Computing Machinery, New York (2011). https://doi.org/10.1145/1958824.1958891

9. Dai, L., Zhang, L., Li, P., Hu, H., Zou, Y.: Study on human errors in DCS of a nuclear power plant. In: Proceedings of the 12th Probabilistic Safety Assessment and Analysis (PSAM12), Honolulu, Hawaii, vol. 40 (2014)

10. Dubus, R., Brock, A.M., Mackay, W.E.: Merging control and feedback? a new design to reduce mode confusions in the cockpit. In: CHI 2023 workshop Automation XP23: Intervening, Teaming, Delegating. Hamburg, Germany (2023)

11. Flanagan, J.C.: The critical incident technique. Psychol. Bull. **51**(4), 327 (1954)

12. Gibson, J.J.: The Ecological Approach to Visual Perception. Houghton, Mifflin and Company, Boston (1979)

13. Greenbaum, J., Kyng, M.E.: Design at Work: Cooperative Design of Computer Systems, 1st edn. CRC Press, Boca Raton (1991)

14. Han, H.L., Yu, J., Bournet, R., Ciorascu, A., Mackay, W.E., Beaudouin-Lafon, M.: Passages: interacting with text across documents. In: Proceedings of the 2022 CHI Conference on Human Factors in Computing Systems, CHI 2022. Association for Computing Machinery, New York (2022). https://doi.org/10.1145/3491102.3502052

15. Han, S.H., Yang, H., Im, D.G.: Designing a human-computer interface for a process control room: a case study of a steel manufacturing company. Int. J. Ind. Ergon. **37**(5), 383–393 (2007)

16. Hutchins, E.: Cognition in the Wild. MIT Press, Cambridge (1995)

17. Kang, D.J., Park, S.: A conceptual approach to data visualization for user interface design of smart grid operation tools. Int. J. Energy Inf. Commun. **1**(1), 64–76 (2010)

18. Kluge, A., Nazir, S., Manca, D.: Advanced applications in process control and training needs of field and control room operators. IIE Trans. Occup. Ergon. Human Fact. **2**(3–4), 121–136 (2014)

19. Lottridge, D., Mackay, W.E.: Generative walkthroughs: to support creative redesign. In: Proceedings of the Seventh ACM Conference on Creativity and Cognition, pp. 175–184 (2009)

20. Mackay, W.: Responding to cognitive overload?: co-adaptation between users and technology. Intellectica **30**(1), 177–193 (2000). https://doi.org/10.3406/intel.2000.1597

21. Mackay, W.: Using video to support interaction design. In: Proceedings of the SIGCHI Conference on Human Factors in Computing Systems, CHI 2002. ACM, New York (2002)

22. Mackay, W.E.: Designing with sticky notes. In: Sticky Creativity, pp. 231–256. Elsevier (2020)

23. Mackay, W.E.: Réimaginer nos interactions avec le monde numérique. Leçons inaugurales du Collège de France, Collège de France — Fayard (2022)

24. Mackay, W.E.: DOIT: The Design of Interactive Things: CHI 2023 Preview. Inria (2023)
25. Mackay, W.E., Beaudouin-Lafon, M.: Participatory design and prototyping. In: Handbook of Human Computer Interaction. Springer, Heidelberg (2023). https://doi.org/10.1007/978-3-319-27648-9_31-1. http://www.hal.science/hal-04108636
26. Mackay, W.E., Fayard, A.L., Frobert, L., Médini, L.: Reinventing the familiar: exploring an augmented reality design space for air traffic control. In: Proceedings of the SIGCHI Conference on Human Factors in Computing Systems, CHI 1998, pp. 558–565. ACM Press/Addison-Wesley Publishing Co., USA (1998). https://doi.org/10.1145/274644.274719
27. Mackay, W.E., Ratzer, A.V., Janecek, P.: Video artifacts for design: bridging the Gap between abstraction and detail. In: DIS 2000, pp. 72–82. ACM (2000)
28. Marot, A.: Perspectives on future power system control centers for energy transition. J. Mod. Power Syst. Clean Energy **10**(2), 328–344 (2022)
29. Mikkelsen, C., Johansson, J., Rissanen, M.: Interactive information visualization for sense making in power grid supervisory systems. In: 2011 15th International Conference on Information Visualisation, pp. 119–126. IEEE (2011)
30. Militello, L.G., Patterson, E.S., Bowman, L., Wears, R.: Information flow during crisis management: challenges to coordination in the emergency operations center. Cogn. Technol. Work **9**(1), 25–31 (2007)
31. Mumaw, R.J., Roth, E.M., Vicente, K.J., Burns, C.M.: There is more to monitoring a nuclear power plant than meets the eye. Human Fact. **42**(1), 36–55 (2000)
32. Nilsson, M., Van Laere, J., Ziemke, T., Edlund, J.: Extracting rules from expert operators to support situation awareness in maritime surveillance. In: 2008 11th International Conference on Information Fusion, pp. 1–8. IEEE (2008)
33. Osiurak, F.: What neuropsychology tells us about human tool use? The four constraints theory (4ct): mechanics, space, time, and effort. Neuropsychol. Rev. **24**(2), 88–115 (2014). https://doi.org/10.1007/s11065-014-9260-y
34. Osiurak, F., Jarry, C., Le Gall, D.: Grasping the affordances, understanding the reasoning: toward a dialectical theory of human tool use. Psychol. Rev. **117**(2), 517–540 (2010). http://www.halshs.archives-ouvertes.fr/halshs-00485348
35. Pertl, M., Rezkalla, M., Marinelli, M.: A novel grid-wide transient stability assessment and visualization method for increasing situation awareness of control room operators. In: 2016 IEEE Innovative Smart Grid Technologies-Asia (ISGT-Asia), pp. 87–92. IEEE (2016)
36. Pietriga, E., et al.: Interaction design challenges and solutions for alma operations monitoring and control. In: Software and Cyberinfrastructure for Astronomy II, vol. 8451, p. 845110. International Society for Optics and Photonics (2012)
37. Porthin, M., Liinasuo, M., Kling, T.: Effects of digitalization of nuclear power plant control rooms on human reliability analysis-a review. Reliabil. Eng. Syst. Saf. **194**, 106415 (2020)
38. Prevost, M.C., Aubin, F., Gauthier, J., Mailhot, R.: Preventing human errors in power grid management systems through user-interface redesign. In: 2007 IEEE International Conference on Systems, Man and Cybernetics, pp. 626–631. IEEE (2007)
39. Prouzeau, A., Bezerianos, A., Chapuis, O.: Evaluating multi-user selection for exploring graph topology on wall-displays. IEEE Trans. Visual Comput. Graphics **23**(8), 1936–1951 (2016)
40. Renom, M.A., Caramiaux, B., Beaudouin-Lafon, M.: Exploring technical reasoning in digital tool use. In: Proceedings of the 2022 CHI Conference on Human Factors in Computing Systems, CHI 2022. Association for Computing Machinery, New York (2022). https://doi.org/10.1145/3491102.3501877
41. Romero-Gómez, R., Diez, D.: Alarm trend catcher: projecting operating conditions in the electrical power grid domain with interactive alarm visualization. In: Proceedings of the XVII International Conference on Human Computer Interaction, pp. 1–8 (2016)

42. Roth, E.M., Mumaw, R.J., Vicente, K.J., Burns, C.M.: Operator monitoring during normal operations: vigilance or problem-solving? In: Proceedings of the Human Factors and Ergonomics Society Annual Meeting, vol. 41, pp. 158–162. SAGE Publications Sage CA, Los Angeles (1997)

43. Salo, L., Laarni, J., Savioja, P.: Operator experiences on working in screen-based control rooms. In: 5th ANS International Topical Meeting on Nuclear Plant Instrumentation, Controls, and Human Machine Interface Technology, Albuquerque, pp. 12–16 (2006)

44. Vicente, K.J., Roth, E.M., Mumaw, R.J.: How do operators monitor a complex, dynamic work domain? the impact of control room technology. Int. J. Human Comput. Stud. **54**(6), 831–856 (2001)

45. Walker, G.H., Waterfield, S., Thompson, P.: All at sea: an ergonomic analysis of oil production platform control rooms. Int. J. Ind. Ergon. **44**(5), 723–731 (2014)

46. Waller, M.J., Uitdewilligen, S.: Talking to the room: collective sense making during crisis situations. In: Time in Organizational Research, pp. 208–225. Routledge (2008)

47. Zhu, J., Zhuang, E., Ivanov, C., Yao, Z.: A data-driven approach to interactive visualization of power systems. IEEE Trans. Power Syst. **26**(4), 2539–2546 (2011)

Visual Representations for Data Analytics: User Study

Ladislav Peska$^{(\boxtimes)}$ ⓘ, Ivana Sixtova ⓘ, David Hoksza ⓘ, David Bernhauer ⓘ,
and Tomas Skopal ⓘ

Faculty of Mathematics and Physics, Charles University, Prague, Czechia
{Ladislav.Peska,Ivana.Sixtova,David.Hoksza,
David.Bernhauer,Tomas.Skopal}@matfyz.cuni.cz

Abstract. One of the characteristics of big data is its internal complexity and also variety manifested in many types of datasets that are to be managed, searched, or analyzed. In their natural forms, some of the data entities are unstructured, such as texts or multimedia objects, while some are structured but too complex. In this paper, we have investigated how visualizations of various complex datasets perform in the role of universal data representations for both human users and deep learning models. In a user study, we have evaluated several visualizations of complex relational data, where some proved their superior performance with respect to the precision and speed of classification by human users. Moreover, the same visualizations also led to effective classification performance when used with deep learning models.

Keywords: Visual representations · Data analytics · User studies · Human-in-the-loop

1 Introduction

In data science and also in data handling in general, we find many cases where raw data (e.g., table entries with many attributes) are difficult to process by humans directly. Having several dozens of attributes (table columns), often with somewhat cryptic semantics, may prevent gaining insights into the data and makes simple tasks such as visual clustering, organization, or classification challenging. In addition, in the era of big data, the problem is not just the high internal complexity of data but also the high data variety expressed in various data models and formats that need to be managed in a unified way.

In this study, we compare several data visualization techniques in their ability to support users to perform simple tasks, particularly to enable users to classify data records into one of the pre-existing classes. Our goal is to understand which visualizations provide the best support for the downstream tasks, or if it is easier for users to work with the raw data directly. Usage of suitable visualizations could also help domain experts with feature engineering that is otherwise affected by the problem of too high dimensionality (the curse of dimensionality [18]). Note that the study does not stand for a comprehensive survey that gives ultimate guide to visualization model selection, it is rather focused at showing the ability of a visualization in the role of data description for both the user and the machine (model).

© The Author(s), under exclusive license to Springer Nature Switzerland AG 2023
H. P. da Silva and P. Cipresso (Eds.): CHIRA 2023, CCIS 1997, pp. 231–243, 2023.
https://doi.org/10.1007/978-3-031-49368-3_14

Moreover, in a recent work [32], the author introduced a vision of a transfer learning framework, where complex data entities are also represented by visualizations, while these are to be used with pre-trained or fine-tuned DCNN (deep convolutional neural network) models for classification tasks and data analytics. Following this idea, the visualizations of data used in this study could be not only suitable for processing by humans, but the very same visualizations could serve as data representations for usage with DCNN models. In other words, we get data representations that a human "sees" in the same way as the machine. Hence, in the study, we also compare the performance of human users and DCNN models when a shared data visualization is used.

1.1 Related Work

Several surveys focused on the techniques of multidimensional data visualization in the past [5,37] and more recently also in the context of data science and big data [23,26], providing a valuable overview of visualization methods, tools, and related challenges.

In visual data analytics, experimental evaluations of visualizations of multidimensional objects initiated with the glyphs, which have a long history and were most popular four decades ago. During this period, several studies examined the perceived similarity of visualizations against the true similarity of objects for various glyph variants, including faces and suns [9,14,35]. Some of the studies have been devoted to the category construction task on an artificial dataset of psychiatric patients, where the participants grouped similar visualizations to identify underlying diagnostic groups [4,25].

More recently, Morris et al. [27] evaluated the effectiveness and pre-attentiveness of several features of Chernoff faces. This experiment indicated that the eyebrow slant and eye size are the most accurate features, and the processing of the face is not pre-attentive.

Another empirical evaluation of glyphs in general, including Chernoff faces, was carried out by Lee et al. [22]. The visualizations of objects were used to help users answer questions about a binary dataset. In this particular study, the glyphs resulted in incorrect and slow responses. Various modern types of glyphs (apart from Chernoff faces) such as leaf glyphs [12], fish glyphs [13] or 3D glyphs [10] have been explored relatively extensively in the literature, but typically evaluated only on by example.

Some studies performed experiments with radial visual representations. Star plots, a variant of radial plots, have been evaluated in the category construction task [11,19,20]. Albo et al. [2] experimentally evaluated different variants of radial plots for several visual analytics tasks, such as lookup, comparison, and relation seeking.

In the past decade, most user studies focused on the effectivity of visual representations of multidimensional data for cluster analysis [8,15,34,39]. There is a partial intersection in utilized visualization techniques between ours and related work, e.g., parallel coordinates. However, the key distinction lies in our task's definition, which requires that visualization techniques can seamlessly display both individual objects and classes of objects, rather than the whole dataset.

To the best of our knowledge, we have not found any recent study to evaluate the performance of various visualization techniques - from the traditional glyphs to modern methods such as scatter plots, on a more general level, i.e., how well they represent the

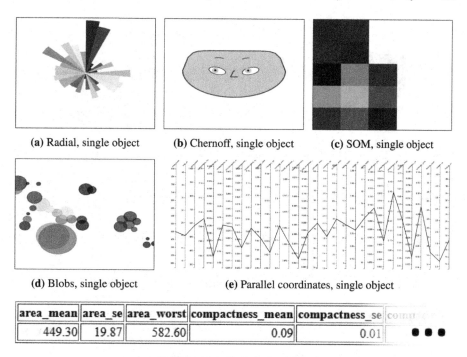

(a) Radial, single object   **(b)** Chernoff, single object   **(c)** SOM, single object

(d) Blobs, single object   **(e)** Parallel coordinates, single object

area_mean	area_se	area_worst	compactness_mean	compactness_se	co···
449.30	19.87	582.60	0.09	0.01	● ● ●

(f) Tabular baseline, single object

Fig. 1. Visualization examples of a single entry for **radial** bar plots, Chernoff **faces**, self-organizing maps (**SOM**), color **blobs, parallel** coordinates plot and original **tabular** values. Note that each visualization represents the same entry from the breast cancer dataset (ID: 48).

underlying data entities and to what extent they allow humans to perform typical data analysis tasks, such as classification.

2 Visualization Methods

In experiments, we considered in total five visualization methods plus a baseline of displaying the raw data in a tabular format. Example visualizations are depicted in Fig. 1.

Radial bar plots belong to the family of radial plots, along with star plots and radar plots. In this plot, attributes of a multivariate entity are drawn as bars originating from a central point where the bar's height is determined by the attribute value. In our visualization method, we also rearranged the bars to put correlated attributes near each other. To this end, we performed hierarchical clustering on the rows of the attributes correlation matrix. Subsequently, we reordered the bars according to the ordering of dendrogram leaves. Additionally, we colorized the bars w.r.t. attributes values (low values in blue tones, high values in orange tones).

Chernoff faces [6] is one of the first attempts to represent a multidimensional object as a single glyph - in this case, a cartoon of a face. Each characteristic of this face, such

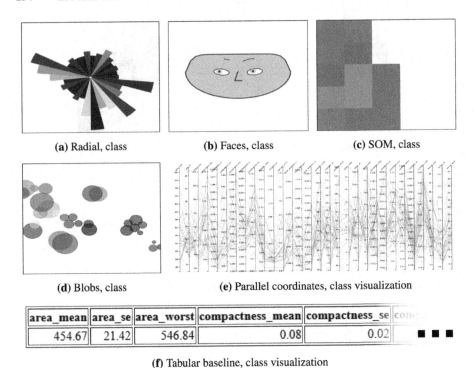

(a) Radial, class   (b) Faces, class   (c) SOM, class

(d) Blobs, class   (e) Parallel coordinates, class visualization

area_mean	area_se	area_worst	compactness_mean	compactness_se	com
454.67	21.42	546.84	0.08	0.02	■ ■ ■

(f) Tabular baseline, class visualization

Fig. 2. Visualization examples of a class. Note each visualization represents the same class (benign) from the breast cancer dataset. This is the class to which the object visualized in Fig. 1 belongs.

as eye shape, nose length, or eyebrows angle, encodes one attribute of the entity, up to 18 attributes. This visualization is based on the idea that a human is capable of registering small changes in facial expressions. In our study, we used a slightly extended method, which also employs the colors of face parts and can encode 22 attributes in total [3].

Parallel coordinates [16] plot multidimensional objects as polylines on parallel axes where each axis represents one dimension. Given an object, the respective positions on the neighboring axis are connected by lines resulting in a polyline representing a given object. This technique allows for simultaneously exploring relationships and patterns among multiple variables, making it useful for data analysis and identifying trends across dimensions.

Given a list of entities, **Self-organizing maps (SOM)** [21] aim to organize them into a regular 2D grid in such a way that similarity among entities translates into the spatial proximity of their positioning. The SOM training is as follows. Each node of the 2D grid is represented as a (randomly initialized) embedding vector of the same length as the representative features of the underlying domain. Then, for a randomly selected entity, the closest node is calculated (w.r.t. L2 distance) and its embedding vector is drawn closer to the feature representation of the entity. The same (with gradually decreasing magnitude) is done also for its neighboring nodes. As such, SOM aims to provide a manifold visualization of the underlying domain.

In our use case, we effectively transposed the problem definition (similarly as, e.g., in [31]): we aimed at visualizing attribute values of a single object, where similar attributes (w.r.t. pairwise L2 distance of attribute values on all objects) should be displayed close to each other. Upon training completion, each attribute is assigned a position in the grid corresponding to the closest node. If multiple attributes are assigned to the same node, their values are averaged[1]. The value of the grid node was color-represented w.r.t. blue-white-red gradient (low values corresponded to blue tones, close-to-average values were depicted in white-ish colors, while high values corresponded to red tones). SOM visualizations were trained w.r.t. 5×5 grids, 10 epochs, initial learning rate $lr = 1$, and neighborhood size coefficient $\sigma = 1$.

Bubble charts and scatter plots are relatively popular in the context of showing relationships between data, and thus became the inspiration for our visualization called **color blobs**. Blobs display individual attribute values using three different aspects. The position of the circle determines the relationship of the attributes, i.e., similar attributes are close to each other. This is achieved using t-SNE [24] where the distance of each attribute is determined by the correlation matrix. The size of the circle represents its actual value. The color of the circle determines the significance compared to the median value so that extremes are more visible.

In order to classify individual entities, it was necessary to provide users with a representation of each class (see Fig. 2). Some visualizations such as *Parallel* have the advantage of inherently allowing multiple records to be easily displayed simultaneously. For others, however, an alternative method had to be chosen. In our case, we chose to use two averaging approaches.

In the case of the *ColorBlobs*, *Faces* and *Tabular* (raw data table) visualizations, we took the average of the values in a given class, and this average representative was subsequently visualized according to the given method. The advantage is that the resulting class visualization looks the same as a single entity visualization. In the case of the *SOM* and *Radial* visualizations, we chose to average the visualizations themselves. This makes the distribution of individual values in a given class more noticeable.

Source codes for the evaluated visualization methods are available from https://github.com/dragoniscz/vizme-gen.

3   User Study

The main aim of the user study was to discover whether the visualizations may simplify the classification tasks (w.r.t. both accuracy and decision times) as compared with the raw-data baseline (i.e., making classification based on the tabular data themselves). Furthermore, we aimed to discover which visualization is most suitable for the task and whether this depends on the underlying datasets and their properties.

---

[1] In order to ensure comparability of attributes, their values were transformed w.r.t. empirical cumulative distribution function.

Table 1. Overview of datasets basic information: intra-δ is the average distance within the class, inter-δ is the average distance between different classes, D index means Dunn index, DB score means Davies-Bouldin score, S score means Silhouette score

Dataset	Classes	Features	intra-δ	inter-δ	D index	DB score	S score
Spotify	2	14	0.087 ± 0.028	0.131 ± 0.025	0.553	1.288	0.324
Cancer	2	32	0.035 ± 0.014	0.052 ± 0.018	0.393	1.246	0.298
Nutrients	25	14	0.030 ± 0.027	0.051 ± 0.030	0.013	6.354	-0.175

The study was conducted online[2] during Spring 2023 using the EasyStudy framework [7]. In the pre-study phase, users received a study description & instructions. Users were also asked to provide their basic demographics (e.g., gender, age, education) and informed consent where they agreed with the study procedure and the publication of anonymized results. Then, users were confronted with a series of classification tasks. In each task, one visualization method was utilized to visualize a randomly selected data record (i.e., object) as well as individual data classes. These were displayed to the participants, whose task was to select the class they thought the object belonged to. The exact prompt was as follows: " Please select the class to which, you think, the input belongs (i.e., select the class visualization most similar to the input visualization)".

3.1 Datasets and Pre-Processing

In the user study, we utilized the following three diverse datasets to instantiate the classification tasks.

Breasts Cancer Dataset [36] is composed of 569 breast biopsy samples; each sample has 32 numerical features describing the cells of breast mass, such as their radius, symmetry, and compactness. There are two target categories - benign and malignant samples.

Nutrients dataset, obtained from [17], contains nutritional data such as the amount of calories, saccharides, vitamins, water, and other elements of 1250 foods. Each entry consists of its name, 14 numerical values representing the nutritional data, and is assigned to one of the 25 classes, such as *Fast Foods* or *Baked products*.

Spotify dataset, obtained from [38], consists of more than 200,000 music tracks across 26 different genres. For simplicity, we limited our experiments to *classical* and *dance* music to keep the overlap between genres to a minimum. Each track consists of 14 numeric and categorical attributes representing the semantic properties of these tracks (e.g., energy, loudness, tempo). The categorical attributes were factorized into numerical values.

Datasets properties are summarized in Table 1. Note that we utilized datasets from highly diverse domains, some containing also non-numerical features, while we kept the volume of features relatively low, so the tabular baseline remains competitive. In

---

[2] The study is accessible from http://hmon.ms.mff.cuni.cz:5002/visualrepresentation/join?guid=JvmOL0_d8aldQyy7wRTzPLJeStoHv5Cc.

order to predict the complexity of the classification tasks, we analyzed the data using several different approaches. First of all, we compared the average distance[3] between elements of the same class (intra-δ) and the average distance between elements in different classes (inter-δ). In the second part, we present standard indices [30] such as Dunn index (D index), Davies-Bouldin score (DB score), and Silhouette score (S score), which represent how compact the classes are with respect to available features. From these characteristics, the Nutrients dataset appears more complex than both Spotify and Breast Cancer datasets. As for Spotify and Breast Cancer datasets, they seem quite comparable, where the Davies-Bouldin score favors the Breast Cancer dataset, but the Dunn index and Silhouette score favor the Spotify dataset.

3.2 Tasks Generation Procedure and Study Flow

During the study definition, we aimed to minimize the effects of varying task complexity and varying user competence on the per-method results. Therefore, we utilized the following within-user study design. For each user, five examples were selected from each dataset at random, resulting in 15 examples in total[4]. Then, we randomly ordered the visualization methods, and for each visualization method, the list of 15 pre-selected examples was iteratively displayed to the user. This setting has the following benefits:

1. Each user evaluates the same set of examples for all visualization methods, so the user bias is minimized.
2. Each method is evaluated w.r.t. the same set of examples, so the task difficulty bias is minimized.
3. All tasks belonging to a single method are evaluated within an uninterrupted sequence, so participants do not have to switch contexts too often.
4. Method's ordering is randomized, so possible carry-over effects (i.e., over time increase/decrease in general capability of users to solve the task) [1] are contained.
5. Thanks to the random example selection, a robust performance estimation can be given.

In addition to the actual classification tasks, we incorporated one attention check for each visualization method (six in total). In particular, one of the class visualizations was presented as an input item, and participants were tasked to select the same class visualization (i.e., the exact duplicate of the input). With this setting, each user evaluated 96 examples in total. Even though each classification task took only a few seconds to complete[5], we did not want to require users to solve more tasks due to possible attention drops in the later stages of the study.

---

[3] In all cases, we have used Euclidean distance. Each feature was converted to numeric value and normalized linearly between 0 and 1.

[4] Note that in the case of *Nutrients* dataset, we also selected a fixed sub-sample of displayed classes: a correct one plus three additional.

[5] Overall, the typical time to complete the whole study was 15–25 min.

Table 2. Overall results of the user study. Best results are bold. Asterisks (*) denote results significantly better to the *Tabular* baseline (p-value ≤ 0.05 w.r.t. Fisher test for accuracy and Moods median test for decision time).

Method	Accuracy	Median decision time (s)
Tabular baseline	*0.760*	*9.103*
Parallel coordinates	0.628	6.325 *
Radial	0.644	4.795 *
SOM	0.685	5.057 *
Color Blobs	0.780	4.460 *
Chernoff Faces	**0.828** *	**3.697** *

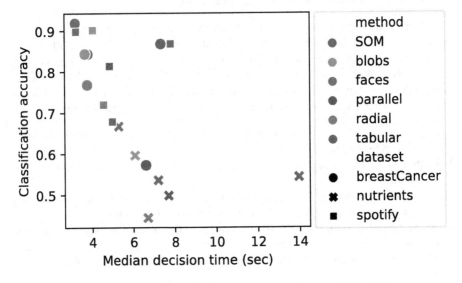

Fig. 3. Accuracy and median decision times for individual visualization methods and datasets.

3.3 Results

The study participants were recruited through Prolific.co service. In total, 121 participants completed the study. We removed 9 participants who failed 2 or more attention checks, resulting in 112 valid users.

Overall study results are depicted in Table 2. *Faces* visualization significantly outperforms all other visualizations (including the *Tabular* baseline) w.r.t. both decision accuracy and decision time. Furthermore, *ColorBlob* model performed slightly better than *Tabular* baseline (no stat. sign.) w.r.t. decision accuracy while significantly outperforming the baseline w.r.t. decision time. Other visualization methods provided a tradeoff of faster decisions but with lower accuracy than the baseline.

We further refined the overall results by considering the individual datasets separately (see Fig. 3). One can observe that the *Faces* method outperforms its competitors on all datasets, with the exception of classification accuracy on the Spotify dataset, where *ColorBlobs* were slightly better (no stat. sign.). As for the individual datasets, both Breast cancer and Spotify datasets were rather easy to decide for users (mean accuracy of 0.80 and 0.81 resp.), while the Nutrients dataset was considerably more challenging (mean accuracy of 0.55)[6]. This corresponds to the estimated dataset complexity, where the Dunn index, Davies-Bouldin score, and Silhouette score are inferior by a large margin for Nutrients as compared to both other datasets.

It is also notable, that median decision times were almost perfectly anti-correlated with the accuracy[7]. The only major exception was the *Tabular* baseline, where decisions were significantly slower for all datasets. We understand this as follows: Despite users spending more time on judging examples from more difficult datasets, or less comprehensive visualizations, they were not able to improve their decisions much.

Finally, the *Faces*, as well as several other visualization methods, on average, exhibited considerably shorter decision times than the *Tabular* baseline. However, it is yet to reveal, whether there exist users who could decide faster while using the *tabular* visualizations. Note that the results contained several outliers (i.e., time to decision of several minutes), which we assume were caused by a temporary change of activity of respective participants rather than by the complexity of the decision. Therefore, in the subsequent analysis, we focused on the median decision time per participant, which reduced the effect of the outliers. Specifically, for each participant, we checked whether the median time to decide was shorter for *Tabular* baseline than for each of *Faces*, *ColorBlobs*, *SOM*, *Radial*, and *Parallel* visualizations. Indeed, such users existed for all combinations, but their volume was rather small (7% for *Faces*, 12% for *ColorBlobs* and *Radial*, 14% for *SOM* and 24% for *Parallel*). We can conclude that, especially for *Faces* visualization, the vast majority of users can utilize it to make faster decisions.

4   Comparison with DCNN Models

The one remaining question is whether the presented visualizations are only suitable for human processing, or whether they also provide a suitable representation for some automated downstream tasks performed e.g. via a fine-tuned DCNN model. Unlike standard similarity approaches, DCNN allows the use of many already trained models with automatic fine-tuning. The goal of comparison is not to find the best DCNN model for this particular task. We are rather interested in the possible correlation between the accuracy rate in user testing and in DCNN approaches. Based on the number and size of the input data, we decided to use a rather small pre-trained network, in particular EfficientNetB0 [33], and fine-tuned it for each dataset and each visualization method. We utilized a 5-fold cross-validation scheme and trained the network for 50 epochs.

The results can be seen in Table 3[8]. We can see that the *Faces* visualization also performs the best across all datasets while being very close to the accuracy of the real

---

[6] Note that because four classes were shown to each user in the case of Nutrients dataset, the accuracy of the random guessing would be 0.25.

[7] Pearson's correlation of -0.57 and -0.94 if the results of *Tabular* baseline are removed.

[8] Note that we only evaluated visualizations that were readily available in PNG format, so we discarded the *parallel* coordinates and raw *tabular* data.

Table 3. Classification accuracy for fine-tuned DCNN models. Best results are bold.

	Breast Cancer	Nutrients	Spotify	Overall
SOM	0.90	0.42	**0.90**	0.74
Color Blobs	0.85	0.42	**0.90**	0.72
Chernoff Faces	**0.95**	**0.48**	**0.90**	**0.78**
Radial	0.85	0.45	**0.90**	0.74

user. Similarly to the user study, we can see that the Nutrients dataset is more challenging than the remaining two. Seemingly, DCNN-based models struggle even more than human participants while performing the classification. Nonetheless, this may be just an artifact of the fine-tuning process, i.e., better results could be achieved if more data is available, or more time (more iterations, while also fine-tuning deeper layers of the network) is spent on the fine-tuning process. For both Breast cancer and Spotify datasets, the DCNN approach slightly outperforms human annotators on average.

5   Discussion and Conclusions

The results of both the user study and the fine-tuned DCNNs supported that the visualizations may serve a dual purpose of both human knowledge acquisition and model-based data processing. For both modalities and all evaluated datasets, Chernoff *faces* outperformed other evaluated visualization methods. Indeed, the main outcome of the paper is the observation that the same visualization method can be successfully utilized both by humans and for subsequent automated processing. We believe the main reason for this is twofold. Humans are well-trained to recognize even small differences in one's face, but also DCNN methods are often trained on datasets comprising many portrait-like images or facial expressions, such as ImageNet [29]. Unlike humans, fine-tuned DCNNs were also well-capable to learn the patterns presented via *SOM* and *Radial* visualizations. So, we can assume that discriminative patterns were presented in these visualizations, but in an incomprehensive or misleading way from the human perspective.

It is important to mention that it was not our goal to train a DCNN model that will achieve state-of-the-art classification accuracy on given datasets, nor to compare it with domain-specific approaches specializing in classification tasks for some of the used datasets. Instead, we wanted to illustrate the potential for dual usage of these generic visualization methods and, as such, assess their suitability as a universal data representation needing no domain-specific processing. This said, even the simple fine-tuning described in Sect. 4 achieved a very good performance as compared to both human annotators and state-of-the-art models. For instance, the state-of-the-art classification accuracy measured on the breast cancer dataset is 0.97 [28], which is quite close to the performance of EfficientNetB0 fine-tuned w.r.t. Chernoff *faces* visualizations (0.95).

Although the results of this study are promising, there are several limitations that should be addressed in future work. First of all, only one related task, i.e., item classification, was evaluated. It is yet to be revealed if the same visualizations are suitable also for other tasks, such as proximity detection, clustering, or data organization. Also, while the utilized datasets come from highly diverse domains, they are all comprised of tens rather than hundreds of attributes. While this simplifies the task if performed on the raw data, a higher volume of attributes may prove challenging for some visualization methods as well. While some methods (e.g., *SOM, Blobs*) have internal mechanisms to deal with the dimensionality issue, others (e.g., Chernoff *faces, Radial, Parallel*) may require some pre-processing such as feature ordering, selection, or merging. We would like to explore this issue and its impact on the methods' applicability in the near future.

Acknowledgments. This paper has been supported by Czech Science Foundation (GAČR) project 22-21696S and by Charles University grant SVV-260698/2023.

References

1. Afchar, D., Melchiorre, A.B., Schedl, M., Hennequin, R., Epure, E.V., Moussallam, M.: Explainability in music recommender systems. AI Mag. **43**(2), 190–208 (2022)
2. Albo, Y., Lanir, J., Bak, P., Rafaeli, S.: Off the radar: comparative evaluation of radial visualization solutions for composite indicators. IEEE Trans. Vis. Comput. Graph. **22**(1), 569–578 (2015)
3. Antonov, A.: ChernoffFace Python package (2022). https://github.com/antononcube/Python-packages/tree/main/ChernoffFace
4. Borg, I., Staufenbiel, T.: Performance of snow flakes, suns, and factorial suns in the graphical representation of multivariate data. Multivar. Behav. Res. **27**(1), 43–55 (1992)
5. Chan, W.W.Y.: A survey on multivariate data visualization. Department of Computer Science and Engineering. Hong Kong University of Science and Technology **8**(6), 1–29 (2006)
6. Chernoff, H.: The use of faces to represent points in k-dimensional space graphically. J. Am. Stat. Assoc. **68**(342), 361–368 (1973)
7. Dokoupil, P., Peska, L.: Easystudy: Framework for easy deployment of user studies on recommender systems. In: Proceedings of the 17th ACM Conference on Recommender Systems, pp. 1196–1199. RecSys '23, Association for Computing Machinery, New York, NY, USA (2023)
8. Etemadpour, R., Motta, R., de Souza Paiva, J.G., Minghim, R., De Oliveira, M.C.F., Linsen, L.: Perception-based evaluation of projection methods for multidimensional data visualization. IEEE Trans. Vis. Comput. Graph. **21**(1), 81–94 (2014)
9. Flury, B., Riedwyl, H.: Graphical representation of multivariate data by means of asymmetrical faces. J. Am. Stat. Assoc. **76**(376), 757–765 (1981)
10. Forsell, C., Seipel, S., Lind, M.: Simple 3D glyphs for spatial multivariate data. In: IEEE Symposium on Information Visualization, 2005. INFOVIS 2005, pp. 119–124. IEEE (2005)
11. Fuchs, J., Isenberg, P., Bezerianos, A., Fischer, F., Bertini, E.: The influence of contour on similarity perception of star glyphs. IEEE Trans. Vis. Comput. Graph. **20**(12), 2251–2260 (2014)
12. Fuchs, J., Jäckle, D., Weiler, N., Schreck, T.: Leaf Glyphs: story telling and data analysis using environmental data glyph metaphors. In: Braz, J., et al. (eds.) VISIGRAPP 2015. CCIS, vol. 598, pp. 123–143. Springer, Cham (2016). https://doi.org/10.1007/978-3-319-29971-6_7
13. Grosse Deters, H., Timm, W., Nattkemper, T.W.: REEFSOM-a metaphoric data display for exploratory data mining. Brains, Minds and Media 2 (2006)
14. Hamner, C., Turner, D., Young, D.: Comparisons of several graphical methods for representing multivariate data. Comput. Math. Appl. **13**(7), 647–655 (1987)

15. Holten, D., Van Wijk, J.J.: Evaluation of cluster identification performance for different PCP variants. In: Computer Graphics Forum, vol. 29, pp. 793–802. Wiley Online Library (2010)
16. Inselberg, A., Dimsdale, B.: Parallel coordinates: a tool for visualizing multi-dimensional geometry. In: Proceedings of the First IEEE Conference on Visualization: Visualization 1990, pp. 361–378. IEEE (1990)
17. Chang, K.: Parallel coordinates Github repository (2023). https://github.com/syntagmatic/parallel-coordinates/blob/master/examples/data/nutrients.csv
18. Keogh, E., Mueen, A.: Curse of Dimensionality, pp. 314–315. Springer, US, Boston, MA (2017). https://doi.org/10.1007/978-1-4899-7687-1_192
19. Klippel, A., Hardisty, F., Li, R., Weaver, C.: Colour-enhanced star plot glyphs: Can salient shape characteristics be overcome? Cartographica: Int. J. Geograph. Inf. Geovis. **44**(3), 217–231 (2009)
20. Klippel, A., Hardisty, F., Weaver, C.: Star plots: how shape characteristics influence classification tasks. Cartogr. Geogr. Inf. Sci. **36**(2), 149–163 (2009)
21. Kohonen, T.: The self-organizing map. Neurocomputing **21**(1–3), 1–6 (1998)
22. Lee, M.D., Reilly, R.E., Butavicius, M.E.: An empirical evaluation of Chernoff faces, star glyphs, and spatial visualizations for binary data. In: Proceedings of the Asia-Pacific symposium on Information visualisation-Volume 24, pp. 1–10 (2003)
23. Liu, S., Maljovec, D., Wang, B., Bremer, P.T., Pascucci, V.: Visualizing high-dimensional data: advances in the past decade. IEEE Trans. Vis. Comput. Graph. **23**(3), 1249–1268 (2016)
24. van der Maaten, L., Hinton, G.: Visualizing data using t-SNE. J. Mach. Learn. Res. **9**(11), 2579–2605 (2008)
25. Mezzich, J.E., Worthington, D.R.: A comparison of graphical representations of multidimensional psychiatric diagnostic data. In: Graphical Representation of Multivariate Data, pp. 123–141. Elsevier (1978)
26. Mohammed, L.T., AlHabshy, A.A., ElDahshan, K.A.: Big data visualization: a survey. In: 2022 International Congress on Human-Computer Interaction, Optimization and Robotic Applications (HORA), pp. 1–12. IEEE (2022)
27. Morris, C.J., Ebert, D.S., Rheingans, P.L.: Experimental analysis of the effectiveness of features in chernoff faces. In: 28th AIPR Workshop: 3D Visualization for Data Exploration and Decision Making, vol. 3905, pp. 12–17. SPIE (2000)
28. Naji, M.A., Filali, S.E., Aarika, K., Benlahmar, E.H., Abdelouhahid, R.A., Debauche, O.: Machine learning algorithms for breast cancer prediction and diagnosis. Procedia Comput. Sci. **191**, 487–492 (2021)
29. Russakovsky, O., et al.: ImageNet large scale visual recognition challenge. Int. J. Comput. Vis. (IJCV) **115**(3), 211–252 (2015)
30. Scitovski, R., Sabo, K., Martínez-Álvarez, F., Ungar, Š.: Indexes, pp. 101–115. Springer International Publishing, Cham (2021)
31. Sharma, A., Vans, E., Shigemizu, D., Boroevich, K.A., Tsunoda, T.: DeepInsight: a methodology to transform a non-image data to an image for convolution neural network architecture. Sci. Rep. **9**(1) (2019)
32. Skopal, T.: On visualizations in the role of universal data representation. In: Proceedings of the 2020 on International Conference on Multimedia Retrieval, ICMR 2020, Dublin, Ireland, June 8–11, 2020, pp. 362–367. ACM (2020)
33. Tan, M., Le, Q.: EfficientNet: rethinking model scaling for convolutional neural networks. In: Proceedings of the 36th International Conference on Machine Learning, pp. 6105–6114. PMLR (2019)
34. Ventocilla, E., Riveiro, M.: A comparative user study of visualization techniques for cluster analysis of multidimensional data sets. Inf. Vis. **19**(4), 318–338 (2020)

35. Wilkinson, L.: An experimental evaluation of multivariate graphical point representations. In: Proceedings of the 1982 Conference on Human Factors in Computing Systems, pp. 202–209 (1982)
36. Wolberg, W., Mangasarian, O., Street, N., Street, W.: Breast Cancer Wisconsin (Diagnostic). UCI Machine Learning Repository (1995). https://doi.org/10.24432/C5DW2B
37. Wong, P.C., Bergeron, R.D.: 30 years of multidimensional multivariate visualization. Sci. Vis. **2**, 3–33 (1994)
38. Hamidani, Z.: Spotify tracks DB (2019). https://www.kaggle.com/datasets/zaheenhamidani/ultimate-spotify-tracks-db
39. Zhao, Y., et al.: Evaluating multi-dimensional visualizations for understanding fuzzy clusters. IEEE Trans. Vis. Comput. Graph. **25**(1), 12–21 (2018)

A Web Platform to Investigate the Relationship Between Sounds, Colors and Emotions

Silvia Dini[1] , Luca A. Ludovico[2(✉)] , Alessandro Rizzi[2] , Beatrice Sarti[2] ,
and María Joaquina Valero Gisbert[1]

[1] Università degli Studi di Parma, Parma, Italy
{silvia.dini,mariajoaquinavalero.gisbert}@unipr.it
[2] Università degli Studi di Milano, via G. Celoria 18, Milan, Italy
{luca.ludovico,alessandro.rizzi,beatrice.sarti}@unimi.it
https://www.unipr.it , https://www.unimi.it

Abstract. This paper presents a novel web platform designed to investigate the relationship between sounds, colors, and emotions, with the overarching goal of enhancing the sensory experience of impaired individuals in visual art museums. Taking advantage of the principles of sensory substitution, the project aims to bridge the gap between auditory and visual perception, allowing individuals with visual or cognitive impairments to engage with visual art through alternative sensory modalities. The platform's architecture is centered around the delivery of short sound stimuli to participants, who then provide feedback on the associations they perceive between these auditory cues and both colors and emotional dimensions. The collected data will be analyzed to discern patterns and correlations, shedding light on how auditory stimuli can be used to evoke visual and emotional responses. This paper outlines the technical and methodological aspects of the web platform, including its design, development, and implementation. It discusses the selection of sound stimuli and the integration of user-friendly interfaces to ensure a seamless experience for participants. Preliminary results from volunteer tests are briefly presented, highlighting intriguing findings regarding the associations between sounds, colors, and emotions.

Keywords: Computer-human interfaces · Chromesthesia · Music · Colors · Emotions · Art

1 Introduction

This paper represents the starting point of a broader study that aims to investigate how people of different ages, educational backgrounds, geographical areas, and cultures react to different sound stimuli and how they intuitively are inclined to link a certain stimulus to a given color and emotion. The motivation behind this research stems from the need to deepen our understanding of the mechanisms involved in the perception and integration of auditory and visual stimuli and their affective interpretation. In fact, by unraveling the complex interplay between these sensory modalities, we can gain insights into the cognitive processes underlying multisensory experiences.

H. P. da Silva and P. Cipresso (Eds.): CHIRA 2023, CCIS 1997, pp. 244–257, 2023.
https://doi.org/10.1007/978-3-031-49368-3_15

Addressing, in particular, the accessibility of museums for people with visual and/or cognitive impairments, the final goal of the project is the intersemiotic translation of the chromatic information of artworks into sounds. For further details on the general project, please refer to [11].

The first research question at the core of this study is the existence of a correlation between colors and sounds. Such a correspondence, if demonstrated, could provide an alternative way to convey chromatic information. The assumption to verify is the possibility of establishing a rule or, at least, a commonly acceptable way to translate color information into sound. In this sense, the first step is to receive initial feedback from normally sighted users on the degree of correspondence between colors and timbres. Another research question concerns the elicitation of emotional states through sounds.

This paper focuses on the design and implementation of a web interface suitable for performing an online experiment on a sample of volunteers. The web framework also provides an easy way to visualize aggregate results gathered from user tests.

The rest of the paper is structured as follows. Section 2 clarifies the theoretical framework of the project; Sect. 3 sheds light on the studies on sound and color historically conducted in both the artistic and the scientific field; Sect. 4 explains how the test was conceived and structured; Sect. 5 describes the web interface designed and made publicly available to conduct such a test online; Sect. 6 provides an insight about the results obtained so far; finally, Sect. 7 draws the conclusions.

2   Theoretical Framework

Taking into account that the acoustic channel is the most developed in blind and visually impaired (BVI) people, to overcome these limitations the approach suggested is to use auditory feedback to sonify chromatic information. As defined by Herman et al. [15], sonification is a technique to communicate information that uses sound to describe data and interactions with no vocal signals in order to facilitate their interpretations. The process of sonification has been explored mainly to improve the orientation and mobility of VIB people because it can rely on non-invasive hardware such as the mobile phone speaker or headphones, it reduces cognitive load and linguistic differences, and it reduces background noise. One example is the *WatchOut* interface developed by the University of Milan, which uses bone-conducting headphones to convey real-time information about the characteristics of an obstacle (distance, position, width, height) as distinct sound properties [24]. Another important stream of research has been conducted by the Hebrew University of Jerusalem, with respect to the adoption of sonification techniques in Sensory Substitution Devices (SSD) for visual rehabilitation. Their idea is to convey visual information to the visually impaired by systematically substituting visual information into one of their intact senses in a non-invasive way [18]. Visual-to-auditory SSD convey visual information via sound, with the primary goal of making visual information accessible to blind and visually impaired people. In particular, they developed the *EyeMusic*, a device that transforms digital images into soundscapes, or auditory representations of images, composed of musical notes, each corresponding to a pixel [1]. The inclusion of chromatic information is the main novelty of *EyeMusic*, demonstrating that color can improve object recognition.

Fig. 1. 3D render of the painting *Work* (1967) by Yamazaki Tsuruko. Image adapted from https://www.metaobjects.org/work/m-plus-sonic-topologies/.

While audio interfaces have been already utilized to convey information with the help of sound effects, particularly in the context of representing the scene of an artwork, there has been a lack of research specifically focused on the colors of the artworks. Notably, color often operates differently in contemporary artwork when compared to more traditional art forms. This is particularly true in the world of abstract art. Unlike representational art, abstract works lack recognizable objects or figures, making it more difficult to establish a connection between visual and auditory elements. Researchers and artists have started to experiment with various approaches to bridge the gap between abstract visuals and sounds. One approach involves using soundscapes or ambient sounds to create an immersive audio experience that complements the abstract artwork. One example is hosted in the M+ Museum of Hong Kong. *The Sonic topologies: Hong Kong* is a 3D reproduction of the painting *Work* by Tsuruko Yamazaki (see Fig. 1). This replica aims to convey the lines, shapes, and colors of the painting by translating this inner language through haptic and audio solutions. It works thanks to a webcam placed on the top of the room that records the position of the index finger on the 3D panel thanks to Machine Learning technologies. The sounds reproduced belong to different areas of the city of Hong Kong, according to a principle of similarity with the features in the painting. Incorporating synaesthetic techniques, such as associating specific sounds or musical notes with colors or visual patterns, can provide a bridge between abstract visuals and auditory sensation, enhancing the viewer's understanding and appreciation of the artwork by creating a multisensory experience. The study presented in the following sections investigates the associations between specific timbres and colors and explores an alternative approach to convey the chromatic information, which would otherwise be inaccessible to VIB patrons.

In recent years, there has been a growing interest among researchers in the practice of sonification as a means of sensory substitution in the field of art. In these cases, this practice involves translating visual information into sound, allowing people with visual impairments to experience and engage with art through auditory means. This approach opens up new possibilities for making art more accessible and inclusive. Bologna et al. [3] developed the *See ColOr* interface, which transforms a small portion of a colored video image into sound sources, by the use of spatialized musical instruments. Cavaco et al. [6] have developed a software application that converts digital images into sound by mapping the hue, saturation, and value attributes of the pixels into audio attributes. Similarly, Proulx et al. [25] have created a sensory substitution system that uses pitch and volume to represent the brightness and height of the image. Pun et al. [26] have explored representing hues in an image through different musical instruments, while also using different rhythms to convey the depth of the elements within the image. The *Eyes-Free Art* project, developed by Rector et al. [27], explores proxemic audio for interactive sonic experiences, like background music, sonification, and sound effects, beyond verbal description.

3 Associations Between Sound and Color

Due to the nature of the experimentation conducted in this first phase, it is worth mentioning some past research on the relationship between color and music. Such an association is often used as an example of the intersensory relations termed *synesthesia* (from the Greek: "to perceive together"), namely the experience of perceiving one sensory modality through stimulation of another. This phenomenon involves a unique sensory experience where information meant to stimulate one of our senses triggers sensations in a different domain (tasting shapes, hearing colors, etc.). According to recent estimates [9,21,29], between 80% and 97% of synesthetes report color-related synaesthesia, such as grapheme–color or music–color, even if synesthesia can theoretically bind any two senses.

One common form of this condition is sound–color synesthesia, also known as *chromes thesia*, where listening to music elicits an experience of colors, ranging from internal feelings to external experiences consisting in superimposing visual color (called *photisms*). A small minority of individuals, including some artists (e.g., Vasilij Vasil'evič Kandinskij and Paul Klee) or some musicians (e.g., Aleksandr Nikolaevič Skrjabin and Nikolaj Andreevič Rimskij-Korsakov) report cross-modal experiences of color while hearing music (Cytowic et al., 2011). For a historical overview, readers can refer to [8,10,14].

The association between music and color has been a subject of interest for both artists and scientists for centuries. Among the earliest to conceptualize a possible correlation between music and color was Pythagoras, the Greek mathematician and philosopher (ca. 550 B.C.) who considered music as a branch of mathematics and is credited with discovering the 3:2 frequency ratio in a perfect fifth interval [10]. Later, Plato and Aristotle also theorized associations between the harmony of colors and sounds. However, the scientific foundation for the connection between light and music was laid by Isaac Newton (1642- 1726) in [20]. Through his experiment on the refraction of white light using a prism, Newton demonstrated that white light could be separated into the colors of the rainbow. Newton mathematically (but rather arbitrarily) divided the visible light spectrum into seven colors (red, orange, yellow, green, blue, indigo, and violet) and, noticing a similar mathematical relationship with the musical scale, he associated these colors with the seven tones in the major scale (see Fig. 2).

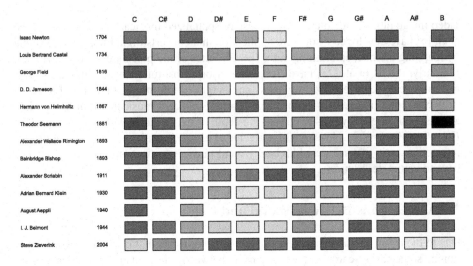

Fig. 2. Fred Collopy's *Three Centuries of Color Scales* [7].

The Jesuit monk Louis Bertrand Castel (1688–1757) broke the association of music and color from cosmological concepts, intervals, or frequencies and undertook a practical realization aimed at combining color and music as an artistic expression, allowing people without the sense of hearing to "see" music. Over the course of about thirty years and through various attempts, the French mathematician and philosopher constructed different models of a colored clavichord called the *Clavecin Oculaire* [5,12,13]. When a key was pressed, small panels would appear above the clavichord, displaying pre-set colors based on the correlation between the musical scale and the chromatic spectrum. Initially, Castel matched the colors of the chromatic spectrum to the notes of the diatonic scale. He later refined his system and presented a range of twelve colors corresponding to the semitones within an octave (see Fig. 2).

Throughout the XVIII-XXI centuries, many other composers and musicians put forth their hypotheses regarding the relationship between color and sound series. The most relevant of them are summarized in Fig. 2, taken from Fred Collopy's *The Rhythmic Light project* [7]. This diagram offers a comprehensive representation of the idiosyncratic nature of synesthesia, illustrating that the correspondences between colors and musical elements are unique to each synesthete and not easily translatable to others.

Alongside these hypotheses, there have been numerous attempts to achieve practical implementations. The advent of electricity and new technologies enabled the exploration of projected light. The most notable color instrument of the last century was the so-called *Colour Organ*, pioneered by Alexander Wallace Rimington (1854–1918). This device did not produce sound; rather, it was intended to connect the tracker of a five-octave keyboard to lens diaphragms and filters for 14 arc lamps [22,28]. The term *Colour Organ* has since become a generic name encompassing all such devices designed to project colored light. This instrument inspired the composer Aleksandr Nikolaevič Skrjabin (1872 – 1915) to incorporate for the first time projected light in a score for orchestra in his synaesthetic symphony *Prometheus: A Poem of Fire* [28].

Over the ages, other pioneers constructed devices or modified instruments like organs and harpsichords to create shifting lights and color mixing. For a detailed exploration of this topic, the reader can refer to [19, 22].

It should be noted that the aim of this part of the project is not to address the population of people affected by synesthesia, but rather to elicit color-related sensations through musical sounds.

4 The Test

In this section, we will describe the structure of the experiment and some design choices. Details about the web implementation will be provided in Sect. 2.

The test has been divided into four sections:

- *Section I* – Introduction;
- *Section II* – User profiling;
- *Section III* – Color–timbre matching, subdivided into 2 steps, namely
  - *Section III.a* – Color wheel, and
  - *Section III.b* – Self-Assessment Manikin;
- *Section IV* – Users' final opinions.

Section I provides an overview of the project and its objectives in particular, it explains that the test forms the basis of a more general project that aims to make artworks accessible to BVI people. In addition, the introduction emphasizes the importance of participants' answers and discourages random choices.

In *Section II*, participants are asked to provide essential personal information such as gender, age group, educational background, country of origin, level of musical practice and experience, as well as any auditory or visual impairments they may have. While ensuring anonymity, this information helps categorizing the data and creating participant profiles for further analysis.

After completing this section, users undergo the actual test through the color–timbre matching interface. The whole test session is made up of 18 units; each unit is structured in the same way and, in turn, is composed of 2 steps. During the first experience, namely *Section III.a*, participants are exposed to a brief auditory stimulus (see details below) and have to instinctively assign the color elicited by the sound picking it from a color wheel. Participants have the freedom to listen to the stimulus as many times as they want and they can change the color until they finalize their decision. In the second step, namely *Section III.b*, participants are expected to assess the emotional dimensions elicited by the stimulus in terms of valence (from negative to positive), arousal (from low to high intensity), and dominance (from submissive to dominant) on 9-point Likert scales. The alternation of the two steps, *III.a* and *III.b*, for each sound stimulus responds to different goals: first, it allows you to instinctively capture, without the need to listen to the sound again, even the emotional aspects evoked by the timbre; secondly, it creates a distance between the choice of color for two consecutive sound stimuli, thus limiting the possibility of mutual influences.

Finally, participants are given the opportunity to share their opinions through yes/no and open-ended questions. To this end, *Section IV* lets users provide feedback and additional information on their experience with the test. Overall, a complete session takes approximately 15 min to complete.

Please note that the goal of this paper is to present the web interface rather than analyze collected data with respect to sound features. However, some considerations emerging from the early results will be reported in Sect. 6.

4.1 Sound Stimuli

The sounds used correspond either to a note in the middle register of a pitched musical instrument or a short sound in the case of an unpitched instrument.

These stimuli, sometimes impulsive and in all cases lasting less than 4 s, are intended to be reproduced through the selected device: headphones, earphones, low-budget/PC speakers, stereo loudspeakers or alternative options. In *Section II*, the user is asked to declare the listening device in use.

A number of different musical instruments were considered to determine the most relevant timbres for the test. Following the Hornbostel-Sachs classification [16], the idea was to pick instruments from each family of musical instruments: Aerophones, Electrophones, Chordopohones, Membranophones, and Idiophones, along with white noise and pink noise.[1] In order to keep the test duration short and, consequently, the user's attention high, the test included only the following stimuli:

- Aerophones – oboe, trumpet;
- Electrophones – electric guitar, sine wave, synth, square;
- Chordophones – harp, piano, violin;
- Membranophones – tympani, bass drum, snare drum;
- Idiophones – tubular bells, vibraphone, triangle, celesta;
- Noise – white noise, pink noise.

As a design choice, there is no predefined sequence of instrumental sounds; instead, auditory stimuli are presented in any user session in random order.

4.2 Colors

The choice of the colors used for the test is based on the nonambiguous color categories identified by Brent Berlin and Paul Kay in 1969 [2]. According to their theory, English has 11 universal basic color terms: red, yellow, green, blue, black, white, gray, orange, brown, pink, and purple. To determine the specific hue to be used, we followed the RGB color model. The RGB (red, green, and blue) cube is an additive color model that involves mixing red, green, and blue channels [17]. According to this model, starting from black, RGB (0, 0, 0), one can reach white, RGB (255, 255, 255), passing through all the color gradations in between.

---

[1] From a formal point of view, white and pink noise are very likely to be additional examples of Electrophone-generated timbres.

Table 1. The list of colors utilized for the test with their red (R), green (G), and blue (B) channel amount in the range of 0–255.

Color name	R	G	B
Red	255	0	0
Orange	255	165	0
Yellow	255	255	0
Blue	0	0	255
Purple	128	0	128
Pink	255	192	203
Green	0	255	0
Brown	150	75	0
Gray	128	128	128
Black	0	0	0
White	255	255	255

In order to implement the test, a specific color shade had to be chosen as a representative of each color category. In the introductory explanation of the test presented to the user in *Section I*, it is clearly stated not to focus on the specific shade but only on the macro-category (e.g., red, green, blue, etc.). For completeness, Table 1 presents the list of specific colors arbitrarily adopted in the experiment along with their RGB code.

As a design choice, colors are presented to the user through filled circles whose centers lie, in turn, on a bigger invisible circle. Moreover, in order to avoid learning and cross-influence phenomena, at each step of *Section III.a* colors are randomly shuffled. The background of the interface is also important to guarantee unbiased results. To this end, the choice fell on a pattern of small white and gray squares alternated. The final interface is shown in Fig. 3.

4.3 The Self-Assessment Manikin

The so-called Self-Assessment Manikin, proposed in [4] and widely adopted in the scientific literature, is a nonverbal pictorial assessment technique used to directly measure valence, arousal, and dominance. Since we also want to measure the emotional associations of participants for each sound stimulus, the manikin can help participants track their personal responses by providing an intuitive visual representation, as shown in Fig. 4. The scale for each dimension ranges from 1 to 9.

5 The Web Interface

The Web interface was designed to reflect the 4-section organization of the test described above. The languages and formats adopted to implement the web pages are compliant with W3C [2] standards. In particular, the pages' structure and static content

---

[2] World Wide Web Consortium, https://www.w3.org/.

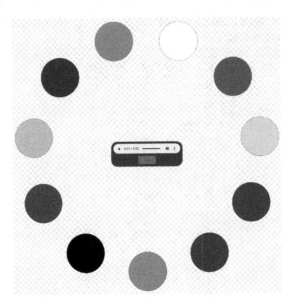

Fig. 3. Interface to select the color associated with the sound stimulus used in *Section III.a.* The order and position of the circles are random.

were written in HTML, the dynamic client-side scripting was realized in JavaScript (e.g., the audio management and the selection of users' choices), the connection and interaction with a database to gather users' answers was made in PHP, and the layout of web pages was carried out through CSS.

The landing page of the web platform is available at http://colorsoundemotion.lim. di.unimi.it/. Interested readers are invited to take the test to increase the number of available responses.

The choice of implementing a software solution from scratch rather than adopting already available online survey tools was motivated by specific constraints and design choices. It was necessary to build an interface capable of reflecting the structure of the test, drawing a very specific interface, randomizing sound and visual stimuli, and collecting results in a custom relational database. Particular attention was paid to responsive design in order to distribute the test as much as possible among interested volunteers by supporting mobile devices, also.

The choice of releasing a web interface was motivated by a number of factors. Among the main advantages is accessibility: web applications are accessible from any device with an internet connection and a web browser. Users can access them on various platforms (desktop, mobile, tablet) without the need to install specific software. Moreover, web applications are typically platform-independent. They can run on different operating systems (Windows, macOS, Linux) without modification, making them versatile and accessible to a wider audience. As another advantage, while offline applications require installation and regular maintenance on individual devices, web applications eliminate this burden; they are centrally hosted, allowing developers to push

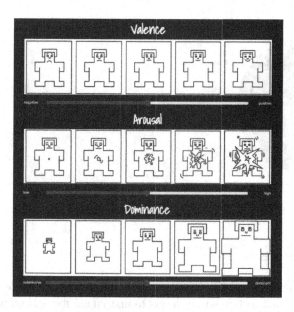

Fig. 4. The Self-Assessment Manikin used in *Section III.b*. The first row represents valence, the second row represents arousal, and the third row represents dominance. The perceived levels, from 1 to 9, are selectable in the web interface through ad-hoc sliders.

updates and improvements seamlessly. Users do not need to manually update their software since they always have access to the latest version. Finally, web applications facilitate collaboration and data sharing among users, regardless of their location. This aspect is particularly relevant to our goals, as we want to gather and compare users' data from different geographical areas and cultures.

Despite these advantages, web applications also have some limitations, such as the dependency on an internet connection and potential performance issues. Fortunately, as it concerns the latter issue, multimedia streams to be delivered in our experiment are very light (a few seconds of MP3 data) and do not present strict real-time constraints.

Concerning interface design, the key page layouts are those for the two parts of *Section III*, shown in Fig. 3 and Fig. 4 respectively. In addition, it is worth mentioning the result page, not intended to be shown to test participants and available in a back-office area, that can be accessed at http://colorsoundemotion.lim.di.unimi.it/results.php. For each of the 18 stimuli, this page presents: i) a pie chart illustrating the distribution of color answers, and ii) a line chart showing the values of valence, arousal, and dominance (see Fig. 5). Graphs have been obtained by parsing database data through the *Google Charts* library,[3] a set of JavaScript-based tools to achieve interactive charts. The results collected so far in the experimentation will be briefly commented on in the next section.

---

[3] https://developers.google.com/chart.

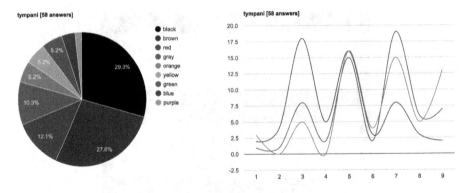

Fig. 5. The pie chart and the line chart used to show results.

6 Early Results

As a premise, please note that this paper is not meant to present a detailed analysis of the data collected so far and much less to understand the reasons why some links between timbres and colors or timbres and emotions emerge.

At the time of writing, a total of 58 participants completed the test (35 females, 22 males, and 1 non-binary). Their age covered categories from ≤19 to 60–69. Only four participants reported visual impairments: "I can't see from my right eye because I recently had a corneal transplant", "Miopia", "Contact lenses (keratoconus)", "Registered blind with some useful sight". Only one participant reported a case of auditory impairment: misophonia, namely a selective auditory sensitivity that implies decreased tolerance to specific sounds or their associated stimuli.

Regarding music practice and listening, 72% of the participants reported that they listen to music very frequently, while 48% of the people never played an instrument. None of the participants reported to play an instrument at a professional level.

A desirable but somehow unexpected result is a clear convergence, for some timbres, toward a color or a color family (namely 2 or 3 similar colors). This is the case with the bass drum, where black + brown + gray (3 colors out of 11) score together more than 76%, the pink noise, where blue + gray score about 64%, and the tympani, where black + brown score about 57%. The result for the white noise, which is either blue or gray for more than 58% of the participants, is also interesting.

Another aspect emerging from the test concerns the interface for *Section III.b.* In fact, despite the theory suggesting a 9-point scale for each dimension of the Self-Assessment Manikin, users rarely used the intermediate position of the cursor between two pictures, instead preferring to target precisely one of the images. The resulting trend in line charts is a wavy one, with local maxima mostly located in correspondence with odd values.

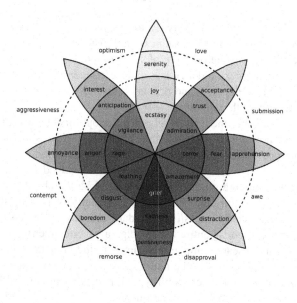

Fig. 6. The *wheel of emotions* proposed by Robert Plutchik in 1980 [23].

7   Conclusion and Future Work

This paper aims to be an early contribution to our understanding of multi-sensory performances involving the combination of auditory and visual stimuli. By investigating the perceptual, cognitive, and emotional dimensions of these experiences, we aim to uncover the potential synergies between sound and color, paving the way for enhanced artistic expression and immersive sensory experiences. This research has implications not only for scientific inquiry but also for the creative industries, offering new possibilities for engaging and captivating audiences in novel and meaningful ways.

In this paper, we have introduced a preliminary test to be conducted on volunteers in order to determine possible correspondences between short sound stimuli and color sensations and between the same sound stimuli and emotional dimensions. We have described the web interface released to gather test results from geographically distributed users and the back-office area to enjoy an easily readable representation of data through pie and line charts.

One of the goals of the general project is to assess the influence of different cultures on associations, but, currently, this aspect is not adequately returned by the result page. Additional test sessions have to be conducted in extra-European countries in order to observe possible cross-cultural influences. Consequently, the back-office interface must be extended to support more refined queries, not only by geographical area, but also by age range, visual or auditory impairment, etc.

An aspect that we want to deepen in future work is the possible use of Plutchik's *wheel of emotions* [23] as an alternative to two different experiments about sound-color association (*Section III.a*) and sound-emotion association (*Section III.b*). This model, proposed by the American psychologist Robert Plutchik in 1980, is shown in Fig. 6.

The eight sectors of the wheel are designed to host as many primary emotions: anger, anticipation, joy, trust, fear, surprise, sadness, and disgust. Each primary emotion has a polar opposite (e.g., joy is the opposite of sadness and fear is the opposite of anger). Additionally, this circumplex model creates a correspondence between an emotion circle and a color wheel. Both colors and primary emotions can be expressed at different intensities and can mix with each other.

A completely new experiment could rely on the adoption of the *wheel of emotions* to let users select the most appropriate slice in response to a sound stimulus. This kind of test, by combining colors and emotions, would halve the duration of a test session and could also serve to either validate or confute the results obtained so far by two separate experiments. In this sense, a possible problem could be the absence from Plutchik's model of some colors, e.g. gray and black, and the difficulty in creating correspondences between shades with specific intensity (e.g., dark green, olive green, lime, etc.) and generic colors that represent an entire family (e.g., a generic green).

In conclusion, this research aims to contribute to the broader research on sensory substitution and its applications in the realm of visual art, demonstrating the promise of technology in enhancing the accessibility and inclusivity of cultural institutions for individuals with sensory or cognitive impairments.

References

1. Abboud, S., Hanassy, S., Levy-Tzedek, S., Maidenbaum, S., Amedi, A.: Eyemusic: introducing a visual colorful experience for the blind using auditory sensory substitution. Restor. Neurol. Neurosci. **32**(2), 247–257 (2014)
2. Berlin, B., Kay, P.: Basic Color Terms: Their Universality and Evolution. University of California Press (1969)
3. Bologna, G., Gomez, J.D., Pun, T.: Vision substitution experiments with see color. In: Ferrández Vicente, J.M., Álvarez Sánchez, J.R., de la Paz López, F., Toledo Moreo, F.J. (eds.) IWINAC 2013. LNCS, vol. 7930, pp. 83–93. Springer, Heidelberg (2013). https://doi.org/10.1007/978-3-642-38637-4_9
4. Bradley, M.M., Lang, P.J.: Measuring emotion: the self-assessment manikin and the semantic differential. J. Behav. Ther. Exp. Psychiatry **25**(1), 49–59 (1994)
5. Castel, L.B.: L'optique des couleurs: fondée sur les simples observations, & tournée sur-tout à la pratique de la peinture, de la teinture & des autres arts coloristes. chez Briasson (1740)
6. Cavaco, S., Henriques, J.T., Mengucci, M., Correia, N., Medeiros, F.: Color sonification for the visually impaired. Procedia Technol. **9**, 1048–1057 (2013)
7. Collopy, F.: Rhythmic light, hue to pitch. https://rhythmiclight.com/visual-musiccorrespondences/hue-to-pitch/ (2004). Accessed 16 May 2023
8. Cuddy, L.L.: The color of melody. Music. Percept. **2**(3), 345–360 (1985). https://doi.org/10.2307/40285303
9. Day, S.: Some demographic and socio-cultural aspects of synesthesia. In: Robertson, L., N. Sagiv, N. (eds.) Synesthesia: Perspectives from Cognitive Neuroscience, chap. 2, pp. 11–33. Oxford University Press, Oxford (2005)
10. Day, S.A.: Synesthesia and Synesthetes. Independently published (2022)
11. Dini, S., Ludovico, L.A., Mascetti, S., Valero Gisbert, M.J.: Translating color: sonification as a method of sensory substitution within the museum. In: 20th International Web for All Conference (W4A '23), April 30-May 1, 2023, Austin, TX, USA, pp. 162–163. ACM (2023). https://doi.org/10.1145/3587281.3587706

12. Franssen, M.: The ocular harpsichord of Louis-Bertrand Castel. Tractrix **3**(1991), 15–77 (1991)

13. Gepner, C.: Le Père Castel et le clavecin oculaire: carrefour de lesthétique et des savoirs dans la première moitié du XVIIIe siècle. Ph.D. thesis, Paris 3 (1994)

14. Hawkins, V.: Music-color synesthesia: a historical and scientific overview. Aisthesis: Honors Student J. **13**(1) (2022)

15. Hermann, T., Hunt, A., Neuhoff, J.G., et al.: The Sonification Handbook, vol. 1. Logos Verlag Berlin (2011)

16. Lee, D.: Hornbostel-Sachs classification of musical instruments. Knowl. Organ. **47**(1), 72–91 (2019)

17. Levkowitz, H.: Color Theory and Modeling for Computer Graphics, Visualization, and Multimedia Applications. Springer (1997). https://doi.org/10.1007/b102382

18. Maidenbaum, S., Abboud, S., Amedi, A.: Sensory substitution: closing the gap between basic research and widespread practical visual rehabilitation. Neurosci. Biobehav. Rev. **41**, 3–15 (2014)

19. Moritz, W.: The dream of color music, and machines that made it possible. Animation World Mag. **2**(1) (1997)

20. Newton, I.: Opticks, or, a treatise of the reflections, refractions, inflections & colours of light. Courier Corporation (1952)

21. Niccolai, V., Jennes, J., Stoerig, P., Van Leeuwen, T.M.: Modality and variability of synesthetic experience. Am. J. Psychol. **125**(1), 81–94 (2012). www.jstor.org/stable/10.5406/amerjpsyc.125.1.0081

22. Peacock, K.: Instruments to perform color-music: two centuries of technological experimentation. Leonardo **21**(4), 397–406 (1988). https://doi.org/10.2307/1578702

23. Plutchik, R., Kellerman, H.: Emotion, theory, research, and experience: theory, research and experience. Academic Press (1980)

24. Presti, G., et al.: WatchOut: obstacle sonification for people with visual impairment or blindness. In: Proceedings of the 21th International ACM SIGACCESS Conference on Computers and Accessibility (ASSETS'19), pp. 402–413. ACM (2019). https://doi.org/10.1145/3308561.3353779

25. Proulx, M.J., Brown, D.J., Pasqualotto, A., Meijer, P.: Multisensory perceptual learning and sensory substitution. Neurosci. Biobehav. Rev. **41**, 16–25 (2014)

26. Pun, T., Deville, B., Bologna, G.: Sonification of colour and depth in a mobility aid for blind people. In: 16th International Conference on Auditory Display (ICAD-2010), pp. 9–13. Georgia Institute of Technology (2010)

27. Rector, K., Salmon, K., Thornton, D., Joshi, N., Morris, M.R.: Eyes-free art: exploring proxemic audio interfaces for blind and low vision art engagement. Proc. ACM Interact. Mob. Wearable Ubiquitous Technol. **1**(3) (2017). https://doi.org/10.1145/3130958

28. Saglietti, B.: Dal clavecin oculaire di Louis Bertrand Castel al clavier à lumières di Alexandr Skrjabin. In: Metamorfosi dei Lumi 6. Belle lettere e scienza, pp. 187–205. Accademia Unviversity Press (2012)

29. Simner, J., et al.: Synaesthesia: the prevalence of atypical cross-modal experiences. Perception **35**(8), 1024–1033 (2006)

Continuous Time Elicitation Through Virtual Reality to Model Affect Dynamics

Francesca Borghesi[1]([✉]) [ID], Vittorio Murtas[2] [ID], Valentina Mancuso[3] [ID], and Alice Chirico[4] [ID]

[1] Department of Psychology, University of Turin, Via Verdi 10, 10124 Turin, Italy
francesca.borghesi@unito.it
[2] Department of Computer Science, University of Turin, Turin, Italy
[3] Faculty of Psychology, eCampus University, Novedrate, Italy
[4] Department of Psychology, Research Center in Communication Psychology, Catholic University of Sacred Heart, Milan, Italy

Abstract. Affective states are constantly evolving, ranging from serenity to excitement. Understanding the dynamic transitions between emotional states, known as *affect dynamics*, is crucial for understanding intraindividual emotional heterogeneity. Various statistical methods have been used to capture and quantify these dynamics, based on longitudinal time series models. However, both the statistical models and experimental design, e.g. Experience Sampling Method, lack a controlled manipulation of the transitions between affective states over time. This study aims to fill this knowledge gap using a meticulous experimental scenario design incorporating controlled affective transitions. For this reason, the study employs Virtual Reality technology to effectively elicit and regulate affective transitions, mimicking real-life situations while offering experimental control. Finally, we proposed an application of the Markovian chain model to analyze affective transition. The study aims to establish a connection between theoretical insights and empirical investigation, providing new avenues for understanding emotional fluctuations within a controlled experimental framework.

Keywords: Affect dynamics · Virtual reality · Psychometrics · Mental flexibility · Markov chain · Markov models

1 Introduction

Affective states refer to changes in behaviour, subjective feelings, and neuropsychophysiological responses associated with emotional experiences [1–3]. These states profoundly shape our perception and reaction to the environment: for instance, our affective states vary over time depending on whether we feel relaxed, bored, engaged or stressed [4]. Russell's Core Affect Model is a pivotal theoretical framework for understanding affective states [2, 5]. According to this model, core affect, the foundational emotional state, is an indefinite and pre-reflective emotional state emerging from our internal experiences, forming the basis of more intricate emotions. This Core affect model can be conceptualized as the "raw material" of emotions, characterized by a lack of specific labels such as happiness or sadness. The Core Affect Model, also called Dimensional model, highlights two fundamental dimensions governing affective states: valence and arousal. Valence reflects how pleasant or unpleasant an experience is, while arousal gauges the level of psychophysiological excitation. These two dimensions form the foundational building blocks for describing and classifying various affective experiences [2, 6, 7] (Fig. 1).

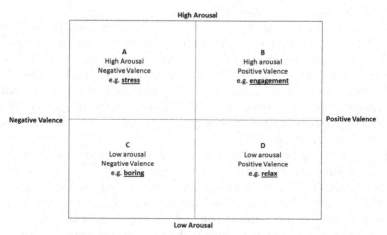

Fig. 1. Core affect model of Russel: each quadrant represents a different affective state [A (e.g. stress)], B [(e.g. engagement)], C [(e.g. boring)], D [(e.g. relax)].

Notwithstanding its significance, the Core Affect Model lacks a comprehensive description of how individuals switch between different affective states. This represents a notable gap in understanding affective dynamics. In other words, this model does not thoroughly address how individuals move from one emotional state to another, failing to capture the dynamic nature of affective experiences [8, 9].

Affective states are perpetually evolving, ranging from moments of profound serenity to states of heightened excitement. For instance, we might feel energetic and elated one day, and calmer or even anxious the next. Understanding the dynamic transitions between emotionally oriented states, yielding intraindividual emotional heterogeneity, has received limited attention [10, 11]. This phenomenon is called affect dynamics, which pertains to how emotions evolve over time, encompassing intensity, duration, frequency, and transitions [9]. Emotions often fluctuate due to external stimuli and evaluation, demanding a comprehensive analysis of affect transitions [8].

The concept of affect dynamics originated within the realm of statistics, aiming to analyze and measure the intricate nature of emotional fluctuations [12]. Researchers sought statistical models that could capture and quantify the dynamics of affective experiences with various approaches including autoregressive models, panel data analyses, Bayesian frameworks, and Markov models [8, 12, 13]. These statistical methodologies aimed to provide insights into how affective states transition over time.

The Experience Sampling Method [ESM] is a highly experimental design that is implemented to conduct intensive longitudinal research. This methodology requires participants to report their thoughts, feelings, behaviors, and/or environment throughout a specific period. In this way, ESM has the potential to facilitate the measurement of both within and between subjects' affects as they evolve. Nevertheless, this methodology lacks a controlled manipulation of all transitions over time since it measured the natural affect transitions of subjects during days without controlling the type of transitions a priori. Consequently, it could be that during a week-long survey, a subject may not encounter the complete spectrum of potential transitions. This limitation hinders making accurate inferences about individuals' affective dynamism.

In this context, the present study seeks to fill this knowledge gap. The study employs a meticulous experimental scenario design that incorporates controlled affective transitions. This innovative approach aims to thoroughly investigate affect dynamics by constructing a priori affect situations that encompass all quadrants of Russel's Core Affect model. Consequently, it enables replicating all potential transitions between affective states within individual subjects. Our proposal entails developing a comprehensive research design employing Virtual Reality [VR] technology to effectively elicit and regulate affective transitions.

The choice of employing VR arises from its unparalleled potential to immerse participants in controlled and dynamic environments, mimicking real-life situations while offering experimental control. Moreover, VR allows us to manipulate affective transitions systematically. For this purpose, we created several VR environments that exhibit dynamic changes over time, encompassing a wide range of all affective transitions. By intentionally manipulating these transitions, the study aims to uncover new dimensions of affective experiences, shedding light on the complex interplay between emotional states and their temporal evolution. Furthermore, VR can induce affective transitions that mirror real-world scenarios while maintaining experimental rigor. This approach enhances the ecological validity of our research and aims to fill the existing gap in incomprehensive methodologies for investigating affect dynamics. This study aims to establish a connection between theoretical insights and empirical investigation, providing new avenues for understanding the intricacies of emotional fluctuations within a controlled experimental framework.

1.1 Eliciting Affective States Through Virtual Reality

Based on stimulus type, affect elicitation includes active and passive approaches. Active methods include behavioral manipulation, social contact, and dyadic interaction [14]. In contrast, passive methods use images such as The International Affective Picture System [IAPS], or emotional facial expressions [15], watching film clips [16], or music stimuli [17]. Due to the importance of immersion in generating emotions by replicating authentic experiences, passive techniques have severe limitations, such as poor sense of presence, poor immersivity, and low realism.

Hence, VR is an exceptional tool for eliciting and studying emotions due to its remarkable potential to immerse participants in meticulously crafted and controlled environments [18–23]. Unlike conventional stimuli such as images or sounds, VR offers an unparalleled multisensory experience, enveloping users in a sensory-rich world that can profoundly influence their emotional states [24] Moreover, VR facilitates the creation of ecologically valid contexts that might otherwise be challenging to reproduce in traditional experimental settings. By mimicking real-world situations, VR can evoke emotions that closely mirror those experienced in everyday life, enhancing the generalizability of findings [18]. The versatility of VR in designing emotional elicitation environments is striking researchers to construct scenarios that precisely provoke specific emotions, allowing for systematic exploration of emotional processes. For instance, VR environments have been creatively designed to elicit different combinations of emotional valence [positive or negative] and arousal [low or high] through various sensory characteristics. For instance, a virtual scenario simulating a crowded and bustling city street can induce anxiety or stress, enabling the observation and analysis of physiological and psychological responses to such situations [25, 26]. Similarly, serene and picturesque natural landscapes can evoke calmness and joy, contributing to a deeper understanding of positive emotions and their underlying mechanisms. In the realm of positive valence and low arousal, VR environments often depict serene and pleasant scenes, such as a sunset on a beach or a tranquil garden in bloom. These settings incorporate warm colors, soothing sounds, and slow movements to evoke a sense of calmness and relaxation [27, 28]. For inducing positive valence with high arousal, VR scenarios might simulate exciting or adventurous experiences, like a thrilling roller coaster ride or an exhilarating hike in a stimulating environment. Dynamic visual and auditory elements and fast-paced movements can enhance enthusiasm and energy [29].

In the case of negative valence and low arousal, VR environments can depict situations of solitude or melancholy, such as a dimly lit, quiet room or a desolate landscape. These environments reduce sensory stimulation to evoke feelings of sadness or melancholy [30]. When aiming for negative valence with high arousal, VR environments may simulate threatening or frightening situations, like a chase experience or an imminent danger scenario. Startling visuals, dissonant sounds, and a sense of urgency can heighten fear and anxiety levels [25, 30, 31]. To measure emotional elicitation, researchers have used behavioural measurement methods, such as the Likert scale e.g. Self-Manikin Assessment [SAM], or physiological ones, such as cardiac variability, skin conductance, or facial electromyography [32–34].

In recent years, the integration of VR into physiological emotional elicitation has brought about innovative applications in the realm of biofeedback - a technique that involves measuring and providing individuals with real-time information about their physiological processes, such as heart rate, skin conductance, muscle tension, or brainwave activity [35, 36]. Consequently, focus has shifted from merely observing virtual environments to actively engaging with and altering physical environments based on our physiological and affective states. In addition to contributing to the growing interest in affect computing, a multidisciplinary field dedicated to developing systems and technologies capable of perceiving, interpreting, and reacting to human emotions and affective states, virtual environments serve as stimuli and modifiers of these affective states in conjunction [37, 38]. By combining real-time physiological monitoring with immersive VR environments, researchers have created a dynamic platform for individuals to gain insights into and regulate their emotional responses [39–41]. For instance, individuals experiencing anxiety can be immersed in a virtual scenario that triggers their specific physiological markers, such as increased heart rate or perspiration [42, 43].This biofeedback-driven approach allows participants to visualize and understand the correlation between their emotional states and physiological changes, empowering them to develop self-regulation strategies.

The idea involves employing affective transitions in a standardized and pre-coded way. Consequently, an experimental design was developed that systematically incorporates and constructs VR environments representing transitions between different affective states. This phenomenon is feasible due to the dynamic nature of environments, wherein the same environment changes its characteristics to elicit and portray a shift in the affective state: from a natural environment with outside, lush birds and trees [positive valence-high arousal] to a bare, and grey natural environment [negative valence and high arousal].

Nevertheless, within biofeedback, the transitions are not predetermined in advance, as they encompass all potential shifts between various affective states and the convergence of arousal and valence levels. Hence, we aim to thoroughly examine and develop dynamic VR environments, considering all conceivable transitions. Through immersivity, sense of presence, and dynamism, we have successfully created ad hoc environments distinct in their ability to influence dynamics.

1.2 Modeling Dynamics in Affect Science

The need to create an experimental design that considers transitions also arises primarily from affect dynamics-new research field that analyzes the variation of emotions over time. In general, affect dynamics, heir to Russel's circumflex model, realizes the model's limitation and statisticality and identifies a critical dynamic solution.

However, affect dynamics is interpreted in statistical terms. The research question is how to analyze affective state changes over time. The most widely used experimental design turns out to be the ESM, which is a methodology of collecting behavioral or physiological data over time, in which several times a day/month more data are collected per subject. Initially, affect dynamics was explored using several methodologies, often leveraging classical time series analysis techniques. These include autoregressive [AR], moving average [MA], autoregressive integrated moving average [ARIMA], and autoregressive conditionally heteroskedastic [ARCH] frameworks.

- Autoregressive [AR] Models: In AR models, the current value of a variable is expressed as a linear combination of its past values. The lag parameter determines the number of past values to consider.
- Moving Average [MA] Models: MA models represent the current value as a linear combination of past prediction errors, obtained by subtracting predicted values from actual values.
- Autoregressive Integrated Moving Average [ARIMA] Models: ARIMA models combine autoregressive, moving average, and differencing components to capture various patterns in the data. Differencing makes the time series stationary.
- Autoregressive Conditionally Heteroskedastic [ARCH] Models: ARCH models capture volatility by assuming the variance depends on past values, revealing patterns of high and low volatility periods.

Within the continuous framework, the derivative of a variable with respect to time, denoted as x', is expressed as a function of the variable itself, f[x]. This function characterizes the rate of change of the variable, encapsulating the intricate interplay of forces that lead to emotional shifts. This representation allows researchers to capture the instantaneous changes in affective states, painting a vivid picture of emotional dynamics beyond the confines of discrete intervals.

Furthermore, the continuous methodology is versatile in accommodating complex systems of equations. Variables can be vectorized to capture interactions and dependencies between multiple aspects of affect simultaneously. This ability to capture intricate interplays enhances the realism of models, offering a more faithful representation of the intricate dance of emotions.

When modeling time series data, several requirements must be met for the model to be appropriate and accurate. These requirements include:

Stationarity: As mentioned previously, time series data must be stationary for most models to work properly. Stationarity means that the statistical properties of the data, such as mean and variance, do not change over time. If a time series is non-stationary, it must be made stationary by differencing or removing a trend or a seasonal component before it can be modeled.

Linearity: Most time series models are linear models, so the relationship between the time series data and the predictor variables should be linear. A non-linear model, such as a neural network or a support vector machine, may be more appropriate if the relationship is non-linear.

Normality: Some time series models, such as the ones based on maximum likelihood estimation, assume that the model's errors are normally distributed. If the errors are not normally distributed, the results of the model may not be reliable.

Independence: Time series data is often correlated, meaning that the value of the series at a certain point in time is dependent on the values of the series at previous points in time. This correlation needs to be considered when modeling the data, and models such as ARIMA are specifically designed to handle correlated data.

Time-Dependent Structure: Time series data often has a clear time-dependent structure, such as trend, seasonality, and cyclical patterns. It is important to consider this time dependence when choosing a model and interpreting the results.

2 Experimental Design

Here we present our experimental design, dividing it into a general descriptive section (2. Experimental design), a specific one on the type and characteristics of the stimuli created (2.1 how to create VR stimuli), one on the type of randomization chosen (2.2 how to randomize), and a last one inherent in the type of data analysis chosen (2.3 how to analyze transition).

In order to comprehensively analyze affect dynamics through the employment of VR, we meticulously designed custom-tailored environments. Based on 12 possible transitions, 6 VR environments, considering outward and return, were created: for the transition from A to B and from B to A, we used the same VR environments, only reversing the effect of transition changes. VR environments were developed with Unity 2021 and deployed for Head Mounted Display.

The core of our methodology involves a dynamic interplay, wherein participants are exposed to a structured sequence of stimuli that traverses various affective quadrants (as illustrated in Fig. 2).

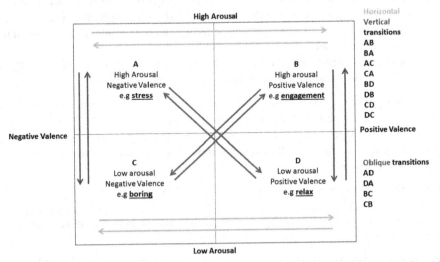

Fig. 2. 12 total transitions, of which 6 VR environments counting outward and return: horizontal and vertical one change only one parameter at a time, oblique both together.

We randomly presented all possible transitions between quadrants to ensure a comprehensive examination of affective transitions. Horizontal and vertical transitions were strategically devised to alter a single parameter while maintaining the other constant. For instance, during transitions from Quadrant A to Quadrant B, a deliberate change in valence occurs while maintaining a consistent level of arousal. Likewise, oblique transitions were purposefully constructed to modify both parameters concurrently. For example, the transition from Quadrant A to Quadrant D involves a shift from high arousal and negative valence to a state characterized by low arousal and positive valence. Participants see the scene firsthand. Each transition lasts 120 s, divided into 30 s presentation of the first block, 60 transitions between the two blocks [the environment changes its characteristics] and 30 s of the last block.

To measure transition between affective states, several key peripheral physiological signals in terms of arousal and valence are measured: corrugator facial electromyography [f-EGM] for negative valence affect, zygomatic f-EMG for positive valence, Galvanic Skin Response [GSR] for arousal [44] (Fig. 3).

However, each VR environment is subjected to a validation pre-experimental phase, using SAM: the aim is to rate each block of affective states individually, measuring arousal-valence-dominance scores.

Each block presentation is static, and they are helpful only to validate the stimuli: for example, after the VR environment of AB transition, A block of VR environment was presented singularly and rated by the subject, the same procedure for B.

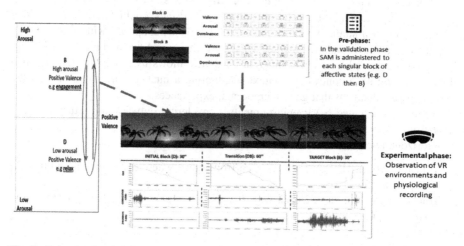

Fig. 3. Behavioral and physiological measures of transition: During VR environments observation we measure physiological parameters (e.g. GSR for arousal, and EMG for valence), and after, for each singular block of affect states, SAM was administered, to measure behavioural arousal-valence-dominance values.

2.1 How to Create Transitions?

By systematically manipulating these transitions within the immersive context of VR, we aim to unravel the intricate dynamics underlying affective experiences and shed light on the underlying mechanisms that govern emotional responses.

The coding of **arousal elements** comprises two crucial dimensions: *'strangeness'* and the manipulation of *dimensionality* [45, 46]. 'Strangeness' encapsulates unexpected elements and piques the subject's curiosity. In contrast, the manipulation of dimensionality involves several components:

- The frequency of elements: This aspect encompasses an augmentation of elements in conditions with high arousal, juxtaposed with a decrease in elements for conditions of low arousal.
- Color: The intensity and hue define central elements within the scene. For instance, flowers, butterflies, and birds contribute to the composition in scenarios marked by high arousal and positive valence.
- Movement: Subjects immersed in the presented scenes experience explorative freedom in high-arousal scenarios. Conversely, subjects are confined to a passive observational role in low arousal conditions, devoid of movement.
- Sound: Auditory experiences complement the scenes, with subjects encountering pleasant sounds like the melodic chirping of birds in instances of high arousal and

positive valence. In stark contrast, scenarios characterized by high arousal and negative valence encompass sounds such as thunder, lightning, and the intrusive buzz of flies.

Conversely, the coding of **valence elements** adheres to established patterns found within existing literature [45, 47]. For example, a landscape could demonstrate positive valence through a sunlit, verdant, and tranquil forest, juxtaposed with a contrasting portrayal of negative valence marked by a dim, rainy, and foreboding forest setting. This intricate interplay of environmental attributes allows us to explore the affective dimensions within a controlled context, facilitating a nuanced investigation into the underlying mechanisms that govern emotional experiences.

Here, we presented 6 VR environments, considering outward and return for each transition.

Horizontal transitions are AB/BA and CD/DC (see Fig. 4):

- Transition from AB/BA: Earth as seen from space where explosions [condition A] alter to butterflies [B].
- Transition from CD/DC: Beach with sea and a few palm trees, changing from gray weather [C] to sunny [D].

Transition AB/BA

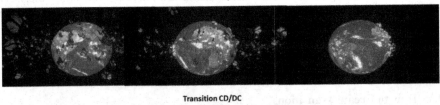

Transition CD/DC

Fig. 4. Horizontal transitions, implemented in VR environments.

Vertical transitions are AC/CA and BD/DB (see Fig. 5):

- Transition from AC/CA: Plain, grey weather and garbage around, falling from the sky [A] to isolated plain with grey weather [C].
- Transition from BD/DB: beach at night with fireworks [B] to beach at sunset [D].

Transition AC/CA

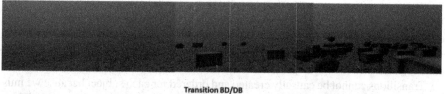

Transition BD/DB

Fig. 5. Vertical transitions, implemented in VR environments.

Oblique transitions are AD/DA and BC/CB (see Fig. 6):
- Transition from AD/DA: Park with lousy weather and flies [A], park with sunny weather [D].
- Transition from BC/CB: Park with sunshine and lush plants flowers [B] to park with cloudy weather, bare [C].

Transition BC/CB

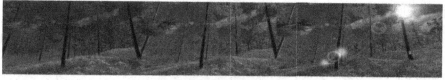

Transition AD/DA

Fig. 6. Oblique transitions, implemented in VR environments.

2.2 How to Randomize Transitions?

When we talk about random sequences, we are used to referring to the randomization we use in creating different sequences for each subject, commonly to avoid the "sequence effect". However, in the experimental designs inherent in affective transitions, we have an additional randomization problem.

Transitions cannot be causally created and ordered for each subject because we must consider the dependency effect between the going and coming transitions [e.g., AB vs, BA]. Considering all 12 transitions means that we consider all transitions the going and coming. This issue is even more pronounced if we use the same environment for the outgoing of a transition (e.g. AB) and its return (e.g. BA), as in our case.

Randomization thus must occur, preventing pairs of transitions from following each other. The methodology employed was as follows and can be generalized to any other study of affect dynamics.

We encoded the sequence of transitions in a one-dimensional data structure, with the going and coming transitions inserted one after the other [for example, AB, BA, AC, CA, AD, DA, BC, CB, BD, DB, CD, DC]. It was easier to set limits on future randomization using this a priori sorting based on pairs. For this reason, we encoded the pairings as integers [1–12]: the algorithm [createShuffledList, see below] generates a random series of numbers by extracting [and removing] them from the beginning pairs. This technique prevents placing starting pairs in adjacent positions by checking on the randomly selected value from the previous iteration. In fact, after selecting an even or odd element from the initial list, the algorithm will choose the next value exclusively from elements other than that value minus one [in the case of even numbers] or plus one [in the case of odd numbers]. When the beginning list has only two elements, the process terminates, randomly putting them into the final sequence. This last point is prone to error: it is possible [with a 10% chance] that the algorithm will leave one of the initial pairs as the last two items. The error is checked after the random list is generated to avoid this: if a pair appears in the last two entries, the sequence is regenerated. A possible pseudocode is presented here:

```
1. Function createShuffledList[size]:
2.      starting_list = Create a list containing ele-
ments from 1 to size
3.      result = Create a new empty list
4.
5.      oldVal = -1
6.      While the length of result is less than size:
7.          newVal = Randomly select an element from
starting_list
8.
9.          If oldVal is not -1 and the length of
starting_list is greater than 1:
10.             If oldVal is even:
11.                 While newVal is equal to oldVal -
1:
12.                     newVal = Randomly select an
element from starting_list
13.             Else:
14.                 While newVal is equal to oldVal +
1:
15.                     newVal = Randomly select an
element from starting_list
16.
17.         Add newVal to result
18.         Remove newVal from starting_list
19.         oldVal = newVal
20.
21.     Return result
22.
23. Main:
24.     a = createShuffledList[12]
25.     While the last element of a is equal to the
second-to-last element of a + 1
26.         or the last element of a + 1 is equal to
the second-to-last element of a:
27.         a = createShuffledList[12]
```

2.3 How to Analyze Transitions?

Affect dynamics has been extensively concerned with measuring affective states over time. However, in an experimental model such as the one proposed, the VR environments created a priori require a type of analysis that accounts for the transitions. Hence, we used Markov Chain models, as reported by [13]. Markov chain is a mathematical model that describes a sequence of events or states where the probability of transitioning from one state to another depends only on the current state and not on previous states. This property is known as the Markov or memory-lessness property: future behavior is determined solely by the current state, and past states have no influence.

In the context of Markov Chains, state transition refers to the process of moving from one state to another. Each state represents a particular situation or condition, and the transition probabilities define the likelihood of moving from one state to another in a single step. This property is particularly relevant for studying affect dynamics, as it allows us to capture the temporal dependencies and transitions between affective states. Our experimental design enables us to calculate and assess the variability across different affective transitions, which can then be normalized and incorporated into the Markov chains. By doing so, we effectively capture the probability of transitioning between blocks while accounting for the total variability. This approach aligns well with the core characteristic of Markov chains, where future states are influenced only by the current state, enabling us to model and understand the affective dynamics within our experimental paradigm. In Markov process, the input structure consists of the transition matrix, where each element [i, j] represents the probability of transitioning from state i to state j in one step. For example, P[A -> B] is the probability of transitioning from the "Stress" state to the "Engagement" state, as expressed below.

$$| P[A \; - > A]P[A \; - > B]P[A \; - > C]P[A \; - > D] |$$

$$| P[B \; - > A]P[B \; - > B]P[B \; - > C]P[B \; - > D] |$$

$$| P[C \; - > A]P[C \; - > B]P[C \; - > C]P[C \; - > D] |$$

$$| P[D \; - > A]P[D \; - > B]P[D \; - > C]P[D \; - > D] |$$

As a result, the matrix's main diagonal represents the probabilities of staying in the same state, indicating stability. On the other hand, the off-diagonal elements represent the probabilities of transitioning between different states, indicating changes or variability between states. This probabilistic representation provides valuable insights into the stability and variability of state transitions within the system being studied. Since the transition probabilities in each row represent the probabilities of transitioning from one state to all possible states in the system, it is a requirement that the rows of the transition matrix sum to 1.

Figure 7 summarizes the structural and graphical elements [a weighted directed graph with transition probabilities as weights] of Markov Matrices, starting with a random sequence of stimulus administration and simulating a practical analysis example for one subject.

Whatever data you input should always be relativized (such that you have 1 as the row sum) with respect to the measure you want to consider, as described below.

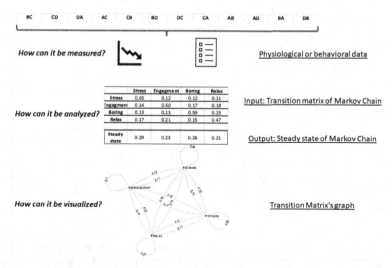

Fig. 7. Mathematical framework of Markov chain, referring to an example random sequence of a potential experimental subject.

Therefore, the primary task at hand involves the identification of methods for computing standardized variability and the creation of an associated relative index that is consistent with the properties of Markov chains.

For this reason, it is essential to incorporate a variability standardized measure encompassing physiological parameters for each VR environment. We can calculate standardized variability measures, based on the inverse of Noise to Signal, quantifying the ratio between the unwanted noise or interference in a signal and the desired signal itself. In this case, it would correspond to the reciprocal of the ratio between the absolute mean of the signal/response and the variability of the signal itself [44, 48]. It consisted of the ratio of the standard deviation of transition and his absolute mean. If the coefficient is close to zero, the standard deviation is relatively small compared to the mean, implying minimal relative variability among the data. Conversely, as the coefficient increases, it exemplifies more significant variability in the data. We called it δ index.

The standardized variability index can be calculated for each transition, considering the 60-second interval spanning across the transition of affective states (Fig. 8). However, in the Markov matrix, it is also necessary to consider state indices for each block, specifically the transition of state A with itself. State transitions (the way in which you remain in the same state in which you are) were measured as the final 30" of each block, representing the most descriptive and informative portion of the elicited affective state, preceding the transition to the next block.

Lastly, the indexes must be relativized within Markov matrices since the row sum must correspond to 1. Hence, the δ indexes can be relativized based on the weighted sum of the various blocks, as in Fig. 9.

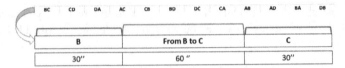

Fig. 8. Time of transition for Markovian chain construction.

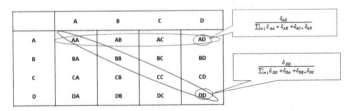

Fig. 9. Theoretical transition matrix with δ index: Firstly, we used δ index to compute a standardised variability index, and then we relativized it, fitting it with Markovian Chain characteristic.

Now our transition matrix is ready to calculate the *steady state vector*, the output structure of Markovian chain. It represents the probabilities of being in each state over an extended period, irrespective of the initial state:

$$\pi_i = [\pi_1, \pi_2, ..., \pi_i,..., \pi_N],$$

where π_i represents the stationary probability associated with state S_i.

In this case, it refers to the long-term equilibrium distribution of probabilities for each affective state, denoted by A, B, C, and D blocks.

The transition probabilities between states influence the steady state and reflect the relative stability or dominance of variability of each affective state in the system. It provides valuable insights into the prevailing variability of affective patterns and their probabilities in the long run. It is calculated after n step. The *steady state* [or equilibrium state] is a state where the system has reached a balance, and the transition probabilities between states no longer vary.

Interpreting the *steady state* in relation to affective states might mean that once a steady state is reached, people have a constant probability of being in a state of stress, engagement, boredom, or relaxation. This can be useful for understanding long-term emotional well-being in a specific context or for assessing the impact of interventions or environmental changes on people's emotions. To calculate the *steady state* in a Markov Chain, you can use the following mathematical formula:

$$\pi = \pi_i * P_{ij}$$

where:

π represents the steady-state probability vector, with each element π_i representing the probability of being in state i in the steady state.

P is the transition probability matrix of the Markov Chain, where P_{ij} represents the probability of transitioning from state i to state j in one step. Solving this equation involves finding the eigenvalues and eigenvectors of the transition matrix P. The eigenvector corresponding to the eigenvalue of 1 represents the steady-state probabilities.

This makes them particularly useful in modelling various real-world phenomena, such as weather patterns, stock market movements, or even text generation in natural language processing.

3 Conclusion

Affective states are mutable and reactive to situational triggers, exhibiting flexible or inflexible traits. Detecting and analyzing affective states in affect dynamics presents complexities. Our study explores the impact of VR on affect dynamics, developing specific settings with transitions that evoke distinct affective states, aligning with Russell's Core Affect. Previously, Affect dynamics used longitudinal experimental and analytical methodologies, in which affective changes unfolded over time and not in a precise analysis of transitions. We propose a tool such as VR, which can emulate and control transitions, and an analysis methodology of deals only with analyzing transitions, Markov chains. As we reflect on the findings and implications of our research, it is evident that we have merely scratched the surface of the potential insights that can be gleaned from studying affect dynamics in the VR realm. The dynamic interplay between virtual environments and affective states holds immense promise for various fields, including psychology, neuroscience, and human-computer interaction.

Looking ahead, several exciting avenues for future research come to light. First and foremost, further investigations could delve deeper into the nuances of affective transitions within VR. By refining our understanding of how VR stimuli influence affective states, we can enhance our interventions' precision in clinical settings. For example, in recent years there has been a renewed interest in affective dynamism with pathologies such as eating disorders, obsessive-compulsive disorders, depressive symptoms and schizophrenia disorders [49–54]. Using a tool such as VR as an assessment tool for affective dynamism could be ecological, realistic, and easily accepted by patients. Moreover, applying Machine Learning and artificial intelligence techniques to analyze affect dynamics within VR holds great potential. Advanced algorithms can enable real-time monitoring and even predictive modeling of affective responses, opening doors to personalized interventions and therapies that adapt in real-time to an individual's emotional needs [12, 55, 56]. Furthermore, ML allows to mix different type of data [from physiological to behavioral one], exploring affect variability comparing traits characteristic e.g., Mental flexibility with physiological ones linked to affect dynamics [57].

In conclusion, our study represents a significant step in unravelling the complex interplay between affective states and Virtual Reality. It highlights the vast potential for future research in this exciting intersection of technology and emotion. As we continue to delve deeper into the fascinating world of affect dynamics in VR, we anticipate that our findings will pave the way for innovative interventions, enhanced well-being, and a richer understanding of human emotions.

Acknowledgment. This research was funded by PON R&I 2014–2020 (ESF REACT-EU).

References

1. Sloman, A., Chrisley, R., Scheutz, M.: The Architectural Basis of Affective States and Processes (2003)
2. Russell, J.A.: Core affect and the psychological construction of emotion. Psychol. Rev. **110**, 145–172 (2003)
3. Puccetti, N.A., Villano, W.J., Heller, A.S.: The Neuroscience of affective dynamics. In: Waugh, C.E., Kuppens, P. (eds.) Affect Dynamics, pp. 33–60. Springer, Cham (2021). https://doi.org/10.1007/978-3-030-82965-0_3
4. Bringmann, L.: Dynamical networks in psychology: more than a pretty picture? (2016). Unpublished
5. Russell, J.A.: A circumplex model of affect. J. Pers. Soc. Psychol. **39**, 1161–1178 (1980)
6. Russell, J.A.: Mixed emotions viewed from the psychological constructionist perspective. Int. Soc. Res. Emotion **9**, 111–117 (2017). https://doi.org/10.1177/1754073916639658
7. Posner, J., Russell, J.A., Peterson, B.S.: The circumplex model of affect: an integrative approach to affective neuroscience, cognitive development, and psychopathology. Dev. Psychopathol. **17**, 715–734 (2005)
8. Hamaker, E.L., Ceulemans, E., Grasman, R.P.P.P., Tuerlinckx, F.: Modeling affect dynamics: state of the art and future challenges. Emotion Rev. **7**, 316–322 (2015). https://doi.org/10.1177/1754073915590619
9. Waugh, C., Kuppens, P.: Affect Dynamics. Springer, Cham (2021). https://doi.org/10.1007/978-3-030-82965-0
10. Kishida, K.T., Sands, L.P.: A dynamic affective core to bind the contents, context, and value of conscious experience. In: Waugh, C.E., Kuppens, P. (eds.) Affect Dynamics, pp. 293–328. Springer, Cham (2021). https://doi.org/10.1007/978-3-030-82965-0_12
11. Lazarus, G., Song, J., Crawford, C.M., Fisher, A.J.: A close look at the role of time in affect dynamics research. In: Waugh, C.E., Kuppens, P. (eds.) Affect Dynamics, pp. 95–116. Springer, Cham (2021). https://doi.org/10.1007/978-3-030-82965-0_5
12. Vanhasbroeck, N., Ariens, S., Tuerlinckx, F., Loossens, T.: Computational models for affect dynamics. In: Waugh, C.E., Kuppens, P. (eds.) Affect Dynamics, pp. 213–260. Springer, Cham (2021). https://doi.org/10.1007/978-3-030-82965-0_10
13. Cipresso, P., Borghesi, F., Chirico, A.: Affects affect affects: a Markov Chain. Front Psychol. **14** (2023). https://doi.org/10.3389/fpsyg.2023.1162655
14. Harmon-Jones, E., Amodio, D., Zinner, L.R.: Social psychological methods in emotion elicitation, pp. 91–105 (2007)
15. Schneider, F., Gur, R.C., Gur, R.E., Muenz, L.R.: Standardized mood induction with happy and sad facial expressions. Psychiatry Res. **51**, 19–31 (1994)
16. Gross, J.J., Levenson, R.W.: Emotion elicitation using films. Cogn. Emot. **9**, 87–108 (1995)
17. Västfjäll, D.: Emotion induction through music: a review of the musical mood induction procedure. Music. Sci. **5**, 173–211 (2001)
18. Riva, G., Malighetti, C., Chirico, A., Di Lernia, D., Mantovani, F., Dakanalis, A.: Virtual reality. In: Capodaglio, P. (ed.) Rehabilitation Interventions in the Patient with Obesity, pp. 189–204. Springer, Cham (2020). https://doi.org/10.1007/978-3-030-32274-8_12
19. Riva, G., et al.: Affective interactions using virtual reality: the link between presence and emotions. CyberPsychol. Behav. **10**, 45–56 (2007). http://www.liebertpub.com/cpb
20. Baños, R.M., Liaño, V., Botella, C., Alcañiz, M., Guerrero, B., Rey, B.: Changing induced moods via virtual reality. In: IJsselsteijn, W.A., de Kort, Y.A.W., Midden, C., Eggen, B., van den Hoven, E. (eds.) PERSUASIVE 2006. LNCS, vol. 3962, pp. 7–15. Springer, Heidelberg (2006). https://doi.org/10.1007/11755494_3

21. Bohil, C.J., Alicea, B., Biocca, F.A.: Virtual reality in neuroscience research and therapy. Nat. Rev. Neurosci. **12**, 752–762 (2011)
22. Somarathna, R., Bednarz, T., Mohammadi, G.: Virtual reality for emotion elicitation–a review. IEEE Trans. Affect. Comput. 1–21 (2022)
23. Mancuso, V., Bruni, F., Stramba-Badiale, C., Riva, G., Cipresso, P., Pedroli, E.: How do emotions elicited in virtual reality affect our memory? A systematic review. Comput. Human Behav. **146**, 107812 (2023)
24. Borghesi, F., Mancuso, V., Pedroli, E., Cipresso, P.: From Virtual Reality to 360° Videos: Upgrade or Downgrade? The Multidimensional Healthcare VR Technology, pp. 549–572, [1AD] (2022). https://services.igi-global.com/resolvedoi/resolve.aspx?doi=https://doi.org/10.4018/978-1-6684-4854-0.ch023
25. Chirico, A., Gaggioli, A.: When virtual feels real: comparing emotional responses and presence in virtual and natural environments. Cyberpsychol. Behav. Soc. Netw. **22**, 220–226 (2019)
26. Chirico, A., Gaggioli, A.: How real are virtual emotions? Cyberpsychol. Behav. Soc. Netw. (2023). https://doi.org/10.1089/CYBER.2023.29272.EDITORIAL
27. Colombo, D., Díaz-García, A., Fernandez-Álvarez, J., Botella, C.: Virtual reality for the enhancement of emotion regulation. Clin. Psychol. Psychother. **28**, 519–537 (2021)
28. Susindar, S., Sadeghi, M., Huntington, L., Singer, A., Ferris, T.K.: The feeling is real: emotion elicitation in virtual reality. In: Proceedings of the Human Factors and Ergonomics Society Annual Meeting (2019). https://doi.org/10.1177/1071181319631509
29. Chirico, A., Gaggioli, A.: Virtual reality for awe and imagination, pp. 1–22 (2023)
30. Felnhofer, A., et al.: Is virtual reality emotionally arousing? Investigating five emotion inducing virtual park scenarios. Int. J. Hum. Comput. Stud. **82**, 48–56 (2015)
31. Slater, M., Wilbur, S.: A Framework for Immersive Virtual Environments [FIVE]: speculations on the role of presence in virtual environments. Presence Teleoper. Virtual Environ. **6**, 603–616 (1997)
32. Schwind, V., Knierim, P., Haas, N., Henze, N.: Using presence questionnaires in virtual reality. In: Proceedings of the 2019 CHI Conference on Human Factors in Computing Systems, p. 12 (2019)
33. Parsons, T.D., Phillips, A.S.: Virtual reality for psychological assessment in clinical practice. Pract. Innov. **1**, 197–217 (2016)
34. Holzwarth, V., et al.: Towards estimating affective states in Virtual Reality based on behavioral data. Virtual Real. **25**, 1139–1152 (2021)
35. Lüddecke, R., Felnhofer, A.: Virtual reality biofeedback in health: a scoping review. Appl. Psychophysiol. Biofeedback. **47**, 1–15 (2022)
36. Mancuso, V., Stramba-Badiale, C., Cavedoni, S., Cipresso, P.: Biosensors and Biofeedback in Clinical Psychology (2022). https://scholar.google.com/scholar?hl=it&as_sdt=0%2C5&q=Biosensors+and+Biofeedback+in+Clinical+Psychology&btnG=
37. Picard, R.W.: Affective computing: challenges. Int. J. Hum. Comput. Stud. **59**, 55–64 (2003)
38. Marín-Morales, J., et al.: Affective computing in virtual reality: emotion recognition from brain and heartbeat dynamics using wearable sensors. Sci. Rep. **8**(1), 1–15 (2018)
39. Gaggioli, A., et al.: Experiential virtual scenarios with real-time monitoring [interreality] for the management of psychological stress: a block randomized controlled trial. J. Med. Internet Res. **16**, e167 (2014). https://doi.org/10.2196/JMIR.3235
40. Gaume, A., Vialatte, A., Mora-Sánchez, A., Ramdani, C., Vialatte, F.B.: A psychoengineering paradigm for the neurocognitive mechanisms of biofeedback and neurofeedback. Neurosci. Biobehav. Rev. **68**, 891–910 (2016)
41. Annerstedt, M., et al.: Inducing physiological stress recovery with sounds of nature in a virtual reality forest - results from a pilot study. Physiol. Behav. **118**, 240–250 (2013)

42. Weibel, R.P., et al.: Virtual reality-supported biofeedback for stress management: beneficial effects on heart rate variability and user experience. Comput. Human Behav. **141**, 107607 (2023)

43. Pallavicini, F., Argenton, L., Toniazzi, N., Aceti, L., Mantovani, F.: Virtual reality applications for stress management training in the military. Aerosp. Med. Hum. Perform. **87**, 1021–1030 (2016)

44. Mauri, M., et al.: Psychophysiological signals associated with affective states. In: 2010 Annual International Conference of the IEEE Engineering in Medicine and Biology, pp. 3563–3566 (2010)

45. Jefferies, L.N., Smilek, D., Eich, E., Enns, J.T.: Emotional valence and arousal interact in attentional control. Psychol. Sci. **19**, 290–295 (2008)

46. Li, B.J., Bailenson, J.N., Pines, A., Greenleaf, W.J., Williams, L.M.: A public database of immersive VR videos with corresponding ratings of arousal, valence, and correlations between head movements and self report measures. Front. Psychol. **8**, 2116 (2017). https://doi.org/10.3389/fpsyg.2017.02116

47. Presti, P., Ruzzon, D., Avanzini, P., Caruana, F., Rizzolatti, G., Vecchiato, G.: Measuring arousal and valence generated by the dynamic experience of architectural forms in virtual environments. Sci. Rep. **12**, 13376 (2022)

48. Rubin, D.I.: Needle electromyography: basic concepts. Handb. Clin. Neurol. **160**, 243–256 (2019)

49. Hawes, M.T., Klein, D.N.: Unique associations between affect dynamics and internalizing and externalizing subfactors: disentangling affective home base and variability (2023)

50. Goicoechea, C.: Shifts in affect dynamics predict psychological well-being (2023)

51. Stapp, E.K., et al.: Specificity of affective dynamics of bipolar and major depressive disorder. Brain Behav. (2023). https://doi.org/10.1002/brb3.3134

52. So, S.H., et al.: Moment-to-moment affective dynamics in schizophrenia and bipolar disorder. Eur. Psychiatry **66**, 1–38 (2023)

53. Dejonckheere, E., et al.: Complex affect dynamics add limited information to the prediction of psychological well-being. Nat. Hum. Behav. **3**, 478–491 (2019)

54. Velkoff, E.A., Smith, A.R.: Temporal dynamics of interoceptive attention and positive and negative affect in adults engaging in disordered eating and nonsuicidal self-injury. J. Clin. Psychol. (2023). https://doi.org/10.1002/jclp.23508

55. Bo, K., et al.: Decoding the temporal dynamics of affective scene processing. Neuroimage **261**, 119532 (2022). https://doi.org/10.1016/J.NEUROIMAGE.2022.119532

56. Valenza, G., Lanata, A., Scilingo, E.P.: The role of nonlinear dynamics in affective valence and arousal recognition. IEEE Trans. Affect. Comput. **3**, 237–249 (2012)

57. Borghesi, F., et al.: Exploring biomarkers of mental flexibility in healthy aging: a computational psychometric study. Sensors (Basel) **23**, 6983 (2023). https://doi.org/10.3390/S23156983

Who Pays Attention to the User Experience Content Embedded in Mobile APP Reviews

Silas Formunyuy Verkijika(✉) 📷

Centre for Applied Data Science (CADS), Sol Plaatje University, Kimberley 8300, South Africa
silas.verkijika@spu.ac.za

Abstract. In recent years, there has been growing interest in understanding what makes a review valuable, as such reviews are vital in guiding consumer and business decision-making. The purpose of this study was to determine the role that the user experience of mobile applications plays in fostering review helpfulness as well as stimulating managerial responses to reviews of these applications. This study proposes a measure of UX richness for online reviews and finds that both positive and negative UX-rich reviews contribute to enhancing the helpfulness of reviews as well as the likelihood that they will receive a response from the application provider. The study further demonstrates the moderating role of UX richness in the prominent effects of review length and review rating on both the helpfulness and managerial response to mobile app reviews. The study culminates with a discussion of the implications of these findings.

Keywords: Review helpfulness · Review response · UX richness · Review length · Review rating

1 Introduction

The importance of online reviews has been widely acknowledged in recent years as reviews are increasingly seen to provide valuable insights about numerous products and services [1]. Reviews provide benefits both to consumers and business/product/service owners. For example, consumers depend on reviews to improve their decision-making, while businesses use reviews to understand customer experiences to better serve their needs [2]. This has increased the use of online reviews as a valuable data source in different business, service, and product settings. One of the areas that benefit from the study of online reviews is mobile apps [2, 3].

In recent years, there has been an increased interest in understanding the engagement features of online reviews. This study focuses on two types of engagement with online reviews that have proven valuable and have become core dimensions in online review literature. The first is understanding the helpfulness of online reviews [4, 5]. There are millions of reviews online, and not all provide the same level of value to consumers. As such, determining the helpfulness of reviews makes it possible for consumers to focus on reviews that are likely to yield benefits in their consumer-decision making. Similarly, businesses depend on review helpfulness to know the dimensions of the consumer experience to pay attention to. As such, online review platforms have provided

H. P. da Silva and P. Cipresso (Eds.): CHIRA 2023, CCIS 1997, pp. 277–295, 2023.
https://doi.org/10.1007/978-3-031-49368-3_17

an engagement feature to capture the helpfulness of online reviews. The helpfulness of a review is generally rated by other consumers [4]. Another engagement feature that is gaining prominence is the managerial response to reviews. Managerial responses are often seen as a means of recovering from service failure or maintaining a good customer relationship [6]. Unfortunately, most companies do not always respond to all customer reviews as it is a costly process [7]. By examining business engagement behaviour, it is possible to have a deeper understanding of what businesses pay attention to. This will assist consumers in adequately framing their reviews for maximum impact and as well as assist businesses in appropriately dealing with consumer complaints.

While there has been an unprecedented growth in studies relating to review helpfulness [4, 5, 8, 9] and review response [6, 7, 10, 11] little attention has been paid to the role of user experience, even for reviews associated with interactive products like mobile apps. The user experience of mobile apps in general is vital for their continued use and the user experience of a product can often be evaluated from online customer reviews [12]. However, to date, there is limited evidence on how user experience content in reviews fosters engagement with online reviews. This study aims to contribute to the user experience and mobile app literature by determining the importance of embedding user experience-rich content in online reviews as a means of fostering engagement.

2 Related Studies

2.1 Review Helpfulness

Review helpfulness is a measure of a user's perception of the value of a given review often characterized in terms of helpfulness votes [4]. Helpful reviews are known to improve consumer intentions to adopt and use a product/service and subsequently lead to increased sales [13]. There is a plethora of studies that have examined the factors that influence review helpfulness. Some of the factors commonly shown to influence review helpfulness include review quality attributes such as review rating, length of the review, emotions, review age, review sentiment, etc. [4, 5].

However, most of the studies on the determinants of review helpfulness have provided mixed findings. For example, although the length of the review has been widely studied, there is still no consensus on whether longer reviews are more helpful [5, 8, 9]. Many researchers have started looking at how the content of reviews influences review helpfulness. For example, using machine learning, [14] identified terms commonly used in fashion reviews that predict the helpfulness of fashion reviews. In the context of an interactive system, user experience is a core aspect of product evaluation and has been shown to feature in product reviews [12]. However, the role of user experience in influencing user engagement with the review is yet to be explored.

2.2 Managerial Response

A managerial response is the reply a business or product/service owner provides to a review by consumers and is generally considered a service intervention strategy [6]. This is considered one of the key engagement features that a service/product owner provides in the online context [11]. Providing managerial responses is an important business function as it contributes to customer satisfaction, trust, the volume, and type of future reviews, as well as the performance of the business [6, 7].

Over the years, there have been efforts to understand the behaviour of managerial response and propose the types of reviews that businesses should focus on responding to since it is costly to respond to all reviews [7]. One factor that has received attention is the polarity of the review, albeit with mixed reactions. Although some researchers propose that businesses should focus on extreme reviews [15], others contend that ignoring neutral reviews in favour of particularly negative extreme reviews can be detrimental to the business [7, 10]. This is because consumers are likely to promote the generation of extremely negative reviews since they believe it will get the attention of the service provider [7, 16], and these can negatively affect the business. Other researchers have highlighted the need to consider the review content, as it provides valuable insights into the intent of the reviewer, as well as specific complaints to address or positive aspects to promote [17]. Managerial response literature has mostly focused on hotel/restaurant reviews with a limited understanding of reviews of interactive systems. In terms of interactive digital systems, user experience is a paramount concern for both consumers and businesses. As such, this study considers user experience worthy of influencing managerial responses.

2.3 User Experience from Online Reviews

User experience (UX) refers to "a person's perceptions and responses that result from the use or anticipated use of a product, system or service." (ISO 9241–210). Over the years, UX has primarily been assessed using questionnaires and interviews [18]. However, there have been several efforts in recent years to extract UX information from online customer reviews [12, 19, 20]. [20] proposed a faceted model for extracting UX information from online user reviews. This approach characterizes UX features in terms of product features, situation features and customer sentiment. [12] used a word frequency approach and implemented the Self-organizing map (SOM) cluster approach to identify words that depicted positive and negative experiences from user reviews. [19] used the linguistic inquiry and word count (LIWC) tool to extract UX elements from online reviews. The UX dimensions proposed by [19] included hedonic values, user burdens, expectation confirmation, pragmatic values, and social values. While these studies provide the basis for the current study, there has not been an attempt to map the studies with extant UX frameworks that have been validated with other forms of data such as surveys and interviews. The present study builds on an existing UX framework with widely validated instruments as the basis for identifying UX content in online reviews.

3 Theoretical Framework

3.1 Conceptualizing User Experience (UX) Richness

Recent studies have started paying attention to the richness of the information embedded in online reviews [21, 22] Content richness measures the informativeness of a review by examining the extent to which valuable information about the product or service is embedded in the review [21, 22]. Prior studies conceptualize the richness of a review by counting the number of words in the review that relate to product or platform features. To achieve this, a dictionary of words related to product and platform features is created and then used to identify the reviews that contain such words. This paper thus relies on the literature that depends on attributes to determine the richness/informativeness of a review [22]. However, instead of focusing on product and platform features, this study focuses on UX-related features.

The first step in characterizing the UX richness of a review is to create a dictionary of relevant UX words. This is achieved by adopting the User Experience Questionnaire (UEQ) as the source of UX-related words [23]. The UEQ uses adjectives to describe the user experience. Each of the dimensions is measured using a combination of positive and negative adjectives. The UEQ is a well-established UX evaluation tool and uses both negative and positive words to describe the UX of a system across six different dimensions. Each positive adjective has a corresponding negative attribute. In this study, we use these attributes as the basis for identifying user reviews that include aspects of user experience. The dictionary words used in the study are shown in Table 1.

Table 1. UX dimensions and associated dictionary words.

UX Dimension	Description	Positive UX words	Negative UX words
Attractiveness	Overall impression of the product. Do users like or dislike the product?	Enjoyable, good, pleasing, pleasant, attractiveness, friendly	Annoying, bad, unlikeable, unpleasant, unattractive, unfriendly
Perspicuity	Is it easy to get familiar with the product? Is it easy to learn how to use the product?	Understandable, easy to learn, easy, clear	Not understandable, difficult to learn, complicated, confusing
Efficiency	Can users solve their tasks without unnecessary effort?	Fast, efficient, practical, organized	Slow, inefficient, impractical, cluttered
Dependability	Does the user feel in control of the interaction?	Predictable, supportive, secure, meets expectations	Unpredictable, obstructive, not secure, does not meet expectations
Stimulation	Is it exciting and motivating to use the product?	Valuable, exciting, interesting, motivating	Inferior, boring, not interesting, demotivating
Novelty	Is the product innovative and creative? Does the product catch the interest of users?	Creative, inventive, leading-edge, innovative	Dull, conventional, usual, conservative

Since the positive and negative words indicate different polarities of the user's experience with the system, this study conceptualized UX richness as two dimensions comprising Positive UX richness and negative UX richness. UX richness is conceptualized as the number of UX dimensions represented in the review.

$$Positive\ UX\ Richness = 6 \sum\nolimits_{(i=1)}^{6} Represent\_PUX_i \qquad (1)$$

$$Negative\ UX\ Richness = 6 \sum\nolimits_{(i=1)}^{6} Represent\_NUX_i \qquad (2)$$

where i is the UX dimension and *Represent_PUX*$_i$ is an indication of whether at least one positive UX word from dimension i is represented in the review. The same applies to negative UX richness with *Represent_NUX*$_i$ depicting whether or not at least one negative UX word for dimension i is represented in the review. As such, the UX richness depicts the diversity of UX dimensions represented in the user's review. To validate this conceptualization, it is expected that the use of positive UX words should be associated with a positive overall rating from the review creator while the use of negative UX should be associated with a lower rating. This was confirmed as indicated in Appendix A, thus showing that the use of UX words by mobile app review creators was congruent with the overall rating they provided for the app (Appendix A).

3.2 Conceptual Framework

Given the importance of user experience to both consumers and system providers [18], it is expected that user experience will be a key consideration in online review engagement. For consumer engagement, we rely on the cue utilization theory to extrapolate the expected relationship. Cue utilization theory posits that consumer perceptions are shaped by the cues they encounter about a given product/service [24]. Users can rely on information from online reviews to identify cues about the quality of a product to determine the trustworthiness or reliability of products [25]. Given that users are often concerned about the user experience of a digital product [18] they are likely to look for signals in reviews that give them insights into the UX of the product. As such, we expect that reviews of mobile applications that provide UX cues will be seen as helpful because they enable users to make better decisions about using the applications.

From a managerial response perspective, we rely on signalling theory to propose the relationship between UX and review response. Since system providers are generally expected to evaluate the user experience of their systems regularly [18] identifying reviews that focus on UX serves as a signal for the reviews that the company should pay attention to, as it enables them to have a better understanding of the system's user experience. By responding to such reviews, system providers demonstrate that they are paying attention to issues of concern that are vital for improved service delivery [6] since they are likely to be actively evaluating the UX of the system [18].

Besides the possible direct effect of UX richness on review helpfulness and response, this study proposes that UX richness can moderate the relationships between review length and review rating with both review helpfulness and response. Review length and rating are two of the most prominent factors that influence the helpfulness and response of a review [5, 22, 26, 27]. For review length, the general perspective is that longer reviews are better because they provide adequate context for the reader and app provider to better understand the issues raised in the review. However, there have been growing concerns that some long reviews are not informative [5, 22], and so might provide limited benefits to both the readers and service providers. Since UX richness makes a review informative by highlighting UX information about the UX of the system, both users and service providers might appreciate such reviews because of the UX cues or signals embedded in them. As such, it is expected that reviews of a similar length might have a differential effect on review helpfulness and review response based on the extent to which UX-rich content is embedded in the review. With review ratings, businesses and consumers tend to promote extreme reviews [5]. However, some reviews tend to have inconsistencies between the content of the review and the rating provided [8]. The bridge such inconsistencies, consumers and service providers can depend on the alignment between the UX content in the review and the associated rating. As such, it is expected that UX-rich content embedded in a review will moderate the effect of review rating on both helpfulness and review response.

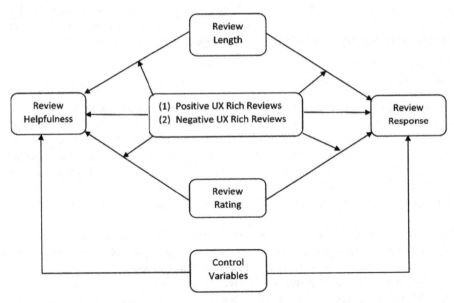

Fig. 1. Conceptual framework of the core relationships.

4   Methodology

4.1   Data and Process

Over 10.6 million reviews were extracted from the 200 apps on the Google Play Store using a Python scrapper. The reviews were preprocessed using natural language processing in line with prior studies [28] and various techniques were applied to extract the core variables used in the study. For example, the Natural Language Toolkit (NLTK) sentiment analyzer was used to determine the review sentiments as well as evaluate the length of the reviews. The different variables extracted from the dataset are described in Sect. 4.2. After data preprocessing two analytical approaches were followed. Linear regression was used to evaluate the factors influencing review helpfulness while logistic regression was used to evaluate the review response. Each approach was selected in alignment with the nature of the dependent variable. Furthermore, the robustness of the findings is evaluated using three machine learning models to determine the accuracy and area under the curve for the proposed models.

4.2 Variables

The variables used in the study are described in Table 2.

Table 2. Variables used in the study.

Variable	Description	Sample Sources
Review Helpfulness	The number of helpful votes received by a review	[8, 27]
Review Response	A review that has received a response from the app provider	[9]
Rating	The star rating of the review ranges from 1 to 5	[20]
Review length	The number of words in the review	[29]
Review Sentiment	The sentiment of the review	
Review Age	The natural logarithm of the number of days elapse from review creation to review collection	[27, 29]
App Type	Binary construct determining if an app falls in a hedonic or utilitarian category	[30]
Revenue model	Binary variable determining if an app is free or paid	[30]
App downloads	The minimum number of times the app has been downloaded	[30]
Positive UX-rich reviews	The number of positive UX dimensions that have been mentioned in the review	-
Negative UX-rich reviews	The number of negative UX dimensions that have been mentioned in the review	-

5   Results

5.1   Descriptive Statistics

Table 3 presents the descriptive statistics of all the variables used in the study. The mean score for review helpfulness was 1.735 with the helpfulness votes ranging from 0 to 49428. This is unlike non-app reviews where it is quite uncommon to find a review with more than 10,000 helpfulness votes. The difference probably lies in the context as mobile apps are easily downloaded and used by millions of users compared to most review studies that focus on restaurants, hotels etc.

Table 3. Descriptive statistics.

Variables	Min	Max	Mean	SD
Helpfulness	0	49428	1.735	5.100
Review length	1	802	13.462	18.195
Rating	1	5	3.733	1.549
Review Age	6	4884	1349.167	967.686
Response	0	1	0.128	0.334
App Type	0	1	0.335	0.472
Review Sentiment	−1	1	0.317	0.435
App Downloads	500	$1.00e + 10$	$1896e^{08}$	$2.997e^{08}$
Revenue model	0	1	0.999	0.009
Positive UX-rich reviews	0	4	0.234	0.450
Negative UX-rich reviews	0	4	0.044	0.212

Data for review length indicates that the shortest review was one word while the longest review was 802 words. The average length of the reviews was 13.462 words. The average rating for the reviews was 3.733. On average, the reviews had been online for 1349.167 days before being extracted. The latest review to be posted had been online for 6 days while the oldest had been online for 4884 days.

Regarding the review response (dummy variable), the mean response rate of 0.128 suggests that only about 12.8% of the reviews had received a response from App providers. Regarding app type, the mean of 0.335 suggests that about 33.5% of the reviews were hedonic apps while the majority were for utilitarian apps. Lastly, the review sentiment had an average sentiment score of 0.317 suggesting that most reviews fell in the positive spectrum.

Concerning the user experience dimensions, the highest number of positive or negative dimensions covered by a single review was 4 UX dimensions. The mean scores of 0.234 and 0.004 suggest that most reviews did not use UX-related words.

5.2 Predicting Review Helpfulness

Table 4 shows the linear regression models predicting the helpfulness of mobile app reviews. Model 1 is the base model with all core variables while model 2 is the interaction model. In line with prior studies, the Review helpfulness variable is log-transformed before performing the linear regression [27].

Table 4. Determinants of review helpfulness.

	Model 1		Model 2	
	Coeff	Std Err	Coeff	Std Err
Control Variables				
Constant	0.9855^{**}	0.019	0.9650**	0.019
Rating	-0.0958^{**}	0.001	-0.0848**	0.001
Rating2	0.0125^{**}	0.000	0.0105**	0.000
Review Age	0.0045^{**}	0.000	0.0044**	0.000
Review Sentiment	-0.0149^{**}	0.000	-0.0157**	0.000
Response	0.0160^{**}	0.001	0.0172**	0.001
App type	-0.0125^{**}	0.000	-0.0127**	0.000
App downloads	-0.0158^{**}	0.000	-0.0156**	0.000
Revenue model	-0.2608^{**}	0.019	-0.2626**	0.019
Review length	-0.4139^{**}	0.001	-0.3888**	0.001
Review length^2	0.1342^{**}	0.000	0.1270**	0.000
Main Variables				
Positive UX Rich Review (PUX)	0.0166^{**}	0.000	0.0679**	0.003
Negative UX Rich Review (NUX)	0.0269^{**}	0.001	0.1076**	0.005
Interaction Effects				
Rating * PUX			-0.0432**	0.002
Rating^2 * PUX			0.0075**	0.000
Rating * NUX			0.0153**	0.003
Rating^2 * NUX			-0.0034**	0.001
Review length*PUX			-0.0423**	0.002
Review length^2 * PUX			0.0133**	0.000
Review length*NUX			-0.1449**	0.004
Review length^2 *NUX			0.0345**	0.001

(continued)

Table 4. (*continued*)

	Model 1		Model 2	
	Coeff	Std Err	Coeff	Std Err
Model Parameters				
Adjusted R^2	20.0%		20.1%	
F-Statistics	$2.232e + 05^{**}$		$1.347e + 05^{**}$	
AIC	$1.739e + 07$		$1.738e + 07$	
Log-likelihood	$-8.6969e + 06$		$-8.6907e + 06$	
Observations	10683594		10683594	

Notes. $^{**}p < 0.01$

Notes. $^{**}p < 0.01$

In terms of the control variables, the data in Fig. 1 shows that all control variables had a significant effect on review helpfulness. Both Review Ratings and Review length have a curvilinear relationship with review helpfulness as observed by the significant quadratic terms. Also observed is that the review age ($\beta = 0.0045$, $P < 0.01$) and review response ($\beta = 0.0160$, $P < 0.01$) had positive effects of review helpfulness while review sentiment ($\beta = -0.0149$, $P < 0.01$), app type ($\beta = -0.0125$, $P < 0.01$), app downloads ($\beta = -0.0158$, $P < 0.01$) and revenue model ($\beta = -0.2608$, $P < 0.01$) had a negative effect on review helpfulness.

Regarding the UX richness of the reviews, it is observed that UX richness of a review has a positive effect on review helpfulness with the effect much stronger for negative UX-rich reviews ($\beta = 0.0269$, $P < 0.01$) compared to positive UX-rich reviews ($\beta = 0.0166$, $P < 0.01$). The interaction effects in model 2 further show that The UX richness of a review moderates the curvilinear effect of review rating and review length on review helpfulness. The nature of these interaction effects is shown in Fig. 3.

The results in Fig. 2 show that while longer mobile app reviews generally tend to be more helpful, the effect is more pronounced for both positive (Panel A) and negative (Panel B) UX-rich reviews. Similarly, the curvilinear effect of review rating on review helpfulness is more pronounced for both positive (Panel C) and negative (Panel D) UX-rich reviews.

5.3 Predicting Review Response

Table 5 presents the logistic regression results for predicting review response. Model 3 presents the outcome of the base model containing all core variables and control variables while model 4 presents the interaction model.

All the control variables have a significant effect on the review response. The review sentiment ($\beta = 0.1184$, $P < 0.01$), review helpfulness ($\beta = 0.0316$, $P < 0.01$) and app type ($\beta = 0.4773$, $P < 0.01$) show a significant positive relationship with review response. On the other hand, review age ($\beta = -0.3178$, $P < 0.01$),), app downloads ($\beta = -0.0270$, $P < 0.01$),) and revenue model ($\beta = -2.4355$, $P < 0.01$),) show a negative relationship with

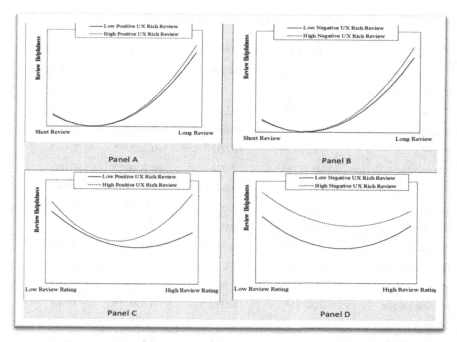

Fig. 2. Moderating effect of UX-richness on the relationship between review length and review rating with review helpfulness.

review response. Both the review rating and review length have a curvilinear association with review response as shown by the significant effects of the respective quadratic terms.

Concerning the main variables, it is observed that both positive UX-rich reviews ($\beta = 0.0296$, P < 0.01) and negative UX-rich reviews ($\beta = 0.1204$, P < 0.01) have a significant positive effect on review response with the latter having the stronger effect. Model 4 further shows that the UX richness of a review moderates the curvilinear effect of both review rating and review length on review response. The nature of these interactions is shown in Fig. 3.

In terms of the interaction with review rating, the data in Fig. 3 show that the probability of receiving a response decreases for reviews with a high rating however the effect is differential based on the UX richness of the review. Positive UX-rich reviews tend to have a high response rate especially when the review rating is lowest (Panel E). On the other hand, the probability of receiving a response is consistently lower for high negative UX-rich reviews (Panel F). In terms of the interaction with review length, it is observed that the curvilinear effect is more pronounced for high positive UX-rich reviews (Panel H) while high negative UX-rich reviews tend to have a lower effect than low negative UX-rich reviews (Panel J).

Table 5. Determinants of Review Helpfulness.

	Model 3		Model 4	
	Coeff.	Std Err	Coeff.	Std Err
Control Variables				
Constant	3.1912**	0.075	3.0545**	0.075
Rating	0.9009**	0.003	0.8909**	0.004
Rating2	−0.2275**	0.001	−0.2227**	0.001
Review Age	−0.3178**	0.001	−0.1109**	0.005
Review Sentiment	0.1184**	0.002	0.1224**	0.002
Review Helpfulness	0.0316**	0.001	0.0350**	0.001
App Type	0.4773**	0.001	0.4787**	0.002
App downloads	−0.0270**	0.001	−0.0274**	0.001
Revenue model	−2.4355**	0.074	−2.4248**	0.074
Review length	−0.1629**	0.004	−0.1109**	0.005
Review length^2	0.0418**	0.001	0.0397**	0.001
Main Variables				
Positive UX Rich Review (PUX)	0.0296**	0.002	0.5107**	0.015
Negative UX Rich Review (NUX)	0.1204**	0.004	0.1359**	0.025
Interaction Effects				
Rating * PUX			0.1144**	0.008
Rating2 * PUX			−0.0278**	0.001
Rating * NUX			−0.3620**	0.015
Rating2 * NUX			0.0439**	0.003
Review length*PUX			−0.3250**	0.008
Review length^2 * PUX			0.0388**	0.002
Review length*NUX			0.5058**	0.016
Review length^2 *NUX			−0.1044**	0.003
Model Parameters				
Pseudo R^2	12.18%		12.22%	
Log-likelihood	−3.7822e + 06		−3.7803e + 06	
Observations	10683594		10683594	

Notes. **p < 001

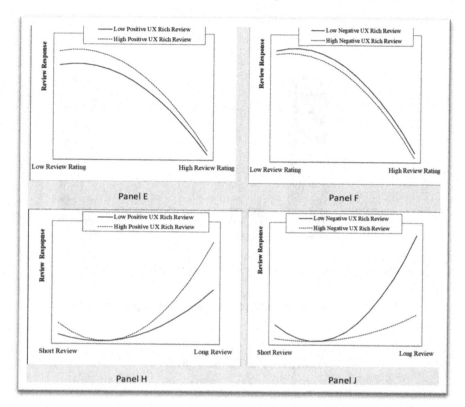

Fig. 3. Moderating effect of UX-richness on the relationship between review length and review rating with review response.

5.4 Classification Analysis

This paper further evaluates how well the proposed models above can be used for the classification of helpful reviews (Table 4) as well as reviews with the likelihood of receiving a response (Table 5). To perform the classification for reviewer helpfulness, the variable is first converted to a binary variable in line with prior studies [31]. The binary variable for review helpfulness is represented as follows: (0) for the reviews that have no helpful votes and (1) for reviews that have at least 1 helpful vote. Since the review response is already a binary variable, no further transformation was needed. The distribution of the prediction classes is shown below (Fig. 4).

Prior studies in review helpfulness and response have mostly processed less than a million reviews thus making the dataset in the study over 10 times that of prior studies. The prediction was performed using three machine learning models namely: Logistic regression (LR), Decision tree (DT) and random Forest (RF). The data below reports the accuracy and area under the curve (AUC) percentages for each of the three models (Fig. 5).

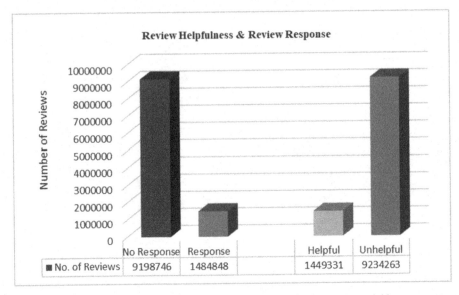

Fig. 4. Distribution of review helpfulness and review response variables.

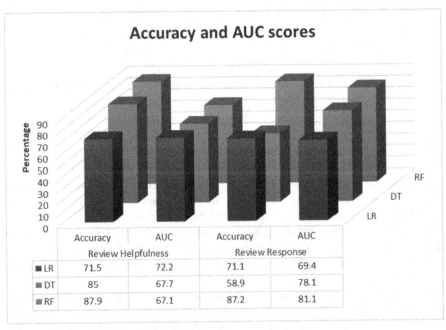

Fig. 5. Classification outcomes for the three machine learning models.

In terms of the review helpfulness, the had the highest level of accuracy (87.9%) while the logistic regression had the highest AUC score (72.2%). In predicting the helpfulness of mobile app reviews [32] found accuracy levels below 70% using semantics, sentiment, readability, structure, and syntax as features. Using the random forest classifier with online reviews from JD.COM, [21] established that the highest prediction accuracy for the combined reviews was 78.5% with an AUC of 82.3%. While the AUC is better than that obtained for the random forest classifier in this study, the accuracy is much lower than in this study. In terms of Review response, this study found that the random forest classifier has the highest accuracy (87.2%) and AUC score (81.1%). Prior studies have only depended on regression models for testing determinants of review response [10].

6   Discussion

Review helpfulness and review response are two vital engagement features that provide significant value for customers and product service providers. To further ignite this knowledge base on these engagement factors, the present study sought to find the role of UX richness as a driver of mobile app review helpfulness as well as managerial response to mobile app reviews. To ensure that the observed relationships are not by chance, this study included a significant number of control variables. It was observed that all the included control variables had a significant effect on both review helpfulness and review response. This validated the importance of including these control variables in the study and supports extant research in this domain [8, 9, 20, 27]. However, the findings are contrary to studies like [33] who failed to find support for the effect of review sentiment and review age on review helpfulness. The introduction of app-level controls (i.e., app type, app downloads and revenue model) also proved to be valued as all had significant effects on review helpfulness and review response. This is in line with prior studies on hotel reviews that have also shown the value of controlling product or business-level attributes when examining the determinants of review helpfulness [5, 26, 27] and review response [11]. After controlling these factors, this study found significant evidence that the proposed UX richness constructs had significant positive effects on review helpfulness and review response. Additionally, the UX richness constructs moderated the effects of review rating and review length on both helpfulness and review response. These findings provide several theoretical and practical implications.

6.1   Theoretical Implications

The theoretical implications of this study are three-fold. First, the results suggest that the inclusion of UX-related words in a review text can significantly increase the helpfulness of the review as well as the likelihood of the review receiving a response. This extends the literature of review content richness by specifying richness attributes relating to the user experience [22]. Prior studies have looked at product and service features to characterize the content richness of a review. However, these studies did not consider content relating to the user's experience of the solution. This study demonstrates that both positive UX-rich content and negative UX-rich content all contribute to the helpfulness or review response. While some studies have attempted to identify the presence of UX-related content in reviews, this is the first study to demonstrate how UX-related information influences the engagement features of a review.

Second, the study identifies the curvilinear effect of review rating and length on both helpfulness and review response. For review length, the majority of prior studies have only examined the linear effect of review length on helpfulness and response [8, 10]. Only recently did [5] demonstrate the existence of a curvilinear effect of review length on helpfulness. However, they found the relationship to be an inverted U-shaped effect. Although this study found evidence of the curvilinear effect between review length and helpfulness, the relationship is a U-shaped effect. These differences might be attributed to the nature of the reviews as Amazon product reviews used by [5] might differ from mobile app reviews from the Play Store. In general, the average app review in the dataset from Amazon is far longer than the average review for mobile apps. Concerning review response, [10] found evidence of the linear effect of review rating and length on review response but not the quadratic effect. This study therefore adds a new dimension to the growing review helpfulness and review response literature.

Third, the study demonstrates the moderating effect of both positive and negative UX-rich reviews on review helpfulness and review response. In terms of review helpfulness, some prior studies have shown that the effect of review length on helpfulness is based on a third moderating factor. Some moderating factors proposed in prior literature include Augmentation changes [5]. This study adds to the growing literature by showing that for reviews with a similar length, those that contain words associated with positive or negative UX dimensions would be more pronounced. The same is also true for reviews with a similar rating. When it comes to review responses, given reviews of a similar length, app providers are more likely to respond to high positive UX-rich reviews and tend to pay little attention to high negative UX-rich reviews. The same is also true for reviews with a similar rating. These findings show the value of UX as an important aspect of reviews that receive attention from both consumers and app providers. For consumers, both positive and negative UX-rich reviews attract more attention, while for the app providers positive UX-rich reviews will receive more attention compared to negative UX-rich reviews.

6.2 Practical Implications

The practical implications of this study are threefold. First, the study guides consumers on what to consider when writing helpful reviews. It is observed that including UX-related words from multiple UX dimensions in a review can increase the helpfulness of the review. By doing so, review creators will be assisting other consumers in making decisions about a given mobile app especially and UX is vital for adoption and continued use. Moreover, review creators can increase the likelihood of receiving a response e to their review by embedding UX-rich content in the reviews.

Second, while reviews that are rated quite low are more likely to get a response [7, 16], it is important to ensure that the review is not only embedded with negative attributes. Providing positive UX words in low-rated reviews will increase the likelihood of getting a response. Lastly, given the importance of UX richness in review content, app providers can regularly analyze the reviews they receive for UX-related information and work towards improving positive aspects and addressing negative aspects. This will provide them with an indication of how other readers might react to the reviews about their app which can assist in promotional efforts of the app. Similarly, app stores can use UX-related content to filter and prioritize reviews to enable consumers to easily see UX-rich reviews as such these are likely to be helpful to them.

7 Conclusion

The importance of online reviews has been widely acknowledged [1, 2], prompting numerous studies to focus on examining the determinants of helpful reviews as well as drivers of managerial response to reviews [4, 5, 10]. However, the majority of prior studies have focused either on products from Amazon or hotel reviews. There has been very minimal effort to evaluate the helpfulness of mobile app reviews. Given that mobile apps are interactive products, this study introduces UX richness as a review ad a vital construct that can help to understand why customers find certain reviews helpful as well as why app providers might respond to some but not other reviews. This is one of the first efforts to demonstrate the importance of writing reviews that focus on the UX of interactive products. The study further demonstrates how the proposed UX richness constructs moderate the effects of review length and review rating on both review helpfulness and review response. These are novel findings that ignite a new discussion on the importance of reviews whose content is rich in terms of describing the UX of the product.

Appendix A

UX Dimensions based on UEQ	Rating model for positive UX words		Rating model for negative UX words	
	B	SE	B	SE
Constant	3.6511^{**}	0.001	3.8307^{**}	0.000
Attractiveness	0.3996^{**}	0.001	-1.6005^{**}	0.003
Efficiency	0.2117^{**}	0.004	-1.3773^{**}	0.004
Perspicuity	0.8083^{**}	0.002	-0.9190^{**}	0.009
Dependability	0.1012^{**}	0.019	-1.6227^{**}	0.054
Stimulation	0.6121^{**}	0.006	-1.1024^{**}	0.011
Novelty	0.8010^{**}	0.011	-0.3644^{**}	0.011
Model Parameters				
Adjusted R^2	2.5%		4.1%	
F-Statistics	$4.565e + 04^{**}$		$7.517e + 04^{**}$	
AIC	$3.926e + 07$		$3.909e + 07$	
Log-likelihood	$-1.9630e + 07$		$-1.9545e + 07$	
Observations	10683594		10683594	

Notes. $^{**}p < 0.01$. Each UX dimensions represents the number of positive or negative UX words from the dimension used in a given review

References

1. Dwivedi, Y.K., et al.: Metaverse beyond the hype: multidisciplinary perspectives on emerging challenges, opportunities, and agenda for research, practice and policy. Int. J. Inf. Manage. **66**, 102542 (2022). https://doi.org/10.1016/j.ijinfomgt.2022.102542

2. Nakamura, W.T., de Oliveira, E.C., de Oliveira, E.H.T., Redmiles, D., Conte, T.: What factors affect the UX in mobile apps? A systematic mapping study on the analysis of app store reviews. J. Syst. Softw. **193**, 111462 (2022)

3. Hussain, A., Hannan, A., Shafiq, M.: Exploring mobile banking service quality dimensions in Pakistan: a text mining approach. Int. J. Bank Market. **41**(3), 601–618 (2023). https://doi.org/10.1108/IJBM-08-2022-0379

4. Chou, Y., Chuang, H.H., Liang, T.: Elaboration likelihood model, endogenous quality indicators, and online review helpfulness. Decis. Support Syst. **153**, 113683 (2022). https://doi.org/10.1016/j.dss.2021.113683

5. Lutz, B., Prollochs, N., Neumann, D.: Are longer reviews always more helpful? Disentangling the interplay between review length and line of argumentation. J. Bus. Res. **144**, 888–901 (2022)

6. Zhao, Y., Wen, Y., Feng, X., Li, R., Lin, X.: How managerial responses to online reviews affect customer satisfaction: an empirical study based on additional reviews. J. Retail. Consum. Serv. **57**, 102205 (2020)

7. Wang, L., Ren, X., Wan, H., Yan, J.: Managerial responses to online reviews under budget constraints: whom to target and how. Inf. Manage. **57**(8), 103382 (2020)

8. Choi, J., Yoo, S.H., Lee, H.: Two faces of review inconsistency: the respective effects of internal and external inconsistencies on job review helpfulness. Comput. Hum. Behav. **140**, 6105701 (2023). https://doi.org/10.1016/j.chb.2022.107570

9. Li, C., Kwok, L., Xie, K.L., Liu, J., Ye, Q.: Let Photos speak: the effect of user-generated visual content on hotel review helpfulness. J. Hosp. Tour. Res. **47**(4), 665–690 (2023). https://doi.org/10.1177/10963480211019113

10. Liu, X., Law, R.: Insights into managers' response behavior: priority and effort. Int. J. Hosp. Manag. **77**, 468–470 (2019)

11. Sheng, J., Wang, Z., Amankwah-Amoah, X.: The value of firm engagement: how do ratings benefit from managerial responses? Decis. Support Syst. **147**, 113578 (2021)

12. Son, Y., Kim, W.: Development of methodology for classification of user experience (UX) in online customer review. J. Retail. Consum. Serv. **71**, 4103210 (2023)

13. Filieri, R., Raguseo, E., Vitari, C.: Extremely negative ratings and online consumer review helpfulness: the moderating role of product quality signals. J. Travel Res. **60**(4), 699–717 (2021)

14. Mahdikhani, M.: Exploring commonly used terms from online reviews in the fashion field to predict review helpfulness. Int. J. Inf. Manage. Data Insights **3**(1), 100172 (2023)

15. Sheng, J., Amankwah-Amoah, J., Wang, X., Khan, Z.: Managerial responses to online reviews: a text analytics approach. Br. J. Manag. **30**, 315–327 (2019)

16. Chevalier, J.A., Dover, Y., Mayzlin, D.: Channels of impact: user reviews when quality is dynamic and managers respond. Mark. Sci. **37**, 688–709 (2018). https://doi.org/10.1287/mksc.2018.1090

17. Surachartkumtonkun, J., Grace, D., Ross, M.: Unfair customer reviews: third-party perceptions and managerial responses. J. Bus. Res. **132**, 631–640 (2021)

18. Albert, B., Tullis, T.: Measuring the User Experience: Collecting, Analyzing, and Presenting UX Metrics. Morgan Kaufmann, Cambridge (2022)

19. Park, E.: Motivations for customer revisit behavior in online review comments: analyzing the role of user experience using big data approaches. J. Retail. Consum. Serv. **51**, 14–18 (2019)

20. Yang, B., Liu, Y., Liang, Y., Tang, M.: Exploiting user experience from online customer reviews for product design. Int. J. Inf. Manage. **46**, 173–186 (2019)
21. Sun, X.Y., Han, M.X., Feng, J.: Helpfulness of online reviews: Examining review informativeness and classification thresholds by search products and experience products. Decis. Support Syst. **124**, 113099 (2019)
22. Wang, Y., Ngai, E.W.T., Li, K.: The effect of review content richness on product review helpfulness: The moderating role of rating inconsistency. Electron. Commer. Res. Appl. **61**, 101290 (2023)
23. Schrepp, M.: User Experience Questionnaire Handbook (2023). https://www.ueq-online.org/Material/Handbook.pdf
24. Kakaria, S., Simonetti, A., Bigne, E.: Interaction between extrinsic and intrinsic online review cues: perspectives from cue utilization theory. Electronic Commerce Research (2023).https://doi.org/10.1007/s10660-022-09665-2
25. Jin, W., Chen, Y., Yang, S., Zhou, S., Jiang, H., Wei, J.: Personalized managerial response and negative inconsistent review helpfulness: The mediating effect of perceived response helpfulness. J. Retail. Consum. Serv. **74**, 103398 (2023). https://doi.org/10.1016/j.jretconser.2023.103398
26. Lee, S., Lee, S., Baek, H.: Does the dispersion of online review ratings affect review helpfulness? Comput. Hum. Behav. **117**, 106670 (2021)
27. Xu, C., Zheng, X., Yang, F.: Examining the effects of negative emotions on review helpfulness: the moderating role of product price. Comput. Hum. Behav. **139**, 107501 (2023). https://doi.org/10.1016/j.chb.2022.107501
28. Verkijika, S.F., Neneh, B.N.: Standing up for or against: a text-mining study on the recommendation of mobile payment apps. J. Retail. Consum. Serv. **63**, 102743 (2021)
29. Akbarabadi, M., Hosseini, M.: Predicting the helpfulness of online customer reviews: the role of title features. Int. J. Mark. Res. **62**(3), 272–287 (2020)
30. Tafesse, W.: The effect of app store strategy on app rating: the moderating role of hedonic and utilitarian mobile apps. Int. J. Inf. Manage. **57**, 102299 (2021)
31. Ma, Y., Xiang, Z., Du, Q., Fan, W.: Effects of user-provided photos on hotel review helpfulness: an analytical approach with deep leaning. Int. J. Hosp. Manag. **71**, 120–131 (2018)
32. Du, J., Rong, J., Michalska, S., Wang, H., Zhang, Y.: Feature selection for helpfulness prediction of online product reviews: An empirical study. PLoS ONE **14**(12), e0226902 (2019)
33. Zhou, Y., Yang, S., Li, Y., Chen, Y., Yao, J., Qazi, A.: Does the review deserve more helpfulness when its title resembles the content? Locating helpful reviews by text mining. Inf. Process. Manage. **57**, 102179 (2020)

Special Session on E3: Enhancing the Esports Experience

Gamers' Eden: The Functioning and Role of Gaming Houses Inside the Esports Ecosystem

alessandro franzó[1]([⊠]) [iD] and Attila Bruni[2] [iD]

[1] University of Milan, 20122 Milan, MI, Italy
alessandro.franzo@outlook.com
[2] University of Trento, 38122 Trento, TN, Italy
attila.bruni@unitn.it

Abstract. The current paper aims to analyse the complex array of practices entailed by teams and esports professionals by looking at one of the most peculiar phenomena of the esports field: gaming houses, i.e., "co-operative living arrangement[s] where several players of video games, usually professional esports players, live in the same residence" [1]. Representing one of the first attempts to assess the role of gaming houses as emerging esports spaces based on new forms of playbour and production of and by users, the paper comprises an innovative adaptation of PRISMA protocol for literature and scoping reviews to shed light on how the technological, material, and social elements are enacted through gaming houses' activities, which mirror the ones entailed by digital platforms. In fact, through the three moves of encoding, aggregating and computing users' interactions [2], gaming houses (re)produce virtual and analogical goods, translating consumer practices and profoundly influencing the broader esports ecosystem. Finally, by framing themselves as ideal hives for pro players, i.e., a prototypical breeding ground for esports professionals, these structures push for new paradigms of work-life balance and users' production, thus leading to a further reflection on the nature of play and working practices in our contemporary network society [3].

Keywords: Esports · Gaming houses · Platforms · Ecosystems · Socio-materiality

1 Introduction

The rise of esports professionals [4–6] and gaming content producers [7–9] has already drawn the attention of social, media and game scholars, which have focused mainly on the spectatorship dimension [10–12] and the emergent identities and cultures associated with gaming [13–16]. On the other hand, labour researchers highlighted the "prosuming" perspective [17, 18], underlining how the gaming industry transforms gamers' consumption practices into processes of production shared within and without the gaming field. What blossomed in the gaming field eventually spilt over the broader society, as displayed by the spreading of gamification among businesses and institutions [19–22].

In such a scenario, esports teams (i.e., groups of professional players that gather to participate in competitions and operate better in the economic market) emerged as relevant organisational actors [23, 24]. Evolving from simpler LAN parties' organisers, these groups of gamers undergo a process of institutionalisation and transformation along trajectories of progressive specialisation [25]. Nowadays, teams usually involve multifaceted activities to increase revenues, like training together and streaming independently; simultaneously, they confront some of the most diffused biases of the field [26] and propose new solutions to the hurdles they encounter [27].

The current paper tries to catch a glimpse over the complex array of practices entailed by teams and esports professionals through their daily grind by looking at one of the most peculiar phenomena of the field: gaming houses, i.e. "co-operative living arrangement[s] where several players of video games, usually professional esports players, live in the same residence" [1]. Depicted as ultimate professionalising tools by many insiders [28], these "houses" offer a privileged empirical ground for assessing how the esports ecosystem adopts new paradigms of work-life balance and users' production [29–31]. Albeit they can respond to different needs [28], these coworking and co-living spaces are the place of continuous refinement of the narratives and identities associated with the figure of the pro players [32]. Moreover, they are also framed as ideal hives to nurture new talents and workspaces for new-fangled professions [33, 34].

Thus, this contribution aims to analyse how gaming houses are composed, administered, and lived. In other words, it will examine how the socio-material matrix [35, 36] embedded in gaming houses influences the houses' (spatial) ecosystem, which allegedly composes the prototypical breeding ground for an esports professional [37]. Then, the literature review will focus on the material aspects and the social structures inside the houses, but also how these are enacted to narrate a professional(ising) trajectory into which these structures play a crucial role [38, 39]. Finally, the last part will highlight how a deeper understanding of these structures may contribute to the current literature on esports as well as offer insights about the embedding of digital technologies in contemporary societies and (new) working practices.

2   Related Works

While scholars have already tackled either the subjective dimension of esports [40–44] or the sociotechnical innovations brought in by esports teams and professional players in the broader gaming scenario [25, 31, 45–47], gaming houses are still an unexplored theme for academia. However, notable exceptions are constituted by the works of Can [37] and Thornham [16]: the former represents an in-depth analysis of the current Turkish esports scene focusing on the role that gaming houses play inside that specific local context, enriched by a reflection on the persistent gender inequality and segregation that these structures seem to reinforce [37]; on the other hand, the latter book by Thornham [16] expands on the issue of gender inside the gaming community by exploring the use of these technologies inside the domestic environments [48, 49], putting the work on the page of current media literature on the theme.

Nonetheless, the latter work brings up a "semantic" problem, as Thornham's research space shares little to no connection to the professional(ised) venture intended by esports insiders with the term "gaming houses". By means of opening up a scholarly discussion on these structures, this paper will address this need for clarification by proposing a first definition of gaming houses, which arises through the lay literature on the theme describing their components and functioning.

3 Methodology

Scholarly approaching gaming houses reveals the scarcity of academic literature regarding these structures. Although many authors have devoted their attention to the competitive scene [25, 30, 50], gaming houses have remained a theme only for insiders and fans. This is why this paper, following some promising results obtained through exploratory inquiries into the Internet, proposes to fill the literature gap by addressing the lay knowledge circulating among gaming communities. However, it was necessary to adapt standard literature review procedures to build a scientific point on such an unstructured body of work. The choice was to use the PRISMA protocol for literature and scoping reviews [51], adapting it to unconventional repositories in order to systematically approach this vast but raw knowledge while maintaining academic reliability.

3.1 Inclusion Criteria

The material included had to talk specifically of gaming houses (i.e., shared households inhabited only by pro players); or other structures devoted to gathering and offering a space to professional gamers; or labelling themselves as "gaming" or "team houses". Consequently, gaming houses were operationally defined as structures, either established by teams or funded by external companies, devoted to hosting pro players temporarily (i.e., bootcamping venues) or permanently (as proper housing solutions) during their playing, training, and living activities. This definition was adopted to distinguish houses from other venues inside the gaming ecosystem (e.g., LAN houses or PC bangs). In addition, the entries chosen for queries reflected the semantic variability found in preliminary searches. Thus, the following keyword combinations were used:

- game house;
- gaming house;
- gaming team house.

3.2 Sources

To fruitfully merge scientific and lay knowledge on gaming houses, the queries were performed on unconventional repositories (accessed through Bing, Google, and YouTube) and then paired with a more common search over the typical academic databases. The scarcity of findings suggested including not only the stricter database Scopus (Elsevier) but also the broader and "messier" Google Scholar, aiming to include even its grey literature and low-tier journals in the review.

To sum up, the following sources have been examined:

- Microsoft Bing (search engine);
- Google Search (search engine);
- YouTube (media platform);
- Scopus (academic database);
- Google Scholar (academic and grey literature search engine).

3.3 Disclaimer on Sources

Acknowledging that one of the major perils of using Internet sources could be stepping in their built-in biases and, more precisely, the possibility that the searching algorithm might influence the results, some precautions were adopted to limit an excessive manipulation of the data: two parallel searches were conducted, keeping the same web browser (Microsoft Edge) but changing the search engine from Bing to Google. Moreover, the Google search engine was linked to a new account to counter past search history effects. Except for the hardly avoidable information related to the IP address and the geolocation of the machine (Northeastern Italy), the two engines differed in the language adopted: Bing ran in the default English, whereas Google in the suggested Italian (because of the IP address)[1].

Moreover, the choice of adding the media site YouTube, even if related to Google Search, was motivated by the large number of videos that emerged in preliminary searches. Indeed, the recognised link between gaming activities and video-sharing platforms like YouTube and Twitch.tv [8, 9, 50] suggested exploring at least one of them: the more extensive database of YouTube and its characteristic of keeping track of videos and comments, a feature lacking in many Twitch channels [53, 54], pushed for its choice.

All searches were carried out over the last week of November 2022, and every result was double-checked and finally consulted during January 2023.

3.4 Search Strategy

Search engines output massive volumes of results (the highest was "around 4.170.000.000 results in 0,47 s", as reported by Google) that could hardly be filtered. The decision was to limit the search to the first ten pages of results to stem this overwhelming amount while keeping the maximum information possible. This was due to time-constraint reasons and the fact that the records seemed to recur consistently after the first pages, reaching near total repetition (i.e., a full page of already shown records) after the tenth one. The same occurred when searching YouTube, Scopus, and Google Scholar, so the same limit criterion was adopted. However, the single-page output on those sites differed, so the threshold was set to 97 results per source to uniform the searches. Indeed, 97 were the records shown in the first ten pages of (both) search engines.

Moreover, technical issues like broken links, search engines malfunctions, or unretrievable material affected the screening, which in some cases hindered the reach of the expected 97 results for each source. Even though these breakages did not constitute a significant issue, the author added 3 more records from hyperlinks or previously retrieved material.

The total number of reports to be screened was still considerable (n = 1354), and the shambolic nature of search engines' indexing made it hard to find clusters of relevant results. Nonetheless, after carefully analysing the 195 relevant studies obtained through deduplication and selection processes (see Fig. 1), some significant axes emerged from the raw knowledge, which will now be presented.

---

[1] The language used for queries has shown to be one of the "local" factors influencing search engines' output [52].

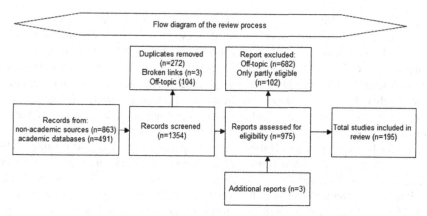

Fig. 1. The diagram summarizes the selection procedure.

4 Findings

A systematic reading of the literature shows how gaming houses represent new opportunities for esports organisations to arrange professional gamers' activities [28] while transforming teams' practices into value-laden products [55, 56]. These organisational configurations sallied from Asian territories [32, 38, 57] and rapidly conquered the rest of the world by narrating themselves as crucial professionalising tools for the field [37, 39, 57]. Gaming houses are displayed as places where professional gamers live and play together [58], as well as modern and innovative economic ventures [59–61].

Drawing from the extensive knowledge gathered by the gaming community, which has been decidedly more productive on the topic, we can recognise several distinctive elements lying behind the houses scattered around the globe, which will help us understand what is intended by the term "gaming house". To navigate the data, the paper will first present a guiding definition of gaming houses, albeit still partial and based on lay knowledge, and then continue their analysis through the proposed theoretical lens of platforms' ecosystemic functioning [2, 62, 63].

4.1 Tracing Gaming Houses' Roots and Defining Them

The Asian background has heavily influenced gaming houses' emergence: mangled in densely inhabited and infrastructured zones, the first goal guiding the creation of these structures was offering an affordable housing solution, which seems to remain a major concern for many teams [64]. Even though the current Korean and Chinese scenes have shifted their focus toward economic sustainability and media production, most Asian organisations still aim to find a balance between endless work and leisure gaming screen hours. Indeed, many insiders claim that life inside these households may become exhausting [65, 66]. On the other hand, a more Western model has diffused lately, more focused on the performance-enhancing opportunities that gathering all players and staff in the same place could give. Following a paradigm that imitates other sports disciplines, many American and European teams' houses emulate sports facilities, starting to criticise the forced co-living for a more flexible "facility model" where gamers gather only for their working (i.e., training) hours. Alongside these two leading and recognisable ideal types, a full assortment of variations for these structures can be found in the different local gaming ecosystems: ranging from the "coerced" model imposed by Riot to the more content-oriented one spreading in the USA, gaming houses seem to maintain operational flexibility that allows them adapting to the diverse needs that gave rise to them.

However, the cornerstones of what defines a gaming house can be summed up as: being a place where (1) professional gamers live together regularly, even if temporarily (i.e., for bootcamps), and (2) they use such spaces for professional gaming (either matches or training); (3) when in use, gaming houses spaces are not accessible by outsiders, except from invited ones or in certain areas (or events). This definition helps discriminate gaming houses from other types of simpler housing solutions adopted by teams [67] and distinguish them from facility-style configurations [68] or other arrangements renting PC stations and other services to (usually amateur) teams and single players [69].

4.2   Gaming Houses as Platformised Environments

Through the literature emerges how gaming houses slowly constructed a general aura of irreplaceability around themselves [57, 70], framing their existence both as a technical and organisational advancement [68, 71] and as an inescapable consequence of esports professionalisation [28, 64]. This central positioning inside the esports ecosystem is obtained through an assemblage of digital, material, and social components, forming these structures' unique environments [72]. Notably, gaming houses seem to mirror platforms' ecosystemic functioning [2, 62, 63], inasmuch they frame their services as life-improving and producing better versions of their "users" (i.e., team members) through encoding, aggregating, and computing the practices entailed in their spaces.

The following paragraphs will expand on this utterance by tackling gaming houses' complex network of components and functions through the theoretical lens provided by Alaimo and colleagues [2, 62]. Paraphrasing Apperley and Jayemane [73], looking at gaming houses through platform studies offers the opportunity to locate them "as the stable object within a complex, unfolding entanglement" of traceable and examinable relations [73]. Approaching the material substrate behind the esports ecosystem through a similar lens will enhance the understanding of these structures as both "standard objects", routinely dealt with by insiders, and "black boxes", to be spread over by deconstructing them into their components [73–75].

This way, it will become clear how the houses' constitutive elements concur in accompanying amateur gamers towards professionalism through three "moves": encoding, aggregating, and computing.

Encode. Gaming houses are engaged in a framing effort, as they constantly try to depict pro players' gaming practices as professional [58, 66, 76]. If this can more easily hold for players, houses strive to enlarge their encoding to broader social communities. As they try to loyalise their fanbase with digital goods, like promo codes and sports merchandise [77], houses often employ community-building tactics [61, 78] and even lifestyle models [79, 80] to enrol followers and fans into the crafting of the professional figure of the pro player.

Digital infrastructures emerge as a crucial asset for this move, as most gaming houses nowadays also involve streaming practices carried by their roster members [81, 82], engage in social media to depict their top players as aspirational stars and funnel participation [81, 83], and cooperate with other influential digital firms to broaden their respective communities [55, 56, 61]. These activities are sustained by external infrastructures, like stable and ultra-fast Internet connection [84], and in-house features, like props and architectural renovations [82, 85, 86], that accommodate technologies and furniture like specific lighting [87, 88] and high-end hardware [89].

This way, the new "hardwired" households [90] become not only used but "prodused" by their inhabitants [17, 18] as they transform into fair-like assemblages of amusements and out-screen diversions aimed at the enhancement of their aesthetic qualities [91, 92]. A "streaming turn" also scaffolded by a human capital made of Hollywood creatives, sports psychologists, physiotherapists, marketing consultants, and video makers [59, 77, 79, 80, 92]. These new figures matched the ever-present managers and coaches, more focused on enhancing players' performance [58, 76, 88, 93]. Thus, this whole new social structure helps teams and players craft contemporary gaming celebrities [7], legitimising gaming and streaming endeavours by offering supporting structures and professionals [58, 94–96].

Even though this shift means translating competitive gaming into a tool (or an excuse) to have more content to work with [77, 88, 97], many pro players care about their personal brand as an asset because of the longer, stabler, and higher revenue that streaming practices ensure over esports winnings or salaries, further reinforcing the encoding of their activity as a professional one [9, 37, 38, 57].

Aggregate. The second move that gaming houses enact is displaying themselves as the elective spatial hubs for hosting the network of actors and objects needed for professional gaming. Indeed, this move frames these structures as an environment housing not only the (freshly defined) professional gamers but also the supporting figures and sustaining materialities, like gyms and relaxation areas [67, 82, 83, 98]. This aggregation process again involves cooperating teams and firms, as they often exchange players (and thus, knowledge and resources) and share partnerships with non-endemic companies [55, 60, 78, 83]. The further inclusion of fans and followers as part of each team community through streaming and social media [50, 58, 81] signals a unique tendency to generate a multilayered and digitally dense ecosystem, inside which gaming houses are positioned, made by the network of these different esports actants [45, 62, 63].

Although the rhetoric of gaming houses tries to detach the figure of the professional gamer from casual ones, the socio-material making of these structures seems undecidedly caught between playing as much as working zones. Although this scenario may challenge the familiar categories that divide play and work [99–101], the fundamental support offered by boundary objects [102] helps navigate the assemblage of objects, actors, and spaces devoted to leisure or work efforts, as they are depicted as equally essential in many gaming houses (self-)presentations [94, 96, 103]. Actually, videos and websites cover houses' playful environments and artefacts, like luxurious pools and old cabinet collections [79, 92, 103], as attractive features for aspiring pros and interested partners [59, 104, 105]. The resulting narrative depicts pro players as enjoying a "totalising" environment [106] where embedded digital infrastructures and physical structures ensnare them between (digital) gaming for professional reasons and playing (analogically and digitally) for leisure. At the same time, this discourse pictures gaming houses as crucial aggregating nodes where all kinds of activities are possible, further framing them as crucial environments for the broader esports ecosystem [28, 39, 64, 65].

Compute. Finally, esports organisations "compute" all the actions occurring among their walls; that is, they extract value from the spatial nodes represented by gaming houses. Pro players, as well as the complex set of practices entailed in these structures, become valuable leverage for connecting with endemic brands and diverse user bases [55, 107, 108]. Moreover, by presenting themselves as broad-ranging digital companies, the organisations behind the gaming houses expand their influence beyond their industrial and economic boundaries, offering interested actors their spatial structures as reliable intermediaries in the exchange of services and products with followers' communities and other gaming firms [78, 109–112].

The appeal of these houses for gaming communities and complementary companies is mainly given by the spatial dimension of their built environment. On the one hand, these structures offer a materiality to collaborating non-endemic firms that position them as unique in a highly dematerialised ecosystem [61, 79, 113], like the one of the gaming industry [45, 114]. On the other hand, the embedding of media and streaming practices, guaranteed by houses' digital infrastructures, material environment and social capital, allows for targeting the respective media audiences [55]. Indeed, the merging of different user communities and their enrolment into the production processes operated through gaming houses both reflect similar tendencies in the media and platform economy [29] and strengthen the reliability of esports organisations, especially the ones backing these structures [60, 78]. In a reinforcing feedback loop, such an intermediary role assumed by gaming houses further establishes a professional "aura" around competitive gamers (i.e., frames them as professionals), who benefit from these processes of industry expansion and stabilisation: not only do they improve esports professionals' economic situation, but they raise significantly the social status associated with the pro player figure [5, 24, 32, 56, 83].

Taking this intermediary role to the extreme, some gaming houses even detached from traditional esports organisations, constituting themselves as rentable hubs for both (amateur-ish) gamers and professional teams. Distantiating from the proper houses outlined in this paper, these hardware-ready facilities offer services like fully-equipped recreative areas, cutting-edge bootcamping venues, and hosting gaming-related events [69, 115–120]. Thus, even though this latter iteration of gaming structures shows a new direction in the meaning associated with these spaces by leveraging the temporary nature of the usage of these places, they display how the know-how behind gaming houses is being morphed to generate novel (economic) actors in the esports ecosystem. As the esports ecosystem evolves through these spaces, the progressive transformation of bigger gaming houses' owners into prominent international media companies [78, 109] gives a sense of how meanings and social relations are endlessly negotiated and adapted to the local (material) features behind their constitutive environments.

5 Discussion

The present study constitutes a first attempt to assess gaming houses' role as platformised spaces [121, 122] that rely on their technological, material, and social elements to embrace gaming's new forms of playbour [100, 123] and production of and by users [29]. Even though it may constitute a limitation for the study, the inclusion of lay sources in the literature review on gaming houses shed light on how the socio-material assemblage composing these structures is enacted through complex organisational processes, which resemble the ones entailed by digital platforms [2, 62, 63]. This body of secondary data showed how through the three moves of encoding, aggregating and computing users' interactions [2], gaming houses not only enrol users as produsers [17] but also (re)produce virtual and analogical goods, translating consumer practices and reshaping the gaming industry [18, 29, 45, 72]. Moreover, it emerged how these structures maintain their role as spatialised nodes in the broader esports ecosystem [45, 124] through a set of boundary-setting tactics [125] that establish gaming houses as core actors in an ever-evolving restructuration of the meanings related to the work-play divide (for further discussion on the innovative, yet ambiguous, power of gaming, see [20, 99, 126, 127]). Nevertheless, it must be noted how these substantial differentiating strategies aimed at separating professional players' activities from amateur(-ish) ones [32, 65, 93, 128] are grounded on the same materialities and digital infrastructures that emancipate gamers from the burden of (traditional) work [64, 129]. Although some insiders and scholars have already warned against the blurring of players' private and public lives [66, 93, 128, 130–132], these shapeshifting qualities allow gaming houses to constantly reposition them and reframe their components along the esports ecosystem and seem to be related to an intrinsic ambiguity belonging to games [133], which is also present in gaming' analogic forerunners (i.e., traditional sports; [6, 58, 134, 135]) and that may represent the focus of further studies.

6 Conclusion

By adapting the rigorous PRISMA protocol to unconventional lay sources, this paper analysed the complex array of practices and actors forming one of esports' most peculiar phenomena, i.e., gaming houses. The fan and insiders' literature showed how these structures frame themselves as ideal hives to nurture cutting-edge workspaces for the new-fangled esports professionals [25, 37, 114]. The paper used the theoretical lens of platforms' ecosystemic functioning [2, 62, 63] to shed light on how the technological, material, and social elements are enacted through gaming houses' activities [72]. As a matter of fact, through the three moves of encoding, aggregating and computing users' interactions, gaming houses embed new forms of playbour [100, 123, 136] and production of and by users [29], as well as constitute themselves as central (material) environments for the esports ecosystem [45, 124, 137]. Finally, the contribution critically engaged with what insiders depict as ultimate professionalising tools to see how their socio-material network led to new paradigms of work-life balance and users' production [20, 29, 31, 129, 137], which may hint at future further reflections on the ambiguous nature of play and working practices in our contemporary network society [3].

References

1. Gaming house (2022). https://en.wikipedia.org/w/index.php?title=Gaming_house&oldid=1127604193
2. Alaimo, C., Kallinikos, J.: Computing the everyday: social media as data platforms. Inf. Soc. **33**, 175–191 (2017). https://doi.org/10.1080/01972243.2017.1318327
3. Castells, M.: The Rise of the Network Society. Blackwell Publishers, Cambridge (1996)
4. Hallmann, K., Giel, T.: ESports – Competitive sports or recreational activity? Sport Manage. Rev. **21**, 14–20 (2018). https://doi.org/10.1016/j.smr.2017.07.011
5. Jenny, S.E., Manning, R.D., Keiper, M.C., Olrich, T.W.: Virtual(ly) athletes: where esports fit within the definition of "sport." Quest **69**, 1–18 (2017). https://doi.org/10.1080/00336297.2016.1144517
6. Kane, D., Spradley, B.D.: Recognizing ESports as a sport. Sport J. **20**, 1–19 (2017)
7. Johnson, M.R., Carrigan, M., Brock, T.: The imperative to be seen: The moral economy of celebrity video game streaming on Twitch.tv. First Monday (2019)
8. Tammy Lin, J.-H., Bowman, N., Lin, S.-F., Chen, Y.-S.: Setting the digital stage: defining game streaming as an entertainment experience. Entertain. Comput. **31**, 100309 (2019). https://doi.org/10.1016/j.entcom.2019.100309
9. Taylor, T.L.: Watch Me Play: Twitch and The Rise of Game Live Streaming. Princeton University Press, Princeton, NJ (2018)
10. Consalvo, M.: Player one, playing with others virtually: what's next in game and player studies. Crit. Stud. Media Commun. **34**, 84–87 (2017). https://doi.org/10.1080/15295036.2016.1266682
11. Hamilton, W.A., Garretson, O., Kerne, A.: Streaming on twitch: fostering participatory communities of play within live mixed media. In: Proceedings of the SIGCHI Conference on Human Factors in Computing Systems, pp. 1315–1324. ACM, Toronto Ontario Canada (2014). https://doi.org/10.1145/2556288.2557048
12. Johnson, M.R., Woodcock, J.: The impacts of live streaming and Twitch.tv on the video game industry. Media Cult. Soc. **41**, 670–688 (2019). https://doi.org/10.1177/0163443718818363
13. Arsenault, D.: Super Power, Spoony Bards, and Silverware. MIT Press, Cambridge (2017)
14. Custodio, A.: Who Are You?: Nintendo's Game Boy Advance Platform. The MIT Press, Cambridge (2020)
15. Dovey, J., Kennedy, H.: Game Cultures: Computer Games as New Media. McGraw-Hill Education, UK (2006)
16. Thornham, H.: Ethnographies of the Videogame: Gender, Narrative and Praxis. Routledge (2016). https://doi.org/10.4324/9781315580562
17. Bruns, A.: Blogs, Wikipedia, Second Life, and Beyond: From Production to Produsage. Peter Lang, New York (2008)
18. Ritzer, G., Jurgenson, N.: Production, consumption, prosumption: the nature of capitalism in the age of the digital 'prosumer.' J. Consum. Cult. **10**, 13–36 (2010). https://doi.org/10.1177/1469540509354673
19. Burke, B.: Gamify: How Gamification Motivates People to Do Extraordinary Things. Routledge, New York (2014)
20. Ferrer-Conill, R.: Playbour and the gamification of work: empowerment, exploitation and fun as labour dynamics. In: Bilić, P., Primorac, J., Valtýsson, B. (eds.) Technologies of Labour and the Politics of Contradiction. DVW, pp. 193–210. Springer, Cham (2018). https://doi.org/10.1007/978-3-319-76279-1_11
21. Jagoda, P.: Experimental Games: Critique, Play, and Design in the Age of Gamification. University of Chicago Press, Chicago (2020). https://doi.org/10.7208/chicago/9780226630038.001.0001

22. Vesa, M., Harviainen, J.T.: Gamification: concepts, consequences, and critiques. J. Manag. Inq. **28**, 128–130 (2019). https://doi.org/10.1177/1056492618790911

23. Gawrysiak, J., Burton, R., Jenny, S., Williams, D.: Using esports efficiently to enhance and extend brand perceptions – a literature review. Phys. Cult. Sport Stud. Res. **86**, 1–14 (2020). https://doi.org/10.2478/pcssr-2020-0008

24. Richelieu, A.: From sport to 'sportainment': the art of creating an added-value brand experience for fans. J. Brand Strateg. **9**, 408–422 (2021)

25. Taylor, T.L.: Raising the Stakes: E-Sports and the Professionalization of Computer Gaming. MIT Press, Cambridge (2012)

26. Johry, A., Wallner, G., Bernhaupt, R.: Social gaming patterns during a pandemic crisis: a cross-cultural survey. In: BaalsrudHauge, J., Cardoso, J.C.S., Roque, L., Gonzalez-Calero, P.A. (eds.) Entertainment Computing – ICEC 2021. LNCS, vol. 13056, pp. 139–153. Springer, Cham (2021). https://doi.org/10.1007/978-3-030-89394-1_11

27. Bucher, S., Langley, A.: The interplay of reflective and experimental spaces in interrupting and reorienting routine dynamics. Organ. Sci. **27**, 594–613 (2016). https://doi.org/10.1287/orsc.2015.1041

28. ESL: Team houses and why they matter. https://web.archive.org/web/20220926170436/http://www.eslgaming.com:80/article/team-houses-and-why-they-matter-1676. Accessed 09 Jan 2023

29. Hyysalo, S., Jensen, T.E., Oudshoorn, N. (eds.): The New Production of Users: Changing Innovation Collectives and Involvement Strategies. Routledge, New York (2016). https://doi.org/10.4324/9781315648088

30. Scholz, T.M.: ESports is Business: Management in the World of Competitive Gaming. Springer, New York (2019)

31. Scholz, T.M.: Deciphering the world of eSports. Int. J. Media Manag. **22**, 1–12 (2020). https://doi.org/10.1080/14241277.2020.1757808

32. Zelauskas, A.: Life of an Esports Athlete in a Team House, https://www.hotspawn.com/dota2/news/life-of-an-esports-athletic-in-a-team-house. Accessed 01 Jan 2023

33. Bányai, F., Zsila, Á., Griffiths, M.D., Demetrovics, Z., Király, O.: Career as a professional gamer: gaming motives as predictors of career plans to become a professional eSport player. Front. Psychol. **11**, 1866 (2020). https://doi.org/10.3389/fpsyg.2020.01866

34. Freeman, G., Wohn, D.Y.: Understanding eSports team formation and coordination. Comput. Support. Coop. Work CSCW. **28**, 95–126 (2019). https://doi.org/10.1007/s10606-017-9299-4

35. Barad, K.: Posthumanist performativity: toward an understanding of how matter comes to matter. Signs J. Women Cult. Soc. **28**, 801–831 (2003). https://doi.org/10.1086/345321

36. Orlikowski, W.J., Scott, S.V.: Sociomateriality: challenging the separation of technology, work organization. Acad. Manag. Ann. **2**, 433–474 (2008). https://doi.org/10.5465/194165 20802211644

37. Can, Ö.: E-sports and Gaming Houses in Turkey: Gender, Labor and Affect (2018)

38. Bago, J.P.: "SANDATA": Dispelling the Myth of the Korean Gaming House: What Lessons the Philippine eSports Industry Can Learn From Our Korean Overlords, https://esports.inquirei.net/13920/dispelling-the-myth-of-the-korean-gaming-house-what-lessons-the-philippine-esports-industry-can-learn-from-our-korean-overloads. Accessed 01 Jan 2023

39. Billy, J.: The Team House Trend. https://dotesports.com/call-of-duty/news/the-team-house-trend-10796. Accessed 30 Dec 2022

40. Huang, J., Yan, E., Cheung, G., Nagappan, N., Zimmermann, T.: Master maker: understanding gaming skill through practice and habit from gameplay behavior. Top. Cogn. Sci. **9**, 437–466 (2017). https://doi.org/10.1111/tops.12251

41. Ash, J.: Technology, technicity, and emerging practices of temporal sensitivity in videogames. Environ. Plan. Econ. Space. **44**, 187–203 (2012). https://doi.org/10.1068/a44171

42. Rambusch, J., Jakobsson, P., Pargman, D.: Exploring E-sports : a case study of game play in Counter-strike. In: 3rd Digital Games Research Association International Conference: "Situated Play", DiGRA 2007, Tokyo, 24 September 2007 through 28 September 2007 (2007)

43. Freeman, G., Wohn, D.Y.: Social Support in eSports: building emotional and esteem support from instrumental support interactions in a highly competitive environment. In: Proceedings of the Annual Symposium on Computer-Human Interaction in Play, pp. 435–447. Association for Computing Machinery, New York, NY, USA (2017). https://doi.org/10.1145/3116595.3116635

44. Scholz, T.M., Stein, V.: Going beyond ambidexterity in the media industry: esports as pioneer of ultradexterity. Int. J. Gaming Comput. Med. Simul. **9**(2), 47–62 (2017). https://doi.org/10.4018/IJGCMS.2017040104

45. Hölzle, K., Kullik, O., Rose, R., Teichert, M.: The digital innovation ecosystem of eSports: a structural perspective. In: Handbook on Digital Business Ecosystems, pp. 582–595. Edward Elgar Publishing, Cheltenham, UK (2022)

46. Kaytoue, M., Silva, A., Cerf, L., Meira, W., Raïssi, C.: Watch me playing, i am a professional: a first study on video game live streaming. In: Proceedings of the 21st International Conference on World Wide Web, pp. 1181–1188. Association for Computing Machinery, New York, NY, USA (2012). https://doi.org/10.1145/2187980.2188259

47. Burroughs, B., Rama, P.: The eSports trojan horse: twitch and streaming futures. J. Virtual Worlds Res. **8**(2), 1–7 (2015). https://doi.org/10.4101/jvwr.v8i2.7176

48. 'Bo'Ruberg, B., Lark, D.: Livestreaming from the bedroom: performing intimacy through domestic space on Twitch. Converg. Int. J. Res. New Med. Technol. **27**(3), 679–695 (2021). https://doi.org/10.1177/1354856520978324

49. Harvey, A.: Gender, Age, and Digital Games in the Domestic Context. Routledge, New York (2015). https://doi.org/10.4324/9781315757377

50. Hamari, J., Sjöblom, M.: What is eSports and why do people watch it? Internet Res. **27**, 211–232 (2017). https://doi.org/10.1108/IntR-04-2016-0085

51. Page, M.J., et al.: The PRISMA 2020 statement: an updated guideline for reporting systematic reviews. BMJ **372**, n71 (2021). https://doi.org/10.1136/bmj.n71

52. Magno, G., Araújo, C.S., Meira Jr., W., Almeida, V.: Stereotypes in Search Engine Results: Understanding The Role of Local and Global Factors. http://arxiv.org/abs/1609.05413 (2016). https://doi.org/10.48550/arXiv.1609.05413

53. Deng, J., Cuadrado, F., Tyson, G., Uhlig, S.: Behind the game: exploring the twitch streaming platform. In: 2015 International Workshop on Network and Systems Support for Games (NetGames), pp. 1–6. IEEE, Zagreb, Croatia (2015). https://doi.org/10.1109/NetGames.2015.7382994

54. Deng, J., Tyson, G., Cuadrado, F., Uhlig, S.: Internet scale user-generated live video streaming: the twitch case. In: Kaafar, M.A., Uhlig, S., Amann, J. (eds.) Passive and Active Measurement. LNCS, vol. 10176, pp. 60–71. Springer, Cham (2017). https://doi.org/10.1007/978-3-319-54328-4_5

55. Brand News: Philips Italia entra nel mondo gaming insieme a Mkers, OMD e Fuse. https://www.brand-news.it/brand/tlc-tech/elettronica-di-consumo/philips-italia-entra-nel-mondo-gaming-insieme-a-mkers-omd-e-fuse/. Accessed 10 Jan 2023

56. Forbes BrandVoice: Mercedes-Benz e gli eSports: una sinergia radicata nel passato e rivolta al futuro. https://forbes.it/2021/12/21/mercedes-benz-e-gli-esports-una-sinergia-radicata-nel-passato-e-rivolta-al-futuro/. Accessed 10 Jan 2023

57. Gaming Houses: The Esports Dream or Nightmare?|OverExplained. (2019)
58. Hood, V.: Life inside a pro-esports team house with Fnatic: streaming, training and burritos. https://www.techradar.com/news/life-inside-a-pro-esports-team-house-with-fnatic-str eaming-training-and-burritos. Accessed 02 Jan 2023
59. Amin, J.: NRG Esports reveals its content house, the NRG Castle|Esportz Network. https://www.esportznetwork.com/nrg-esports-reveals-its-content-house-the-nrg-castle/. Accessed 03 Jan 2023
60. DBusiness Daily News: Detroit's Rocket Mortgage Sponsors Esports Online Gaming Competition, Builds 100 Thieves Team House in California. https://www.dbusiness.com/daily-news/detroits-rocket-mortgage-sponsors-esports-online-gaming-competition-builds-100-thieves-team-house-in-california/. Accessed 03 Jan 2023
61. Samsung Newsroom Italia: Samsung annuncia la nascita dell'eSport Palace un luogo unico nel suo genere in Italia e residenza dei Samsung Morning Stars. https://news.samsung.com/it/samsung-annuncia-la-nascita-dellesport-palace-un-luogo-nel-suo-genere-in-italia-e-res idenza-dei-samsung-morning-stars. Accessed 03 Jan 2023
62. Alaimo, C., Kallinikos, J., Valderrama, E.: Platforms as service ecosystems: lessons from social media. J. Inf. Technol. **35**, 25–48 (2020). https://doi.org/10.1177/0268396219881462
63. Kapoor, K., ZiaeeBigdeli, A., Dwivedi, Y.K., Schroeder, A., Beltagui, A., Baines, T.: A socio-technical view of platform ecosystems: systematic review and research agenda. J. Bus. Res. **128**, 94–108 (2021). https://doi.org/10.1016/j.jbusres.2021.01.060
64. workaccno33: Gaming Houses. Why? https://www.reddit.com/r/leagueoflegends/com ments/1s5jpi/gaming_houses_why/. Accessed 01 Jan 2023
65. GOOD LUCK HAVE FUN: Life in an esport gaming house with Schlinks, https://www.tim eslive.co.za/sport/2017-11-27-life-in-an-esport-gaming-house-with-schlinks/. Accessed 03 Jan 2023
66. Izento: CLG Biofrost talks buying a house, work-life separation, and the double-edged sword of gaming houses. https://www.invenglobal.com/articles/8493/clg-biofrost-talks-buying-a-house-work-life-separation-and-the-double-edged-sword-of-gaming-houses. Accessed 03 Jan 2023
67. Retegno, P.: Dentro la Gaming House del Team Forge. https://www.redbull.com/it-it/esport-dentro-la-gaming-house-del-team-forge. Accessed 02 Jan 2023
68. Byrne, L.: The changing face of gaming houses and esports training facilities. https://esp orts-news.co.uk/2019/01/16/gaming-houses-esports-facilities/. Accessed 02 Jan 2023
69. MOBA Milano - Gaming House & eSports Cafè. (2017)
70. AFP: Inside a gaming house: How an elite eSports team hones its skills under the same roof. https://scroll.in/field/912364/inside-a-gaming-house-how-an-elite-esports-team-hones-its-skills-under-the-same-roof. Accessed 02 Jan 2023
71. Vivere in una "gaming house", la nuova frontiera degli eSport. (2019)
72. Franzò, A.: STS Invaders: gaming as an emerging theme for science and technology studies tecnoscienza. Ital. J. Sci. Technol. Stud. **14**, 155–170 (2023)
73. Apperley, T.H., Jayemane, D.: Game studies' material turn. Westminst. Papers Commun. Cult. **9**(1), 5 (2012). https://doi.org/10.16997/wpcc.145
74. Montfort, N., Bogost, I.: Racing the Beam: The Atari Video Computer System. The MIT Press, Cambridge (2009)
75. Montfort, N., Consalvo, M.: The Dreamcast, console of the avant-garde. Loading. J. Can. Game Stud. Assoc. **6**, 82–99 (2012)
76. Carmone, A.: Mercedes e Mkers aprono a Roma la "palestra" per i gamers, https://it.mot or1.com/news/546560/merceds-mkers-gaming-house-rome/. Accessed 03 Jan 2023
77. Touring: The MOST EXPENSIVE Gaming Facility In The World! TSM's Esports Performance Center (2022)

78. QLASH: QLASH. https://qlash.gg/. Accessed 09 Jan 2023
79. We Built the BEST Gaming Facility in the World! (MILLION DOLLAR TOUR) (2020)
80. ADC Group: Stardust lancia Dsyre, la nuova gaming house italiana. Al Museo della Permanente di Milano esposto l'NFT Stardust. https://www.adcgroup.it/e20-express/news/industry/industry/stardust-lancia-la-nouva-gaming-house-italiana-al-museo-della-permanente-di-milano-ssposto-linft-dedicato.html/. Accessed 02 Jan 2023
81. Di Donfrancesco, G.: Abbiamo visitato la gaming house dei Mkers a Roma, https://it.mashable.com/6649/come-e-gaming-house-mkers-roma. Accessed 01 Jan 2023
82. The MOST LUXURIOUS GAMING FACILITY in INDIA | First Glimpse at S8UL 2.0 ONE MILLION $ FACILITY (2021)
83. FIRST LOOK AT T1'S NEW GAMING FACILITY IN GANGNAM (English Tour). (2021)
84. TheFuriees: Origen's gaming house. www.reddit.com/r/leagueoflegends/comments/2srksn/origens_gaming_house/. Accessed 03 Jan 2023
85. GamingLyfe.com: The Swifty Gaming House Gets an Upgrade! https://gaminglyfe.com/the-swifty-gaming-house-gets-an-upgrade/. Accessed 03 Jan 2023
86. Santin, F.: I vantaggi di vivere in una gaming house per giocatori esport? Ce li svela FaZe Swagg! https://www.everyeye.it/notizie/vantaggi-vivere-gaming-house-giocatori-esport-ce-svela-faze-swagg-587638.html. Accessed 03 Jan 2023
87. ETERNAL FIRE GAMING HOUSE VLOG (2022)
88. TOURING THE BEST GAMING HOUSE IN ESPORTS! (2019)
89. Team Secret LoL EXCLUSIVE GAMING HOUSE Sneak Peek (2020)
90. Taylor, N.: Hardwired. In: Sharma, S., Singh, R. (eds.) Re-Understanding Media, pp. 51–67. Duke University Press, Durham (2022)
91. TOUR DELLA QLASH HOUSE! GAMING HOUSE PIU' GRANDE D'EUROPA?! (2019)
92. NRG's New $10,000,000 Gaming Fantasy Factory | NRG Castle Full Facility Tour. (2020)
93. Sledge, B.: Excel Esports' new BBC documentary shows the struggles of living in a gaming house. https://www.theloadout.com/excel-esports/gaming-house-struggles. Accessed 10 Jan 2023
94. Revealing The New $30,000,000 FaZe House (2020)
95. The BEST $1,000,000 Gaming House Tour in Vegas | TSM Rainbow Six Siege (2021)
96. TOURING THE BEST CONTENT HOUSE IN GAMING ft. CouRage, Valkyrae, Nadeshot & BrookeAB. (2020)
97. DSYRE: DSYRE | Esports, Streetwear, Intrattenimento. https://dsyre.com/. Accessed 10 Jan 2023
98. Khám phá NRG GAMing House TRIỆU ĐÔ (2022)
99. Kerr, A.: The Business and Culture of Digital Games: Gamework/Gameplay. SAGE Publications Ltd., London (2006). https://doi.org/10.4135/9781446211410
100. Kücklich, J.: Precarious Playbour: Modders and the Digital Games Industry. Fibreculture J. (2005). https://five.fibreculturejournal.org/fcj-025-precarious-playbour-modders-and-the-digital-games-industry/
101. Törhönen, M., Hassan, L., Sjöblom, M., Hamari, J.: Play, Playbour or Labour? The Relationships between Perception of Occupational Activity and Outcomes among Streamers and YouTubers (2019)
102. Star, S.L., Griesemer, J.R.: Institutional ecology, 'Translations' and boundary objects: amateurs and professionals in Berkeley's museum of vertebrate zoology, 1907–39. Soc. Stud. Sci. **19**, 387–420 (1989). https://doi.org/10.1177/030631289019003001
103. Marsh, J.: Botez Sisters, JustAMinx, And CodeMiko Unveil Brand-New Envy House. https://www.ggrecon.com/articles/botez-sisters-justaminx-and-codemiko-unveil-brand-new-envy-house/. Accessed 03 Jan 2023

104. Di Felice, G.L.: Mkers Gaming House: la casa dei Pro Player e il simulatore da 40.000 euro - HDmotori.it. https://www.hdmotori.it/mercedes-benz/articoli/n546855/mer cedes-benz-mkers-gaming-house-esport/. Accessed 02 Jan 2023

105. LA GAMING HOUSE DE TEAM HERETICS - ESPECIAL 1 MILLÓN (2019)

106. Goffman, E.: Asylums: Essays on the Social Situation of Mental Patients and Other Inmates. Anchor Books, Garden City (1961)

107. ENCE: ENCE Gaming House. https://www.ence.gg/article/ence-gaming-house. Accessed 10 Jan 2023

108. Team Liquid's NEW EU Alienware Training Facility! (2020)

109. 100 Thieves: 100 Thieves. https://100thieves.com/. Accessed 09 Jan 2023

110. Macko Esports: Macko Esports - The org #DrawnToDare. https://www.mackoesports.com/. Accessed 10 Jan 2023

111. Mkers: Mkers. https://shop.mkers.gg/. Accessed 10 Jan 2023

112. NRG: NRG Esports|Home. https://www.nrg.gg/. Accessed 10 Jan 2023

113. Schiavella, U.: Mkers Gaming House Powered by Mercedes-Benz, https://www.gazzetta. it/Auto/10-11-2021/mkers-gaming-house-powered-by-mercedes-benz-4202326729847. shtml. Accessed 02 Jan 2023

114. Johnson, M.R., Woodcock, J.: Work, Play, and Precariousness: An Overview of the Labour Ecosystem of eSports. Media Cult. Soc. **43**, 1449–1465 (2021). https://doi.org/10.1177/016 34437211011555

115. 1337Camp: 1337 Bootcamp/Gaming House. https://1337.camp/en. Accessed 02 Jan 2023

116. East, T.: Dentro il Red Bull Gaming Sphere di Londra. https://www.redbull.com/it-it/red-bull-gaming-sphere. Accessed 03 Jan 2023

117. Esport Palace. https://esportpalace.it/. Accessed 02 Jan 2023

118. The GameHouse. https://www.coexistgaming.com/gamehouse. Accessed 02 Jan 2023

119. Ring, O.: Step inside the OG team house. https://www.redbull.com/int-en/og-team-house-tour-video-and-q-and-a-red-bull-esports. Accessed 01 Jan 2023

120. The Bug Game House: The Bug Game House. https://www.thebuggamehouse.com/. Accessed 10 Jan 2023

121. Nieborg, D., Poell, T.: The Platformization of Making Media. In: Deuze, M., Prenger, M. (eds.) Making Media: Production, Practices, and Professions, pp. 85–96. Amsterdam University Press (2019). https://doi.org/10.1017/9789048540150.006

122. Poell, T., Nieborg, D.B., Duffy, B.E.: Platforms and Cultural Production. John Wiley & Sons, London (2021)

123. Goggin, J.: Playbour, farming and leisure. Ephemera **11**, 357–368 (2011)

124. Yström, A., Agogué, M.: Exploring practices in collaborative innovation: unpacking dynamics, relations, and enactment in in-between spaces. Creat. Innov. Manag. **29**, 141–145 (2020). https://doi.org/10.1111/caim.12360

125. de Certeau, M.: The Practice of Everyday Life. University of California Press, Berkeley (1984)

126. Consalvo, M.: Kaceytron and Transgressive Play on Twitch.tv. In: Jørgensen, K., Karlsen, F. (eds.) Transgression in Games and Play, pp. 83–98. The MIT Press (2019). https://doi. org/10.7551/mitpress/11550.003.0009

127. Taylor, N.T.: Now you're playing with audience power: the work of watching games. Crit. Stud. Media Commun. **33**, 293–307 (2016). https://doi.org/10.1080/15295036.2016.121 5481

128. Jacobs, H.: Here's what life is like in the cramped "gaming house" where 5 guys live together and earn amazing money by playing video games. https://www.businessinsider.com/inside-team-liquids-league-of-legends-gaming-house-2015-4. Accessed 01 Jan 2023

129. Pedersen, V.B., Lewis, S.: Flexible friends? Flexible working time arrangements, blurred work-life boundaries and friendship. Work Employ Soc. **26**, 464–480 (2012). https://doi.org/10.1177/0950017012438571

130. Andrejevic, M.: The work of watching one another: lateral surveillance, risk, and governance. Surveill. Soc. **2**, 479–497 (2004)

131. Duffy, B.E.: The romance of work: Gender and aspirational labour in the digital culture industries. Int. J. Cult. Stud. **19**, 441–457 (2016). https://doi.org/10.1177/1367877915572186

132. Stanton: The secret to eSports athletes' success? Lots -- and lots -- of practice, https://www.espn.com/nfl/story/_/id/35343574. Accessed 30 Dec 2023

133. Sutton-Smith, B.: The Ambiguity of Play. Harvard University Press, Cambridge (1997)

134. Red Bull Team: Erena è il paradiso del simracing. https://www.redbull.com/it-it/gaming-house-erena. Accessed 02 Jan 2023

135. Sacco, D.: exceL Esports open LoL training facility at Twickenham Stadium & explain why they're leaving their gaming house behind. https://esports-news.co.uk/2019/01/05/excel-training-facility-twickenham-stadium/. Accessed 02 Jan 2023

136. Taylor, N., Bergstrom, K., Jenson, J., De Castell, S.: Alienated playbour: relations of production in EVE online. Games Cult. **10**, 365–388 (2015). https://doi.org/10.1177/1555412014565507

137. Johnson, M.R., Woodcock, J.: Work, play, and precariousness: an overview of the labour ecosystem of esports. Media Cult. Soc. **43**, 1449–1465 (2021). https://doi.org/10.1177/01634437211011555

The Communication Effectiveness of AI Win Prediction Applied in Esports Live Streaming: A Pilot Study

Minglei Wang[✉]

College of Media and International Culture, Zhejiang University, Hangzhou, China
wangmingleie@zju.edu.cn

Abstract. AI win prediction is widely used in the live streaming of Esports games, with the assumption that it is capable of significantly enhancing the viewing experience and providing valuable information to spectators. However, there is very little empirical research to demonstrate the actual attitudes and feelings of spectators towards AI win prediction. This paper describes an ongoing study from the perspective of communication effectiveness that aims to bridge this gap and explore some possible influencing factors, which could provide a scientific basis for better presenting AI prediction information in future Esports live streaming, thus further improving the viewing experience and engagement of spectators. This study has not yet officially begun on a large scale, so this paper reports primary results from in-depth interviews with 12 hardcore fans of League of Legends, as a pilot study for the formal survey experiment. The perceived usefulness, the balance between credibility, accuracy, and dramatic effects, and the anthropomorphic image are mainly discussed.

Keywords: AI win prediction · Esports spectators · Esports live streaming Viewing experience

1 Introduction

In recent years, the Esports industry has become a new type of mass culture and entertainment consumption, especially among young people. Esports competitions rely heavily on live streaming. Therefore, creating a good viewing experience for the audience is the goal pursued by practitioners in the fields of Esports and live streaming. Researchers from different disciplines have also carried out a series of studies on the viewing experience of Esports fans, such as the motivation and paying behavior (Ma et al. 2021; Wang 2022; Wohn and Freeman 2020), as well as the psychological process of watching the games (Meng-Lewis 2022). Additionally, there have been various technical works and design efforts aimed at enhancing the quality of live streaming, including modifying perspectives in first-person shooter games (Li et al. 2022) and providing more detailed statistics about games and players (Block et al. 2018; Kokkinakis et al. 2020).

Currently, the widespread use of artificial intelligence (AI) has had a significant impact on the Esports industry and is expected to continue to grow in the coming years.

© The Author(s), under exclusive license to Springer Nature Switzerland AG 2023
H. P. da Silva and P. Cipresso (Eds.): CHIRA 2023, CCIS 1997, pp. 315–325, 2023.
https://doi.org/10.1007/978-3-031-49368-3_19

One of the most prominent applications is AI win prediction, which is widely used in pre-competition gambling, live streaming of the competition, and other processes (Chan et al. 2022). For spectators of Esports, measuring the advantages and disadvantages between two teams in a game can be challenging, particularly compared to traditional sports competitions. This is due to the dynamic nature of Esports games, where conditions can change rapidly, and important events can occur simultaneously in multiple locations, making it difficult to predict the outcome of the game.

Therefore, it is believed that AI win prediction developed by neural networks and other machine learning algorithms can allow the audience to follow up on the development of the game more easily, thus enhancing viewability and viewer engagement (Kugler 2022). There is a lot of research that is focused on optimizing models and algorithms to further improve the accuracy of predictions (Akhmedov and Phan 2021; Yang et al. 2022; Ke et al. 2022; Zhao et al. 2022). These developments are expected to provide more valuable insights for Esports enthusiasts and play a more important role in enhancing the viewer experience. What's more, the application of AI win prediction has also been adopted in traditional sports competitions such as football and basketball, providing a more precise and data-driven analysis of the performance of the athletes (Fialho et al. 2019).

In the technical research domain, it is widely assumed that AI win prediction has the capacity to significantly enhance the viewing experience, providing audiences with valuable information. However, there has been little evaluation of the genuine feelings and attitudes of spectators towards AI win prediction. There remain many uncertainties, such as whether the audience is likely to believe that AI prediction is helpful for watching a game, the situation in which it is useful, and the factors that influence their attitudes and feelings. Even the most basic issue, of whether AI win predictions are always noticed when they appear, has not yet been systematically proven. Research by Hodge et al. (2019) suggests an interesting paradox associated with win prediction: if its accuracy is too low, an audience would afterward have no trust in the functionality of these predictions. In contrast, if AI can predict the result of a competition completely correctly, the audience would gain less emotional stimulation from unexpected outcomes in the competition. However, to date, there is no follow-up research into this paradox.

The new technical method of AI win prediction presents a new form of information during the live streaming of Esports games. Systematic and in-depth research of an audience's genuine reactions and preferences of AI win prediction and its influence factors is needed to learn about this new phenomenon, suggesting the shape of the implementation of useful and worthwhile AI-powered processes in the media and entertainment sectors. From the perspective of communication effectiveness, this study seeks to provide a better understanding of the ideal conditions for the display of AI win prediction during the course of live streaming, allowing the development of more effective strategies to attract and satisfy Esports spectators.

2   Method

In many Esports games and competitions, League of Legends (LOL) is one of the most mature and influential brands, with a large fan audience worldwide. The LOL Pro League in China (LPL) is one of the most famous and exciting leagues. According to an official report, the number of Chinese Esports users is expected to reach 450 million in 2023. Therefore, this study selects Chinese Esports fans who like watching LPL live streaming as research participants to explore their attitudes towards AI win prediction and viewing experience. Although there are certain regional limitations, it still has reference significance for global Esports events.

This study aims to conduct a survey experiment, in which participants can be recruited from various LPL fan communities (mainly through social media platforms such as Weibo, Tieba, Hupu Forum, and WeChat groups). These samples will be randomly assigned into different groups and exposed to different stimulus materials, which are expected to be pictures or short videos of Esports live streaming including AI win prediction under diverse conditions. After watching these materials, the participants' attitudes and feelings will be measured through scales. In addition, the viewing motivation and behaviors (e.g., the frequency of watching the live streaming), as well as some sociodemographic variables, will also be collected. During data analysis, the main focus is on exploring the impact of experimental conditions on the viewing experience, while also examining whether other variables have mediating or moderating effects during the viewing process.

However, when it comes to the factors in the experimental groups, due to the lack of literature that can be referenced before, a pilot study is necessary to carefully understand the spectators' true thoughts and concerns. This paper has conducted semi-structured in-depth interviews with 12 hardcore fans who have been watching LPL live streaming for more than five years with high frequency. The reason for choosing to obtain reliable opinions from experienced viewers is because they are loyal viewers of the live streaming of the events, and only then can they pay sufficient attention to all aspects of the live content, whose demand for improving the viewing experience is also the strongest. The specific information of the respondents is shown in Table 1.

The average interview time for each person exceeded one hour, and the topics were mainly around their reactions and thoughts after seeing AI win prediction during the viewing period. Some of the most important questions are: "Have you noticed the AI prediction appearing in the live streaming?" (If not, the researcher would provide them with stimulating materials, such as figures in Sect. 3.3.) "Overall, what is your opinion on it?" "Do you think it is useful? In what situations is it most useful?" "Can you easily understand it" "Do you believe its predicted results?" "Do you remember the previous Colonel KI (see specific explanations in Sect. 3.3)?". Further questions were inquired based on the respondents' answers. In addition, the interviewees were also asked for some personal information, including sociodemographic characteristics, the length of time spent watching the game live and their motivations, whether they play games and their gaming level, as well as AI literacy. It will not recruit more participants until it reaches saturation in terms of opinions and content.

All the responses were recorded. The researcher encoded and organized these contents, summarizing the same viewpoints in the responses to structural questions, and paying special attention to the correlation between different viewpoints and their characteristics. At the same time, some meaningful elements were extracted from the responses to open-ended questions, which may be helpful for further experiments as different influencing factors.

Table 1. Respondent's personal information.

No.	Gender	Age	Highest education level (including current state)	Since which year start watching LPL competitions	Whether to play LOL games and the highest-ranking level[a]
F1	Male	25	Undergraduate	2012	Yes. Challenger
F2	Male	25	Undergraduate	2015	Yes. Diamond
F3	Female	28	Undergraduate	2018	Yes. Silver
F4	Male	23	Graduate	2013	Yes. Platinum
F5	Female	25	Graduate	2017	Yes. No ranking
F6	Male	29	Undergraduate	2014	Yes. Platinum
F7	Male	26	Graduate	2015	Yes. Gold
F8	Male	28	Undergraduate	2013	Yes. Diamond
F9	Male	26	Graduate	2014	Yes. Gold
F10	Female	22	Undergraduate	2016	Yes. Diamond
F11	Female	25	Graduate	2018	Yes. No ranking
F12	Male	20	Undergraduate	2013	Yes. Diamond

[a]The Ranked system in League of Legends is divided into nine different tiers, from low to high: Iron, Bronze, Silver, Gold, Platinum, Diamond, Master, Grandmaster, Challenger.

3 Primary Results from the Pilot Study

3.1 Perceived Usefulness

Whether people accept a new technology often requires consideration of both usefulness and ease of use. Because win prediction driven by AI in Esports games is a new form of technology, both aspects are carefully questioned.

Given that AI win prediction is directly presented during the live streaming of a competition in the form of line charts, the spectators effectively act as receivers, not being required to learn specialized methods or skills to use the application. As a result, in terms of perceived ease of use, interviewees concur that the information brought by AI win prediction is clear, straightforward, and understandable.

However, for crucial perceived usefulness, interviewees show inconsistent opinions, which are closely linked to their viewing motivations and individual characteristics. Seven of the interviewees believe that AI win prediction is beneficial for watching a game, largely because it provides them with more data to help them better analyze the game's situation. These interviewees typically watch and enjoy Esports matches in order to learn about game-playing skills or to support their favorite team; they often pay great attention to data statistics about professional players and game champions. Some examples are as below:

"I mainly hope that my favorite team can win the game… Seeing the winning rate provided by AI can help me have an expectation of the result in advance. If the winning

rate is high, I feel more at ease. But if the winning rate is low, I will try to prepare for the failure." (F5).

"I have always been very concerned about the statistical data of players, which can reflect their level of strength. I think AI may also be inferred based on the past data, which can reflect a current trend, so I think it is quite helpful." (F8).

Further, four of these interviewees proactively mention that the occurrence timing of AI win prediction is critical. F4, F5, and F7 all agree that seeing the prediction at the beginning of the game is very important, due to it being based on the line-up (i.e. the process of banning/picking champions and their collocation levels), which is not usually fully understood by individual spectators. Thus, the prediction can work as a useful tool to discern the advantages of one team over the other regarding the line-up.

In addition, during the early stage of a game, when there is no large gap between the two teams (such as kills and deaths, destruction of turrets, etc.), predictions at this point play a big role in helping the audience understand the game's dynamics. The leading way for a layman to evaluate the situation is to compare the proportion of kills and deaths between the two sides, while there are fewer group battles during the early stage (at this point the routes of the Jungle are the biggest consideration), resulting in some spectators easily being lost, like what F9 describes, *"it seems like nothing happened but in reality, the gap had already been widened"*. AI win prediction during this stage can therefore provide good support, enabling viewers to catch the competition process. In contrast, during the game's later stage, the situation often becomes so clear to the audience that the effect of AI win prediction in this situation decreases significantly, unless the game is particularly close.

However, three skillful players(F2, F10, F12) believe that they can easily understand a game's situation by themselves; for them, AI win prediction at any stage can not provide them with more help. There are also two female interviewees(F3 and F11) with limited gaming experience who tend to focus on the performance of their favorite players when watching live streaming, so they pay less attention to AI win prediction, regarding it as unnecessary, as F11 says, *"... I mainly focus on watching the players I like, paying attention to the scenes where they show up (especially those shots with their faces, in which I really enjoy watching their expressions) or the champions they play with. Although the AI winning rate will appear directly on the screen, I think it doesn't seem to have much effect, maybe? I feel like whether it appears or not, everything is the same to me, so it actually doesn't matter... What I am more concerned about is the player's appearance and whether he can show his skills. Perhaps some cool first-angle shots showcasing the champion's actions are more attractive."*

3.2 Credibility, Accuracy, and Dramatic Effects

The audience's attitudes towards AI win prediction, either as a form of technology or as a form of media information presented during live streaming, are both associated with the issue of trust. In terms of technology, if users trust AI technology, they are more inclined to regard it as useful, while it also positively influences their attitudes and behavioral intentions (Sánchez-Prieto et al. 2020). From the perspective of media information, the media's credibility has always been an interesting topic. Some studies investigate the credibility of AI-generated news, especially the evaluation of its fairness, accuracy, believability, and comprehensiveness (Lee 2020).

As a result, trust in AI win prediction is a key issue that the researcher is concerned about during the interviews. Despite interviewees usually having a high level of AI literacy (which may be associated with their educational background), such as knowing about big data and speech recognition, they do not hold a relatively high level of trust in AI technology. However, as a form of media information presented during live streaming, the credibility of AI win prediction is generally acceptable. The interviewees basically agree that AI win prediction is fair, believable, detailed, and, to some extent, accurate. This is related to the fact that, in the Esports context, the data and algorithms used by AI systems for win prediction are largely based on historical outcomes and current performance within games and matches; they avoid addressing controversial issues such as bias and ethics.

The accuracy of AI win prediction is essential in determining its credibility. All interviewees concur that, if predicted outcomes were to differ from actual results at all times, their trust in AI win prediction would inevitably decrease. Official statistics indicate that, overall, current AI win predictions are accurate in most cases. However, the interviewees usually take little notice of these correct examples, taking them for granted and not perceiving them as a great success. Instead, the mistakes are noteworthy because these cases involve the competition's dramatic effects. F4 explicitly states, "*I feel that AI prediction has a dramatic function. It is that prediction increases the drama of the game.*"

For most audiences, when a team has an overwhelming advantage, being defeated by the other team makes the game more thrilling and exciting. At least 5 interviewees clearly say that, when AI predicts certain results, such as a team having a 70% or higher probability of winning, they will be more willing to see the competition turn around, leading to incorrect forecasts.

This is consistent with the win prediction paradox mentioned in the introduction section. Accuracy is closely linked to the degree of credibility; but if accuracy reaches 100%, the audience may lose their desire to continue watching. There are perhaps two options for maintaining the audience's curiosity and engagement. One is to adjust the accuracy to a certain level by modifying models and algorithms, and the other is to deliberately predict some extreme outcomes that can be easily changed by players' behaviors in the game, though the latter can easily be regarded as an intentionally exaggerated arrangement by the directors. In conclusion, although accuracy is an essential factor in the public's perception of AI win prediction, it should not be the only consideration. Further research is required to strike a balance between credibility, accuracy, and dramatic effects.

3.3 The Anthropomorphic Image

During the 2018 LOL World Championship, LPL officials reached strategic commercial cooperation with Kentucky Fried Chicken (KFC) to create an image of Colonel Harland Sanders, which was called Colonel KI (as shown in Fig. 1). Each time the winning rate curve of an AI prediction was displayed during live streaming, the image of Colonel KI would appear to the left of the curve, usually accompanied by a comment from him,

as shown in Fig. 1 below. Commentators would also say: "Colonel KI predicted.......".
Overall, the Colonel KI character acted as a virtual anchor, responsible for reporting the
AI win prediction.

Unfortunately, in 2023, after the termination of the cooperation between KFC and
LPL, Colonel KI 'retired' gracefully. After his 'retirement', some simple advertisements
(words and pictures), or a mascot image of the new commercial partner (e.g., a puppy)
are often positioned to the left side of the AI win prediction graph (as shown in Fig. 2).

Since all the interviewees have gone through the above process, the researcher is
curious about whether this change is perceived by the interviewees, thus asking them
if they still remember Colonel KI. Surprisingly, nearly everyone shows familiarity with
Colonel KI. Especially for F6, when asked directly "Have you noticed the AI prediction
?" he can not recall it at first; but he understands immediately when the researcher
explains the AI prediction with Colonel KI as an example. F6 even says, "*I used to
watch games alone in the past years, and sometimes I could treat Colonel KI as an old
friend who had accompanied us to watch Esports games.*" F1 and F5 also express that
sometimes they would miss Colonel KI slightly after his disappearance. In contrast, none
of those messages appearing simultaneously with with AI winning rate since 2023 can
be remembered by the interviewees, which indicates that the current advertisements and
images can not attract the spectators as much as Colonel KI did.

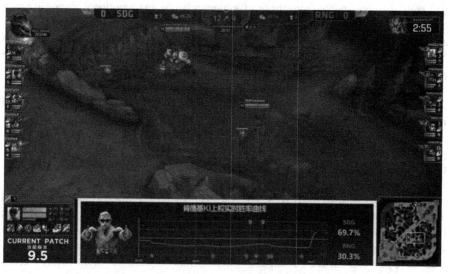

Fig. 1. AI win prediction line graph with the image of Colonel KI.

The researcher speculates that this may be related to anthropomorphism. The term
'anthropomorphism' refers to the attribution of a human form, characteristics, and/or
behavior to non-human entities such as robots, computers, and animals (Bartneck et al.
2009). The 'uncanny valley' theory proposes that when robots become more human-like
in appearance and movements, humans' emotional response to them becomes increasingly positive and empathetic up to a certain point, after which the response rapidly

Fig. 2. AI win prediction line graph with advertisements.

becomes intense revulsion. However, if their appearance and movements continue to be barely distinguishable from those of a human being, the emotional response again becomes positive, close to the level of human-human empathy. Therefore, the highly anthropomorphic image of Colonel KI might have sparked a parasocial relationship between the audience and him, meanwhile also making it easier to let the audience pay attention to the AI win prediction that was broadcast by Colonel KI.

However, because of the constantly-evolving nature of the competition and the limitations of early technology, the competition seemed to be often reversed after Colonel KI gave his prediction, impressing the spectators strongly. Over time, general spectators thought that Colonel KI was putting on the persona of 'Du Nai', which refers to the person who always predicts the opposite (of what is true). Six of the interviewees mention a once popular joke: *"If you bet on the opposite outcome to Colonel KI's prediction when gambling before the competition starts, you will soon be able to afford a villa by the sea"*. Because Colonel KI's 'Du Nai' had left a deep impression on viewers, it also caused them to regard his prediction accuracy as relatively low, which could even be seen as a deliberate program effect. F7 describes it this way: *"Many times Colonel KI had predicted that a team is about to win, the team would lose horribly at last. He must have jinxed the team. Sometimes I doubt if Tencent Esports[1] deliberately created it behind the AI."*

Overall, compared to other kinds of images or simple prediction information with no attachments, it appears to be easier to provoke the audience's emotional response to AI win prediction 'broadcast' by a human-shaped virtual anchor image, which is beneficial for building long-term and stable relationships with viewers, while the presence of this social attribute means that there is also a stronger reaction when an AI win prediction makes a mistake.

---

[1] It is generally believed that the operator of LPL is Tencent Esports.

4   Conclusion and Future Work

When asking firstly about the respondents' attention to AI win prediction they are generally aware that such thing has appeared in the live streaming. Even if occasionally someone can not remember it for a moment, they can immediately recall it after providing stimulating materials. However, overall, AI win prediction has not become a very important part of their viewing experience. In comparison, in the live streaming of Go competitions, AI win prediction has almost become the most crucial factor. There is a large audience who do not understand the rules of Go at all, but they can judge the situation based on the changes in AI winning rate after the players' every step, which can trigger a large amount of discussion on social media platforms, and even the commentary heavily relies on it for commentary. Therefore, the potential of AI win prediction in Esports competitions still needs to be further explored.

In the current interviews, these hardcore fans' general attitudes towards AI win prediction go from neutral to positive, without any particularly negative feelings. The perceived usefulness of AI win prediction is dependent on viewing motivations and personal characteristics to some degree. Meanwhile, the timing of the AI win prediction's appearance is critical. The credibility and accuracy of AI win prediction are interrelated, but the dramatic effects expected by the audience should also be taken into account. The format of reporting AI-predicted outcomes with an anthropomorphic image as a virtual anchor may help increase the audience's attention and emotional reactions. Given that the interviews are not completely finished yet, the attitudes and feelings of spectators towards AI win prediction and possible influencing factors will be further explored and summarized at a later stage. Through such a pilot study, what the viewers truly care about can be discovered to prepare for the large-scale survey experiment.

In the formal experiment, different experimental levels will be set according to each of these influencing factors, and participants will be randomly assigned to these groups and their attitudes towards AI win prediction will be measured through surveys. For example, in terms of the anthropomorphic image, a humanoid virtual anchor image will appear along with the graph of predicted winning rates in Experimental Group 1, with a cartoon animal image appearing in Experimental Group 2 and only AI prediction information presented in the control group. As for the time point of the appearance of AI win prediction, it can be considered to be divided into 3 groups: before the start of the match, before the appearance of the second Rift Herald[2], and after the average level of all the champions reaches level 16 or something like that. In addition to the main effects respectively, whether these factors have interaction effects can also be tested.

LOL is one of the most popular Esports competitions in the world. The Chinese Esports market is also one of the global largest markets. Through a survey of Chinese fans of LOL, this study hopes to empirically verify people's actual feelings and attitudes towards AI win prediction in the live streaming of Esports games and explore effective

---

[2] The Rift Herald is a powerful neutral Monster in the battleground. Slaying the Rift Herald will grant the player specific ability. If not killed in advance, it will disappear permanently at 19:45 in a game, or 19:55 if in combat.

influencing factors, which will provide a scientific basis for better presenting AI prediction information in future live streaming, thus further improving the viewing experience and engagement of spectators.

References

Akhmedov, K., Phan, A.H.: Machine learning models for DOTA 2 outcomes prediction (2021). arXiv preprint arXiv:2106.01782

Bartneck, C., Kulić, D., Croft, E., Zoghbi, S.: Measurement instruments for the anthropomorphism, animacy, likeability, perceived intelligence, and perceived safety of robots. Int. J. Soc. Robot. **1**, 71–81 (2009)

Block, F., et al.: Narrative bytes: data-driven content production in Esports. In Proceedings of the 2018 ACM International Conference on Interactive Experiences for TV and Online Video, pp. 29–41, June 2018

Chan, L., Hogaboam, L., Cao, R.: Artificial intelligence in video games and esports. In: Chan, L., Hogaboam, L., Cao, R. (Eds.) Applied Artificial Intelligence in Business: Concepts and Cases, pp. 335–352. Springer International Publishing, Cham (2022). https://doi.org/10.1007/978-3-031-05740-3_22

Fialho, G., Manhães, A., Teixeira, J.P.: Predicting sports results with artificial intelligence–a proposal framework for soccer games. Procedia Comput. Sci. **164**, 131–136 (2019)

Hodge, V.J., Devlin, S., Sephton, N., Block, F., Cowling, P.I., Drachen, A.: Win prediction in multiplayer Esports: live professional match prediction. IEEE Trans. Games **13**(4), 368–379 (2019)

Ke, C.H., et al.: DOTA 2 match prediction through deep learning team fight models. In: 2022 IEEE Conference on Games (CoG), pp. 96–103. IEEE, August 2022

Kokkinakis, A.V., et al.: Dax: Data-driven audience experiences in Esports. In: ACM International Conference on Interactive Media Experiences, pp. 94–105, June 2020

Kugler, L.: How AI is driving the Esports boom. Commun. ACM **65**(9), 17–18 (2022)

Lee, S., Nah, S., Chung, D.S., Kim, J.: Predicting ai news credibility: communicative or social capital or both? Commun. Stud. **71**(3), 428–447 (2020)

Li, J., Li, M., Wen, Z.A., Cai, W.: Understanding the challenges of team-based live streaming for first-person shooter games. In: 2022 IEEE Games, Entertainment, Media Conference (GEM), pp. 1–6. IEEE, November 2022

Ma, S.C., Byon, K.K., Jang, W., Ma, S.M., Huang, T.N.: Esports spectating motives and streaming consumption: moderating effect of game genres and live-streaming types. Sustainability **13**(8), 4164 (2021)

Meng-Lewis, Y., Lewis, G., Lin, Z., Zhao, Y.: Examination of esports fans' live streaming experiences using an extended expectation-confirmation model: a case study of the King Pro League. Int. J. Hum. Comput. Interact. 1–16 (2022). https://doi.org/10.1080/10447318.2022.2141008

Sánchez-Prieto, J.C., Cruz-Benito, J., TherónSánchez, R., García-Peñalvo, F.J.: Assessed by machines: development of a TAM-based tool to measure AI-based assessment acceptance among students. Int. J. Interact. Multimed. Artif. Intell. **6**(4), 80 (2020)

Wang, W.: Returning for skill or popularity? The demand for Esports match replay. Int. J. Sports Mark. Spons. **24**(2), 295–310 (2022)

Wohn, D.Y., Freeman, G.: Live streaming, playing, and money spending behaviors in Esports. Games Culture **15**(1), 73–88 (2020)

Yang, Z., et al.: Interpretable real-time win prediction for honor of kings—a popular mobile MOBA Esport. IEEE Trans. Games **14**(4), 589–597 (2022)

Zhao, C., Zhao, H., Ge, Y., Wu, R., Shen, X.: Winning tracker: a new model for real-time winning prediction in MOBA games. In: Proceedings of the ACM Web Conference 2022, pp. 3387–3395, April 2022

Using Audience Avatars to Increase Sense of Presence in Live-Streams

Tomáš Pagáč[1(✉)] [iD] and Simone Kriglstein[1,2] [iD]

[1] Faculty of Informatics, Masaryk University, Botanická 68a, 60200 Brno,
Czech Republic
`469165@mail.muni.cz`
[2] AIT Austrian Institute of Technology GmbH, Giefinggasse 4, 1210 Vienna, Austria

Abstract. Social interactions and the sense of presence are important
for the spectatorship experience in live-streams. In large audiences, communication gets harder and viewers participate less. This paper explores
the possibility of representing an audience using animated avatars to
increase the sense of presence and potentially move some traffic from
the chat window to the avatars. We discuss the motivations for and the
challenges in creating an audience avatar interface.

Keywords: Live-streaming · Spectatorship experience · Avatar

1 Introduction

This paper explores ways to better immerse large audiences in a live-stream
by representing the viewers using avatars. To motivate this research direction,
we begin with discussing the issue from the perspectives of viewer motivation,
presence, and participation.

Hilvert-Bruce et al. [16] explored the social motivations of viewer engagement
on Twitch [41]; social interaction and a sense of belonging were the most consistent and strongest motivators. The authors' model explained twice as much of
the engagement of participants who preferred smaller channels – the authors suggest that smaller channels provide richer social interactions and a greater sense of
community. A study into offline and streamed esports events by Neus et al. [33]
found that both ways of consumption are similar but cannot substitute one
another. Specifically, offline attendees were motivated by the social aspect more
and also more satisfied with the event. The authors suggest that the organizers
have limited options in an online environment and the experience depends more
on the users' own efforts. This indicates online esports events could be improved
by bringing the environment and social options closer to an offline event. On
the other hand, a study by Lessel et al. [21] found that users were overall satisfied with elements available on streams, though relevantly, 15 of 20 top-voted
elements were related to interactivity.

Many kinds of presence can be achieved in virtual environments; we can make
a distinction between the sense of a physical environment, interaction with genuine humans, and authentic representation of self [19]. For example, to emulate

H. P. da Silva and P. Cipresso (Eds.): CHIRA 2023, CCIS 1997, pp. 326–337, 2023.
https://doi.org/10.1007/978-3-031-49368-3_20

the experience of attending an esports tournament, a stadium with a crowd of cheering people using avatars that authentically represent the spectators could be shown. A distinction can also be made between emulating real and artificial reality – for example, a streamer can record their real appearance or use a vTube [28] character with made-up characteristics. Defining social presence as the perception that viewers are connected and interacting with genuine individuals, Chen and Liao [7] found it has an effect on watching intention, and is in turn affected by interactivity, sense of community, and emotional support. Similarly, Zheng et al. [46] found a positive impact of social presence and interactivity on flow, which in turn positively impacted continuous watching intention and purchase intention. Defining copresence as the sense of being and acting with others, using qualitative analysis Diwanji et al. [9] found viewers to show considerable copresence, mainly through the nature of their chatting behavior. The quantitative analysis found very little copresence – the authors suggest it currently cannot be measured due to its contextuality. In a study specific to esports, Meng-Lewis et al. [45] found spatial presence and copresence had a positive effect on the intention to continue using the platform. Copresence also had a positive effect on satisfaction, but only a part of spatial presence did – the sense that participants could carry out actions in the environment had an effect, but the sense of being physically present did not. In summary, having the sense that other viewers are genuine individuals and being able to connect and interact with them has positive effects, while emulating the physical environment of the venue might not have an effect. Do note that currently, unless a viewer actively participates in chat or other interactive features, there is little to show they are a genuine individual.

When the number of active viewers rises too high, communication can turn into 'crowdspeak' [12] or start breaking down, viewer participation and information value of messages decreasing [4]. Flores-Saviaga et al. [11] found that larger streams (7 703 to 21 678 average viewers), having the most viewers in total, had the least participatory audience members and 58% of audience members only participated in chat for one day. Celebrity and tournament streams (21 678+ viewers) featured short but frequent messages at 2.45 messages per second, often containing custom emotes. The authors suggest that streamers in the latter category were able to professionally manage the audience and therefore keep them participating, though at the level of 'crowdspeak'. Grace H Wolff et al. [14] found that on Twitch [41], audience size had a negative association with viewer's participation and subscriptions per capita, while use of bits was not related. In contrast, moderator activity had a positive association with participation, subscriptions, and bits per capita. Lu et al. [25] found that while audience size has a positive effect on total tipping revenue, the effect does not scale linearly. The authors suggest splitting chat rooms to keep the audiences smaller (assuming it does not reduce the streamer's performance). These results show that large audience sizes indeed have negative effects on viewer behavior, and it is possible to reduce the effects by managing the audience effectively.

We discussed the importance of viewer interaction, the sense of social presence and community, and how large audiences can have a negative impact on them. Using audience avatars could improve the situation. The initial idea came from comparing streams to offline events. In offline events, there is a crowd of people – the communication might not be clearer than 'crowdspeak', but the crowd's reactions and energy are visible. On a stream, we can see how fast the chat is moving and how long the messages are. Active viewers are only distinguished by their usernames, and passive viewers are only a number in the viewer count. We believe that displaying the audience as a crowd of avatars could increase the sense of presence in viewers. Even passive viewers would be in the crowd, giving a better representation of the audience. Animated reactions or emotes could be used to offload traffic from the chat while giving the avatars more character. The avatars could be customized to add a sense of authentic self presence. Last but not least, the streamer would get visual feedback on the attitude of the audience, as well as an increase in sense of social presence. In this paper, we explore the design challenges in representing audience avatars on live-streams.

2   Related Work

We can get informed on the properties of avatars from virtual reality (VR) research, as it has been an important topic there. Heidicker et al. [15] found that avatars animated by real movement exhibited larger copresence than avatars with predefined animations, but there was no significant difference between avatars with whole body and ones with only head and hands. Aseeri and Interrante [2] found that 3D scanned and video seethrough avatars exhibited higher copresence than an avatar made of a head-mounted VR device and controllers. Neither study could confirm a difference in social presence between the avatars. Do note that in these studies, copresence was a sub-scale of social presence. Additionally, Dubosc et al. [10] found that facial anthropomorphism had no significant impact on social presence, but more anthropomorphic facial properties led to higher perceived attractiveness and higher performance in tasks.

There is research on the use of avatars in (non-VR) games too. Mancini and Sibilla [30] explored avatar creation in multiplayer online role-playing games – a relevant finding is that the more the avatar was similar to the player, the more the player identified with it. Birk et al. [6] found that players identifying with their character were more immersed and motivated to continue playing. A study into the effects of age on avatar preferences found that, among other things, different age groups preferred different visual styles of avatars and had different attitudes toward customization [34].

Research on other features that can increase the sense of presence in streaming is also relevant. The use of vTube characters is a growing phenomenon where streamers use avatars to form an artificial identity [20,28]. The avatars are highly expressive as their body and facial expressions can be controlled by motion tracking. The magic of vTube characters lies in the artificial identity performed by the streamer [28], so their use by the audience might not be interesting. However, as most devices have web cameras, it would be possible to animate audience avatars using motion tracking.

Danmu or danmaku (chat messages scrolling over the video) [22,23] are popular in some eastern Asian countries. They are similar to audience avatars in that they can both display individual reactions to content over the video. Li et al. [22] found that danmu improved the number of views of esport videos and positively affected viewer engagement. Other phenomena occurring on streams include streamers thanking the viewer and mentioning their nickname if they donate or subscribe [31]. On some platforms, viewers can send gifts with messages, animated effects, or sounds [29]. All these features could increase the sense of social presence in the audience, as they draw attention to authentic interactions with individual viewers.

Finally, we look at some existing Twitch extensions that have use cases similar to audience avatars. Pando [13] features a pet that the viewers can interact with, which may add the sense of artificial social presence [19] to the stream. Viewer Geolocation [8] displays what countries the viewers come from, possibly adding some sense of togetherness to groups from the same country. There are also many extensions that add more interactivity, for example by reading viewer messages aloud or adding audience participation games. Stream Avatars [3] is the only one featuring audience avatars among the extensions we found. It features customizable and controllable audience avatars drawn over the streamed video. There are also minigames played using the avatars. Instead of being a background addition to any type of content, the extension seems to aim to take a central spot in the interaction between the streamer and the audience. Moreover, with a larger audience, the avatars may overlap each other or an important part of the video. This extension could be considered in further research the compare the advantages and drawbacks of various features. We discuss this and other challenges of designing the audience avatar interface in the next section.

3   Challenges

In this section, we discuss the challenges in designing an audience avatar interface. They are the four essential issues of where to display the avatars, how to display them, what they can do, and how they are controlled. We discuss them to understand the trade-offs caused by design decisions and to be able to test these in future studies.

3.1   Screen Space

Firstly, there is a lack of available screen space, no matter how the audience avatar interface actually looks. The key elements of live-streams are the live video and chat. On platforms such as Twitch [41] or Kick [17], the video is next to the chat with only a small space left for information about the stream (Fig. 1 left). There are also extensions that duplicate the chat to overlay the video [36],

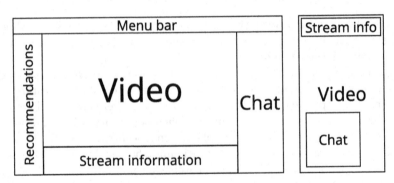

Fig. 1. Approximate layouts of live-stream interfaces: Twitch and Kick on the left, Instagram and Tiktok on the right.

making the chat visible when the video is viewed in full-screen mode. On other platforms such as Instagram [32], TikTok [38], or the discontinued Periscope [24], the video takes up the full screen and chat messages are laid over it (Fig. 1 right). In both types of interfaces, there is no free space left over; extensions on Twitch can appear under the video (accessible by scrolling) or over the video [40], or be rendered into the video itself [18].

The use of a second monitor or a mobile device with a companion app would circumvent the issue. We do not discuss this approach here as we aim to improve the basic experience without any special equipment.

Overlaying the audience avatars over the video is a straightforward approach (Fig. 2 top-left). Danmu/danmaku discussed in Sect. 2 are an example of a video overlay. They have positive effects on some viewers, but some refuse to watch danmaku videos due to the visual clutter [44]. Game-specific overlays are highly desired [21], but they have the advantage of being carefully designed to enhance spectatorship experience for a single game. In research, novel interfaces such as StreamWiki [26], StreamSketch [27], or Snapstream [43], use overlays, pop-up windows, custom windows around the video, or a customized chat window. They do not interfere with the content, because the content is tailored toward using the novel interface. A general interface would have to be adjustable by the streamer or viewers to avoid covering important parts of the video.

Having the interface rendered directly into the video in broadcasting software would give the streamer complete control over the space it takes up and allow them to draw more important elements (such as a webcam) over it (Fig. 2 top-right). The extension Stream Avatars (discussed in Sect. 2) uses this approach. The disadvantage is that the interface cannot be a default feature of a streaming platform, the streamer has to set it up in their broadcasting software.

There is the option to overlay the interface over elements other than the video (Fig. 2 bottom-left). This would prevent the avatars from covering the content, making them cover arguably less important features instead. The limitation of this approach is that the video covers most, on some platforms all, of the screen, so there might not be enough space for avatars. Chat messages might be shown

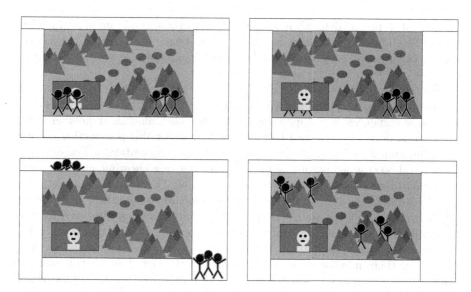

Fig. 2. Options to display audience avatar interface. Top-left: video overlay. Top-right: overlay integrated in video. Bottom-left: overlay around the video. Bottom-right: avatars integrated into the content.

directly next to avatars representing the chatting users, freeing the space taken up by the chat window, but adding more visual clutter.

Finally, audience avatars can also appear directly inside the content, as done in the game Minion Masters [5], which allows the avatars to perfectly fit in the environment (Fig. 2 bottom-right). In research, Robinson et al. [35] used physiological data of the audience to directly influence the streamed content, avoiding cluttering the interface. This could be a great way to engage the audience for example in esports tournaments, where the audience avatars only have to be implemented for the game in the tournament.

In summary, there is no optimal solution to get enough usable screen space. The more the avatars are integrated into the content of the stream, the better they can be displayed without interfering with other elements.

3.2 Visuals

Secondly, designing the visual representation of the avatars is of critical importance. As the goal is to increase the sense of presence in the audience (specifically social and spatial presence), the avatars must be perceived as representing genuine individuals. As discussed in Sect. 2, avatars animated by real movement and avatars represented by a human body exhibit higher copresence than avatars with predefined animations and those represented by a head-mounted VR device and controllers. Non-human avatars with anthropomorphic features did not reduce copresence. Therefore the avatars should have visible anthropomorphic (or humanlike) features and the ability to be (or appear to be) animated by authentic (not predefined) movement. Within these constraints, avatar visuals can be simplified to reduce visual clutter. Determining a visual that has the desired features while causing as little clutter as possible is a subject for future research.

However, popular live-streams can have tens of thousands of concurrent viewers. Displaying so many avatars would only create visual clutter. In offline events with large audiences, it is impossible to see what each individual member of the audience is doing – the crowd blends together. Using this perspective, we can forgo individual avatars and use a more abstract representation. For example, users could be grouped according to their behavior (e.g. cheering, clapping) with each group being represented by one crowd visual. The limitation is that there may be a loss in the expressiveness of individual viewers. On the other hand, in offline events with large audiences, people can only have more involved interactions with the people in their immediate surroundings. Using this perspective, we can only display the part of the audience around each user's avatar. As a limitation, there may be a loss in expression of the crowd as a whole, such as 'Mexican waves' carried out at stadiums. Additionally, the position of individual avatars becomes more important to the spectatorship experience.

Fig. 3. Grouping avatars: examples with 240 avatars of two colors. They represent distinctly visualized or animated avatars. Top-left: no grouping. Top-right: the same avatar types are close together. Bottom-left: groups of an avatar type are merged into a larger avatar. Bottom-right: groups of avatars are represented by an abstract 'crowd' visual.

Restricting the view to only a small part of the audience can be done at any time. But grouping and abstracting the avatars is more involved. In the first place, there must be a criterion to group by. If the avatars can be moved by the users, they can organize themselves and forcefully moving them into groups does not make sense. In the opposite case, avatars could be grouped by their visual style (if there are multiple styles or customization) or by their animation. With multiple visual styles, similar avatars can be moved closer together (Fig. 3 top-right). This seems ideal for dividing fans of opposing teams, as they would be divided in a real stadium. Grouping based on animations reacting to content is harder, as the reactions of users can change quickly. It might be more appropriate to move the avatars based on overall behavior or level of activity instead of immediate reactions.

If there are too many avatars, similar avatars can be merged into one (Fig. 3 bottom-left). The ratio of merging and effects such as avatar scaling could be proportional to the size of the audience to maintain the desired crowd density. Alternatively, individual avatars can be replaced with an abstracted visual of a crowd (Fig. 3 bottom-right). This approach could be more visually pleasing, as the visuals can be prepared in advance to represent different crowd densities well. The first approach needs a scheme for shared control of merged characters, while the second approach needs to represent varied animations with one visual. Both approaches lead to some loss of individuality for the users, but preserve the sense of a crowd.

3.3 Interactivity

Thirdly, the abilities of the avatars need to be considered. As discussed previously, the avatars must be perceived as representing genuine individuals, which means they should (appear to) reflect users' attitudes towards the events happening on the live-stream. In a real crowd, this is achieved by moving the body (waving hands, dancing, etc.) and making sounds (clapping, yelling).

Avatars can be animated to show body movements. The simplest approach of allowing the users to select from predefined animations would also make it easier to coordinate multiple avatars or merge them to reduce clutter. Animating avatars by users' movement (e.g. by webcam body tracking) could increase the sense of copresence, but is more challenging to implement and could exclude users without compatible hardware. An additional option to increase the expressiveness of avatars is to display chat messages or just emotes near the sender's avatar.

Giving the users the option to make sounds could easily create a distraction from the content. User-triggered sounds can be limited for example by requiring currency [1]. In the context of avatars, sounds can be tied to animations and played after aggregating the state of the whole audience, potentially using different sounds based on audience size – this would eliminate trolling and the cacophony of each individual user making a sound.

The movement of the avatars can also play an important role. Avatars entering and leaving the screen could represent users entering and leaving the live-stream. If users can control their avatars' movement, they can form groups, for example, based on the team they cheer for. On the other hand, this could lead to less optimal distribution of avatars on the screen or trolls trying to cause chaos.

3.4   Control

Finally, the users need to be able to control the avatars. Live-streams already contain many interactive elements, such as video controls and chat input field, that need to remain accessible. Twitch even has documentation for the recommended placement and sizing of interface elements on desktop and mobile devices [39]. It is extremely important to keep mobile users in consideration, because 35% of Twitch users access it from the mobile app [42], while Instagram and TikTok are the two most downloaded mobile apps [37].

The simplest way to control something on a live-stream is via chat commands. It is easy to implement and adds no new interface elements. For activating animations, the experience is not seamless as the users have to remember the command for each animation. Using emotes as commands could reduce the load of remembering commands. On mobile devices, if the selection of animations is extremely limited (e.g. cheering and booing), an accelerometer can be used to trigger animations by shaking or moving the device.

Using a mouse or touch interface to move the avatars is problematic if the avatar interface is overlaying other interactive elements. On a computer, keyboard control schemes from games can be used, but this is not practical on devices without a physical keyboard.

4   Discussion and Future Work

We discussed the main known challenges in designing an audience avatar interface. Many of the issues are faced by all live-stream interface extensions and stem from adding features onto an interface that is already full of attention-drawing and interactive elements. The actual challenges largely depend on whether the avatars should be integrated with the live-streaming platform, with the broadcasting software, or with the content, and also on the degree of interaction and the desired role of the avatars.

We first plan to design a basic audience avatar interface and compare its effects to the currently used stream interfaces and to an interface with danmaku. Based on the results we will research how to complement the avatar interface's strengths, and how to design visuals and animations to represent large groups of avatars. We will also study the trade-offs of overlaying or replacing existing interface elements, such as the chat window, with the avatar interface.

5   Conclusion

In this paper, we explored the motivations, related research, and challenges behind representing live-stream audiences using avatars. We believe this to be a good direction toward improving the spectatorship experience, specifically the sense of social presence. We plan to study the effects of using audience avatars and explore various designs based on the discussed challenges.

References

1. Sound Alerts: Sound alerts twitch extension (2023). https://www.soundalerts.com
2. Aseeri, S., Interrante, V.: The influence of avatar representation on interpersonal communication in virtual social environments. IEEE Trans. Visual Comput. Graphics **27**(5), 2608–2617 (2021). https://doi.org/10.1109/TVCG.2021.3067783
3. Stream Avatars: Stream avatars (2023). https://www.streamavatars.com/
4. Nematzadeh, A., Ciampaglia, G.L., Ahn, Y.Y., Flammini, A.: Information overload in group communication: from conversation to cacophony in the twitch chat (2019). https://doi.org/10.1098/rsos.191412
5. BetaDwarf: Minion masters stream features (2022). https://www.minionmaster.com/streamerboost/
6. Birk, M.V., Atkins, C., Bowey, J.T., Mandryk, R.L.: Fostering intrinsic motivation through avatar identification in digital games. In: Proceedings of the 2016 CHI Conference on Human Factors in Computing Systems, CHI '16, pp. 2982–2995. Association for Computing Machinery (2016). https://doi.org/10.1145/2858036.2858062
7. Chen, J., Liao, J.: Antecedents of viewers' live streaming watching: a perspective of social presence theory **13**, 839629 (2022). https://doi.org/10.3389/fpsyg.2022.839629, https://www.ncbi.nlm.nih.gov/pmc/articles/PMC9008234/
8. CommanderRoot: Viewer geolocation (2023). https://dashboard.twitch.tv/extensions/9zqhb3hba48m0c382uno7k2t74isfi-1.2.0
9. Diwanji, V., Reed, A., Ferchaud, A., Seibert, J., Weinbrecht, V., Sellers, N.: Don't just watch, join. in: exploring information behavior and copresence on twitch **105**, 106221 (2020). https://www.sciencedirect.com/science/article/pii/S0747563219304406. https://doi.org/10.1016/j.chb.2019.106221
10. Dubosc, C., Gorisse, G., Christmann, O., Fleury, S., Poinsot, K., Richir, S.: Impact of avatar facial anthropomorphism on body ownership, attractiveness and social presence in collaborative tasks in immersive virtual environments. Comput. Graph. **101**, 82–92 (2021)
11. Flores-Saviaga, C., Hammer, J., Flores, J.P., Seering, J., Reeves, S., Savage, S.: Audience and streamer participation at scale on twitch. In: Proceedings of the 30th ACM Conference on Hypertext and Social Media, HT '19, pp. 277–278. Association for Computing Machinery (2019). https://doi.org/10.1145/3342220.3344926
12. Ford, C., et al.: Chat speed OP PogChamp: practices of coherence in massive twitch chat. In: Proceedings of the 2017 CHI Conference Extended Abstracts on Human Factors in Computing Systems, CHI EA '17, pp. 858–871. Association for Computing Machinery (2017). https://doi.org/10.1145/3027063.3052765
13. cvs-gaming.nl: Pando (2023). https://dashboard.twitch.tv/extensions/fubh5p0lrwei0v4w4ncs2rnlqw455h
14. Wolff, G.H., Shen, C.: Audience size, moderator activity, gender, and content diversity: exploring user participation and financial commitment on twitch.tv (2022). https://doi.org/10.1177/14614448211069996
15. Heidicker, P., Langbehn, E., Steinicke, F.: Influence of avatar appearance on presence in social VR. In: 2017 IEEE Symposium on 3D User Interfaces (3DUI), pp. 233–234 (2017). https://doi.org/10.1109/3DUI.2017.7893357

16. Hilvert-Bruce, Z., Neill, J.T., Sjöblom, M., Hamari, J.: Social motivations of live-streaming viewer engagement on twitch **84**, 58–67 (2018). www.sciencedirect.com/science/article/pii/S0747563218300712, https://doi.org/10.1016/j.chb.2018.02.013
17. Kick: Kick (2023). https://www.kick.com/
18. Lain: OBS-stream layout tutorial (2023). https://obsproject.com/kb/stream-tutorial-1-game
19. Lee, K.M.: Presence, explicated. Commun. Theory **14**(1), 27–50 (2004). https://doi.org/10.1111/j.1468-2885.2004.tb00302.x
20. Lehtovirta, S.: Creating a VTuber avatar (2023)
21. Lessel, P., Altmeyer, M., Krüger, A.: Viewers' perception of elements used in game live-streams, pp. 59–68 (2018). https://doi.org/10.1145/3275116.3275117
22. Li, F., Wang, W., Lai, W.: The social impact from Danmu-insights from Esports online videos **18**(1), 441–456 (2023). www.mdpi.com/0718-1876/18/1/23. number: 1 Publisher: Multidisciplinary Digital Publishing Institute.https://doi.org/10.3390/jtaer18010023
23. Li, Y., Guo, Y.: Virtual gifting and Danmaku: what motivates people to interact in game live streaming? **62**, 101624 (2021). https://linkinghub.elsevier.com/retrieve/pii/S0736585321000630, https://doi.org/10.1016/j.tele.2021.101624
24. Licoppe, C., Morel, J.: Visuality, text and talk, and the systematic organization of interaction in periscope live video streams. Discourse Stud. **20**(5), 637–665 (2018). https://doi.org/10.1177/1461445618760606
25. Lu, S., Yao, D., Chen, X., Grewal, R.: Do larger audiences generate greater revenues under pay what you want? Evidence from a live streaming platform. Mark. Sci. **40**, 964–984 (2021). https://doi.org/10.1287/mksc.2021.1292
26. Lu, Z., Heo, S., Wigdor, D.J.: StreamWiki: enabling viewers of knowledge sharing live streams to collaboratively generate archival documentation for effective in-stream and post hoc learning. Proc. ACM Hum.-Comput. Interact. **2**, 1–26 (2018). https://doi.org/10.1145/3274381
27. Lu, Z., Kazi, R.H., Wei, L.Y., Dontcheva, M., Karahalios, K.: StreamSketch: exploring multi-modal interactions in creative live streams. Proc. ACM Hum.-Comput. Interact. **5**, 1–26 (2021). https://doi.org/10.1145/3449132
28. Lu, Z., Shen, C., Li, J., Shen, H., Wigdor, D.: More kawaii than a real-person live streamer: Understanding how the otaku community engages with and perceives virtual YouTubers. In: Proceedings of the 2021 CHI Conference on Human Factors in Computing Systems, CHI '21, pp. 1–14. Association for Computing Machinery (2021). https://doi.org/10.1145/3411764.3445660
29. Lu, Z., Xia, H., Heo, S., Wigdor, D.: You watch, you give, and you engage: a study of live streaming practices in china. In: Proceedings of the 2018 CHI Conference on Human Factors in Computing Systems, CHI '18, pp. 1–13. Association for Computing Machinery (2018). https://doi.org/10.1145/3173574.3174040
30. Mancini, T., Sibilla, F.: Offline personality and avatar customisation. Discrepancy profiles and avatar identification in a sample of MMORPG players. Comput. Hum. Behav. **69**, 275–283 (2017). https://doi.org/10.1016/j.chb.2016.12.031,https://www.sciencedirect.com/science/article/pii/S0747563216308524
31. Johnson, M.R., Woodcock, J.: "And today's top donator is": how live streamers on twitch.tv monetize and gamify their broadcasts (2019). https://doi.org/10.1177/2056305119881694
32. Meta: Instagram live producer (2023). https://about.instagram.com/blog/tips-and-tricks/instagram-live-producer
33. Neus, F., Nimmermann, F., Wagner, K., Schramm-Klein, H.: Differences and similarities in motivation for offline and online eSports event consumption

34. Rice, M., et al.: Comparing avatar game representation preferences across three age groups. In: CHI '13 Extended Abstracts on Human Factors in Computing Systems, CHI EA '13, pp. 1161–1166. Association for Computing Machinery, New York (2013). https://doi.org/10.1145/2468356.2468564
35. Robinson, R.B., Rheeder, R., Klarkowski, M., Mandryk, R.L.: "Chat has no chill": a novel physiological interaction for engaging live streaming audiences. In: Proceedings of the 2022 CHI Conference on Human Factors in Computing Systems, CHI '22, pp. 1–18. Association for Computing Machinery (2022). https://doi.org/10.1145/3491102.3501934
36. Logitech Services S.A.: Chat box overlay for twitch (2023). https://streamlabs.com/desktop-widgets/chat-box
37. Statista: Most downloaded apps worldwide 2022. https://www.statista.com/statistics/1285960/top-downloaded-mobile-apps-worldwide/
38. TikTok: Tiktok live features (2023). https://www.tiktok.com/creators/creator-portal/en-us/what-to-know-about-live/live-product-features/
39. Twitch Interactive, Inc.: Designing extensions –twitch developers (2023). https://dev.twitch.tv/docs/extensions/designing/
40. Twitch Interactive, Inc.: Extensions –twitch developers (2023). https://dev.twitch.tv/docs/extensions/
41. Twitch Interactive, Inc.: Twitch (2023). https://www.twitch.tv
42. TwitchTracker: Twitchtracker (2023). https://www.twitchtracker.com/statistics
43. Yang, S., Lee, C., Shin, H.V., Kim, J.: Snapstream: snapshot-based interaction in live streaming for visual art. In: Proceedings of the 2020 CHI Conference on Human Factors in Computing Systems, CHI '20, pp. 1–12. Association for Computing Machinery (2020). https://doi.org/10.1145/3313831.3376390
44. Chen, Y., Gao, Q., Rau, P.L.P.: Watching a movie alone yet together: understanding reasons for watching Danmaku videos (2017). https://doi.org/10.1080/10447318.2017.1282187
45. Meng-Lewis, Y., Lewis, G., Lin, Z., Zhao, Y.: Examination of Esports fans' live streaming experiences using an extended expectation-confirmation model: a case study of the king pro league (2022). https://doi.org/10.1080/10447318.2022.2141008
46. Zheng, S., Chen, J., Liao, J., Hu, H.L.: What motivates users' viewing and purchasing behavior motivations in live streaming: a stream-streamer-viewer perspective **72**, 103240 (2023). www.sciencedirect.com/science/article/pii/S0969698922003332, https://doi.org/10.1016/j.jretconser.2022.103240

Initial Developments of Teamwork and Mental Health Focused Minigames for the Purpose of Esports Training

Danielle K. Langlois[1]([✉])[iD] and Simone Kriglstein[1,2][iD]

[1] Faculty of Informatics, Masaryk University, Botanická 68a, 60200 Brno,
Czech Republic
dlanglois@mail.muni.cz
[2] AIT Austrian Institute of Technology GmbH, Giefinggasse 4, 1210 Vienna, Austria

Abstract. Esports professionals have to cope with a lot of stress and really need to be in sync with their teammates in order to perform at their highest capability. As part of an ongoing project, we are working toward a battery of minigames aimed at helping esports professionals train their teamwork skills and improve their mental health. Proposed ideas include modules focused on meditation, teaching coping mechanisms for difficult social scenarios via visual novel, and synchronized breathing exercises. Each of these has positive points and negative points. With these ideas, we hope to further develop several engaging minigames which can later be user tested.

Keywords: Esports · Esports training · Game design · Human computer interaction

1 Introduction

It should be obvious, but professional esports players are an important asset that the esports industry ought to invest in throughout the training process. There are many varying ideas related to which training areas should pull more focus.

For example, one review [2] of several studies found that several mental health related areas were of high importance for professional esports players. These areas included avoiding loss-related rumination, game/life separation, using good coping mechanisms when faced with harassment, and keeping a growth-oriented mindset [2]. Another review paper [8] found that playing esports games do not seem to have a specific impact on psychophysiological stress responses. However, the authors of that paper recommend further research in the domain of esports and stress [8]. A later paper by some of the same authors also found that people who play esports cope with stress by focusing on performance [9]. A different study also found that team cohesiveness could be improved by improving communication, preparedness, and good social climate [10]. Finally, another publication found that esport players could benefit from access to the psychological interventions designed for traditional athletes to train coping skills [13]. Clearly, all of these domains are worthy of further study.

Recently, we designed and executed a survey study meant to ask esports specialists and fans where they thought training was lacking and looked at how much they agreed (submitted for publication). Two areas repeatedly reported were teamwork and mental health. We intend to follow-up on these results by developing training modules focused on teamwork and mental health. Our primary research question is "what are some minigame designs which are helpful and relevant to improving training related to teamwork and mental health of esports professionals and those pursuing professional esports?" The following paper details some proposed ideas for the development of a battery of minigames meant to help in these specified areas.

2 Related Work

Past research has found support for meditation as an intervention that can help in the domain of mental health [5,14]. For example, one meta analysis published in 2014 examined clinical trials featuring meditation as an intervention [5]. The results of this meta analysis indicated that meditation programs helped to reduce negative dimensions of mental health (like stress and anxiety), but they noted that there was still more testing to do to completely understand meditation as an intervention [5]. Another meta analysis focusing specifically on "Mantra-Based Meditation" (MBM) was published eight years later [14]. In this meta analysis, researchers found similar results to the 2014 meta analysis. They observed a noticeable reduction in anxiety and stress when MBM was involved. They also observed that there were small improvements in depression and "mental health-related quality of life". The 2022 meta analysis also found some trends involving improvement in burnout, insomnia, and substance use, though they report that the number of studies measuring these variables is low [14].

There is also a great deal of precedent for breathing exercises being used to combat stress and anxiety [3,6]. There are also many different types of preexisting breathing exercises available for implementation. These include pursed-lip breathing [12], paced breathing, coherent/resonance breathing, resistance breathing, unilateral/alternate nostril breathing, "moving the breath," and breathing with movement [3]. Each of these is different, and may be useful in different circumstances.

Stress related coping strategies are also an area of interest [1,4,17]. Many esports games are known to involve "toxic" behaviors like name-calling or "griefing" [1]. This also requires players to cope with being a target of such behaviors. One paper found that although many games provide tools to report or reward behaviors, players often do not use these systems [1]. Still, they have to cope with stressors. Researchers have, in the past, examined people's existing coping strategies and examined how to construct new, positive behaviors. For example, one intervention amongst students introduced a resilience program to physiotherapy students. This intervention, based on Cognitive Behavior Therapy, resulted in positive outcomes [4]. Another project sought to increase patient confidence in hospital settings via a visual novel [17]. They found that playing their game resulted positive outcomes, but only for participants with gaming experience or high game engagement [17].

3   Requirements

We have a few requirements for the design and development of these minigames. Many of these requirements come partly from our prior research and partly practical considerations.

- The minigames should try to prompt engagement. We can design many interventions, but if they fail to engage and interest players it is a moot point [17].
- Low cost development. We want to try and keep our development costs as low as possible, thus we plan to use platforms which we can use for free like Unity, Blender, or Godot. Development cost should also be low in terms of time. We do not have the capability to spend multiple years on one minigame.
- Low barrier to entry for players. We are hoping to develop minigames which do not require an excessive number of peripheral products. However, we need to fully explore our options, thus we will try to thoroughly examine as many options as possible and select the more accessible option. We hope to try and develop minigames that require a computer and little else (tower, monitor, mouse, keyboard, and headset). We want our interventions to be accessible to esports professionals and people trying to become esports professionals, who might have limited means. This is something we found to be important in a prior study (submitted for publication).
- The purpose of the minigame should be clear and obvious. The game itself should transparently be related to teamwork and mental health. We hope that this will lend us face validity in future user testing.
- The minigames should not be too repetitive. They should be targeting different aspects of teamwork and mental health. These are multifaceted phenomena and they deserve multifaceted approaches. This is clearly visible in our related work, in which teamwork and mental health is approached in a variety of manners [1, 3–6, 10, 13, 14, 17].

4   Minigame Concepts

We propose the creation of a battery of minigames to help train teamwork and mental health coping skills. The following sections detail three of the ideas we are currently working toward developing, though we are open to new ideas as well.

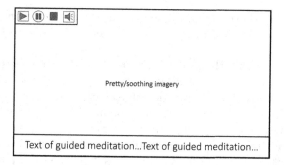

Fig. 1. An image of the proposed user interface for Game Concept 1, in which users would follow a guided meditation.

4.1 Concept 1: Meditation

This minigame would include guided meditation modules for participants. Players would sit in front of a screen displaying various moving backgrounds (like the waves on a beach, an old forest, or perhaps a snowy day) and hear guided meditations encouraging them to relax. Meditation is clearly related to mental health [5,14]. It also would be unlikely to require a lot of additional products or an excessive amount of development time as the project could be altered and simplified depending on the timeline.

Mechanisms. This design would be more dependent on verbal instructions, soothing sounds, and pleasant imagery in short bursts. We are still examining what currently is available on the market as well. It may be worthwhile to look into options for measuring physiological feedback like heart rate or breathing pattern. Unlike Concept 3, meditation is less oriented around completing a task or "wining" and more about the simple experience of meditation. Thus, while we are classing it as a "minigame" it might be better described as a guided experience. Figure 1 shows one idea for what the user interface may look like.

Conceits. At this point we are not considering special stories of conceits around meditation. It is simply meant to introduce and assist with a practice meant to help esports players with mental health. We hope that pairing these guided meditations with pleasant imagery and sounds will make meditation as a practice more approachable and desirable.

4.2 Concept 2: Teamwork and Social Coping Skills

We already know that esports professionals deal with stress and harassment [2]. As previously stated, one study found that playing a visual novel game meant to teach confidence in hospital settings led to positive outcomes for participants, but only for participants with gaming experience or high game engagement [17].

Thus, our target of esports professionals and those who want to be esports professionals might be perfect for a similar intervention due to built-in gaming experience.

This minigame takes the form of a visual novel that involves short modules meant to help teach players healthy coping and communication skills. In this game the players go through a series of scenarios and have multiple healthy and unhealthy options to cope with and communicate about the scenario. For example, a player may be prompted by Character 1 to "punish" a teammate (Character 2) for making a mistake and the player has to choose how to cope with that situation. If they do not want to take part in the punishment team cohesiveness with Character 1 will decrease, but "punishing" Character 2 could result in a loss of cohesiveness with Character 2. Further, the scenario could be complicated with further options, like what kind of "punishment" is employed and if there are additional teammates involved. Also, how does the player character cope with the social stress of the scenario? Hopefully, the idea would be that participants can test and learn about multiple approaches to these kind of stressful team based scenarios.

We are currently using the open source program Twine [7] to help draft our decision trees for the visual novel. A draft of one of these decision trees is featured in Fig. 2.

Mechanisms. The strength of the visual novel format is that it can be used to clearly communicate what it is about (by literally, writing about the item directly), and is flexible enough to be used for a variety of topic areas. We think that maintaining the same cast of characters throughout multiple modules will help to keep players engaged, especially if the separate modules are all part of an overarching story. Visual novels are also pretty easy to use and understand, so it should have a low barrier to entry. Right now, we are planning on using the open source program Ren'py [15] for development of this visual novel.

Conceits. Currently, we are developing one consistent scenario/cast of characters on which to base multiple visual novel "chapters"/lessons. The player character will play as a newly signed esport athlete to an existing team, the "Capricious Coatis", or, potentially, the "Sea Angels". We have some early mock up logo sketches featured in Fig. 3. The player then needs to get to know and practice with their team. Right now we are loosely building the team to contain 10 athletes on an A and B roster of five athletes each, including the player character. We also are planning on a Coach, Manager, and a event host character (who will "host" events, conduct interviews, and potentially communicate public perception to the player).

4.3   Concept 3: Team Breathing

The last of our proposed minigames involves a game in which two participants engage in a controlled breathing exercise using some specific breathing technique.

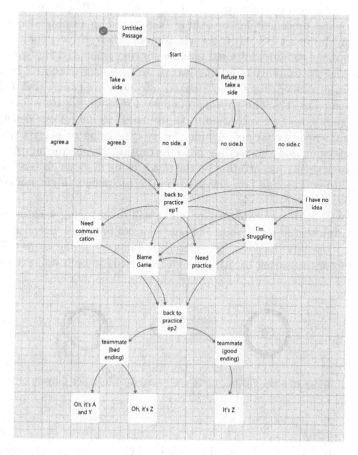

Fig. 2. A Screenshot of an early draft in Twine showing a decision tree for Game Concept 2's Visual Novel.

Fig. 3. A sketch of some potential logos for the fictional esports team in the visual novel.

In different modules the participants would breathe in unison or concurrently. Or, different breathing techniques could be used in different modules. There is already some precedent for breathing being used in gaming situations, for example, in Mariokart DS [11] there was a mode where players could blow into their microphone to add additional balloons during gameplay. Researchers have also looked as the usability of adding breath and a means of control in VR [16]. Another project called "Life Tree" looked into creating games that facilitated breathing exercises [12]. They make a number of recommendations for designing breathing games, and we will attempt to use these to inform our development. Some recommended strategies include clearly expressing to players what their assigned breathing pattern will be, not interrupting players during play (this is likely to break their concentration on the task), using in-game objects to provide feedback, and considering how the peripheral attachments might impact player experience [12].

We hope that this multiple person game will be engaging with our different conceits and potential for introducing new types of breathing exercises. We also would like to avoid additional peripheral products by trying to use a headset microphone for measuring breath, though this needs to be tested extensively.

Fig. 4. Still image of some initial mock-ups created to instruct players on breathing.

Mechanisms. We have a number of proposed visual cues for this team breathing. These are largely informed by existing applications related to breathing. Figure 4 shows some of these visual cues.

As previously mentioned, it might also be interesting to use different types of breathing exercises for different "minigames" or even different "levels" of the same minigame.

It may also be preferable to abandon these designs altogether and integrate the feedback more tangibly into the game world rather that a heads-up display (HUD). One research team found that integrating the breathing feedback into game events itself is less distracting for the player. However, the same publication recommends that it is important to communicate to the player what their breathing pattern should be [12]. A basic mock-up for what this structure might look like is included in Fig. 5 and Fig. 6. In this illustrated example, the color-fill inside of the circles would grow/shrink and change colors as a guide for the player's breathing.

Fig. 5. An image of the proposed user interface for the team breathing game where players are breathing via pursed-lip breathing in an alternate pattern.

Fig. 6. An image of the proposed user interface for the team breathing game where players are breathing via pursed-lip breathing in unison.

Conceits. We have loosely developed three general conceits for the team breathing game. The first, called "Tides", is a game in which players breathe in sync with crashing waves. The second and third conceits are based in the idea of thermal regulation. In game concept 2, called "Hatchery," players are breathing in a controlled manner in order to keep a clutch of eggs at optimal temperatures. When the module ends, players are rewarded by the eggs hatching and baby animals emerge. These could be real-life animals or fantastical animals. Game conceit 3 is referred to as "Forge Friends" or "Bellows Buddies". It is similar to Game conceit 2, but instead of hatching eggs, players are playing as dragons who are keeping a blacksmith's hearth at optimal temperatures for weapons and tools to be forged. Figure 7 shows a sketch of some potential dragon player characters.

Fig. 7. A sketch of dragon player characters for game concept 3, "Forge Friends/Bellows Buddies" .

346   D. K. Langlois and S. Kriglstein

5 Discussion

Once these minigames are developed, we plan to conduct user tests to see if they would truly be useful additions to esports training programs. If they do prove useful, this would mean that such interventions should be made accessible for people in the esports space. It may also be useful to test these minigames on other populations to see if they are useful among other populations. For example, introducing these interventions to people with severe social anxiety or chronic stress.

The general limitation of these ideas is that they are not able to cover every aspect of mental health and teamwork communication struggle that exists. Further, it is really only set up for one to two simultaneous players right now. We might extend to trying to design for more in the future, but are trying to create a proof of concept within limited parameters.

5.1 Positives and Negatives

There are positives and negatives to each of our concepts, which we explored to answer our research question. The meditation module, for example, is a simplistic concept. This is simultaneously positive and negative. Because it is simple we hope it will be widely applicable, and we hope players will even consider adding regular meditation as a part of their self care routines. However, its simplicity may lead players to not be as immersed. Another positive is that most players have likely heard of the concept of meditation before, so they will hopefully have a better idea of what to expect going into the game.

For Concept 2, the teamwork and social coping visual novel also has a list of positives and negatives associated with it. Among the positives, it likely will not require a lot of extra resources to create a pilot version with minimal backgrounds and character models. Another positive is that it will hopefully allow us to clearly communicate information to the player. Further, previous research has found that visual novels are effective for people who are experienced gamers, which our target population is already by definition [17]. A potential negative would be if our target player base fails to be fully engaged they may not get as much out of the intervention. We will have to be conscious in balancing narrative and education. Further, it is worth noting that a full version of a visual novel will require quite a few assets, with backgrounds and character models being the most obvious.

Each conceit of Concept 3 (Breathing Games) have both positives and negatives as well. For "Tides" (where players breathe in sync with the tides and another player), the positives are that we could probably use preexisting assets instead of needing to animate, we also think that it is an easy idea to explain to players. The negatives would be that it might not be as engaging as the other options and might be repetitive with our idea for the meditation module. For "Hatchery" (a game where player breathing keeps a clutch of eggs at a steady temperature) the pros and cons are different. The positives would include that most of the gameplay would probably not require extensive animation as the primary visual would be static eggs. There would also be a solid case for replayability because players could hatch new patterns/colors/species. The negatives are that some people may be afraid of various animals that emerge from eggs and it would likely require a lot of assets even if they are static images. It may also be harder to explain. Finally, "Forge Friends/Bellows Buddies" (a game in which players play as a dragon and their breathing is used to regulate the temperature of a forge while weapons and tools are being created) has the major negative of likely being the most labor/asset intensive since it would probably require fire animations, images of the forging process, etc. The positives, however, are that it is probably the most engaging, a dragon breathing fire is a logical connection, and changes to what tool or weapon is being forged encourages repeatability.

6 Conclusion

In order to improve esport professionals' mental health and teamwork skills, we have begun designing a battery of minigames aimed at training these areas. Prior research, both our own and other researcher's work led us to the areas of teamwork and mental health [2,8–10,13]. We further decided to focus on the following domains within the mental health arena: meditation, breathing exercises, and learning social/stress coping skills as we think we can focus on them and add components associated with teamwork and communication. We think that we will be able to create engaging minigames out of these concepts and hopefully, in the future, we will be able to assess their impact on esports professionals.

References

1. Adinolf, S., Türkay, S.: Toxic behaviors in Esports games: player perceptions and coping strategies. In: CHIPLAY (2018). https://doi.org/10.1145/3270316.3271545
2. Bányai, F., Griffiths, M.D., Király, O., Demetrovics, Z.: The psychology of Esports: a systematic literature review. J. Gambl. Stud. **35**, 351–365 (2019). https://doi.org/10.1007/s10899-018-9763-1
3. Brown, R.P., Gerbarg, P.L., Muench, F.: Breathing practices for treatment of psychiatric and stress-related medical conditions (2013). https://doi.org/10.1016/j.psc.2013.01.001
4. Delany, C., Miller, K.J., El-Ansary, D., Remedios, L., Hosseini, A., McLeod, S.: Replacing stressful challenges with positive coping strategies: a resilience program for clinical placement learning. Adv. Health Sci. Educ. **20**, 1303–1324 (2015). https://doi.org/10.1007/s10459-015-9603-3
5. Goyal, M., et al.: Meditation programs for psychological stress and well-being: a systematic review and meta-analysis. JAMA Intern. Med. **174**, 357–368 (2014). https://doi.org/10.1001/jamainternmed.2013.13018
6. Jerath, R., Crawford, M.W., Barnes, V.A., Harden, K.: Self-regulation of breathing as a primary treatment for anxiety (2015). https://doi.org/10.1007/s10484-015-9279-8
7. Klimas, C.: Twine (2009). https://twinery.org/. Accessed 4 Oct 2023

8. Leis, O., Lautenbach, F.: Psychological and physiological stress in non-competitive and competitive Esports settings: a systematic review (2020). https://doi.org/10.1016/j.psychsport.2020.101738

9. Leis, O., Lautenbach, F., Birch, P.D., Elbe, A.M.: Stressors, associated responses, and coping strategies in professional Esports players: a qualitative study. Int. J. Esports 1 (2022)

10. Musick, G., Zhang, R., McNeese, N.J., Freeman, G., Hridi, A.P.: Leveling up teamwork in Esports. Proc. ACM Hum.-Comput. Interact. 5, 1–30 (2021). https://doi.org/10.1145/3449123

11. Nintendo: Mario kart ds. [Game] (2005)

12. Patibanda, R., Mueller, F., Leskovsek, M., Duckworth, J.: Life tree: understanding the design of breathing exercise games. In: CHI PLAY (2017). https://doi.org/10.1145/3116595.3116621

13. Poulus, D., Coulter, T.J., Trotter, M.G., Polman, R.: Stress and coping in Esports and the influence of mental toughness. Front. Psychol. 11, 628 (2020). https://doi.org/10.3389/fpsyg.2020.00628

14. Álvarez Pérez, Y., et al.: Effectiveness of mantra-based meditation on mental health: a systematic review and meta-analysis. Int. J. Environ. Res. Publ. Health 19, 3380 (2022). https://doi.org/10.3390/ijerph19063380

15. Rothamel, T.: Ren'py (game engine) (2004). https://www.renpy.org/. Accessed 4 Oct 2023

16. Sra, M., Xu, X., Maes, P.: BreathVR: leveraging breathing as a directly controlled interface for virtual reality games. In: Conference on Human Factors in Computing Systems, vol. 2018-April (2018). https://doi.org/10.1145/3173574.3173914

17. Yin, L., Ring, L., Bickmore, T.: Using an interactive visual novel to promote patient empowerment through engagement. In: Foundations of Digital Games (2012). https://doi.org/10.1145/2282338.2282351

Power to the Spectator: Towards an Enhanced Video Game Stream Discovery Experience

Laura Herrewijn[ID] and Sven Charleer[(⊠)][ID]

AP University of Applied Sciences and Arts, Ellermanstraat 33, 2060 Antwerp, Belgium
{laura.herrewijn,sven.charleer}@ap.be

Abstract. Game streaming platforms like Twitch could benefit from more user control and transparency in recommendations. In this paper, we highlight the importance of allowing users to customise their streaming experience through three design goals: Social Interaction, Captivation, and Knowledge Acquisition, the latter addressing both skill improvement and serendipity. We discuss the preliminary results of our on-going iterative and user-centred design process aimed at improving the exploration experience for game spectators. More specifically we report on the results of co-design research to explore the parameters necessary for game spectators' enhanced control over their game stream discovery experience.

Keywords: Esports · Spectator experience · Video games · Twitch

1 Introduction

The act of watching video games has become very popular, with leading game streaming platform Twitch [11] reaching a daily viewer count of 30 million people watching content generated by 7.4 million streamers per month [5]. As the variety of streamers and games on these game streaming platforms grows, users have to find their way through massive libraries of broadcasts to find a stream that caters to their specific interests. We posit that the existing searching and browsing tools of game streaming platforms-like keyword searches and sorting by popularity-may be insufficient for helping game spectators find a stream or community they can relate to.

Prior research has shown that there are a variety of reasons for watching game streams, ranging from pure entertainment and pastime, a need for community engagement and social-emotional support, to discovering new games and learning from the gameplay of expert players [1,2,4,9,14,20,23]. Different games and game streams tend to satisfy different spectator motivations. For instance, competitive games attract spectators looking to learn new strategies but these fast-paced streams often leave little room for social interaction, while sandbox games' slow pace welcomes interaction between streamer, spectator and community [9,20]. In addition to that, game spectators also value the personal attributes of the streamer and stream, like personality, skill level, gender, style, and audience type [9,18,19,21].

L. Herrewijn and S. Charleer—Both authors contributed equally to this research.

H. P. da Silva and P. Cipresso (Eds.): CHIRA 2023, CCIS 1997, pp. 349–360, 2023.
https://doi.org/10.1007/978-3-031-49368-3_22

As such, every type of game spectator has a different set of requirements when looking for a stream which can furthermore vary from session to session [9]. Previously, our research has gained more insight into these spectator needs by investigating game spectator characteristics, searching behaviour, motivations and stream(er) affordances of game spectators on Twitch by means of a survey study [9]. The results of the survey suggest that finding a new stream to watch on the platform is not a straightforward process due to the limitations of its user interface. The existing method on Twitch of organising streams by recommendations, games/game categories, viewer count, and "Recently started" does not adequately address the diverse motivations and needs of spectators.

Based on the results of the survey, we have therefore suggested a series of design goals to improve the spectator experience in the game stream discovery phase (and provide a more personalised searching experience), using Twitch as a case study [9]. These design goals give examples of which attributes or metadata the game spectator should directly or indirectly be given control of during their exploration experience. In this paper, we go a step further and explain our iterative and user-centred process of designing a new Twitch exploration interface that implements the aforementioned design goals. Specifically, the following research question takes centre stage: *which design choices can improve the search and exploration experience of video game spectators on Twitch?*

2   Related Work

Plenty of research has focused on the motivation behind and experience of watching streams. While entertainment is a major motivational factor when watching esports [24], people also watch professionals at play to learn how to improve their own skills [23, 24]. To support spectators in making sense of complex, fast-paced gameplay, streaming platforms such as Twitch [11] help spectators by augmenting the viewing experience through visual overlays, while professional esports streams such as ESL [6] visualise game metrics during tournaments to facilitate viewer understanding of in-game events. Live dashboards and companion apps can provide the spectator with even more live insights and predictions [2, 10] while post-game visualisations help both spectator and player to learn about successful and less successful tactics [23]. Next to entertainment and learning, spectators have a wide range of motivations to participate in streams [14]. Often they are simply looking for communities to interact with or want to become immersed in the streamer's game through innovative ways of interactivity [17]. They wish to support their esports teams or watch to gain in-game rewards ("drops") [15, 24].

Research shows that YouTube spectators value both personality and physical attractiveness of YouTubers [13]. Similarly, Guo et al. [7] discovered that streamer popularity is influenced by characteristics such as attractiveness, competence, and communication style. Beauty, expertise, and humour, as well as community, interactivity and emotional support attract spectators [3]. While this research explains what motivates spectators to choose specific streams, little research focuses on how platforms facilitate bringing the user to their specific niche stream.

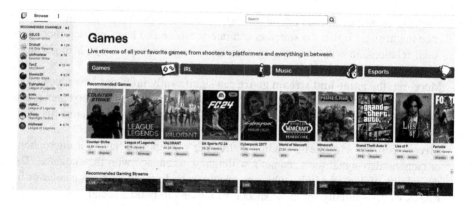

Fig. 1. The current browsing interface of game steaming platform Twitch

Game streaming platforms rely heavily on recommendations but provide little control to the user. Twitch's browsing structure, for example, prioritises current subscriptions, followed channels, and recommendations (see Fig. 1). In addition, it allows users to filter by game, game category and viewer count. This "black box" approach means the user has no insight into the process behind the suggestions [16]. We have learned [9] that Twitch users often browse through streamers they follow, navigate specific game titles, or search content by typing in keywords in the search bar, but also that they find streamer attributes such as personality and speaking style very important when choosing content to engage with: factors that are currently very difficult to include in searches on the platform. In line with prior research on recommender systems of other platforms [8,12,22], we therefore posit that allowing users to understand and tweak their proposed recommendations can create a more efficient and enjoyable user experience.

3   Design Goals

In our previous paper [9] we have defined three design goals to improve the exploration experience of the stream spectators, based on the insights garnered from our survey and pertinent literature: 1) **Social Interaction**, 2) **Captivation** and 3) **Knowledge Acquisition**. In this section, we elaborate further on these goals.

3.1   Design Goal 1: Social Interaction

The first design goal is to foster enriching social interactions. This includes the interactions between spectator and streamer, as well as among the spectators themselves since connecting with others is a big reason why people watch streams. To help spectators find streams that match their social preferences, it is important that the metadata includes an indication of how interactive a stream is. Therefore, we proposed to focus on several key attributes [9]:

- First, the **viewer count** can hint at how approachable a streamer is. A smaller audience might suggest that the streamer can interact more and have a closer, more personal relationship with viewers. In contrast, a larger audience-which might need moderators-indicates a lively, socially active community.
- Moreover, the **game and stream genre** can significantly influence how much room there is for community participation. For instance, slower-paced sandbox games and casual streams tend to encourage spectator participation, helping spectators find new, socially cohesive communities.
- **Stream context** attributes-including a streamer's setup, like having a microphone or camera-also signal the streamer's willingness to engage with the audience. The availability of donation links, which enable financial interaction, plays a noteworthy role as well, especially for those spectators looking to build a social and emotional connection.
- Additionally, allowing spectators to tailor their searches based on **personal traits** of the streamer, including personality, appearance, gender, and sexual orientation, can further streamline the process of finding relatable streamers and communities.
- Finally, recognising the importance of **chat atmosphere** is crucial; spectators who prioritise community engagement value a friendly atmosphere, a quality that can potentially be evaluated through community ratings or user profile reviews.

In focusing on these attributes, our goal is to address motivations like "Community Engagement" and "Social and Emotional Support" [9], aiming to cater to various spectator types or personas including "The Social Player" and "The Streamer-Focused Observer" as conceptualised by Shuck et al. [18]. This approach strives to create a platform where every spectator can find a community that resonates with them, enhancing the overall user experience.

3.2   Design Goal 2: Captivation

The second design goal focuses on holding the attention of spectators who are looking for fun, a break from monotony, or simply a distraction. Even though Twitch's current recommendation system might suit this audience to some extent, we believe that a more tailored approach that allows spectators to fine-tune their searches based on personal preferences and current mood could be highly beneficial. Depending on whether spectators want active engagement or just a chilled watching experience, they might choose a stream based on various aspects like the streamer's setup, looks, unique personality, or the vibe in the chatroom. To address this, we proposed the categorisation of streams based on the following attributes [9]:

- First, the **game and stream genre** significantly impact a spectator's choice. Our survey revealed that spectators seeking an escape from reality often prefer Role-Playing games and "Let's Play" streams, viewing them as an entertainment source and a means to unwind. This sentiment is echoed by Sjöblom et al. [20], which noted the role of First-Person Shooter games in facilitating tension release.
- Second, the streamer's **personal traits** are a dominant factor; spectators are drawn to streamers with qualities like attractiveness, skill, humour, and enthusiasm. In fact,

our survey highlighted the streamer's personality as the most critical element in influencing the choice of streams.

With these attributes, we aim to target motivations such as "Entertainment" and "Pastime and Habit" [9] and cater to the needs of spectator personas such as Cheung and Huang's "The Entertained" and "The Bystander" [4]. By focusing on the outlined attributes, the design goal seeks to foster a dynamic and immersive viewing environment where spectators can find streams that not only entertain but also resonate with them on a personal level.

3.3 Design Goal 3: Knowledge Acquisition

The third design goal addresses those spectators who watch streams to improve their gaming skills and knowledge. It can be subdivided into two impulses: Skill Improvement and Serendipity. **Skill Improvement** looks at the spectators wanting to learn how to play and get better at specific games, while **Serendipity** focuses on discovering new games or learning about newly released video games [20].

Many streamers, including both professional esports players and seasoned "casual players", share their gaming expertise and use their platforms to teach their followers. Spectators often tune in to these streams to learn new techniques and strategies from their favourite players and to get information on new games, assessing whether they satisfy their expectations before making a purchase.

To help spectators navigate through the many streams available, especially when exploring recently released or trending games, we proposed two key attributes that could guide users in choosing the most informative streams:

- First, highlighting the **streamer's skill level** can be instrumental. Spectators who want to improve their skills often watch competitive games. To help them find skilled players, we suggest using information from esports player rankings and offering a general streamer skill rating. This could be determined through crowd-sourcing or streamers rating their own skills. Importantly, in-game rankings in online competitive games can be used as an objective measure of skill levels, helping spectators make informed choices.
- Second, emphasising the **game and stream genre** can be a deciding factor in the learning experience. "How to Play" streams and Multiplayer Online Battle Arena (MOBA) games, prevalent in esports, serve as valuable resources. They provide detailed insights into expert strategies and game mechanics, satisfying spectators' desire to learn [20].

By focusing on these attributes, we aspire to nurture a space that encourages "Learning and Skill Improvement" and "Game Discovery" [9], meeting the needs of personas such as "The Curious" and "The Pupil" by Cheung and Huang [4]. This approach aims to match the streaming environment with viewers' learning needs, making it easier for them to find streams that are both educational and relevant to their gaming goals.

4   Designing for Enhanced Spectator Experiences

To further these design goals of enhanced social interaction, captivation and knowledge acquisition experiences, it is essential to undertake user evaluations to precisely define the range and scope of the necessary parameters and ideas for new exploration interfaces. Therefore, we are currently in the process of conducting an iterative user-centred design study. This study consists of several phases:

1. A **listing of (categories of) parameters** that could be beneficial to guiding users' search on game streaming platforms such as Twitch for the three defined experiences, based on our initial survey research [9];
2. **Designing a new exploration interface** for Twitch, taking into account these parameters;
3. **Conducting co-design research** with users of game streaming platforms, gathering feedback on the benefits, drawbacks, and usefulness of the parameters and the design;
4. Optimising the design of the exploration interface based on the co-design feedback;
5. Performing a large scale user evaluation of the final design.

   Phases 1–3 have been carried out already and will be discussed in the remainder of this paper. Phases 4–5 are still in progress.

4.1   Listing Parameters

Based on the insights from our survey research and the design goals we put forward [9], we created an initial list of categories of parameters for each experience (i.e. Social Interaction, Captivation and Knowledge Acquisition, with the latter being further subdivided into Skill Improvement and Serendipity). The list of categories per experience is shown in Fig. 2. For example, the experience of Social Interaction lists the categories Streamer, Streamer Context, Community, Game Genre, and Game Name.

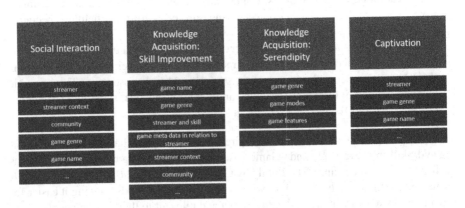

Fig. 2. Experiences as defined in our previous research [9] and their potential categories to tweak recommendations when browsing Twitch

Per category we furthermore defined a list of parameters. These parameters define the actual search filters or recommender system tweaks/weights the user can modify for a more focused result while exploring streams. As an example, the tweaks listed within Community are viewer count, follower count, chat atmosphere, and chat per second. Streamer Context includes parameters such as the presence of a microphone, camera, hardware specifications, social media links, while the category Streamer encompasses skill, gender identity, personality, etc.

4.2 Designing a New Exploration Interface

We also created an initial design prototype for a new exploration interface for Twitch, based on the design goals of our previous work [9] and our initial parameter list (see Fig. 3). Central to our design is the inclusion of four clearly labeled buttons at the top of the interface. These buttons represent the different types of experiences a user might be seeking: social interaction, skill improvement, captivation, and serendipity, providing a straightforward way for users to start their browsing journey based on their interests at that moment.

To complement this, we introduced a sidebar that houses a detailed list of parameters that can be expanded or collapsed according to the user's preferences. This feature allows users to fine-tune their search criteria, enabling a more personalised and efficient browsing experience. The sidebar is designed to adapt to individual preferences, helping users find content that suits them best with minimal effort. Through this two-part design approach, we aim to create a user experience that is both simple and deeply

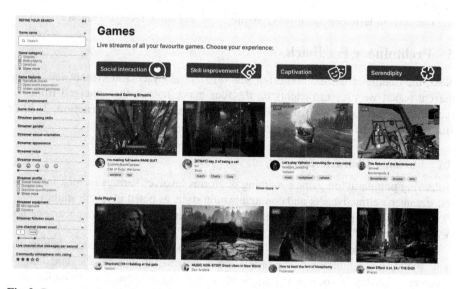

Fig. 3. Prototype of a Twitch exploration interface with a focus on the spectator experiences "Social Interaction", "Skill Acquisition", "Serendipity", and "Captivation". The sidebar provides a list of tweaks to refine the results even further

customisable, encouraging more satisfying and relevant engagements with the Twitch platform.

4.3 Conducting Co-Design Research

In order to gather user feedback on our list of parameters and design prototype, we have conducted co-design research with six participants who play games themselves and are active video game spectators as well (5 male, 1 female, age range 24–43 years old). All participants had experience watching streams through the platforms Twitch or YouTube.

The first goal of this session was to gather initial feedback on our list of categories and parameters for each type of experience. Examples of each category were explained orally and the participants received the list on paper, including examples of tweaks/parameters within each category. We encouraged the participants not to limit themselves to the technical and practical feasibility of the parameters on the list or any new parameters they could think of, but that the required metadata for such parameters could potentially be gathered from the streams through manual extraction, streamer input, machine learning, etc. The usefulness of the resulting parameters will be evaluated again through a large-scale online questionnaire.

Our second goal was to gather feedback and ideas for a user interface design to facilitate both user flow based on preferred experience (Social Interaction, Captivation, Skill Improvement, Serendipity) as well as user control regarding recommendation. To this end, we let users think about the optimal user interface and flow themselves, after which we presented them with our own design prototype and asked them for their evaluation.

The session lasted approximately 90 min, and was audio recorded and transcribed.

5   Preliminary Feedback

Next, the findings from the co-design session were analysed and synthesised. In the current paper, we present insights on the four major themes that emerged from our participants' feedback: 1) **Streamer Characteristics**, 2) **Social Interaction**, 3) **Skill Improvement**, and 4) **User Experience**.

5.1   Streamer Characteristics

Achieving popularity on game streaming platforms involves various factors, including the streamer's attractiveness and communication style, as noted in recent studies [3,7]. Consequently, our proposed parameters encompass both the physical appearance and personality traits of the streamer.

Participants acknowledged that these parameters carry certain risks, such as the potential for discrimination or the promotion of unrealistic physical standards among streamers. Conversely, they also highlighted the benefits, including the ability for spectators to find streamers who better align with their own identity, cultural backgrounds or experiences. To gain deeper insights into the utility and ethical implications of these parameters, we plan to subject them to more comprehensive evaluations on a larger scale.

Parameter Examples. *Gender identity, sexual orientation, hair colour, eye colour, clothing style, piercings, tattoos, makeup, posture, voice type*

5.2 Social Interaction

Participants proposed moving beyond basic statistics such as the number of viewers and instead advocated for exploring parameters that offer a more accurate representation of chat room activity. They recommended examining the spectator count over specific time intervals, such as the past week or month. This approach could not only reveal the stream's growth trajectory, highlighting trending streamers, but also forecast chat engagement levels. While chat participation may require some time to ramp up, predicting activity would disregard the initial cold start of live stream chats when users are searching for active streams.

Nevertheless, participants acknowledged the advantages of a simple viewer count. They pointed out that lower chat participation allows for more direct interaction with the streamer, while busier chat rooms often necessitate moderators, making direct engagement with the streamer challenging. Spectators seeking a more intimate connection with the streamer might opt for those with smaller communities.

In addition, we proposed a parameter to assess the quality of the chat, such as identifying whether it is characterised by toxicity or fosters a positive atmosphere. Participants recommended employing crowd-sourcing methods to collect data on chat quality, thereby assisting in the evaluation of this aspect.

Parameter Examples. *Viewer count, follower count, recent number of viewers, chat atmosphere, level of chat activity.*

5.3 Skill Improvement

Participants noted that they refrain from utilising platforms like Twitch for "educational" purposes and instead prefer to rely on prerecorded instructional content found on YouTube. This situation presents an opportunity for live streams, especially considering that participants also pointed out that numerous esports players maintain personal streams on Twitch.

In terms of refining skill enhancement methods, a streamer's online ranking emerged as a quick gauge of their proficiency in a specific game. This allows spectators to delve deeper into specific parameters, such as game mode or difficulty level, and even the particular class or weapon employed by the streamer. This provides valuable insights on how to elevate one's gameplay within these precise settings and at a higher skill tier. Additionally, some games incorporate training modes, as seen in the Street Fighter series, making such streams an excellent source of targeted guidance for skill improvement.

Another suggestion involved streamers who are dedicated to teaching and willingly share their knowledge. Here, crowd-sourcing could play a pivotal role in evaluating and rating a streamer's teaching aptitude and willingness, providing a reliable metric for potential viewers seeking educational content.

Parameter Examples. *Ranking, game mode, level, map, weapon, class, character, difficulty level.*

5.4   User Experience

The initial prototype received positive first impressions. Users appreciated the straightforward approach of presenting four motivations at the top of the screen, finding it inviting and clear. However, the sidebar, which contained a lengthy list of parameters that could be expanded or collapsed based on user preferences, felt overwhelming to participants. One participant even mentioned that they tend to dismiss similar interfaces instantly.

Participants proposed a wizard-like approach: when selecting a motivation, users would have the choice to either view the results directly or be guided through the parameters they want to modify. They acknowledged that this step-by-step process might become tedious if repeated frequently, so presets were suggested. These presets would allow users to save their preferred parameter settings for future use, streamlining their search experience on subsequent visits.

Regarding skill acquisition, one participant suggested the ability to easily delete presets related to this motivation when a user loses interest in a particular game.

One participant suggested archetypes to represent different types of streamers, their audiences, and the content they offer. It was also proposed to explore character creation approaches, which would tie into the numerous parameters related to streamer appearance, offering a more engaging and enjoyable way to search for the ideal streamer.

Examples of User Experience Tweaks. *Wizards, presets, archetypes, character creation.*

6   Conclusion and Future Work

This paper presents an ongoing design study aimed at improving the exploration tool for video game spectators. With platforms like Twitch continuous growth, conventional methods such as keyword searches and popularity-based sorting are inadequate in providing a personalized and gratifying user experience. In response to these challenges, we have introduced three key design goals: Social Interaction, Captivation, and Knowledge Acquisition. These goals are intended to enrich the exploration journey for stream spectators, addressing their diverse requirements.

Our ongoing user-centered design study involves gathering feedback from experienced stream spectators. This process has yielded valuable insights, such as the expansion of control parameters and user interaction approaches to streamline the discovery process.

Our goal is to create an environment where each viewer can effortlessly find streams and communities that resonate with their preferences, thereby enhancing their overall viewing experience. To achieve this, we will combine the feedback acquired during our co-design session with the findings from our prior work, enabling us to advance our iterative user-centered design process. Building upon these insights, we will develop new designs that will eventually undergo a comprehensive evaluation involving video game spectators. Subsequently, the resulting design will be assessed for its feasibility, usefulness, ethical implications, and potential impact.

References

1. Cabeza-Ramirez, J.L., Sanchez-Canizares, S.M., Fuentes-Garcia, F.J., Santos-Roldan, L.M.: Exploring the connection between playing video games and watching video game streaming: relationships with potential problematic uses. Comput. Human Behav. **128**, 107130 (2022). https://doi.org/10.1016/j.chb.2021.107130
2. Charleer, S., Gerling, K., Gutiérrez, F., Cauwenbergh, H., Luycx, B., Verbert, K.: Real-time dashboards to support esports spectating. In: Proceedings of the 2018 Annual Symposium on Computer-Human Interaction in Play, pp. 59–71. ACM (2018)
3. Chen, J., Liao, J.: Antecedents of viewers' live streaming watching: a perspective of social presence theory. Front. Psychol. **13**, 839629 (2022). https://doi.org/10.3389/fpsyg.2022.839629
4. Cheung, G., Huang, J.: Starcraft from the stands: understanding the game spectator. In: Proceedings of the SIGCHI Conference on Human Factors in Computing Systems, pp. 763–772 (2011). https://doi.org/10.1145/1978942.1979053
5. Dean, B.: Twitch usage and growth statistics: how many people use twitch in 2022? (2022). https://backlinko.com/twitch-users. Accessed 13 June 2023
6. Turtle Entertainment GmbH. ESL (2018). www.eslgaming.com. Accessed 16 Apr 2018
7. Guo, Y., Zhang, K., Wang, C.: Way to success: understanding top streamer's popularity and influence from the perspective of source characteristics. J. Retail. Consum. Serv. **64** (2022). https://doi.org/10.1016/j.jretconser.2021.102786
8. Harper, F.M., Xu, F., Kaur, H., Condiff, K., Chang, S., Terveen, L.: Putting users in control of their recommendations. In: Proceedings of the 9th ACM Conference on Recommender Systems, pp. 3–10. ACM (2015)
9. Herrewijn, L., Charleer, S.: Spectator LF streamer: facilitating better stream discovery through spectator motivations and stream affordances. In: Proceedings of the 2023 Annual Symposium on Computer-Human Interaction in Play. ACM (2023). in Press
10. Hoobler, N., Humphreys, G., Agrawala, M.: Visualizing competitive behaviors in multi-user virtual environments. IEEE Visualization **2004**, 163–170 (2004). https://doi.org/10.1109/VISUAL.2004.120
11. Twitch India Inc. Twitch (2023). www.twitch.tv/. Accessed 23 Aug 2023
12. Jin, Y., Tintarev, N., Verbert, K.: Effects of personal characteristics on music recommender systems with different levels of controllability. In: Proceedings of the 12th ACM Conference on Recommender Systems, RecSys 2018, pp. 13–21. ACM, New York (2018). https://doi.org/10.1145/3240323.3240358
13. Korres-Alonso, O., Elexpuru-Albizuri, I.: Youtubers: audience identification with and reasons for liking them. In: Icono14, vol. 20 (2022). https://doi.org/10.7195/ri14.v20i1.1761
14. Kriglstein, S., et al.: Be part of it: spectator experience in gaming and esports. In: Extended Abstracts of the 2020 CHI Conference on Human Factors in Computing Systems, pp. 1–7 (2020)
15. van der Molen, K.: Valorant and the platformization of free-to-play games. Press Start **8**(2), 21–43 (2022)
16. Parra, D., Brusilovsky, P.: User-controllable personalization: a case study with setfusion. Int. J. Human-Comput. Stud. **78**, 43–67 (2015). https://doi.org/10.1016/j.ijhcs.2015.01.007

17. Ramirez, D., Saucerman, J., Dietmeier, J.: Twitch plays pokemon: a case study in big g games. In: Proceedings of DiGRA, pp. 3–6 (2014)
18. Schuck, P., Altmeyer, M., Krüger, A., Lessel, P.: Viewer types in game live streams: questionnaire development and validation. User Model. User-Adapt. Interact. **32**, 417–467 (2022). https://doi.org/10.1007/s11257-022-09328-9
19. Shen, Y.C.: What do people perceive in watching video game streaming? eliciting spectators' value structures. Telematics Inf. **59**, 101557 (2021). https://doi.org/10.1016/j.tele.2020.101557
20. Sjöblom, M., Törhönen, M., Hamari, J., Macey, J.: Content structure is king: an empirical study on gratifications, game genres and content type on twitch. Comput. Human Behav. **73**, 161–171 (2017). https://doi.org/10.1016/j.chb.2017.03.036
21. Sjöblom, M., Törhönen, M., Hamari, J., Macey, J.: The ingredients of twitch streaming: affordances of game streams. Comput. Human Behav. **92**, 20–28 (2019). https://doi.org/10.1016/j.chb.2018.10.012
22. Verbert, K., Parra, D., Brusilovsky, P., Duval, E.: Visualizing recommendations to support exploration, transparency and controllability. In: Proceedings of 2013 International Conference on Intelligent User Interfaces, pp. 351–362. ACM (2013)
23. Wallne, G.: Enhancing battle maps through flow graphs. In: 2019 IEEE Conference on Games (CoG), pp. 1–4. IEEE (2019)
24. Yu, W.B., Beres, N.A., Robinson, R.B., Klarkowski, M., Mirza-Babaei, P.: Exploring esports spectator motivations. In: CHI Conference on Human Factors in Computing Systems Extended Abstracts, pp. 1–6 (2022)

Author Index

Printed in the United States
by Baker & Taylor Publisher Services